Honest To Goodness

Honest To Goodness

An Ethical and Spiritual Odyssey

MARTIN PROZESKY

Foreword by John Bluck

RESOURCE *Publications* • Eugene, Oregon

HONEST TO GOODNESS
An Ethical and Spiritual Odyssey

Copyright © 2019 Martin Prozesky. All rights reserved. Except for brief quotations in critical publications or reviews, no part of this book may be reproduced in any manner without prior written permission from the publisher. Write: Permissions, Wipf and Stock Publishers, 199 W. 8th Ave., Suite 3, Eugene, OR 97401.

Resource Publications
An Imprint of Wipf and Stock Publishers
199 W. 8th Ave., Suite 3
Eugene, OR 97401

www.wipfandstock.com

PAPERBACK ISBN: 978-1-5326-6536-3
HARDCOVER ISBN: 978-1-5326-6537-0
EBOOK ISBN: 978-1-5326-6538-7

Manufactured in the U.S.A. 02/20/19

Permission to use copyright material in this book is gratefully acknowledged to the following: Darton, Longman and Todd Ltd., for the passage in chapter 1 from John Baker's book *The Foolishness of God*; 1517 Media for passages from *Luther's Works*, volume 30, published by Concordia, and volume 36, published by Fortress Press; the academic journal *Alternation* for part of my article "Is the Secular State the Root of our Moral Problems in South Africa?"; the *Journal for the Study of Religion* for part of my article "Homo Ethicus: Understanding the Human Nature that Underlies Human Rights and Human Rights Education"; *The Witness* newspaper for the following articles of mine published in it at various times: "When Great Rivers Converge," "The Return of the Comet," "A New Home for Questioning Christians," and "Reading and Misreading the Bible"; also to ProgressiveChristianity.org for permitting me to quote the "Eight Points" from its website; the University of KwaZulu-Natal Press and SCM Press for the passage from my book *A New Guide to the Debate about God*, called "A Christian Understanding of the Divine"; Porcupine Press for a quotation from my book *Warring Souls;* and Globethics.net for an extract from my chapter "Universities, Cultural Diversity and Inclusivity" in its book *Ethics in Higher Education: Values-driven Leaders for the Future*.

Scripture quotations marked (ESV) are from The ESV® Bible (The Holy Bible, English Standard Version®), copyright © 2001 by Crossway, a publishing ministry of Good News Publishers. Used by permission. All rights reserved.

Scripture taken from the HOLY BIBLE, NEW INTERNATIONAL VERSION® NIV®. Copyright © 1973, 1978, 1984, 2011 by Biblica, Inc.™ Used by permission of Biblica, Inc.™. All rights reserved worldwide.

"NIV" and "New International Version" are trademarks registered in the United States Patent and Trademark Office by Biblica, Inc.™.

Every aspect of creation affects, effects, impacts upon the furtherance of creation's project—from the delicate ecosystems, the orbits of the planets, the birth and death of stars, and the swirl of galaxies, to the expansion of the universe itself ... Creation as a project was not finished on the sixth day—it's still ongoing, evolving, adapting ... Always it is emerging, like grace and in line with God's providential foresight ... life doesn't just pulsate; it pulsates in a direction towards its ultimate thriving.

(Graham Ward, *How the Light Gets In*)

And on the eighth day he said, "In perfect goodness I have created humankind in my own image, so that my people can make their own ways to me if they use my gifts of conscience, intelligence and freedom to choose goodness over evil, light over dark, and love over all."

(Martin Prozesky)

Let us take up the fragments of our traditions and use them like flint to light up new campfires, where strangers like dreams are welcome, where new worlds are unearthed with each new friend, and where each moment trembles with the birth of creation.

(Art Dewey, *The Fourth R*)

At last the horizon appears free to us again, even granted that it is not bright; at last our ships may venture out again, venture out to face any danger; all the daring of the lover of knowledge is permitted again; the sea, our sea, lies open again; perhaps there has never yet been such an open sea.

(Friedrich Nietzsche, In *The Portable Nietzsche*)

My heart is in the Church of England, with all its beauty and deep sense of holiness, but not my mind, which is repelled by its unreal dogmatic doctrines.

(Alister Hardy, *The Divine Flame*)

Surely goodness and love shall follow me all the days of my life.

(Psalm 23:6, ESV)

Contents

Acknowledgements | ix
Foreword by John Bluck | xi
Preface | xv
Apologia for an Odyssey | xix

Part I: Formative Factors

Chapter 1
Goodness | 3

Chapter 2
Youthful Awakenings | 9

Chapter 3
Theological Studies 1963-1969 | 15

Chapter 4
Academic Life | 34

Chapter 5
Themes and Thinkers from Multi-Disciplinary Research | 76

Chapter 6
Researching Religion | 114

Part II: Conservative and Liberal Christianity in the Light of Great Goodness

Chapter 7
Essentials of Conservative Christianity | 145

Chapter 8
Is Conservative Christianity sufficiently ethical? | 158

Chapter 9
Essentials of Liberal Christianity | 185

Chapter 10
An Ethical Critique of Liberal Christianity | 191

Part III: Progressive Christianity as an Ethical Faith and Practice

Chapter 11
Overview of a Goodness-based Faith | 201

Chapter 12
Ultimacy, Perfect Goodness and the Concept of God | 208

Chapter 13
Jesus and his Revolution | 223

Chapter 14
The Jesus Movement Today and a Global Goodness Project | 246

Epilogue | 279
Bibliography | 281
Index | 295

Acknowledgements

THANKS ARE DUE TO the following for their help in the research and preparation of this book. They are my colleagues and friends in the Faculty of Theology and Religion at the University of the Free State, especially Fanie Snyman, Francois Tolmie and Rian Venter, and, for administrative assistance in various ways, Ingrid Mostert, Ronel Ellis and Marina Oberholzer. Sue Broers and Sarah Jenkinson at Trinity College, Oxford, arranged accommodation for me there, and the Bodleian Library staff greatly assisted my research. I have also been assisted by the library staff at the University of KwaZulu-Natal and at St Joseph's Oblate Scholasticate in Cedara, KwaZulu-Natal. I am also grateful to Judith Brown, formerly Beit Professor of Commonwealth History at the University of Oxford, for assistance in connection with the spirituality of Mahatma Gandhi.

The experiences, both personal and academic, that have led to this book go back to my early boyhood, as will be seen, so I owe a very great debt of gratitude to the many who helped me along the way, most of them no longer with us. Along with my immediate family members and friends, they include Peter Hinchliff, Leslie Houlden, Robert Craig, Alec Burkill, Vic Bredenkamp, Lloyd Geering, John B. Cobb Jr., and John Hick. My thanks also go to those who kindly read parts or even all of the book in draft and provided me with much beneficial feedback. They are Bishop John Bluck in New Zealand, and Professor Rian Venter at the University of the Free State who first suggested that I write a spiritual autobiography, and thus paved the way to this book. Bishop Bluck also kindly wrote the Foreword. I remain, of course, responsible for my use of that feedback, and of all my other sources.

Next, I must record thanks to those who helped see this book into print. They are Christopher Merrett for checking the text, and the staff at Wipf and Stock Publishers for their encouragement and expertise in seeing the book into print, namely Matt Wimer, Daniel Lanning, Ian Creeger and their editorial, typesetting, production, and other colleagues. As always, my wife Elizabeth has been wonderfully supportive in ways too many to mention.

Foreword

Bishop John Bluck

THERE ARE PLENTY OF promoters promising the end of Christianity, the death of God, the obsolescence of Jesus and the irrelevance of the church. Professor Martin Prozesky is not one of them. This book is unlike other explorations of our post-Christian landscape. He treats the conservative and liberal theologies that formed his life with great respect, even though he has left them behind. Both brands fall short for Martin, having explored them both from the inside, with a foray or two on the way into neo-orthodoxy and religious humanism. He's served his time in them all and even though ending up at the radical and progressive end of the spectrum, he remains in his own words, "a nostalgic exile from church life."

It's this sympathy and respect for more traditional expressions of Christian faith that makes this book so useful and challenging to those of us who still inhabit churches. Martin has some hard things to say about the old landscape, but he says them in a way that we who still belong back there, can hear. I can imagine that his great-grandfather, a pioneering missionary for the Berlin Missionary Society in South Africa, could have read this book and revelled in the debate that followed, while disagreeing with his great-grandson's conclusions.

There are many things in this book that we who still belong to more traditional forms of church need to address: our compromise with Caesar and the market forces of greed, power and environmental abuse; our timidity in meeting other world religions as authentic expressions of God, our reluctance to let go understandings of the divine that deny science, defy justice, and ignore history.

In a rigorously argued and scholarly way, Martin shows us where re-thinking and re-imaging is overdue and offers a framework for that. In his language, it is about joining a new Jesus movement that is goodness based, community creating, ethically committed and action oriented.

But what is it that will inspire and drive such a movement and make it more than good intentions and worthy words, a warmed-up version of Moral Rearmament? Has it got anything to do with religion as we have known it?

There are times in the book when religion is worn lightly. "All religion," he tells us, "can be explained naturalistically as a human, cultural creation that doesn't require the existence of spiritual beings." But before we're left floating away on the sea of faith in a post Christian boat, Martin's argument is fuelled by life changing inspirations. For example, he calls us to trust, as he most clearly does himself, "a powerful sense of being in the uplifting presence of an inexhaustible goodness, or blessing, seeking to be as open as possible to its creative power." Such a blessing has encompassed Martin's life from boyhood.

And where does this inspiration come from? In the new vocabulary Martin offers us, it comes from a Godhead of sheer goodness; "the mysterious, inspirational generosity that upholds and infuses all things, the creativity that fosters everything good, beautiful and true, the truth that enlightens and directs all living beings."

Reasonable Christians of whatever brand might well want to add a sentence or two about such a God. But who would want to argue with such a statement? And if we could agree on such statements as a starting point, would they not provide a more fruitful dialogue than the doctrinal divides that continue to tear Christianity apart?

What this book offers is a chance for people of all sorts and conditions of faith, from the devout to the doubters, whether you hold tight or sit light to the old tenets, to try on a new wardrobe and experiment with some new names. And even if you decide to revert to the old labels and put on your old clothes again, the experience of trying on something new will leave you richer for the experience.

Honest to Goodness is best read with a novel, also written by Martin, that is really a companion volume to this theological text. *Warring Souls* is a story about what happens when religious faith is governed by ethical passion—and when it isn't. It follows the adventures of Sarah Williams, a radical professor of Christian Ethics, colliding with evangelical opponents. At one point she rescues two of these opponents from near death in a snow storm, and has to answer what all that had to do with God.

"The rescue on Sunday wasn't planned," she tells her college community. "What I do know is that the saving goodness we call God is real. Neither danger nor death can defeat it, and we must be part of its goodness. That is what Easter means. It isn't something long ago and far away. It is everywhere and anywhere. Always."

The novel anchors the theological book, just as Martin's own pilgrimage of faith anchors them both, in his lifelong experience of a force that will not let him go. Martin calls that force "supreme goodness." With his love for astronomy he looks at the stars through his telescope and marvels at "the ultimate good that there is this reality at all." He believes with all the passion of a true believer that there is "such a rich, ultimate reality, pervasively present and available in the universe and in human life and it is truly, literally supremely good."

Desmond Tutu is one of Martin's heroes. He remembers the then archbishop answering a radio host who asked him what he meant by God, saying "God is all that is beautiful, good and true." You could build a theology on any part of that answer but it's the notion of goodness that excites and drives Martin the ethicist. This book is the culmination of a lifetime of following that drive, and sharing that excitement in a deeply personal way.

His work is a gift worth embracing for all sorts and conditions of believers and especially for those who struggle to find faith at all.

John Bluck
(Rtd) Bishop of Waiapu
Aotearoa New Zealand

Preface

HONEST TO GOODNESS IS a progressive, Abelardian and experiential metatheology. It emerges on this eighth day of creation from a lifetime of ethical, spiritual and intellectual exploration of Christianity. In a world crying out for all the good it can get, it culminates in the last chapter in what I see as humanity's greatest need and opportunity, which I call the goodness project. This would be a cooperative, global initiative to understand and promote all that is caring, beautiful and true, as never before, and to understand and transform all that is not. It will require research, activism, networking, education and organizational capacity. Joining this project with all its immense resources will, I believe, express and extend the mission of the movement founded by Jesus of Nazareth.

Goodness is portrayed in the chapters that follow as the sublime reality behind our word "God," with Jesus of Nazareth as the superlative ethical and spiritual revolutionary whose vision and program of action the whole world needs. I show the extent to which both the conservative and liberal parts of the church could promote the goodness project, and identify grave problems in what C.S. Lewis called "mere Christianity" in his much-loved book of that title, when seen in the fullest light of rigorous, ethical scrutiny. I measure traditional Christianity against the norms of the greatest moral goodness, and show ways of renewing what is found wanting.

Why do I speak of it as the Christianity of the eighth day of creation? The answer lies in the creativity it involves, or rather the rediscovered creativity that builds a faith tradition and certainly built traditional Christianity until core beliefs hardened into dogmas, allegedly the same forever. To speak of an eighth day of creation picks up the symbolism of the biblical narrative of creation, in which the Creator rested from the work of creation on the seventh day, the same Creator who, according to the Bible, made humanity in the divine image and likeness. What else can that mean but that we human beings are gifted with creative powers of our own, and gifted therefore also with the responsibility to share the ongoing work of creation, so wonderfully described by theologian Graham Ward in the quotation at the start of this book, symbolized here as the eighth day of creation.

The term "Progressive Christianity" names a recent, semi-organized development in the churches which is relevant to the conclusions I had myself reached about traditional Christianity. While this preface is not the place for an account of my studies and experience of it—that is given in chapters 5 and 6—a brief explanation at this point is necessary. It is an approach to Christianity that is inclusive, innovative and informed. It was reportedly started in the USA in the 1990s to provide a home in the church for people who were no longer convinced by traditional doctrines and were either on the fringes of church life or already outside it, but who still wanted a rich faith experience in the tradition that goes back to Christ. Initially called the Center for Progressive Christianity, it is now often referred to as ProgressiveChristianity.org, and has a following in the USA, Britain, Australia, Canada, New Zealand, Ireland, and in very small numbers in South Africa. Most important, it prioritizes ethical practice as the heart of the Jesus movement, not doctrine, creed, ritual or institution, which makes it a highly promising development for a book that prioritizes ethics. Among those whose work has influenced this development, the following may be cited: Friedrich Schleiermacher, Lloyd Geering, John B Cobb Jr., Bishop John Shelby Spong, and the eminent New Testament scholars Marcus Borg and John Dominic Crossan.

As for the concept of an Abelardian approach, the intention in using the name of the important but also controversial medieval French theologian, Peter Abelard (1079–1142), is to echo his view that Christ saves through his moral influence, which moves those who respond to it to make it part of their own lives.[1] Such a view does not deny that the death of Jesus on the cross is a saving event, for as an act of supreme self-sacrifice it can be seen as a climactic part of the powerfully moving, moral quality of his life. The emphasis this puts on goodness is obvious and is directly relevant to the central concern of this book, which is to explore, embrace and live by the greatest goodness possible, and in its light offer my conclusions about Christianity.

Honest to Goodness is experiential because it is the fruit of my own spiritual and ethical experiences going back to boyhood, greatly deepened, broadened and enriched by many years of research into issues in theology and related disciplines.

---

1. Burkill, *Christian Thought*, 174–76; McGrath, *Christian Theology*, 337–47.

I call it a metatheology for two reasons. First, what I offer involves a significant shift from the concept of God that is usually the focus of theology; and secondly because what I offer after such theology is experienced as a reality above and beyond the concept of a supreme being, which the familiar concept of God is mostly taken to involve. What I offer is not unlike what Oxford's Trevor Williams has called critical theology, as distinct from confessional theology, in a recent publication.[2]

In my 1992 book *A New Guide to the Debate about God*, I evaluated the arguments of both believers and skeptics about the soundness of the traditional Christian concept of God. My evaluation ended boldly but also humbly with the following words, very slightly edited: "What cannot validly be claimed is that the established Christian concept of God is rationally preferable to its secular rival, or equally supported by evidence and rational argument. In reaching this conclusion on the basis of all the available evidence and by means of rules of judgment which Christians themselves endorse, I am of course acutely aware of how vast is the ocean I have tried to chart and how small my ship and her instruments. That ocean is doubtless too mysterious to yield all its secrets to any one person's fathoming."[3]

The present book resumes that fathoming, confident that a deeper truth than the lesser ones held by both traditional believers and liberals, and certainly by their atheist critics, lies waiting beyond the horizon of the great ocean of our existence. *Honest to Goodness* is thus the fruit of spiritual experiences and extensive academic research extending for over fifty years, of which only the most relevant parts are presented. That earlier research is used in this book because of its abiding value, along with the most recent available work. It has been about religion in general, Christianity in particular, religion's main atheist critics, and above all about multi-disciplinary ethics, both theoretical and applied. These investigations have also been informed by many discussions with internationally eminent scholars in those fields, as will be clear in the following pages.

Honest to Goodness offers a critical and constructive contribution to creative thinking about the ethics of Christian belief and practice, as I have encountered them in the Episcopal, Anglican and other, non-Catholic, traditions. My contacts with Catholicism since boyhood, while always very pleasant, lack the depth that would enable me write with any scholarly authority about that world, though I know that some of what I say in parts II and III also applies there. While the book is offered as a scholarly work, at the same time it aims at clarity of expression with a minimum of technical,

---

2. Williams, "What Makes You Think?" 250–59.
3. Prozesky, *New Guide*, 173.

academic language. This policy echoes the advice of F.L. Lucas about style, where he wrote that "the gardens and porticoes of philosophy are hung with philosophers entangled in their own verbal cobwebs," adding that clarity is mainly acquired "by writing to serve people rather than impress them."[4]

Adding his formidable weight to this advice was the celebrated South African writer Alan Paton. I was fortunate enough to meet him socially in my then home city of Pietermaritzburg in about 1978, and later in our divinity department at the former University of Natal, which he visited for information about Francis of Assisi. I took the opportunity to ask for his advice about good writing. He told me there were two main principles. The first was that the three key words for a writer were "clarity, clarity and clarity," and second that he revised his own writing at least six times before sending it to his publishers or the press. I have tried to follow his advice and sometime revise my work even more than six times, and never less than three.

Being creative and deeply personal in its basic approach, *Honest to Goodness* must be understood and judged as such. Let me offer a modest parallel with the method of Mahatma Gandhi's autobiography, writing these words on the very day of the 125th anniversary of the early winter South African morning of June 7, 1893, when he was forced off a whites-only railway carriage at the station in Pietermaritzburg. He called his book *An Autobiography: The Story of my Experiments with Truth*. While my own book is only semi-autobiographical, there is a parallel in that I am both its underlying research object, but also its researcher. It is therefore not primarily a critical engagement with scholarly literature relating to its coverage, although it does so engage with plenty of such work, ending in November 2018. It is particularly concerned with the writings of conservative theologians, for reasons explained in the introduction, as the footnotes and bibliography both attest.

On the liberal Christian side, Keith Ward's 1991 book *A Vision to Pursue: Beyond the Crisis in Christianity* has been both informative and inspiring, as will be seen in part III of the present book. His depth of ethical and spiritual insight was a great encouragement for the writing of my own journey.

While I have made every effort to ensure that *Honest to Goodness* is supported by academic research, it is therefore not written just for scholars and spiritual leaders, but also for any deeply thoughtful reader who believes that what Jesus of Nazareth started is enormously important for today and tomorrow's wider world.

4. Lucas, *Style*, 12, 62.

Apologia for an Odyssey

AN ODYSSEY IS A long journey to where we truly belong. This I see as a supreme and seemingly inexhaustible goodness. Goodness is therefore the touchstone of all that follows, for nothing can matter more. It is our word for whatever effects anything beneficially, like a cooling breeze after a sweltering day, the rains that end a drought, a helping hand and a sudden recovery from a serious illness. We *feel* its presence, and welcome it, being by nature sentient, valorizing beings, who cannot but welcome whatever brings those benefits. Goodness, moreover, ranges from the most familiar and minor of those benefits to the most powerful and mysterious, and everything in between. It is thus part and parcel of our daily lives and experiences on this planet, and not in the least like Plato's notion of the Good, especially as given in his *Republic*, as belonging to an ideal world of forms removed from the physical world, and thus beyond empirical experience. Instead, my stance is akin philosophically to Aristotle and especially Alfred North Whitehead.[5]

An apologia is an introductory explanation of what a book offers. *Honest to Goodness* is about Christianity today and perhaps tomorrow. It contends that goodness, especially in its richest and most mysterious form, is the reality that drives everything that is noble and lastingly valuable in our existence, with religion as an enduringly important but never perfect human product of its power, a power that works within us, with us, around us, and ultimately also beyond us. Goodness is the crowning value of our existence, and to its transforming power everything we have and do must conform, including our religious beliefs and practices.

It will be shown that central aspects of traditional Christianity, based on the creeds of the church, including its concept of God, the way it understands Jesus, sin and evil, salvation and the Bible, all fall short of the great goodness at its heart and of the way Jesus embodied and taught it.

---

5. Copplestone, *History of Philosophy I:I*, 201.

This includes the Christianity that C.S. Lewis called "mere Christianity" in the classic statement of a conservative Christian position to which I have already alluded, and which Alister McGrath has confidently identified with evangelicalism.[6] It will also be shown how Christianity could grow into much greater conformity with that great and glorious goodness, using as criteria only those espoused by Christianity itself. These criteria are principally love, justice and truth, the chief constituent values of moral and spiritual goodness.

Basing my understanding of Christianity on goodness does not imply any blindness to the reality of its opposite, for evil is also all too real, even in religion itself. The world is disfigured and threatened by insidious, destructive forces whose nature and power are insufficiently recognized, and are even accepted by too many as beneficial, like ways of making staggering amounts of money for the few and impoverishing the many. That is why it is so important for us to align ourselves totally with all that is caring, beautiful and true in order to oppose evil and, wherever possible, defeat it by the power of the good. For an impressive account of what this ugly and destructive reality is, and of its main forms, there are few better guides than John Hick, even though it is now over fifty years since he wrote his landmark study in a 1966 book called *Evil and the God of Love*. His account is summarized in the part of chapter 5 that deals with our need for a better understanding of evil.

*

The Christian faith is mostly seen from two antagonistic perspectives, the perspectives of the committed insider and of the skeptical and at times hostile outsider. This book and the interpretation of goodness that governs it come from a different standpoint, that of a spiritual explorer. You could also call me as author something of a nostalgic, ecclesial dissident, except that I never dissented from the living heart of the faith as I know it, set out later in this book.

It is important that most of my experience of Christianity has taken place in South Africa, both under and after apartheid. That experience made it abundantly clear that Christianity can be shockingly ambivalent about central ethical values like truth and socio-economic justice, for apartheid was both the handiwork and the implacable foe of orthodox, Bible-reading, church-going Christians, making it a haven for both moral saints and apartheid's supporters and agents. Sadly, never did I find in the church

---

6 McGrath, *Evangelicalism*.

of my experience much appetite for rigorous self-criticality and even less for an appreciation of other faiths.

For someone with a resolutely independent, probing mind, the church of my experience has at times seemed more suited to kindly tunnel vision than to people who persist in asking awkward, wide-ranging questions. Not surprisingly, therefore, I was led away from my spiritual homeland by beliefs, values, attitudes and practices I could not and cannot in all honesty accept, but I am still held by the memory of a kindness I found in the church that I cannot let go. Not only has this involved contact with people like Desmond Tutu and other heroes of conscience; it also involves the influence of many other wonderful, caring, truth-loving believers from the ranks of family, friends and colleagues.

From my self-exiled perspective I find, after many years of careful study and countless consultations with a wide range of experts both conservative and liberal, that intellectual and moral honesty lead me to a seemingly strange conclusion about the faith I once embraced so wholeheartedly. What is that conclusion? It is that the criticisms of those hostile outsiders, of whom Richard Dawkins and other militant atheists are only the most recent, while often half-baked and ill-informed, are in certain key respects correct; but to my knowledge they are very seldom taken seriously enough in the churches. As I show later in this book, the core beliefs of traditional, conservative Christianity, taken at face value, cannot all be true, just as these critics so confidently assert. At the same time, I also find that the critics are completely mistaken if they think they have fatally damaged the living heart of the faith launched by Jesus of Nazareth. It is as valid and important today as it was at the hands of its founder. The tragedy is that so many mainline Christians, those in America perhaps most of all, whose sincerity is not in question, seem not to know what I am calling the living heart of their faith. My conclusions about that living heart are set out in detail in part III of this book.

What I have found, striving now for the best ethical living and responding to a new age of information about religion in general, and about Christianity and the Bible in particular, is that Christianity itself is now made up of two seemingly irreconcilable strands and one that sits somewhere between them. There is the conservative faith of my younger years, and a vastly smaller and much younger radical strand called Progressive Christianity, where I now sense a possible spiritual home. Between them is the liberal Christianity that I embraced in my student years and for a time afterwards, until I began to study and at times also experience religion in the light of every available source of relevant modern knowledge, and engage with people of other faiths. For me, liberal Christianity proved unstable, and I now see it as in need of further liberalization in a radical direction. While I discuss and assess liberal faith and its founding father, Friedrich Schleiermacher, in the chapters that follow, it is mainly the conservative and progressive forms of Christianity that concern me, with the dominant conservative side being the main subject of part II, followed in it by shorter chapters about liberal Christianity. The fledgling radical version is the subject of part III. While what I say is offered to Christians anywhere, it is offered most of all to those in America as the heartland of the fundamentalist and evangelical Christians that Frances FitzGerald has described in such great detail in her recent book,[7] and as the birthplace of the progressive Christian movement.

The two strands that primarily concern me, conservative and radical, can be likened to the secure faith of spiritual settlers and the risky, questing faith of spiritual pioneers. For the former, faith is mostly comfort; for the latter, faith is mostly adventure. I well remember how the former required of me a trusting acceptance of what loving parents and a caring church taught me was the most important truth of all, the truth they sincerely believed would determine my eternal life, but which I now clearly see to be mistaken. I am grateful for the comforting memory of its assurance of salvation, for uplifting worship and loving fellowship, even if I can no longer embrace those comforts.[8]

Very different is the path that led me to the radical position I now hold. It has required a restless hunger for truth and goodness, a questioning attitude prepared to explore all relevant knowledge discovered by the revolution of the mind that has gathered strength in recent centuries, and above all it has required a passion to believe and serve only that which is truly and deeply good. I find, sadly, that the traditional Christianity that shaped me has not adequately opened its mind and, worse, its heart, to the truths of the knowledge revolution and to the world's need for justice and peace. I find that the new Christian radicalism is far closer to Jesus himself and the great spiritual and ethical movement he launched, even more so than the brave, liberal orientation that was once my own. And I find that the traditional, conservative version of Christianity has fallen short of being the powerful force for good in the world that it could and should see as its true mission, a mission supported by appropriate ritual and fellowship, but not dominated by them. I call this traditional form of faith Conservative Christianity in this book because the word "conservative" means that which has traditional authority and resists change.

---

7. FitzGerald, *Evangelicals*.
8. Seliger, "Frontier Theology," 10–12.

Apologia for an Odyssey

It is very important that I make myself as clear as possible about what I mean by the term "Conservative Christianity." It refers to the set of beliefs and related practices based on its way of reading Scripture and on the Nicene and Apostles' Creeds, as further defined in the twelve points below, and I see it as including two basic positions: extremely conservative believers like biblical fundamentalists, and evangelicals (who include conservative, moderate and more liberal members), who now appear to be numerically the biggest part of non-Catholic Christianity. I do not include theological liberals in the churches in what I am calling Conservative Christianity because they are the result of the liberalizing movement that has developed since the Enlightenment, whereas the other two go back to the fourth century at least, when the Nicene Creed was formulated and adopted, and the biblical canon settled.

All of the members of these strands of Christian belief regularly recite the Nicene and Apostles' Creeds in their worship, even though the liberals would interpret some clauses like the reference to hell symbolically. Many liberals also reject the claims to exclusive, saving truth of fundamentalists and evangelicals.

Specifically, I see Conservative Christianity as being defined by the following twelve characteristics, with some variation in the way the beliefs in hell, the virgin birth of Jesus, the resurrection, the ascension, what salvation requires of us, biblical inspiration and other religions are interpreted, variations that are certainly the case with liberal Christians I have known or studied.

1. The only God is the Holy Trinity of Father, Son and Holy Spirit.
2. God the Trinity is personal, holy, infinite, all-loving, perfectly good and all-powerful.
3. There is life after death, either eternally with God in the joys of the spiritual realm which believers call heaven, or in the eternal separation from God spoken of as hell in the Gospels and Creeds.
4. We humans are sinners who merit the righteous judgment of a holy God so that we cannot inherit eternal life with him after we die, but face the eternal consequence of our sins called hell, as variously interpreted.
5. God the Son became incarnate of the Virgin Mary as Jesus Christ for our salvation.
6. Jesus Christ, by his life, death on the cross, and resurrection is the only Savior.

7. Only by faith in Christ and participation in the church can anybody be saved from being eternally lost.

8. Christ rose bodily from the dead, appeared to his followers, ascended into heaven and will come again in judgment.

9. No other religion or philosophy can provide salvation.

10. The church is the body of Christ, founded by him as the sole vehicle of the truth about God, Christ, the Bible and salvation.

11. The Bible is no mere human creation but is God's uniquely inspired word.

12. God requires of us that we love one another and live loving lives, governed by the values that love requires, such as truth, justice and forgiveness.

My spiritual and ethical pilgrimage involved much more than I have so far mentioned. I found that there has been a major revolution in how to understand and use the Bible, a revolution which is poorly understood and even ignored by too many traditionalists, with very grave ethical consequences. I find that its ideas about God are fatally mistaken in several key respects, though not the sheer delusion alleged by their atheist critics. I find that the beliefs of Conservative Christianity about salvation cannot be true and, worse, are deeply unjust when judged by Christianity's own core values of honesty and love. And I believe that its practice as a church must be dramatically overhauled in certain significant respects in order to bring itself back to Jesus himself and the divine reality he embodied, chiefly its preoccupation with ritually praising God. Among other liberations this brings is liberation from a long and terrible history of anti-semitism that is rooted in the core doctrines of traditional orthodoxy. So I conclude that Conservative Christianity now needs another reformation to extend and deepen the one started by Martin Luther in 1517 and continued by the other leading reformers, John Calvin especially.[9]

Christianity is thus no longer one faith but two. The older one is the Christianity of traditional belief as given in the Nicene Creed, with its two conservative variants of fundamentalism and evangelicalism. Sharing its central beliefs and main ritual practices but in a much less rigid and undogmatic way is Christian liberalism, which is sometimes hard for me to pin down. It has been growing for the past few centuries inside its older sibling. Now some of its more radical members find themselves increasingly outside their older and far larger sibling, giving us what I see as virtually a second

---

9. de Gruchy, *John Calvin*, 201–31.

Christian faith. It is the faith of the eighth day of creation, producing a new synthesis of faith, ethics and knowledge, and offering a way to a more ethical future for Conservative Christianity, provided its members and leaders can choose spiritual adventure, governed by goodness, above religious comfort governed by conformity and security. For me it is an adventure of salvation from a spiritual dead end to a space of liberation that is beyond traditional Christian theism, liberalism and also atheism, as I explain later in this book.

By way of anticipation of what I propose in the chapters that follow, here is what I wish to say to the various strands of belief that I describe, evaluate and seek to help change. To all of them, may goodness govern, guide and where necessary change everything in your faith and practice. To fundamentalists, may you free your devotion to Scripture for the illuminating power of goodness and discover the Bible's true meaning. To evangelicals, may you liberate your faith in Christ as savior from everything that falls short of the greatest love and truth. To liberals, please continue to transform your understanding of God, Christ, salvation and the Bible from everything that is less than as loving and good as it can be, and please don't stop halfway. To radicals and progressives, as the main but not sole group to whom this book is directed, please work more on the social and practical implications of your ethical values and your new vision about what is ethically believable. Lastly, to atheists, full marks for rejecting bad theology and spurious beliefs, and for your commitment to ethics, but zero marks for the sometimes smug superficiality and often unfairness of your views of theism and religion in general.

In this way the present book seeks to bring together all I have learnt from Christianity, other religions and many ethical traditions, philosophy, history and science about being ethically spiritual and spiritually ethical, into a unified vision of a supreme goodness, the fountainhead of all that is good in both religion and secular life. Its foundations will be the personal and academic formative factors, as theologian John Macquarrie once called them, which have taken me from youthful fundamentalism and evangelicalism, with their comforting delusions, to an ever-widening circle of concern, involving acceptance of the truth and moral goodness in other faiths and philosophies, to where I am today, seeking to serve goodness as the governing principle of life.[10]

These formative factors are presented in part I of the book. They led me to the conviction that the "mere Christianity" of my early years, and also some aspects of the liberal theology that followed it, do not survive the ethical critique that is presented in part II. It is very important that this

10. Macquarrie, *Principles*, 4–18.

critique be understood as no mere theoretical exercise by an armchair philosopher of religion, but is the result of lived experiences of goodness over a long period of time. That is the reason for having part I in this book. The formative factors in question are the reality of pervasive goodness; my own spiritual, ethical and intellectual experiences from boyhood to adult life; the call of conscience in faith and politics; philosophy; the results of the knowledge revolution about the cosmos and human nature; religion with its deep and surface structures; Christianity and its Bible; all of them supported by a commitment to honest probing and creative thinking, and above all by the beauty and power of goodness itself. These influences, comprising experiences and studies of both Conservative and Liberal Christianity under the transforming power of the good, are recounted in the following chapters, but before that it is essential to focus on goodness itself.

PART I

Formative Factors

Chapter 1

Goodness

CELEBRATING GOODNESS

IN A POWERFUL BOOK written more than a generation ago, England's Bishop John Austin Baker wrote a memorable passage about goodness. With his and his publisher's permission it is reproduced here, very slightly edited to fit the present context.

> "Sorrow is at most only one half of reality. In a thousand, often surprising ways our humanness is matched to its environment, and enabled to find it good; indeed, the ways in which humankind finds or makes its pleasures are far more varied than its pains.
>
> "There is the relish of food and drink; the satisfaction of hard, tiring work alternating with rest, leisure, sleep; the precious sense of physical health. There are the joys of love, of friendship, and of family life, the pride and excitement stirred by the achievements of one's children, fellow-workers, and neighbours, one's nation or others, be it in football or philosophy, outrigger racing or space exploration. Almost every nation takes pleasure in music and dance, in making things that are beautiful or useful, in solving problems. There are the delights of the senses. Visual beauty—not only present in the people and the works of art or Nature generally agreed to be beautiful, but liable to descend with a sudden nuance of the light, even if only for a short while, on the most unlikely objects; and the more acutely or wholeheartedly we look, the less bored or sated we are with what we see. Beauty of touch—the feel of polished wood,

of water through the fingers or swilling all over you, of the solid earth under you, of the sheets of muscle in a horse's neck. Beauty of hearing—an old song worn to a perfect line by centuries, ripples against a running boat, a bird, a drum, a smooth powerful motor. Beauty of smell—wine, the first frost, green things after rain, the fur of a healthy animal . . .

"The pleasures already mentioned are of the kinds open to all societies, poor or rich, simple or sophisticated, in every continent. Once we start investigating those peculiar to each culture or sub-culture—pop music and pigeon-racing, bullfighting and beer, Stravinsky and stamp-collecting—there are more than enough entries for a large encyclopaedia. And that in itself tells us something of enormous importance about our experience of the world. Are we to count only the hate, never the love, only the ugliness, never the loveliness, only the misery, never the joy?"[1]

GOODNESS EXPLAINED

As the governing value of this book, goodness must now be more carefully explained. According to philosopher Richard Robinson, to deem anything good is "to reach an attitude towards it, an evaluation of it, and a decision how to behave with regard to it. It is to choose it," adding the important insight that the "beginning of wisdom is to value something for itself."[2] Goodness is valued for itself in the experiences underlying this book because it is like a many-faceted diamond, precious for itself, and for the many beautiful forms that are its facets.

The living heart of goodness for us as human beings is well-being, which stands, subjectively, for the many profoundly fulfilling, meaningful and happy experiences that matter most to us, and objectively for the surrounding contexts that make them possible. The three main facets of goodness, in the judgment of this book, are love, which entails active concern, compassion and a dedication to justice for all; truth, which requires honesty, attested evidence and reason; and freedom, understood as both creativity and as a willingness to seek fulfilment in new ways that do no harm. Experiencing any of these and embracing them leads to behavior that expresses and extends them to others, and also receives them from others.

---

1. Baker, *Foolishness of God*, 54-55.
2. Robinson, *Atheist's Values*, 24, 32.

These values are ones that Christianity itself teaches; they are also taught by other ethical traditions, as earlier research of mine demonstrated.[3]

A book called *Honest to Goodness* clearly sets very great store by the pursuit of truth, so something needs to be said now about truth, a value that the Bible itself centralizes, in John 8:32 and in numerous other passages. The standpoint of this book is that there is an ethical duty for everybody to seek the fullest possible truth, understood as beliefs that can be confirmed by evidence and logical reasoning of the kind that are open to everybody. This is what it means to love God with all your mind and not just all your heart and strength, and its clear implication is that deference to authority cannot be the primary method of truth-seeking. Here again Richard Robinson provides a helpful insight with these words: "Complete submission to authority is a grave irresponsibility" and when he adds that truth "is something like the accumulation of acceptable statements, the pursuit, formation and possession, of *as many* acceptable statements as possible."[4]

As a philosopher Robinson not surprisingly regards reason as the greatest virtue, whereas in Christianity love is deemed the greatest virtue, but his definition of reason, which plays a decisive part in this book, is nonetheless fully compatible with the love that Christianity and other faiths require. He defines it as love of truth, respect for reasons, consistency, deductiveness (meaning acceptance of the logical implications of our beliefs), preference for probability, tentativeness (as opposed to dogmatism), respect for evidence, submission to criticism, impartiality (meaning balanced objectivity), and the lessening of misery.[5]

The goodness of which Bishop Baker wrote so eloquently is within us, among us and beyond us. We experience it daily, hourly and even continuously when we put our minds to it, in the wondrous ways that give us well-being. Life itself and all living things are good, as is the existence of the cosmos in its stunning grandeur. Love is a very great good, in the Christian faith the greatest of all. Good also is our ability to be aware of our worlds and to recognize and create beauty; and, for our own good and of others, also the ability to recognize and transform ugliness and evil. The ability to know and value truth is another very great good, both in itself and because without it other goods diminish and even perish. The ability to find ways of facing and handling adversity, alone and with others, is yet another good, as is the joy of sharing whatever makes life very precious.

---

3. Prozesky, *Conscience*, 98-145.
4. Robinson, *Atheist's Values*, 65, emphasis added.
5. Robinson, *Atheist's Values*, 73-74.

Goodness is present in the people who enrich our lives all the time and in the structures of society that give it stability, order and justice. We experience it in all the unearned and unexpected blessings that come to us, like a seemingly miraculous deliverance from deadly peril, a welcome job offer, a chance meeting that leads to love, marriage and a family, rains that end a long drought, the breath-taking beauty of the universe and a tiny flower that catches the eye next to a path in the mountains, and in so many other ways which touch us all, unbidden, throughout our lives. And most wondrous of all is the ability to recognize and value goodness itself, a supreme blessing that gives us our bearings and direction, underlying the countless specific ways we experience it throughout our lives. Encountering these realities evokes gratitude and at times amazement; it offers us opportunities to enhance goodness around us and in ourselves, and it invites us to ponder its ultimate source.

From, or perhaps through, a handful of rare individuals over the past few thousand years there have flowed powerful rivers of goodness that have changed the world and still do, mostly as an inherent part of their spiritual influence. Moses on Mount Sinai, according to the Hebrew Scriptures, received the moral guidance of the Ten Commandments. I once heard a Hasidic rabbi explain that on the holy mountain he received a vision of an inexhaustible compassion, a vision that not only shaped Judaism but also Christianity. As the eminent New Testament scholar John Dominic Crossan has said, the entire prophetic tradition involves an "insistent divine demand for distributive justice" for all and not just for Israel.[6] In India there was Gautama Siddharta's experience of enlightenment about the way to overcome suffering, which made him the Buddha and gave rise to yet another great river of goodness, best known today in the person of the Dalai Lama.

Some five centuries after the Buddha, Judaism gave birth to a great new river of goodness with a message and practice of divine love as a world-changing ethic, given to the world in and by Jesus of Nazareth, who fed the hungry and healed the sick, and whose earliest followers experienced the life-giving Easter truth that his spirit, message and example had not been defeated by the horror of his crucifixion. Still later came a further great stream from Prophet Muhammad's hearing and reciting of the words of the Qur'an, receiving them as from the very heart of Allah himself.

Nearer our own time came the moral outrage felt by Karl Marx at the pitiless exploitation of workers by their employers in the mines and factories of nineteenth-century Europe; the women and men of conscience who started and led the movement to end slavery; also Gandhi's great experiment

---

6. Crossan, *How to Read the Bible*, 110.

with truth and the power of the soul known as *satyagraha* to overcome injustice.[7] At much the same time brave women began the demand for equal treatment with men, launching another great stream of goodness in the world. Then we saw the dramatic force of Martin Luther King's courage and his great speech of a dream for a better world which so inspired all who struggled against racism, like Nelson Mandela and Desmond Tutu. For me personally, listening some years ago to Jonathan Sacks, then a chief rabbi, and the Dalai Lama, and knowing Desmond Tutu, were personal experiences of a very great good.

Sometimes these spiritual and ethical encounters have a power and intensity that is so great that they surpass our ability to understand and express adequately. Then they leave us speechless and full of wonder as we search for ways to express them as best we can. We find ourselves using metaphors, like calling a sense of protective divine presence a good shepherd. Notice how even physics sometimes employs seemingly contradictory models, for example by explaining light as both particle and wave, for that which is outside the world of familiar experience and language. Such, certainly, is the case with peak spiritual experiences of great and wondrous goodness.

There is, therefore, indeed good news: goodness, both mysterious and accessible, is at work in the world, inspiring, inviting and empowering our active commitment. It enlightens and does not mislead or deceive; it never enslaves but attracts by its beauty; it never discriminates unfairly but is there equally for us all, like the force of gravity or the sunshine. And if further evidence of its power and presence is needed, the following instances should suffice: existence rather than nothingness; order in the cosmos rather than chaos; life and not just dead matter; consciousness and its gift of self-consciousness; intelligence with the ability to discern truth and falsehood; conscience and morality; creativity leading to beneficial change but also involving sufficient stability to give us confidence of worthwhile, painstaking achievement; beauty, vision, hope, and spirituality. As I have already suggested, these precious realities can be likened to the facets of a beautiful diamond, but unlike diamonds which are costly and for the few, they are available freely and in abundance for everyone, everywhere, and at all times.

Although I have been privileged to spend nearly all my adult life in the academic world, the experiences that took me to my present sense of the crowning power and beauty of goodness and its decisive relevance for faith were as much before and outside that world as within it, so those experiences must now also be described. No explanation is needed for including

---

7. Brown, "Gandhi," 97; *Prisoner of Hope*, and *Gandhi in South Africa*, 21–33.

what my academic studies and research revealed to me. It is the personal part of the formative factors in the next chapters that need a word of explanation. I include this part because it is these personal experiences that led me to my present conclusions about Christianity, strongly reinforced by the academic side.

Chapter 2

Youthful Awakenings

THE WONDER OF THE STARRY HEAVENS

IN MY NINTH YEAR I discovered something that, quite unknown to me, pointed my life in the direction of my present conviction that the natural *is* the supernatural and not something different, and not far less important. I discovered the fascinations of the solar system from the pages of an illustrated encyclopedia brought home one day by my father, and not yet from the clear night skies of our South African home town of Oudtshoorn. Observing those night skies came later. The pages on astronomy in the encyclopedia featured an artist's impressions of the surface of the Moon as seen from an imaginary spacecraft of the future, as well as images of the planets based on telescopic observations. I was captivated by the craters and mountains of the Moon, a ruddy Mars with a polar ice cap, and Saturn's rings.

So began a love of the starry heavens that led during my high school years to my first glimpse of Jupiter and its four large moons through a telescope, and from that experience to building my own reflecting telescope, with an 8-inch primary mirror that I painstakingly ground and polished, and had silvered. It is a love that remains strong today, except that I now have a sophisticated, computerized telescope and get most of my information about astronomy from NASA's amazing space probes to Mars and the outer planets, and from the Hubble telescope. It has also led to the understanding of the cosmos that modern astrophysics has given us, with major implications for how to think of creation. So from a young age the phrase "the heavens" took on an astronomical meaning that fascinated me much more than its usual religious connotation. I give my resultant ethical and spiritual understanding of the cosmos in chapter 5.

MY FIRST BIBLICAL INSPIRATION

Not long after that youthful awakening to the marvel of the star-filled heavens in 1954 came my earliest spiritual experience, which also connected with my interest in astronomy and has given direction to my life ever since. It happened later that year on my tenth birthday. Early in the morning while I was still in bed my father, who loved his Bible, brought me the gift not just of my first Bible but, even more meaningful for me, the gift of what he had written in it. He opened it at Daniel 12:3, which I recall went as follows, in whatever version that was: "They that be wise shall shine as the brightness of the firmament and they that turn many to righteousness, as the stars forever and ever." In the margin, next to these words, he had written in his beautiful handwriting, "God's promise." Given my existing passion for the starry heavens, those biblical words could not fail to seem as if they were meant for me personally.

Ours was then a fundamentalist home in which the Bible was seen, quite literally, as the directly inspired Word of God. The human writers whose names appear in it were believed to be no more than transmitters of what was divinely revealed to them. But even as a boy this view of the Bible began to trouble me. While I found some parts truly inspiring, like Daniel 12:3, others, like the book of Numbers, struck me secretly as too boring to be the sort of thing a God of perfect wisdom would communicate. A questioning tendency about Scripture had already begun to make itself felt and would continue to do so, affecting what I could believe. My university education would encourage and fuel it, as I relate later.

HEEDING THE POWER OF CONSCIENCE ABOUT POLITICAL EVIL AND RELIGION

In my 2007 book called *Conscience: Ethical Intelligence for Global Well-Being*, I defined conscience as the inner voice of ethics, of right and wrong, good and evil, adding that we can think of it as a built-in guidance system in our search for the morally good life. Then I continued as follows.

> "It is the uncomfortable feeling we get, or should get, when we tell a lie, speak cruelly, cheat on somebody, use our fists, double-park, break a promise, or do any of the many things we know are

wrong. It is also the warm and noble feeling that comes when we do the right thing—standing up for a friend, being loyal to a team-mate or to a partner at home, or in business, giving time, effort and money to those in need, or insisting on the truth, especially when it costs us something to do these things."[1]

More ambitiously but with good reason, I now extend that definition to the belief that conscience—or our moral sense in practice—is the cosmos manifesting in us its potential for goodness.

This way of understanding conscience arises from two sources. The first one is my university studies and later research as a university professor, including the research that led to my first book.[2] I present the fruits of that research in chapters 5 and 6, which deal with the theoretical foundations of my conclusions about Christianity. The other source is my experience of the power of the moral sense in both politics and religion, which I began to feel in my boyhood. Here are some highlights of those experiences, starting with religion, after which I turn to politics.

ENCOUNTERING THE JEWISH COMMUNITY IN THE "LITTLE JERUSALEM"

At much the same time as my first fascination with astronomy and my first Bible, my growing sense of right and wrong began to reshape my Christian faith itself, an influence that continues to this day. Our town was home to a substantial Jewish community, earning for itself the label of the "Little Jerusalem," and several of my classmates were Jewish. In time friendships with them developed, especially with one of them who became a very close friend. I soon learnt that these Jewish people were fine, upstanding members of the community with a deep faith and strong ethic of their own.

At home, however, our then very evangelical and biblically fundamentalist faith declared that only by accepting Christ could anybody find salvation and eternal life. Deeply troubled at the dreadful thought of damnation awaiting these Jewish people, I turned to my father for guidance, asking how that could possibly be fair. His answer remains one of my greatest experiences of the power of ethics. Given his very evangelical and conservative Christian faith, he should, to be true to its beliefs, have said something like "That is what the Bible says," but he didn't. His own conscience and trust in a God of perfect goodness overrode his beliefs when he replied by asking me

---

1. Prozesky, *Conscience*, 19.
2. Prozesky, *Religion and Ultimate Well-Being*.

if I thought I was more just than God. "Of course not," I replied, to which he responded by telling me that if I saw a problem of justice here, then how much more would God with his perfect justice see it, so there wasn't a problem. I could leave things to God's justice.

That satisfied me and began my journey out of our then evangelical orientation. Now, as I think back to the defining moments in my early life, I can see in them the transforming power of goodness manifesting itself as justice and other values that change even deeply held religious beliefs, once that power begins to rule our lives.

APARTHEID AS UNCHRISTIAN

Strongly influenced by my parents, by our Anglican parish priest and curate, and also by the moral stand being taken against apartheid by leading figures in our church like Father Trevor Huddleston and Archbishops Geoffrey Clayton and Joost de Blank in Cape Town, I came to abhor the many signs of ugly racism in the community in that time of the rampant, early apartheid state. Many whites openly referred to black people as "kaffirs," the equivalent of "niggers" in the USA, or as *Hotnotte* (from "Hottentot") in the case of members of the so-called colored community, comprising people of mixed and Malayan ancestry, and they demanded a servile response from them.

At home my father was calling apartheid a national sin and in my senior high school years I was openly expressing the conviction that racism was unchristian. I did so most strongly at a conference near Cape Town of youth leaders from schools all over what was then our Cape Province. It was hosted by that city's government-supporting Afrikaans daily newspaper, *Die Burger*. A number of other youth leaders, mostly Afrikaans-speaking, supported me but others were hostile, none more so than one who I shall simply called Magda.

I had just spoken of apartheid as unchristian and she rose to announce that "in Romans 8:31, Paul says that if God is for us who can be against us, so Martin Prozesky is in conflict with the Word of God!" She eyed me distastefully as she sat down. I got up and replied that St Paul was referring to the tiny, embattled Christian communities of the very early church, not white South Africa, but I could see that Magda was unconvinced. She had been taught that the Bible speaks directly to her people and did not need to be contextualized. To my relief an Afrikaans-speaking and very senior figure in the province's education hierarchy and his wife came to me at the end of the conference and gave me a word of encouragement for being willing to think critically about our affairs.

There was sometimes a valuable benefit from such early experiences of objecting to injustice by showing respect and courtesy towards black people. One incident stands out in my memory. It took place on a Saturday morning in my high school years. I was washing my father's car in the road outside our home when I saw an older colored woman of about my mother's age walking towards where I was working. I smiled politely at her as she passed. She stopped and said the following in a friendly voice in Afrikaans, the language of most of her community at that time. "If Sir (*Meneer*) can smile at us like that at us brown people, then Sir need never fear us." She returned my smile and walked on as I mumbled my astonished but grateful thanks. It was an important early lesson of the power of even little acts of goodness, mine but especially hers.

Two books by prominent anti-apartheid Christians added powerfully to the moral influence on me of home and church in relation to political injustice. The first was Trevor Huddleston's book *Naught for your Comfort*, based on his experience of the state's terrible treatment of black people in an area of Johannesburg then called Sophiatown, when it forced them out of their homes to flatten the area for a new suburb for whites, which it gloatingly re-named Triomf in Afrikaans (meaning Triumph).[3]

Even more powerful for me was Nobel Prize winner Albert Luthuli's book *Let my People Go*, which appeared in 1962, my final year at high school. Its powerful echo of the biblical words of Moses to the Pharaoh greatly inspired me and many others, even though one of my school teachers sneeringly dismissed Luthuli as an *Outa*, a patronizing Afrikaans word for an older black man. Written by a black South African Christian and the leader then of the African National Congress, later to be led by Nelson Mandela, Luthuli's book confirmed my belief that being a Christian was first and foremost a duty to oppose injustice and other evils.

DISCOVERING PHILOSOPHY

A classroom in the old Boys' High School in Oudtshoorn, now housing the town's fine museum, might not seem a likely place for a spiritual experience, understood as a powerful sense of inspiration, least of all involving philosophy, but that is indeed what happened in my penultimate high school year. Our English teacher, Sam Bosman, was a great favorite of ours with his vivid way of saying things, wide-ranging interests and silvery mane of hair. One

3. Huddlestone, *Naught for Your Comfort*.

day he broke away from literature and told us about the French philosopher René Descartes, quoting his famous dictum of *cogito ergo sum*, meaning "I think, therefore I am." I was captivated. It was as if a whole new, brilliantly lit world of insight and possibility had opened for me, a world where careful, resolute thinking about things would be my mainstay and guide. From later university studies of thinkers like Pascal, Kant and Whitehead, I would come to see the limitations of such an exclusive reliance on rationality, but my faith in the power of logical thought that was kindled that day at school has never left me.

Nor did I have any doubts about wanting to become a priest. I was a very devoted Anglican worshipper and had been accepted by the Bishop of George, my home diocese, as a candidate for the priesthood. This led to theological studies from 1963 to 1966 at Rhodes University in the compact city of Grahamstown, now renamed Makhanda. Those years changed my faith and the direction of my life in ways of which I had no inkling as I set off eagerly by train for my studies early in 1963.

Chapter 3

Theological Studies 1963-1969

GRAHAMSTOWN NESTLES IN A valley with low hills all around the little city. In glorious, early morning sunshine on the Sunday of my arrival, the train wound its way slowly down a long, curving route to the station. I was entranced by the sight of the campus and the many church spires of the City of Saints, as it was then also called. There I encountered new faiths and philosophies, inspiring Christian opponents of apartheid, the critical method of interpreting the Bible that finally ended my boyhood innocence about Scripture. Perhaps most important of all in my student life at Rhodes, within two days of my arrival I received advice which would later change the direction of my life.

ADVICE AT REGISTRATION

Here is what happened. I entered the study of the Dean of Divinity, Professor William Maxwell, for my registration and a listing of the courses I would study that first year. Maxwell, a stocky Presbyterian from Scotland given to bow ties and snuff, was the professor of Systematic Theology. We shook hands and he introduced me to the Anglican professor of Church History, Peter Hinchliff, who acted as a mentor for Anglican ordinands like me. Maxwell looked at my school results, turned to his colleague and said, "Dr Hinchliff, this man should teach." Thereupon he listed my courses and added the words "BD to follow," Peter Hinchliff concurring. The Bachelor of Divinity degree was for future scholars and church leaders. So the man who would in his lectures encourage me to read voraciously, planted in my mind a seed that would germinate and grow into a much changed career from the one in the priesthood I then so eagerly expected, but it would take another seven years for that expectation to end.

FAREWELL TO BIBLICAL LITERALISM

The end of my boyhood notions about the Bible began in the lectures on what we all called the Old Testament, completely oblivious of how offensive that term is to Judaism. They were given by a dour but kindly Scot named Willie Cosser. Early in the course Dr Cosser announced as his topic "The moral problems of the Old Testament," in which he took us through a number of events involving cruelty and deception. The most notable was the account in 1 Samuel 15:33, of the prophet Samuel vengefully hacking Agag, the captured king of the Amalekites, in pieces, as the older translations have it, unlike the softened rendering of the New International Version of the Bible.

I was initially shocked by the lectures, having a very patchy knowledge then of that part of the Hebrew Scriptures and quite unaware of these moral problems. As our New Testament lecturer never mentioned any ethical problems about its twenty-seven books, like its ambivalence about slavery and gender justice, I soon got over that first reaction. In any case, I already believed that Christianity was the true Israel, not the one we were taught had rejected Christ. Only later in my life did I fully discern the serious moral problems of such a dismissive view of Judaism in the New Testament itself.

Dr Cosser also explained that the critical study of the Bible was a judicious, probing approach, alert to possible ethical, historical and theological difficulties, and not something essentially negative. He told us that the responsible, informed study of Scripture must start by approaching the biblical texts as we would any others and not as privileged writings exempt from questioning scrutiny. I was at first much disturbed by this approach, given my view of the Bible, but in time my mind took over and the method began to reveal far greater depth in Scripture than my erstwhile, rather naive reading had done. In any case, my faith was not threatened, probably because I had long seen Christianity primarily as a force for good in the world, as I have already mentioned, and not primarily something that stood or fell with a fundamentalist attitude to Scripture.

During my later studies and lecturing I found much confirmation from eminent biblical scholars of what Dr Cosser had taught us. Thus Dennis Nineham could write that we needed a new type of New Testament scholarship which assumes as a working hypothesis "that all past events form a single causally interconnected web and that no event occurs without this-worldly causation of some sort."[1] In other words, our understanding of events recounted in Scripture must be informed by a knowledge of the culture, history and even geography of the time. Significantly, Nineham added the following on the same page: "It would still be possible to see the God whose hand is everywhere behind the first-century events."

Until those Biblical Studies classes at Rhodes University I had no idea of how the Bible came about. Like most others I was interested in what it said, not where and when the biblical writers operated, other than having a vague sense that they wrote under the direct guidance of the Holy Spirit. Dr Cosser, in introducing us to the concept of the canon of Scripture, began an important process of discovery for me about how the sixty-six books of the Protestant Bible came about, and were ultimately deemed the official, inspired Scriptures of Christianity in the fourth century. I remember being intrigued by the fact that for several centuries the early Christians, who suffered much persecution and martyrdom, managed without the Bible as contemporary Christians know and use it, for nothing like it existed. That insight took me even further from my erstwhile youthful assumption that biblical faith meant basing your life uncritically on the words of Scripture. As David Stacey sharply puts it, "no religious group that values learning can be satisfied with the ploughboy's understandings."[2]

Such an approach to the biblical texts perforce changes the idea of inspiration from a process allegedly involving divine dictation, which denies any meaningful human influence in the message supposedly so given. I liked David Stacey's definition, which I read years later, that inspiration is "what happens when an exceptionally gifted person has moments of supreme insight," because it points to a Deity who respects and uses the brains he has created.[3] In time I also discovered the enormous importance of understanding the historical, cultural and even geographical contexts in which the biblical writers operated and by which they were affected, an interpretive principle prompted by the following apt question by Stacey: "How can one know what the Bible means, unless one comprehends Hebrew social and family structure?"[4]

I wrote this chapter in the 500th anniversary year of the start of the Protestant Reformation and am happy to find from my records of Stacey's work that Martin Luther held that when problems in the biblical texts are

---

1. Nineham, *Use and Abuse*, 22.
2. Stacey, *Interpreting the Bible*, 8.
3. Stacey, *Interpreting the Bible*, 45.
4. Stacey, *Interpreting the Bible*, 15.

discerned, "Scripture must be used to interpret Scripture."[5] My own conclusion here is that the central biblical message is about a God of perfect goodness and love, so I am using that as my norm to judge what is spiritually and ethically acceptable and what is not, when I evaluate Conservative and also Liberal Christianity, and interpret the Bible, later in this book.

CHRISTIAN ACADEMICS AGAINST APARTHEID

In my boyhood most of Oudtshoorn's white population supported apartheid. It was soon clear that things were different at Rhodes University, especially in the Faculty of Divinity and in the Department of Philosophy. Three of my lecturers there proved particularly influential.

In Basil Moore we divinity students had an inspirational young lecturer in systematic theology. This was less for his radical theology, with his admiration for Paul van Buren's book *The Secular Meaning of the Gospel*, published in 1963, than for his brave passion for an ethical faith that totally rejected apartheid. For this he and his family paid dearly as first the university council excluded him and then the country drove them into exile in England and Australia, a fate that would profoundly affect my life in 1969, as I recount later.

Here is one example of Basil Moore's passionate denunciation of apartheid. An open symposium had been organized on the campus about Christian National Education or CNE, the system imposed by the government on the country's public schools. I recall my father, who was himself in education, dismissing CNE as being "a big N, a small E and no C." At the symposium a local politician, who supported apartheid, argued that it was in fact Christian. A visibly angry Basil Moore, using the New Testament passage about Satan tempting Christ with the offer of state power (Matt 4:8—10), dramatically and repeatedly dismissed that notion with the following words, strongly emphasising the last one: "The New Testament rejects CNE and state control as *satanic!*"

Another speaker at that symposium was the philosophy professor, Daantjie Oosthuizen. He was also an inspirational Christian figure who would greatly enrich my life a few years later, as I describe in the next chapter. Daantjie, as he was universally called, was well-known as an Afrikaner Christian who bravely and publicly opposed apartheid, but who also remained a loyal, worshipping member of the local Dutch Reformed Church, a denomination then notorious in our eyes for its purportedly biblical support for apartheid. There was talk that even the ministers there avoided

---

5. Stacey, *Interpreting the Bible*. 87.

friendly contact with him because of his opposition to their political stance, and perhaps also because his wife Anne was Jewish.

Just as opposed to the politics of the day was Peter Hinchliff. He too left us in no doubt that being a Christian had serious ethical implications for the priesthood. Although much younger than his professorial colleagues in the faculty, he set the best example of scholarly achievement by writing books and acquiring the prestigious Doctor of Divinity degree from Oxford, where he had studied. It was he whose actions ended the intention for me to study at Rhodes for a BD after my theological BA. Correctly, he told me that going to Oxford would be better for me, advised me to apply successfully for admission to Trinity, his old college there, and went out of his way to help me find the necessary funds.

In these ways my most important academic guides at Rhodes deepened and extended the strongly ethical orientation my religious life had acquired in my Oudtshoorn schooldays, and opened to me the prospect of being both a priest and a scholar. As I look back to those student years in Grahamstown, I see there the gently powerful workings of a goodness, in and through those mentors, taking charge of my life. By then I knew and loved the famous prayer of St Francis of Assisi, "Lord make me an instrument of Thy peace . . ." but I did not then know that the Hebrew word that is translated as peace—*shalom*—has a much richer meaning, signifying a goodness that is more than just calm and quiet, involving a shared enrichment of life based on the finest values, where enmity and harm are no more. Rhodes also taught me that *shalom* was not the exclusive gift of my own Christian faith or of Judaism.

ENCOUNTERING MORALLY STRONG BUDDHISTS AND ATHEISTS

In my first year at Rhodes I was assigned a room in a residence for first year men that was then called Jan Smuts House. To guide us young freshers, or Inks as we were called then, we had a number of student councillors. One of them, Johan Maree, later a sociology professor at the University of Cape Town, was a keen Christian and ran a small prayer and Bible study group, which I joined. Fortunately for us, Johan's was a liberal faith. He showed this by encouraging us to think widely about Christianity and at one session he introduced us to another senior student, named Harry Farmer. Harry hailed from what was then called Southern Rhodesia, now Zimbabwe, and was a Buddhist. He gave me my first encounter with a non-biblical faith, telling us quietly about the Buddha and the spiritual path he launched. Though not then drawn to what I heard, and intrigued that there could be a religion without belief in a God, I was impressed by Harry's quiet, dignified sincerity, and knew that my mental world had been enlarged.

That change was dramatically extended for me later in the year by a remark in class one day by the philosophy lecturer who took us for logic, Cedric Evans. Students majoring in Systematic Theology like me were required to take at least a year's course in philosophy. I welcomed that but other divinity students were less keen on being required to know something about ancient Greek philosophers like Thales and Anaximander, moral philosophy and logic.

Cedric was a liberal in political matters and a person of notable moral courage. Even so I was much taken aback, and some of my fellow theology students shocked, when our lecturer, departing briefly from symbolic logic, announced boldly that he had never sinned. Noting our startled looks, he said, as I clearly recall, "Sin is a theological concept. It means transgressing the commands of God. I am an atheist because I believe there is no God, so I can't transgress his commands, for they can't exist. I have, unfortunately, sometimes done wrong, for wrong-doing is an ethical concept, not dependent on religious beliefs, but I haven't sinned."

That was my first encounter with an atheist. His moral courage and clear reasoning impressed me much more than the uneasiness I felt about his rejection of my belief in God. Like Harry Farmer, Cedric Evans was pushing me towards a still wider sense of reality, one where religious faith not only changed and even sometimes went out of the window, but where moral goodness remained strongly in place.

Over the years I have forgotten most of the formal logic Cedric Evans taught us, but I've never lost the importance of his conviction that moral goodness can and does thrive without religion. Little did I know it then, but what I now know to be the limitless power of the good was taking me a step further away from the comfortable captivity of my immature faith. I could not then see Cedric as a spiritual liberator. I do now and am grateful.

From that early experience I would, later in my academic career, make a point of examining the arguments of various atheists past and present, as I explain in a subsequent chapter, in order to ensure that my studies of Christianity and other theistic faiths were as balanced as I could make them, and not confined to the views of believers, however uncomfortable such an approach might be.

THE IMPACT OF *HONEST TO GOD* IN 1963

The next liberator during my studies at Rhodes was a bishop of the Church of England, John A.T. Robinson, with his sensational little book *Honest to God*. It quickly became a best-seller, reportedly with more copies sold than any other theological book, and was soon being translated into other languages. Not long after its appearance, a newspaper in the nearby city of Port Elizabeth carried a long article about it, and our Anglican chaplain at Rhodes, Father John Barnett, arranged a Saturday morning of discussion about the book for members of the student Anglican Society.

We met at St Bartholomew's Church, of which John was also rector. It was there that I heard him reporting Robinson's dismissal of the idea of God as "an old man in the sky." I remember during a tea break standing at the gate of the churchyard and gazing up at the clouds in the blue sky above and acknowledging to myself that they were indeed empty of such a being. Reading the press article and later the book itself confirmed that recognition, but Robinson's proposal that instead we should think of God as the ground and depth of being made little sense to me. On the other hand, his view of Jesus as an ethical leader of immense importance appealed to me very much. Concerning God, what the famous English bishop, whom I would later encounter in person during his visit to South Africa in 1977, did achieve for me was to help me see my faith as a creative journey for pioneers, not a haven for settlers, as it is for many others whom I greatly respect.

EARLY EXPERIENCES AT OXFORD

After my BA degree at Rhodes I had the privilege of taking my theological studies further at Trinity College, Oxford. There I had three outstanding dons as tutors: Leslie Houlden for the New Testament, John Baker, whose lyrical celebration of goodness was quoted above, for the Old Testament, and for doctrine the dazzlingly brilliant David Jenkins, later to become Bishop of Durham. Well I remember him once saying that a theology that is not also a powerful ethic cannot be Christian. I would later find lasting inspiration in the opening words of one of his books where he wrote that "God is either a gift or a delusion."[6]

My two years at Oxford, besides being academically very rigorous and rewarding, aided my spiritual journey into a more inclusive, more ethical selfhood in four main ways. The first was new multi-faith friendships.

6. Jenkins, *Living with Questions*, 1.

I quickly became friends with wonderful, caring Japanese students, one of them with a background in both Shinto and Zen. In him especially I encountered a gentle, refined and sensitive nobility that owed nothing to Christianity or western culture. As with my boyhood Jewish friends and encounters with Harry Farmer and Cedric Evans at Rhodes University, he and other Japanese friends showed me that the realm of goodness is deeper, richer and more inspiring than the impression I'd received from my Christian nurture.

A similar enrichment came from a Muslim fellow student who hailed from Damascus and was studying Arabic literature for a postgraduate degree. From his refined manner and knowledge of Islam I received my first personal lesson about his faith and the Qur'an, when he told me of its great, poetic beauty in Arabic and the fact that Prophet Muhammad was illiterate. I remember thinking long and hard about that revelation, pondering the amazing reality of such a person giving voice to such beauty of words and beliefs. How could that happen unless he was indeed divinely inspired, a possibility orthodox Christian doctrine struck me as ruling out entirely.

NEW CHRISTIAN FRIENDS

At the same time, new Christian friendships were adding their influence to my experience of moral goodness. Four of these stand out for their lastingly rich impact on me and my life's work. The first one happened early in December 1966. It was occasioned, of all things, by the annual rugby match between Oxford and Cambridge Universities at Twickenham in London, to which a contingent of Oxford supporters like me had travelled by coach. On alighting at the stadium I chanced, if that is the right word, to encounter somebody who introduced himself as Hays Rockwell, an Episcopalian priest on sabbatical at Oxford from America with his family.

We soon became very good friends and it was he, later to become an Episcopalian bishop of great moral courage and spiritual depth, who opened the way for me to spend a year after Oxford at the former Episcopal Theological School, or ETS, in Cambridge, Massachusetts, starting in September 1968. Our friendship continues to the present, enhanced by times together both in the USA and South Africa over the years, rich in itself but also rich in the way my time at the ETS, since re-named the Episcopal Divinity School and now, alas, closed down in Cambridge, led to other ways in which the power of goodness took me where I needed to be and not where I believed I should be, as I relate later.

The second of these friendships happened after Trinity College had closed for the winter vacation of 1966 and I needed somewhere to stay. My college tutor and its chaplain, Leslie Houlden, arranged for me to spend a few weeks in a small guest room at an Anglican community of Franciscan brothers, called the House of the Divine Compassion, in Plaistow, then a poor suburb in the east end of London. A number of the brothers were social workers helping drug addicts, others maintained the place, cooking and cleaning, all of them under the spiritual leadership of a remarkable man called Brother Bernard, whose welcoming serenity drew me to him and gave me my first living glimpse of the loving path of service and self-sacrifice pioneered in Christianity by Francis of Assisi. If ever there were instruments of God's peace, they were Brother Bernard and his fellow brothers.

As winter's grip tightened, the days grew shorter and it was very cold. Heating was minimal and the meals, taken with the brothers, were very basic, but the love and warmth I experienced from them and the gentle wisdom of Brother Bernard far outweighed the physical discomforts. Most memorable of all was Christmas dinner. The brothers welcomed a number of outsiders to join us, a few of them vagrants off the street, another one a lonely old man who had no living relatives. One of the vagrants sat next to me and I struggled to cope with the strong smell of clothes and a body that hadn't had a wash for a very long time. What saved me from recoiling was seeing how Brother Bernard and the other brothers accepted similar guests with a welcoming warmth that made me ashamed of my reaction and helped me to accept the man next to me the way they were doing. Kindness, I was being taught, ranks higher by far than fragrance.

There was another South African guest from Trinity College at the House of the Divine Compassion who was the third of my new Christian friends at Oxford. He was Stephen Gawe, my first black friend and a fellow Anglican. He had been persecuted in South Africa for anti-apartheid activity and received a banning order, which severely curtailed his life. Sympathizers at Oxford put up the money to award him a scholarship, so he left his homeland on what was known as an "exit permit"—permission to leave but not return. We became good friends and from his kindly, gentle Anglican faith I saw for myself the cynical dishonesty of the apartheid belief that people like him were, or could be, furthering the aims of atheistic communism. Compassion, I knew unforgettably, was not only a place of love and care in the bleak stretches of the east end of London, but a reality that could change everything if we will but let it govern our lives and work with it.

In time at Oxford I became friendly with a few others from the South African anti-apartheid community, both black and white, secular and religious, liberals and Marxists. Meetings and social occasions with them were my first experience of the fulfilment that would come to our homeland after apartheid. They showed that people with different belief-systems could be united by a shared ethical vision of justice and acceptance, demonstrating vividly for me that ethical values are more important than other aspects of culture, and certainly more important than ethnic differences. I was learning that while these differences exist and can divide us, especially when they are prioritized, a shared commitment for the ethical values of respect, justice, the truth and active concern for others can reduce them to relative insignificance.

BERLIN IN 1967

In the Easter vacation of 1967 I found a very different but equally memorable place to stay. A recently widowed cousin of my father's was living in West Berlin. She wrote that I was welcome to spend a few weeks at her home. She was born and grew up in South Africa and it was there that she married a German missionary who had been sent to work in South Africa. An accident led to the loss of a leg for him and to a recall back to Germany, eventually to a pastorate in Pomerania in the east of the country. There they had endured the rise of Nazism and World War II, and then became refugees, seeking to escape the vengeful soldiers of Stalin's Red Army on foot early in 1945. They ended up, safe at last, in the American zone of West Berlin where he was later appointed assistant pastor at the imposing Lutheran church in the suburb of Neukölln. He died a few years before my visit.

Along with the kindness of my aunt, three experiences of the power and potential of ethical commitment stood out in my weeks in Berlin. One was being taken by a visiting South African missionary through the infamous Checkpoint Charlie into East Berlin, where he had a meeting at the headquarters of the Berlin Missionary Society, where my Prozesky great-grandfather had trained for missionary work in South Africa in the 1860s. While the meeting took place, an elderly driver, also a Christian, gave me a tour of the city in a rattling Trabi car. What struck me more than the fear that I detected and felt for myself, was that old man's answer when I asked what it was like to live under East German communism. He replied that he had lived since 1933 under relentless dictatorships, indicating that with faith and courage you can endure anything. Well I remember how he urged me to stop taking pictures whenever the police or soldiers were in sight, which was often.

The second Berlin experience took place at the infamous Wall near the Brandenburg Gate. I had climbed up some wooden steps to a platform next to the Wall. From there I could look into East Berlin, noting the sentry towers with helmeted guards who viewed me and others through their binoculars. Between the Wall and them I could view the desolate death strip alongside the Wall and its rolls of barrier wire, impediments to would-be escapers. Near me on the western side black crosses and notices had been placed on the Wall to commemorate people who had died trying to scale it from the east, shot by those steel-helmeted border guards.

It was a desolate experience. That feeling swiftly changed when soon after clambering down I found a brochure about West Berlin at a nearby kiosk, featuring a quotation from Mahatma Gandhi, which I recall saying "I want the winds of all cultures to blow freely in my face." The effect of those words was very great, coming as they did at that hideous wall of separation and reminding me painfully that apartheid South Africa was also doing its level best to prevent the experience Gandhi had in mind, just as effectively as the Berlin Wall.

The third experience in Berlin was a visit after Easter to the monument to murdered victims of the Nazi terror at Plötzenzee in the north-west of the city, not far from today's Tegel airport. Among those murdered there by hanging were men and women involved in anti-Hitler activity, most notably in the failed assassination plot against the Führer of July 20, 1944. They also numbered, although I did not then know this, members of the Kreisau Circle, a resistance group founded in 1940 and led by the Silesian aristocrat and devout Lutheran, Count Helmuth James von Moltke, as I would discover after returning to Oxford. The count was hanged there on 23 January 1945.

Well I remember the grim execution chamber. A steel bar extended from side to side about three meters above the floor. Attached to it were eight large, steel hooks, the actual method of hanging being the particularly terrible one of garrotting. A rope noose around the neck of the victim was suspended from those hooks and the victim left hanging like that, causing suffocation and a slow, agonizing death, some of their deaths reportedly being filmed for Hitler's viewing.

Nearby I also visited the Regina Maria Martyrium, a Catholic memorial which included an open-air courtyard, surrounded by a tall, concrete wall. Into that wall, spaces for letters spelling out a number of place names had been chipped and filled with packed nails about six inches long, perhaps like those used by the Romans for crucifixions. Among the names were Golgotha and Auschwitz, along with others associated with oppression, terror, and murder. Whether it was one of them or whether I added it in my mind I cannot now recall, but Sharpeville became fixed in my mind and memory as I viewed those names, because of the massacre there in 1960 of protesting black South Africans by the apartheid police. I do not know if those nails remain where I saw them in 1967.

AN OXFORD FRIENDSHIP THAT WOULD TRANSFORM MY LIFE

Back at Oxford came the close contact with my philosophy professor at Rhodes, Daantjie Oosthuizen, the fourth of my Christian friendships there. It came in my final term after Easter 1968. He was there for part of a sabbatical and I had found accommodation for him in a flat in the same North Oxford, red-brick mansion where friends and I were staying. Even though I was then devoting most of my time to preparation for what is called Schools at Oxford, the daunting, successive days of morning and afternoon final examinations for one's degree, and he was equally immersed in research with his friend, the eminent philosopher Gilbert Ryle, we found time to meet in the evenings for endless discussions which mainly centered on ethics. He opened my eyes to key parts of Immanuel Kant's moral philosophy, to ways of making notes while thinking an issue through logically, and especially to the moral courage of Christians who were part of the failed resistance and plot to assassinate Hitler on July 20, 1944.

The person who inspired him most in that plot, with its savagely brutal consequences for the plotters that I have already mentioned, was not the brave, martyred theologian Dietrich Bonhoeffer, who was not directly involved, but Count Helmuth von Moltke. From Daantjie Oosthuizen I got the deeply moving words of the count's last letter to his wife before his execution, where he wrote that he had stood before the fanatically pro-Hitler and so-called People's Judge, Roland Freisler, just as a Christian. Well aware of Daantjie's courage in publicly rejecting apartheid in circles that supported it back in Grahamstown, I could sense, as he told me about von Moltke and that last letter, that he identified deeply with those heroic German Christians who stood up publicly against Nazism, murderers of millions of members of his own wife's Jewish faith, and others.

After that final term at Oxford he and his family moved to the USA to spend the rest of his sabbatical at Brown University in Providence, Rhode Island, until the end of 1968. As I relate below, we were able to continue our friendship while he was there, until the family returned to Grahamstown where he had been appointed Dean of Arts with responsibilities that included theological students, with consequences early in 1969 that would unexpectedly affect my life. These I describe later. Daantjie's sudden death a few months after his return to Rhodes was a devastating shock and loss to all of us who loved and esteemed him.

DISCOVERING FRIEDRICH SCHLEIERMACHER AT OXFORD

One further experience at Oxford helped me move yet further from the world of traditional beliefs. This was a detailed study of the ideas of the founder of modern, liberal theology, Friedrich Schleiermacher (1768—1834). While the syllabus I was following required a study only of his doctrine of the person and work of Christ, I was interested enough to dig a lot deeper by reading his most famous early work, *On Religion: Speeches to its Cultured Despisers*, first issued in 1799, and revised several times afterwards, especially in 1806, the version I used then and still have,[7] since retranslated by Terrence N. Tice and others.[8] It was a step that changed my understanding not just of Christianity but of religion in general.

Three of his proposals struck me as especially important. Briefly, they are that experience is central to the life of faith; that religious beliefs, including belief in a personal deity, are secondary, variable parts of religion that are shaped by the cultures in which they arise; and thirdly that the clue to the unique significance of Jesus is the strength of his awareness of the divine. His own words later in his career about this were these: "The Redeemer, then, is like all men in virtue of the identity of human nature, but distinguished from them all by the constant potency of His God-consciousness, which was a veritable existence of God in Him."[9] Here I found a Christian thinker who not only understood the burgeoning new world of critical philosophy, the critical study of the Bible, literature and science, but welcomed that world of new knowledge, and redefined religion accordingly. Those Oxford studies of Schleiermacher were the beginning of later research for my doctorate, with results that are described in chapter 6.

STUDIES IN AMERICA

Having obtained my Oxford degree, later to become an MA in the Oxford manner, I began my time as a seminary student on a generous international scholarship at the Episcopal Theological School in Cambridge,

---

7. Schleiermacher, *Speeches*.
8. Tice, *Addresses*.
9. Schleiermacher, *Christian Faith*, 385.

Massachusetts, starting in September 1968. While there, where I had stimulating further academic studies at both the ETS and at Harvard Divinity School, new formative experiences also made themselves felt. Three of them helped me understand that goodness can work in unexpected and even unwelcome and distressing ways, but nonetheless be a lasting blessing.

We seminarians were assigned to parishes in the greater Boston area to be guided in church work by a parish priest. Mine was the Church of the Good Shepherd in the suburb of Waban, a lengthy trip from Cambridge on the network of underground and surface railroad lines in the greater Boston area. After the morning Eucharist one snowy Sunday the rector, Bill Foley, who with his artist wife Marilyn became lifelong friends, gave me a list of addresses and said that I should call at each. He gave me little detailed guidance about what to do or say at them, except that I should take them as I found them. Here is my account of what happened that morning, written some years later, very slightly edited.

> "At the first address, of a couple unknown to me, I was received by an elderly woman who expressed great appreciation at my presence; unknown to me the owner of the house had died during the night and she was there comforting his widow. Both women thought I had come to offer support as a would-be priest, and I sensed with a strange urgency that I must not say otherwise in their grief. But the truth was crystal clear to me: I had gone reluctantly and routinely; this house was first on my list. My visit was to them something totally different: a sign of the prompt caring of the local Episcopal parish. As such my presence seemed valuable, and I felt this very strong urge not to tell them the truth about my personal situation.
>
> "This incident is one of the most important I have experienced. I knew then that there are sometimes forces at work in and through us far greater than we conceive in our egocentricity and ignorance, forces for the good of others and perhaps also ourselves, and that for me to have insisted on telling those two tear-flecked ladies my little tale of accidental succour would have been as gross an act of selfishness and egoism as I can imagine. I learnt that while one must never deceive oneself, it is not necessarily good always to tell the whole story as seen from one's own standpoint. For the first time I had experienced a powerful reality at work in pastoral service, and from then on I have known, and not just believed, that theism cannot be merely subjective illusion."

Looking back as I write now to that Sunday, I can still see in my mind the bright sunshine on the fresh, deep snow and remember the crisp cold of the morning on my face as I walked to that sorrowing home. I also remember feeling deeply shaken by what happened and sensing, for the first time, that I had been the instrument of a power for good far greater than my own. I thought intuitively then that it was the Holy Spirit, and not mere good luck on my undeserving part. The experience had another lesson which I was very slow to understand: my shortcomings as a pastor. I had felt no great eagerness to do those house calls, perhaps because they would be new experiences and I had a natural shyness about initiating such encounters.

By strong contrast, what I enjoyed most as a trainee seminarian in that parish was preaching. I have a good speaking voice and had been a prize-winner in speaker's competitions at high school and Rhodes University, besides relishing the opportunity to use the beauty and power of words. The comments of parishioners and especially of Bill Foley after my sermons were very positive indeed. Here too I was slow to discern an emerging pattern in my activities, that I was more suited to teaching than to pastoral care.

Little did I then know that a golden opportunity to show me the way ahead lay just around the corner that winter. This was the second pivotal experience in my time at the ETS. It came late one evening after I had attended a play in Cambridge. On arriving at my room in Lawrence Hall at the ETS I found a card on the door knob telling me that a cable was waiting collection at the offices of Western Union. My immediate reaction was anxiety. What else would such a cable mean in all likelihood than bad news from home? A restless night and hurried breakfast followed till at last I could hurry off for my cable.

To my huge relief and amazement it did not bring bad news but a total and thrilling surprise. It was from Rhodes University telling me that they urgently needed a temporary lecturer in systematic theology, and asking if I could come immediately at their expense. My reaction was in sharp contrast to the reluctance I had felt in Waban about those pastoral visits. I was elated, excited and very eager to accept the request. As soon as I could meet him, I presented the request to the Dean of the ETS, Professor Harvey Guthrie and a few other faculty members with whom I was studying. All were supportive, telling me this was a great opportunity to experience lecturing. Harvey Guthrie even assured me that my place and funding at the ETS would be held over for me to return to afterwards.

So it was that I could almost immediately send a cable back to Rhodes to accept the invitation and, with the help of the ETS, arrange the long flight via London, Johannesburg and Durban to Port Elizabeth, the airport nearest to Grahamstown. The only obstacle to my departure was the arrival right then, over the whole north-east of the USA, of a massive, three-day snowstorm, which closed Boston's Logan airport for a number of days and lay almost as deep as car roofs along the streets of Cambridge.

As soon as flights resumed I was on my way, arriving exhausted but excited at Port Elizabeth. There I was met by David Novitz, a great Jewish friend from our school days, then working on a master's degree in philosophy, together with my late, younger sisters Linda and Leonie, also then studying at Rhodes. Ever since receiving that cable at the ETS I had wondered what lay behind the urgent need for my services. Now I heard it from David and my joy changed to dismay. He told me that at the instigation of the Dean of Arts, my friend and mentor Daantjie Oosthuizen, Rhodes had cabled me to return urgently to help out. The reason for the staffing crisis was partly the recent retirement of Professor William Maxwell, but the main reason was the highly controversial refusal of the university council to approve the senate's recommendation for a permanent appointment of my erstwhile lecturer Basil Moore.

David Novitz explained that Daantjie and my Anglican mentor at Rhodes, Peter Hinchliff, had felt that I would accept the situation once it was explained to me on my return, the situation being far too complex for even a lengthy cable. Most important for me was hearing that Basil Moore himself supported the invitation to me. With very mixed feelings I accepted the situation and launched into the challenge of preparing my first lectures, doing what I found I did best, lecturing to interested divinity students about things that mattered greatly to us.

So, from what I and many others saw as a grave injustice to Basil Moore, I began an academic career that has spanned nearly forty years. I loved lecturing and found that I was good at it. My appointment there was temporary but the full-time post was made available for applications. Many urged me to apply but I declined for two reasons. The main one was that I did not want a post that had wrongfully been denied to Basil Moore. I knew that the reputation for academic competence I had been able to develop at Rhodes was itself indebted to that wrong. The second reason was that I was still an ordinand of the Diocese of George and wanted to complete my training for the priesthood at the ETS. So I returned to Cambridge early in December 1969.

FACING MY LIMITATIONS FOR THE PRIESTHOOD

It was back in Massachusetts that the third transforming experience of my time at the ETS came, in my second winter there. The remaining part of what I needed for the BD degree was called Clinical Pastoral Education, or CPE, a three-month internship in a chosen field of pastoral care. I opted for hospital chaplaincy training at the vast Massachusetts General Hospital, over the Charles River from Cambridge in Boston itself. While I found the theoretical training and insight into medical matters fascinating, like being allowed to observe surgery along with the medical students, I found the work of visiting seriously ill patients very difficult.

One of them probably saved me from what would have been a very bad mistake, namely proceeding to ordination and the priesthood, and perhaps even from the tragedy of the middle-aged priest who knows he is a failure but cannot escape his situation except by recourse to the brandy bottle.

This is what happened. I had been given a list of patients to care for pastorally. One of them was an elderly black woman who was, I was told, dying of cancer. I found her in great pain when I introduced myself at her bedside. She took in the chaplaincy badge I was wearing, which I still have, and said, "You're God's man, Chaplain. You can make the pain go away. Pray!" My heart sank. I no longer believed in miracle cures, but I did my best as she closed her eyes, closing mine as well and asking God to be with her and support her with his love. I ended with the usual "Amen," pronouncing it the American way.

She opened her eyes, was silent for a short while and then abruptly said, "The pain ain't gone. You're no damn good!" I felt shattered and powerless. She was right. If getting miracle cures as a pastor was what was needed, I was in the wrong place and I knew it. In the days that followed I talked through my sense of failure with kindly and wise advisers both at the hospital and at the ETS, where I had a room, especially with Dean Harvey Guthrie, with whom I still have contact. My New Zealand friend John Bluck, later to be a bishop in his home country, helped me enormously by trying every argument he could against my leaving America, to make sure I wasn't overlooking something important, and then accepted that I was right to go. The upshot was acceptance by all that it would be best for me, with my heart no longer in what I was doing, to discontinue the programme and return to South Africa, which I immediately did.

The plan on my return was for me to proceed in mid-year to the former St Paul's Theological College in Grahamstown for a semester before being made a deacon at the end of 1969 and thereafter ordained to the priesthood. In the meantime I needed to find work to sustain me. I had always been fascinated by the world of printing and publishing, and my father had a contact with a senior Cape Town publisher at the firm of Maskew Miller, so I wrote to him and asked about work. He replied promptly with a job offer. Thus began my experience over the next eighteen months of the business world, initially as an editorial assistant at Maskew Miller, then with the Cape Town branch of Oxford University Press as its Text Book Editor.

While still at Maskew Miller I wrestled with whether I could continue towards the priesthood. The happiness and fulfilment of my lecturing at Rhodes the previous year and the difficult experience at Massachusetts General Hospital weighed heavily on my mind, causing great emotional distress. A meeting with my bishop in George began to help resolve the dilemma. I had asked if the diocese would provide me with a car as I wanted to do as much parish visiting as possible, knowing from my Waban experience that this was very important, no matter what I might feel. I remember the puzzled, slightly sad look on his face as he replied, his tone kind but also firm. "I am not ordaining you to be a social worker but to celebrate the sacraments," he said. In response I knew that I had a different sense of priestly priorities, the ritual side counting less for me than preaching and caring, so I was greatly troubled.

Back in Cape Town I could discuss my problem and the great distress it was causing me with my concerned and deeply caring fiancée Elizabeth, soon to be my wife. I also sought guidance from my parish priest. Somewhat abruptly he told me that anyone who puts his own interests above his duty is not to be trusted, advice that merely made things worse for me. So I prayed desperately for help. It came quite suddenly in a remark by my older sister Frieda, to whom I also confided my problem. She asked me why I thought I should continue towards ordination. I replied that I saw the priesthood as a wonderful way to do good.

Sensing, correctly, that I felt no joy in my answer, she said, "There's nothing worse than reluctant charity." The truth of her remark worked its magic right there and then. We were standing on the balcony of her sixth floor flat in the suburb of Rondebosch. I remember glancing from her to the sunlit view of those beautiful, nearby Cape Town mountains as I felt a great weight leaving me and a sense of relief and liberation taking over in my emotions and mind. I knew with complete assurance what to do. Not long afterwards I met my bishop again and told him that I couldn't continue to ordination. Somewhat to my surprise, he didn't seem perturbed at all as he nodded and wished me God's blessing. I had underestimated his wisdom.

The work and my new publishing colleagues were stimulating but I found myself longing to be able to lecture again. Seeking a way to that life I arranged to meet Professor John Cumpsty, the first head of the new Department of Religious Studies at the University of Cape Town, and explained what I was seeking. He told me that while I was qualified to work in his department he needed a specialist biblical scholar, which ruled me out.

Then came another of those remarkable, unsought developments that prove so immensely beneficial. My brother Oskar was then teaching German at the University of Stellenbosch. He sent me an advertisement for a lectureship in my area of academic competence at the University of Rhodesia, as it was then named, in the former Salisbury, now Harare. I was immediately interested but also hesitant. Given my liberal, anti-apartheid political views, I had serious misgivings about moving to a country governed by the Rhodesian Front party under Ian Smith, a regime which struck me as little better than our white South African government on racial matters. Once more I turned to John Cumpsty for advice. He said that academic posts were extremely scarce and that if I really wanted an academic career, I could not afford to pass this opportunity over. "You don't have to be there for life," he added. "You just have to get on the ladder and start climbing."

I heeded his advice, applied and got the job. We moved to Salisbury in July 1971 for the beginning of an academic career. I left that post to return to South Africa at the end of 1976 for reasons explained in the next chapter, to a more senior position in Pietermaritzburg at the University of Natal, now re-named the University of KwaZulu-Natal. From there I took early retirement at the end of 2007 to concentrate on ethics training and writing. It was a great joy to me while still at the University of KwaZulu-Natal to make contact after many years with Basil Moore. In that way I was able to begin a fine friendship with him and to have a small part in the decision of a new and very ethical Rhodes University to award him an honorary doctorate in 2012.

Chapter 4

Academic Life

NORTH OF THE LIMPOPO

So it was that in the former Rhodesia my fledgling academic career could resume and, as I see things now, deepen the experiences of goodness that have been described so far at the multi-racial and cosmopolitan University of Rhodesia. I was appointed to lecture in comparative religion and also to teach an introductory course on the Old Testament, as it was also called there. Both fields were rich in ethical implications. Once again I not only read about other faiths but encountered impressive members of them. Buddhists like Harry Farmer whom I had met at Rhodes in 1963 and Rob Nairn in the School of Law were particularly important because they gave me my first extended encounter with people who were not theists like me, but whose spiritual, philosophical and ethical depth was unmistakable.

So began a scholarly and personal encounter that included a careful study of Marxism. Rhodesia did not ban Marxist works, unlike apartheid South Africa with its paranoia about communism, so I was able to read what I needed and come to understand and appreciate the power of the atheist conscience when directed especially at the evil of economic exploitation. I discovered that Marx's famous dictum that religion is the opium of the masses refers to the use, or misuse as many would say, of religious beliefs to dull the pain of poverty and injustice, using the promise of a heavenly reward in the afterlife.

It is worth noting the longer passage from which that famous dictum comes. Writing at the end of 1843 and early in 1844, Marx began an essay about religion by declaring that "the criticism of religion is the presupposition of all criticism." He then went on to assert the following: "Religion is the sigh of the afflicted creature, the soul of a heartless world, it is also the spirit of spiritless conditions. It is the *opium* of the people. The abolition of religion as the *illusory* happiness of the people is the demand for their *real* happiness. The demand to abandon the illusion about their conditions is the *demand to give up a condition that requires illusions*. Hence criticism of religion is in embryo a *criticism of this vale of tears* whose halo is religion."[1]

In the years after these studies of Marxism I made a point of facing up to the criticism of religion by other atheists, of which Richard Robinson's was the most instructive, as I show later in this book.

My work on the Hebrew Scriptures in those years reminded me of Willie Cosser's lectures at Rhodes, about the prophetic principle of speaking truth to power as the gift of Judaism to Christianity and the wider world.[2] I found powerful parallels between the way the great classical prophets of ancient Israel like Elijah and Nathan railed in the name of a God of justice against political and economic evil, and the voices of protest then being raised bravely against the same evils in Rhodesia and South Africa. Being in full support of the yearning of my students, nearly all of whom were black, for liberation from racist control over their country, I lost no opportunity to link the words and deeds of those ancient Hebrew prophets with the prevailing situation. This greatly strengthened my existing conviction that Christianity was more important as a source of ethical action than for comforting ritual.

One classroom event stands out for me. It happened when the guerrilla war against the Smith regime was well under way. I had been lecturing about Moses and the Exodus, and focused my attention on the narrative about Moses at the burning bush that was not consumed by the flames. There, according to Exodus chapter 3, Moses received the divine name and the message of divine deliverance for his oppressed people in Egypt. In a moment of creativity I attempted a symbolic interpretation of the story, suggesting to the class that perhaps the burning bush was a symbol for an event in the mind and soul of Moses, in which he felt a fiery outrage at oppression and a sense of mighty empowerment to act for the liberation of his people. Today I would use the language of conscience and the power of goodness for that experience.

---

1. Marx, *On Religion*, 35–36.

2. Nolan, *Jesus Today*, 2006; see Denis, "Thirty Years Later," and "Timeboundness and Prophetism."

At the end of the class one of the Shona students whom I shall simply call Ezra came to me, his eyes shining, and told me he felt inspired by my interpretation. I thanked him and left for my study. Over the next days and week I noticed that he was no longer attending my lectures. Concerned that he might be ill I asked the class about him. One of the older students came to me at the end of the lecture and told me that Ezra had gone on a scholarship to Lusaka. I knew what that meant, for a scholarship at the Zambian capital was a coded way of telling me he had left to join the guerrillas in their fight against the forces of the Smith regime. I remember being deeply shaken and also deeply moved by this news as I connected it with my interpretation of the burning bush story.

Over the years I have often thought of brave, inspired Ezra, wondering what befell him. Did he reach the guerrillas out in the bush and if so was he welcomed or treated as a spy and executed, as I have heard happened to some would-be volunteers? Was he welcomed and did he later die in combat? Did he return home in triumph when his country achieved liberation in 1980 and became Zimbabwe? I shall never know but at least I can tell his story and remember him with pride and humility, but also with an acute sense of how important it is for educators to understand the power, for good but also ill, of what they say to those who look to them for more than just knowledge, but also for guidance. I was fortunate indeed to have just that guidance myself at that time.

Doctoral research and my first publications

My scholarly head of department in the former Salisbury, Professor Alec Burkill, impressed on me that I must swiftly embark on research for a doctorate and start publishing if I wanted to rise in the academic life. He advised me to select a challenging issue for my doctorate and also to set myself the goal of becoming the best in the world about it. The relevant university rules, modelled on those of the University of London of which the Salisbury campus had originally been a constituent college, required evidence of a reading knowledge of at least two relevant languages other than English. I already had that in German, so Burkill required me to achieve the required proficiency in French as well, even though I'd done a year of Introductory French as part of my BA at Rhodes. So I enrolled for a year-long refresher course and successfully sat a translation exam of a philosophical passage about Hegel.

For my doctoral topic I selected Schleiermacher and narrowed that down to exploring the enigma of how such a radical thinker with a revolutionary view of both religion and the Christian faith could have emerged from a significant early involvement with late eighteenth- century Moravian pietism, a very conservative form of Christianity.

Alec Burkill set me a fine example as a supervisor when I was writing my chapters. Not only did he read and comment on them promptly, never taking longer than about two weeks per chapter and even doing so while in England on sabbatical, but he also insisted on meticulous attention to language as well as content. Aided also by university-funded research visits to libraries and expert scholars in England, the USA and Germany, I was able to complete the research, most of it in German, and submitted my dissertation successfully for examination by the end of 1976. My DPhil was awarded *in absentia* early in 1977, for by then we had returned to South Africa, as I relate below.

Burkill's advice about publishing proved just as valuable. It spurred me to research and present a paper for the Salisbury Theological Club. I was drawn to the philosophy of religion in which the nature of religious language was a leading concern at the time, so I chose that as my topic. Gratified by the feedback I received, I sent it to the *Scottish Journal of Theology* and was delighted when it was immediately accepted and published.[3] Then I wrote an article on some of my findings about Pietism in the Reformed tradition to which Schleiermacher belonged. I sent it to the *Journal of Ecclesiastical History* which also accepted it unchanged.[4] These two successes based on my supervisor's advice gave me the assurance I needed that I was indeed capable of published scholarly work.

Meeting Desmond Tutu

Another valuable experience of the time in Rhodesia was meeting Desmond Tutu and the beginning of a long association with him as mentor, role model and friend. He was then based in London and working for an organization that supported theological education at a number of African universities, including mine. His work involved visits to those campuses and I was deputed to meet him and show him around the university when it was our turn for a visit.

I had first encountered him very briefly in my 1969 year as a lecturer at Rhodes University. He had returned from his theological studies at King's College, London, to teach at the erstwhile Federal Theological Seminary in the nearby town of Alice. A small group of us at Rhodes drove there to hear

---

3. Prozesky, "Context and Variety."
4. Prozesky, "Emergence of Dutch Pietism."

him give a lecture on the work of Rudolph Otto, whose book *The Idea of the Holy* is a classic. I vividly remember him quoting Otto's famous Latin phrase about the Holy as the *mysterium tremendum et fascinans*, meaning "an awesomely great and attractive mystery."[5] We returned to Rhodes that evening sure that we had heard an important new voice in church and society, and so it has certainly proved, but it was only some years later at the University of Rhodesia that I had the privilege of beginning a friendly link with the person who would become South Africa's greatest prophetic voice of conscience against apartheid and other evils.

Advice about ethics and law

One of my older friends at the University of Rhodesia was Harry Silberberg, a senior member of the School of Law and later the author of a well-known textbook on the law of property in South Africa. He and his wife were Jewish and had left an increasingly menacing Germany in 1938. Like all the Jews who managed to leave, their relatives who remained all perished in the Nazi genocide. Appreciating Harry Silberberg's fine values, wisdom and experience of evil, I asked what he saw as the relationship between ethics and law. His answer has become a permanent part of my own understanding of this matter, and I have quoted it many times in my ethics teaching down the years. He told me that at its best, law is only a minimal ethic. What this means is that legality is never a sufficient basis for moral goodness, though it can certainly be a morally sound component of it; moreover legality can at times be the very opposite of moral goodness. There are such things as evil laws, like Hitler's, and the racist, unfairly discriminatory laws of apartheid South Africa, white Rhodesia and elsewhere.

Harry Silberberg's advice also means that for moral strength we must look elsewhere than just to legislators and lawyers of integrity. Some would say that religion provides what law at its best cannot, but against that is the evidence that religion can itself in important respects be ethically unsound, as with Christianity when it took nearly nineteen centuries to condemn slavery. The conviction underlying this book is that the domain of the good itself, independent of any religion or philosophy, is the answer, as I argued at length in my 2007 book *Conscience: Ethical Intelligence for Global Well-Being*, contending that our moral values come from the kind of social, inter-related beings we are. The guidance I received all those years ago from my Jewish mentor in the former Salisbury stood me in good stead when I

---

5. Otto, *Idea of the Holy*, 144.

started thinking about the proper place of religion in a post-apartheid South Africa, a challenge I describe later in this chapter.

Researching Christian atheism

By the 1960s and 1970s secularization, understood not just as the process of removing institutions like education from the control of religion, but more radically, for some people, as spelling the end of belief in a spiritual realm, seemed to many intellectuals to be an unstoppable force in western societies, a conviction already being confidently proclaimed by secular humanists and Marxists. Among those who shared this conviction was a group of Christian thinkers who began to explore what they saw as the secular meaning of Christianity. John Robinson and Paul van Buren have already been mentioned in connection with my time as a divinity student at Rhodes University. They were joined by Harvey Cox at Harvard University[6] and then by other American radicals[7] who announced and explored what they called "the death of God," using a phrase adapted from Nietzsche.[8]

Alerted to their work by media reports and journal articles, I set about researching this "Death-of-God" group and presented a public lecture at the University of Rhodesia about it, later publishing a revised version as a journal article after we had returned to South Africa.[9] In this way I encountered the thinking of some eminent academics in the Christian world who had embraced atheism not because "of the absence of the experience of God, but because of the experience of the absence of God," as I quoted the striking words by William Hamilton.[10]

By then I was deeply immersed in the work of Schleiermacher, with its demonstration of a way of engaging positively with secular culture without being captive to it, so I could not share their embrace of outright atheism. Much more instructive was the Christian radicalism of New Zealand's Lloyd Geering and England's Don Cupitt, whom I encountered in person and print some years later. All the same, my studies of the works of leading atheists, then and subsequently, convinced me that their criticisms of theism had to be taken very seriously. On re-reading Bishop John Robinson's short book calling for a new reformation while writing the present book, I was much impressed by his own critical but open-minded engagement with atheism in

---

6. Cox, *Secular City*.
7. Altizer, *Gospel of Christian Atheism*; Hamilton, *Radical Theology*.
8. Nietzsche, *Thus Spoke Zarathustra*.
9. Prozesky, "Divine Absentee."
10. Prozesky, "Divine Absentee," 44.

an appendix called "Can a Truly Contemporary Person *not* be an Atheist?"[11] but I miss in his work the kind of synthesis of goodness and the concept of God that I offer in part III.

Conscientious objection and returning to South Africa

The power of conscience led to the end of those valuable and mostly happy years at the University of Rhodesia, despite our strong dislike of the country's politics. Foreign residents like me were permitted to work there but couldn't vote and could be deported with a mere twenty-four hours' notice. That happened to some of my university colleagues who were also critical of the minority, racist regime then in power, one of them a married man with a young family, like me. As the bush war of liberation, which young Ezra had left to join, spread and the regime became increasingly desperate, it began the injustice of conscripting foreigners, people who had no vote and could be summarily ejected from the country.

Never will I forget the day I received my call-up papers, as we called the draft system, with the order to report for training at army barracks in the city of Bulawayo. I knew those papers would come and I also knew I would refuse, not just because of the gross injustice of expecting people with no political rights and no security of residence to endanger their lives in this way, but most of all because I considered it deeply wrong to support an unethical political system, worst of all by bearing arms for it. So I immediately resigned and we prepared to return to South Africa.

I set about seeking an academic position there and to our huge relief finally received an offer of a temporary position, at senior lecturer level, to teach philosophy of religion in the former Department of Divinity at the University of Natal in Pietermaritzburg. It came from Professor Vic Bredenkamp, its kindly and tireless departmental head, among whose extremely valuable contributions to my work was to encourage the following of the phenomenological method of studying religions, which I explain later in this book. I accepted the offer without hesitation even though we had experienced much that was very enriching in Rhodesia. We loved our travels around that beautiful country; we made some special friends; I had nearly completed my doctoral dissertation; we had close relatives on my wife's side of the family and very enjoyable times on the cricket field, which included my only century and my best ever bowling figures. In Professor Robert Craig we had an outstanding vice-chancellor, and our first child was born there, making us a small but very happy family.

11. Robinson, *New Reformation*, 106-22.

On the other hand, there was no way in which I could in good conscience risk life or limb for a deeply unjust cause. So we sold the house we loved, parted with family and friends and left Salisbury with very mixed feelings just after Christmas in 1976. The last part of the drive from Fort Victoria, today's Masvingo, to the Beit Bridge border at the Limpopo River found us in a long convoy, escorted by the army with spotter aircraft above to protect us from the guerrillas known to be in the area. The soldier who briefed us before the drive began at first light glanced at our little son in his car seat and told us that in the event of Terry, as he called the bush fighters, opening fire we were to hit the ground immediately with him. Then followed the most nerve-wracking three or four hours of our lives, till with huge relief we were back in South Africa. Even the fierce, midday heat of the Limpopo valley and the nearby mining town of Musina seemed welcome after that ordeal.

Filled with relief, I was in no position then to reflect on what was happening to our lives and my work. I do now, as I look back, and once more I can see all too clearly how the power of conscience, and behind it the far greater power of goodness, was driving our existence. Still at the time a conventionally liberal Christian believer and regular church-goer, I might have acknowledged that my life was an unfolding story not just of academic theology, but of lived, fallible ethics and faith in a guiding God.

THE YEARS AT THE UNIVERSITY OF NATAL

Early in 1977 I took up my temporary post in Pietermaritzburg and was later able to apply successfully for a permanent appointment. Racism in apartheid South Africa was worse than in Rhodesia but at least I was a citizen and could not be summarily deported, and could continue to see the academic life, even in an all-white university in those days of rigid segregation, as a wonderful opportunity to open minds to truths the state would rather people did not know, including truths about the ethical and unethical practice of religion. Professor Vic Bredenkamp's unfailing supportiveness, even when my critical probing took me to positions he did not share, certainly helped my career develop further, but first I must describe one of the most liberating events of my years in Pietermaritzburg.

My own Good Samaritans

It happened painfully but unforgettably one winter morning in 1978 and thus during the heyday of apartheid. As a young academic with limited means and a wife and two little sons to provide for, all I could afford as a second vehicle was a motor scooter, leaving our six year-old family car for my wife to use. Early that morning I was on my way to the university campus, enjoying the lively zip of the bike as I throttled up a road past a row of modest suburban houses in what was then a whites-only neighborhood.

Very suddenly a small fox terrier appeared from a nearby gate and rushed out at me, barking wildly. In an instant I knew I must brake and swerve or hit the animal. Instinct took over and I braked but too strongly. The bike lurched sideways, enough to miss the dog but also enough to go down, sending me flying. As I fell one of the rubber handlebar grips struck me above the left eye, just under my crash helmet. The skin burst open and blood poured down my face. Badly shaken but, I quickly realized, with no broken bones, I stood slowly up. The dog was nowhere to be seen, doubtless satisfied by a scoreline of Dogs 1 Humans nil. With blood running down my face and the fallen scooter at my feet, I must have looked a mess. I needed help immediately to get medical attention for the injury. That was long before the arrival of cellphones so I depended on passers-by.

Nobody emerged from the nearby houses. A few cars passed me, driven by whites like me. Then a car pulled up. An Indian man and woman got out and hurried towards me. I vividly remember the red dot on her forehead, a custom of the Hindu community to signify marriage. The man gave me a neatly folded handkerchief to press to the cut over my eye and to wipe blood from my face, pulled my bike to the sidewalk, and shepherded me to the car. It was then that I noticed that it was a taxi. Under apartheid laws at that time it was a taxi for "non-whites" and carrying me was against the law. But without hesitation my two Indian benefactors took me, a white from the Christian community, to a whites-only city hospital, saw me to the casualty desk and quietly disappeared.

An hour later, with a bandage swathed around my head and some memorable bruises, I was fetched by an anxious Vic Bredenkamp, retrieved my undamaged Honda and decided that I was fit for work. Later that day I found the Indian woman in charge of the taxi that had come to my help to give my rescuers my thanks and to return a fresh handkerchief. She graciously declined any payment for the taxi ride or reward for her two Good Samaritans.

What I knew for sure then was that my circle of concern had been dramatically enlarged by that warm-hearted Indian couple. Years later I could record that a life-changing message had been sent unforgettably to me that morning: "Welcome to the world you have just entered and must serve in your work, a world where kindness transcends colour, culture and creed." The memory of that morning's experience has moved and inspired me ever since. I have spent forty years studying, encountering, teaching and writing about the world's great belief- and value-systems, both religious and secular, from Australian Aboriginal to Zen and Zulu, seeking to understand how to work for a world where conscience transcends colour, culture and even creed, and transforms evil into lasting good, a world governed by goodness, not greed. This book is a result.

Four world-class mentors who became friends

Another great enrichment in my career in those Natal years was encountering four world-class religious thinkers and writers who became mentors and friends. They were John Hick, Lloyd Geering, John B. Cobb Jr, and Don Cupitt, though my contacts with him, while also very stimulating, were less extensive than with the other three. Hick was already then arguably the world's most important philosopher of religion because of his groundbreaking work on the problem of evil for belief in a loving God, already mentioned in this book, and for his pioneering work on the implications of religious pluralism for belief in the sole and exclusive validity of any one faith.[12] His guidance and friendship continued to the end of his life, leading to several visits to his home in Birmingham, and included three scholarly gifts that continue to bear fruit more than thirty years later.

The first one happened in 1980 when he was a visiting professor in our department in Pietermaritzburg at the invitation of Professor Vic Bredenkamp. I was then hard at work in my post-doctoral investigation of the nature of religion, pondering both the great differences that separate the various religions and their important similarities. Apartheid's theoreticians contended that humanity's ethnic and cultural differences were too fundamental for co-existence ever to be harmonious, so that it was best to segregate the different communities in South Africa.

Was religion a case in point, I wondered, drawing on my research into comparative religion in the former Rhodesia? What could be more fundamentally different about believing that there is a God and believing that there isn't, as in parts of Buddhism, as the Dalai Lama himself once confirmed to me at a meeting in Durban many years later. Nonetheless, I wanted to see if there were valid grounds for showing that despite such differences, there was in fact a shared, basic identity to all religion and thereby deny apartheid one of its most important attempted justifications, namely that our differences are deeper than any commonalities.

---

12. Hick, *God has Many Names*.

I was walking back to our department from the university library one day in 1978 when quite suddenly the answer came to me. I even remember the exact words that came to my mind. "That's it! That's the mother lode!" I was referring to the thought that the core of religion wasn't belief at all, but values, above all the value to people of the promise of a supreme blessing that all religions offer in one way or another. I immediately set about exploring all the information about religion I could find, concentrating not on their teachings but on religious experience the way Friedrich Schleiermacher had pioneered in 1799 and which William James, Edwin Starbuck and Sir Alister Hardy had so richly documented in their later studies of religious experience.[13]

Soon I had my idea ready for testing and after presenting a first version as a paper at the first conference of the Association for the Study of Religion in Southern Africa in 1978, I developed it further and, knowing that John Hick would be coming to our department, sent it to him for critical comment. His encouraging responses and suggestions for some changes of wording would in themselves have been invaluable, but his main response took my academic career to an altogether higher level. He told me he thought I should develop my ideas about the nature of religion into a book and that he wanted it for the prestigious series of which he was general editor, the Library of Philosophy and Religion of the Macmillan Press in London. Needless to say, I lost no time setting to work to deepen and extend my research and was able to have a year's sabbatical in 1982, spent first in Claremont, California, where Hick taught for half of each year, researching and testing my ideas, and the rest of the year in Oxford writing the book. It was published in London and New York in 1984 and provided my work with a conceptual foundation that continues to inform my work on religion and ethics. The gist is explained in chapter 6.

Hick's visit to our department was not without controversy because he had recently edited and been a co-author with six other British theologians, one of them Don Cupitt at Cambridge, of a sensational 1977 book called, somewhat misleadingly, *The Myth of God Incarnate*. For many people the word "myth" means a mistake or delusion, as in the phrase "the myth of white superiority." Hick and his co-authors had in mind the technical meaning of the word, according to which a myth is a symbolic story or narrative involving supernatural beings that points to a deeper truth.

In the preface of a subsequent book which Hick and Paul F. Knitter co-edited a few years later, the two of them gave a helpful explanation of the word "myth." This is what they wrote: "We are calling 'Christian uniqueness'

---

13. James, *Varieties*; Starbuck, *Psychology of Religion*; Hardy, *Spiritual Nature*.

a "myth" not because we think that talk of the uniqueness of Christianity is purely and simply false, and so to be discarded. Rather, we feel that such talk, like all mythic language, must be understood carefully; it must be interpreted; its 'truth' lies not in its literal surface but within its ever-changing historical and personal meaning."[14]

According to Hick in the 1977 book, the definition of Jesus Christ in the Nicene Creed as the only-begotten Son of God who came down from heaven and was incarnate of the Virgin Mary and made man, "is only one way of conceptualizing the lordship of Jesus, the way taken by the Greco-Roman world of which we are the heirs."[15] He immediately added that in our time with its far wider horizons, "it is proper for Christians to become conscious of both the optional and the mythological character of this traditional language." On reading these words I heard a clear echo of Schleiermacher's contention that doctrine is a secondary and variable part of faith, not its heart.

Among other influences on me by Hick and his co-authors, *The Myth of God Incarnate* encouraged me to work on two issues that are still central to Christianity. They are how best to understand and express the significance of Jesus, and how to define the place of beliefs and doctrines in the spiritual life of Christianity and, for that matter, any faith. Two books came my way at that time that would richly influence this central interest of mine about Jesus. They were *Jesus before Christianity: The Gospel of Liberation* (1976), by the Catholic theologian Albert Nolan, and Humphrey Carpenter's 1980 book called *Jesus*. I return to these two books in chapter 13, and to Nolan's more recent book about the spirituality of Jesus, where I give my own interpretation of Jesus.

Christology was thus much on our minds at the time of Hick's visit, so I proposed to my departmental colleagues that we organize a conference about it during his visit on what we decided to call Cross Currents in Contemporary Christology. It was held on July 25-26, 1980 at the former University of Natal in Pietermaritzburg. Papers by a range of speakers, with comments by Hick, generated much lively and valuable discussion, and were subsequently published.[16]

My own contribution carried the title "Christology and Cultural Relativity."[17] It gave me an opportunity to explore the status of our language about Jesus in precisely the wider, contemporary, global context Hick had

14. Hick and Knitter, *Myth of Christian Uniqueness*, vii.
15. Hick, *Myth of God Incarnate*, 168.
16. *Journal of Theology for Southern Africa*, 35, June 1981.
17. Prozesky, "Christology," 44-67.

mentioned in his chapter in *The Myth of God Incarnate*, and reveals the powerful influence of Schleiermacher's assertions about the variable status of doctrine on my own thinking, as the following quotations from my paper clearly show.

> "There is no doubt in my mind that traditional Christian beliefs and their christological centre-piece were magnificent in the circumstances of their origin. They won and held the loyalty of an entire civilization for over fifteen centuries. But circumstances have changed. Our mental and religious horizons are immensely bigger than those in which Christianity was born and grew to maturity. Demands are now being made of religion which the old beliefs cannot meet. Therefore Christianity faces the urgent challenge of producing a new religious vision and presence, adequate to the experiences and requirements of the present age and nourished by more than just the insights of the past."[18]

The paper ended with a clear indication of my sense that far wider horizons were summoning us to what I called religious map making, new, much better informed than our traditional ones, but always provisional. I wrote that when "the new comprehensive map of reality is available we shall be able to identify what ails us and establish what relief Jesus of Nazareth can give to a thirsty, contemporary, culturally plural world. I personally suspect that the enquiry will lead to an increased rather than a diminished appreciation of the Galilean. But perhaps I have spent too long beside the Jordan and too little at the Ganges or the Tugela, or on the sea itself."[19] John Hick's support for the paper after I had delivered it gave me every encouragement to proceed towards that new spiritual cartography, of which this book is a result.

The second of the three great blessings from Hick led to my contact and friendship with another internationally eminent scholar, New Zealand's radical religious thinker, Lloyd Geering, now Sir Lloyd, a friendship that continues to the present. During Hick's time in our department he was reading a recent book which he urged me also to read. It was Geering's *Faith's New Age*, which gave me an historical perspective on the way religion has developed since ancient times, which I explain later in my account of today's understanding of religion in chapter 6. His vision of the modern period

---

18. Prozesky, "Christology," 44.

19. Prozesky, "Christology," 67. The Tugela is the main river of my part of South Africa.

opening the way to a new kind of faith was also a great encouragement for my own, increasingly radical, understanding of it.[20]

In *Faith's New Age*, since revised and re-issued in America under the title *Christianity at the Crossroads* in 2001, Geering provided a rarely comprehensive account of the context of contemporary and early modern religion, including its atheist critics. This enabled my studies of atheism that had begun in earnest in Rhodesia with Marx to develop further through Geering's accounts of the thought of the Baron d'Holbach (1723 –89), David Hume (1711– 76), and especially Friedrich Nietzsche (1844– 1900), whose main works I would study later.[21] Other atheists whose rejections of theism I studied afterwards are Bertrand Russell, Antony Flew, who subsequently rejected atheism, Jean-Paul Sartre, and, most recently, A.C. Grayling, Richard Dawkins, and J.E. Schellenberg, besides others. I found it impossible to dismiss these powerful thinkers as misguided, but at the same time concluded that they were attacking problematic *concepts* of God without understanding what drives religion, including theistic religion, which, as I explain later, is much richer, deeper and more important than any of those problematic concepts.

Not long after discovering Geering's work I encountered him personally, again the result of John Hick's support. Hick recommended that I be invited to present a paper at an international conference on "God: the Contemporary Discussion" in Maui, Hawaii, at the end of 1981. It was there that I met Lloyd. The conference was organized into a range of theme groups and the one I chose included him. Initially I found him rather formal but that changed completely when he heard my paper, "Groundwork for a theistic quantum jump," later published with a different title.[22] I argued for a radical change in our beliefs about God and mentioned that apartheid was strongly supported by many of traditional Christian believers in South Africa.

To my huge relief Geering was very supportive and, having discovered my anti-apartheid views, welcomed me as a friend. His country had, just six months before we met, been very deeply divided by the visit of a top rugby team from my then legally racist country, and people like Lloyd had campaigned passionately to have it stopped. Thus began a personal and scholarly friendship that grew over the years, enriched by Lloyd's gifts of critical comments on my work and copies of his visionary books about the future of faith in an environmentally endangered world. Above all, Lloyd gave me the priceless gift of encouraging me to develop my radical ideas as rigorously

---

20. Geering, *Faith's New Age*.
21. Geering, *Faith's New Age*, 92-96, 189-193, 300-319.
22. Prozesky, "Critique."

as possible and welcomed the results. In South Africa I might then perhaps have been a lone, very radical Christian voice but not in Geering and Hick's world of international Christian scholarship.

The third contribution to my scholarly development from John Hick followed immediately after the conference in Hawaii. Knowing that I had a year's sabbatical in 1982, he had encouraged me to spend at least part of it in Claremont, California, where he was teaching at the Graduate School, and put me in touch with John Cobb, the world's leading process theologian at the School of Theology there. The result was a semester in Claremont in which I could research my book and also immerse myself in the work of the process theologians, guided by John Cobb. Before then I had only a superficial understanding of process theology. Those Claremont studies began to reveal to me that these highly competent Christian scholars, building on the philosophy of Alfred North Whitehead (1861– 1947), were showing very persuasively that the church had developed a concept of God that was deeply flawed on theological and ethical grounds, out of alignment with the message and example of Jesus himself.

Of many highly stimulating discussions about theology and ethics with John Cobb, two stand out. In the first one I asked why he and other process theologians continued to use the word God when they meant something so unlike the usual meaning of an omnipotent, eternally unchanging deity. I will never forget his answer. "Why should we surrender the most important word in the world's religious vocabulary to those who misuse it?"

In another conversation I asked what he saw as the most important problems facing America, expecting him to say something like racism, violence or gender injustice, but he didn't. Without hesitating he said that it was saving the environment. Puzzled, I asked him why. He replied that if we didn't save the environment we wouldn't have a world in which to overcome other serious problems like gender injustice and racism. He added that under President Ronald Reagan, environmental damage was worsening. Reagan, with his aggressively capitalist passions, had reportedly said of America's beautiful redwood forests that when you've seen one redwood tree you've seen them all. That was evidently in response to protests against big business wanting a free hand to clear-cut those majestic trees for profit. So began a concern for the good of the environment that led in due course to the introduction of course content on environmental ethics at my home campus.

My sense of ethical priorities has been permanently enhanced by John Cobb's friendship and wisdom, which began to channel great goodness into my life in those months in Claremont in 1982. Little did I know at the time that two new books of his would greatly extend his influence on me. The first to appear was his book about the way Christianity and Buddhism can be mutually enriching.[23] It draws on John's scholarly and personal involvement with Buddhism which goes back to his early years when his parents were Methodist missionaries in Japan. He showed, with great sensitivity to both faiths, that Christians can learn much from the philosophical power of Buddhism, and that they can offer Buddhists much about the need for ethical engagement with this world's problems. So impressed was I by this book that I wrote an appreciative review article about it with my colleague at Rhodes University, Professor Felicity Edwards.[24]

The second book was a gift copy by John Cobb and his co-author Herman E. Daly. It was about a new global economy and appeared in 1989 and again in 1994. Its 500 pages revealed a rare depth of economic understanding and creativity in mapping a sustainable global future that gives hope that humanity can achieve an enduringly worthwhile future for itself on a safe planet.[25] Shortly after issuing this book, Cobb produced a shorter, more popular statement of his vision.[26] Together with its more technical predecessor it gives significant support to those of us who believe that goodness is not something controlled by churches, temples, mosques and synagogues, but must be found and fostered in the market place, politics, the environment and everywhere else.

After the time in Claremont the rest of my 1982 sabbatical was spent at Oxford. It was while there that I read Don Cupitt's 1980 book *Taking Leave of God*. Soon afterwards I met him during a visit to Oxford for the filming of an episode of his BBC television series, *The Sea of Faith*, which gave rise to an organized following in a number of countries called the Sea of Faith movement, when he kindly set aside time for me. We met again a number of times over the years and I read all his books as he developed a post-modern spirituality and religious philosophy with a powerful ethical component. Of those books I consider his *Solar Ethics* of 1995 the most important for my work, with its memorable, sustained use of the symbolism of the sun for the greatest goodness, because the sun spends its entire existence pouring forth its light, warmth and gravitational power, making life and well-being possible for us, and taking nothing back.

In another of his books I found the striking idea that in our time the world is moving from the mode of the soldier to the mode of the artist, signifying a shift from cultures of obedience and dependency to cultures of

---

23. Cobb, *Beyond Dialogue*.
24. Prozesky and Edwards, "Review Article."
25. Daly and Cobb, *For the Common Good*.
26. Cobb, *Sustaining*.

liberated creativity. We see this change in the march of democracy and the demise of traditional monarchies, but I have not at the time of writing been able to track the quotation down in his books. Part III will show the very great ethical significance of this major cultural shift for the future of the movement begun by Jesus of Nazareth.

As my account of contacts with these four Christian mentors shows, I have found their writings and personal influence very significant and lastingly helpful, though not always with complete agreement on my part about some aspects of their thought. For example, I considered that Hick's work attended too little to the challenge of secularism, unlike Geering's. I have also been unable to enter as much as I'd like into the world of process philosophy so superbly done by John Cobb, and I have some serious concerns about the post-modern outlook which Cupitt has embraced, along with his rejection of theism.

At the same time as these contacts, I continued to study the conservative side of Christianity, through personal discussions with influential evangelical leaders like Michael Cassidy in South Africa and especially England's Michael Green during his visits to South Africa, and in their writings, with great appreciation for their friendly responses and integrity. I had long since ceased agreeing with the beliefs of this side of Christianity but saw it as an important academic duty to keep myself informed about it. Much later I would find the work of Oxford's Alister McGrath, with his voluminous output, and to a lesser extent that of England's Anglican bishop and academic, N.T. Wright, immensely beneficial in keeping me aware of their theological world, as will be made clear in part II.

Buddhist encounters

Hitherto my awareness of Buddhism had been limited to the personal contacts already described at Rhodes University and in Salisbury, and to what I had studied about it at the University of Rhodesia. That changed at the University of Natal through contact with a leading, Durban-based Buddhist, Louis van Loon. He attended the first conference of our new Association for the Study of Religion, at which I presented the first version of my explanation of religion with its strong emphasis on religion as a source of supremely enhanced well-being. Afterwards he introduced himself and said he saw my paper as pure Buddhism.

Intrigued, I decided afterwards to deepen my experience of Buddhism and attended a number of short courses at the beautiful Buddhist Retreat Centre, which Louis had founded, near Ixopo in the southern part of our province, which welcomed people of any faith. While I benefited from the deeper understanding of Buddhist teaching and philosophy at those sessions, especially the central role of compassion in Buddhist ethics, it was the practical instruction about meditation practice that was most valuable. I loved the sense of gentle, mindful calm and greater awareness of things it produced, along with some ability to control the tendency of my mind to be distracted by things like bird song or the wind in nearby trees, and bring my consciousness back to just being aware. Thus began a spiritual practice that has been with me ever since, now focused on awareness of goodness in all its wonderful ways of operating in and around us.

A near-fatal incident

A few years after meeting John Hick, Lloyd Geering and John Cobb, something happened that still amazes me. By then I was riding a light motor bike to work through the lively, early morning traffic of the city of Pietermaritzburg. As I approached a busy intersection along Boshoff Street, with the traffic lights facing me on green, I slowed down but was still going at a steady speed when I saw a car approaching from the other side. The driver was saying something to the passenger next to him, his head turned slightly towards him, and was indicating to turn across my lane. Then, to my horror, he didn't stop to wait for me to pass but began to turn directly into the space I was entering. No matter how much I braked, a bad collision was inevitable.

I remember with crystal clarity my reactions. "So this is how I die," I said desperately to myself as an anguished, wild cry burst involuntary from me. Then everything seemed to go into very slow motion even though what happened could not have taken more than a split second. I saw the car coming straight at me as I tried to brake, certain that I would be hit and probably killed. And then I found myself stopped safely on the side of the street ahead of me, shaking like a leaf but completely untouched.

As I have already related, I had previously experienced a fall from my motor scooter when I had braked too sharply to avoid a small dog, so I knew what it was like to come flying off the machine and hit the road, though I was only slightly injured by that fall. This was something very, very different, with a moving car and my motor bike at running speed seemingly heading for a direct collision that somehow never happened.

I have no awareness whatever of the split seconds between my despairing sense that I was about to be killed and finding myself trembling at the roadside. Does the mind shut down its awareness to block the horror of an impending crash, so that I was completely unaware of the narrowest of escapes, or of how that escape could possibly have happened? Did something else happen? By that period of my life I had long stopped believing in divine miracles, heavily influenced by David Hume's brilliant philosophical refutation of claims that they happen. I accept that I shall never know and I also accept that sometimes things happen about which it is best to keep an open mind and accept that the workings of the universe far surpass our present understanding. Maybe there are encompassing powers, as my doctoral mentor Alec Burkill once wrote, that far exceed our own, from which sometimes come deliverances which we can receive with the deepest gratitude and humility, accepting them also as ultimately mysterious.[27]

A mystical experience

If mystical experiences mean being taken to a level of insight beyond any usual kind, then I have certainly had them. They are events in which I felt that I'd been drawn into awareness of a brighter, clearer, glowing world, and that I was somehow part of it and even inside it, and not just seeing it from outside.

The first happened in mid-1985, just before a conference on "Salvation and the Secular" at the Pietermaritzburg campus, for which I was preparing a contribution. Here are the relevant parts of my handwritten account of that experience, dated Sunday, August 24, 1986, from 10 to 10.30 a.m., and slightly edited on grounds of language and spelling. The first part sets the scene for the mystical experience itself.

> "I had taken up as my own contribution the whole problem of Christianity, apartheid and the salvation of South African society from the evils of apartheid. My investigations led me to acknowledge that apartheid was in one sense the antithesis of a religion about perfect love, but in another a partial consequence of Christianity's themes of elitism and exclusivism in the matter of salvation through Christ alone. I gradually laid bare a realization of the appalling extent to which a presumed vehicle of the most sacred things can in fact work diabolically . . . namely the idea that a God of perfect love, goodness and power could possibly institute the means of salvation into the world in a way that is grotesquely unfair to most humans.
>
> "The discovery shook me very deeply and led me to see in apartheid an event of Christian deicide—the only metaphor strong enough for the revelation that had risen in my

27. Burkill, *Faith, Knowledge and Cosmopolitanism*, 7.

consciousness, and one which could point, like the crucifixion, to the possibility of a new life, a new Easter, while still very aware that the present reality is that evil had ruled our very concept of God, and had therefore killed it for me as a believer in even-handed dealing, an essential part of goodness and love.

"With these deeply haunting and disturbing thoughts in mind I drove home one twilight, and as I stopped the car on our driveway and turned off the engine I had a sense, quite suddenly, of having, as it were, penetrated through the utmost limit of our Christian theism, as if I had found there a terrifying wrongness, and then broken through to the other side, to the far side of this God . . .

"And what I then experienced as I sat there at the wheel of the car in the twilight of that June evening, was no more the desolation and anxiety of that deicidal event, but something deeply different, something deeply good and benign—a sort of atmosphere aglow and warming in a wonderfully relaxing and reassuring way, as though I had gone beyond the last structures and restraints and distortions into a sky of the spirit, open, empty, totally peaceful, alone yet comforted, a solitude of welcome, a limitless, horizon-less space of freedom and goodness, an enduring glow of reposeful exhilaration."

Writing about the world's soulscapes

Scholarly publications are intended, quite rightly, to be read by other scholars whose critical appraisal they must survive. They are not light reading. While this is good for academic excellence it can have the effect that scholarly findings remain largely unknown to the broader public. Theological writing can be very technical, as any reader of Paul Tillich's three volumes of *Systematic Theology*, or the dozen or so hefty volumes of Karl Barth's *Church Dogmatics* will know. Here the great gap between the academic library and the church pew is not the only problem, for the gap often also exists between scholars on one hand and priests, ministers and pastors on the other. If a scholar, troubled by the gap, writes more accessibly the way John Robinson did with *Honest to God*, the result, as he certainly found, can be heavy scholarly criticism and even dismissal as being superficial. My sympathies, as I mentioned in my preface, are with the goal of seeking both clarity and depth; indeed I sometimes suspected that obscure academic writing was masking untidy thinking. After all, if you muddy the waters nobody will see how shallow they might be.

A way to overcome this problem was given to me very unexpectedly in mid-1988 when Richard Steyn, editor of the Pietermaritzburg daily then called *The Natal Witness*, asked me to arrange a small team to write the weekly "Saturday Talk" column for the paper, a team that would write in a way that reflected something of the main faith traditions of the city. I found very competent people to write about Christianity, Islam and Hinduism, so Richard suggested that I write about other belief-systems. This I did, discussing a wide range of beliefs including religious humanism, secular humanism and atheism. So began a venture into the world of writing for the broader public, not just for my local newspaper but in time for others, including some of the country's Sunday papers. The venture continues to the present, with over 200 of my articles on spiritual and ethical topics having been published.

While these articles certainly helped me write more accessibly, they had two other consequences. The first one was the response of readers which ranged from enthusiastic approval to, on a few regrettable occasions, nasty condemnations. Both responses intensified when the paper, renamed *The Witness*, began to print small photos of its writers alongside their articles. Now total strangers could recognize me, and I began to experience welcome smiles from them but also some hard looks of disapproval. A few times the hostile responses were hurtfully vicious but these negative reactions were far outweighed by the positive ones, like requests for me to collect some of my articles into a small book. I did this in 1997 and my little book *Soulscapes: A Book of Spiritual Explorations* was the result, followed in 2003 by a second such collection called *Frontiers of Conscience: Exploring Ethics in a New Millennium*.

The other consequence of writing about a wide range of faiths and philosophies, with an increasing emphasis on their ethical common ground, was to deepen and enrich my own understanding of those world-views. Goodness, I was writing, is indeed a truly global reality, whereas our faith traditions and philosophies are at most just provinces on the world map of beliefs, despite claims to the contrary, for none shows any sign of being embraced by people of all cultures. That there is a lesson here about faith itself is clear.

Opposing religious discrimination

The next formative ethical experience concerned the ceremonies of the university at that time. These were at the start of the academic year to welcome new students and at its graduations. The practice was for the Head of the

Department of Divinity to open the ceremonies with a Christian prayer. In the department itself the policy was to teach students about the various religions in an even-handed, empathetic way, yet at its official ceremonies the university was behaving like an extension of the church. Some of us, myself included, saw this as unfair discrimination against people of other faiths or none. As departmental colleagues we then began a process of contesting those prayers, which led in the end to them being dropped altogether. Looking back I am chastened by the fact that I, then a regular church-goer, was so slow to see that there was a problem. That makes me acutely aware that one's religious comfort zone can easily be a barrier to seeing moral problems about religion itself.

Opposing the misuse of the Bible

As I have already explained, I had by then long been very aware that the misuse of the Bible was itself in some important ways part of the problem of moral wrong in South Africa and elsewhere, when it is cited to justify evils like racism, sexism and violence. All of us who rejected apartheid knew that it had the support of influential parts of the churches in South Africa and their leaders, who contended that the Bible itself justified apartheid. Although Scripture was not my field, along with many others I was well aware that Scripture was being abused in this way, and began to look for ways to help counter it. My best opportunity came when, in 1986, I was asked to deliver the College Lecture, a weekly event open to the public on the Pietermaritzburg campus that was intended to focus on important issues in society. I chose as my topic the morally divided role many white Christians were playing in the country, many supporting apartheid, others opposing it.

My title was "Is Apartheid Destroying Christianity's Credibility? A New View of Religion in our Time" and a packed lecture theatre which even included the Vice-Chancellor faced me as I delivered it, contrasting the heroic Christian stand against apartheid with the powerful support other Christians, no doubt also sincere, were giving the racist government of the day. I noted the important reality that both sides claimed biblical justification, making it something of an ambivalent guidebook.

It was what happened afterwards, days after the applause had died away, that gave my lecture a truly remarkable exposure to the strange way goodness sometimes works. David Robbins, a senior journalist from *The Natal Witness*, had attended my lecture. He interviewed me afterwards and wrote an account of it for the paper, under the headline "The Bible: Ambivalent Guide Book." He showed me the courtesy of running the article past me before publication and I saw nothing in it that was inaccurate. It appeared on April 14, 1986. Little did I expect the great anger it caused certain readers, for some of whom Scripture was the unblemished Word of God. News of their reactions soon reached me. Then came the strange way goodness can make itself felt.

For that we must move, a while later, to Christchurch, New Zealand, where David Novitz, my close Jewish friend from our boyhood and Rhodes University days, whom I have already introduced, was lecturing in philosophy at the local university.

He phoned me at my university study quite unexpectedly and told me a strange tale. An uncle of his whom I had never met was in charge of prosecutions in my home province. A day or so earlier this uncle had phoned David, something he had never done before. A puzzled David told me what followed. "Hello David," began his uncle, "this is your uncle in Pietermaritzburg. Interesting things your friend Martin has been saying, David. Goodbye David," and ended the call. Just what was going on here, both David and I wondered. After putting the phone down I surmised that the uncle's phone call might be a word of caution to me in a country where the powers that be did not take kindly to any chipping away at a key pillar of support from their apartheid policies, but it was only years later when the uncle and I had become friends after he had retired that the puzzle was explained.

He told me that he had been visited in his office by a delegation of conservative local clergymen. Righteously angered by my views as reported in the press article about my recent lecture, they wanted me to be charged with blasphemy, an extremely rare but possible measure in South Africa in those days. He declined to prosecute but knew that I needed to be made aware that I had made some serious enemies. Professional ethics prevented him from contacting me personally about this but there was nothing to stop him giving his nephew in New Zealand a careful hint, and trust that a puzzled David would pass it on. As a man of moral principle his conscience made him sympathetic to my views, so he sought and found a professionally acceptable way of alerting me to danger.

I already knew then that the notorious Special Branch of the police, charged with security matters, kept a file on me, and I knew that the apartheid state could easily judge my views as falling foul of its law prohibiting anybody from supposedly furthering the aims of communism. After all, they might reason, anybody who says the Bible is faulty is clearly attacking Christianity, which is exactly what the communists want. I also remembered the vicious treatment meted out to Basil Moore by the state years before, forcing him and his family into exile, so I understood that I needed henceforth to heed Scripture in Matthew 10:16, and be as shrewd as serpents and innocent as doves.

Gender justice

Somewhat later the university began to experience the academic movement against gender discrimination, led by women academics, one of them a departmental colleague. With many others I see this development as one of a handful of the most important manifestations in recent times of the power of the good to engage and progressively transform whatever harms our existence. It had valuable ethical consequences for me personally. I became aware of feminist theologians like Mary Daly, Rosemary Radford Ruether, and Ursula King, and their books, laying bare the extent to which patriarchy was a seriously corrupting presence in religion.[28]

By then I had become head of department and was able to arrange for two of these leading women scholars to visit the department. They were professors Ursula King and Rosemary Radford Ruether, whose excellent scholarly qualities and friendship ensured that a concern for the ongoing evil of male domination in society and religion would be a permanent part of my thinking. It was also an inspiration to give my fullest support to the creation of Gender Studies courses on our campus in Pietermaritzburg. To this day I rate the Honours level course in Gender and Religion that my colleague Dr Alleyn Diesel and I taught to a brilliant group of women as one of the most stimulating I had given in my entire career.

Christianity's patriarchal heritage

With the 500th anniversary of the start of the Protestant Reformation in mind as I wrote these words in 2017, it is instructive to look into the contribution of the Protestant Reformation to gender ethics. South Africa's Lutheran theologian, Dr Detlev Tönsing, kindly emailed me as follows about Luther and the position of women, with the punctuation very slightly edited: "He was of course a child of his time. However, in his writing *On Marriage* he did advocate that men should also change the diapers of their children. He had great respect for his wife and attempted to leave the property they owned to her in his will—which was at the time not legally possible. He allowed his wife great authority to run the household and finances according

---

28. Daly, *Gyn/ecology*; King, *Faith and Praxis*; Ruether, *Sexism and God-Talk*.

to her decisions. With Phillip Melanchthon, he advocated the establishment of schools, primary and higher, for girls as well as boys."

In Luther's *Sermons on the First Epistle of St Peter*, of 1522, the great reformer put the following question: "Should no distinction be made among the people, and should women, too, be priests?" This Luther answered as follows: "As St Paul says in Gal. 3:28, you must pay no attention to distinctions when you want to look at Christians. You must not say: 'This is a man or a woman; this is a servant or a master; this person is old or young.' They are all alike and only a spiritual people. Therefore they are all priests. All may proclaim God's Word, except that, as St. Paul teaches in 1 Cor.14:34, women should not speak in the congregation. They should let the men preach, because God commands them to be obedient to their husbands . . . If, however, only women were present and no men, as in nunneries, then one of the women might be authorized to preach."[29]

Similar words occur in Luther's 1521 treatise on *The Misuse of the Mass*: "The person who wishes to preach needs to have a good voice, good eloquence, a good memory and other natural gifts; whoever does not have these should properly keep still and let somebody else speak. Thus Paul forbids women to preach in the congregation where men are present who are skilled in speaking, so that respect and discipline may be maintained; because it is much more fitting and proper for a man to speak, a man is also more skilled at it. Paul did not forbid this out of his own devices, but appealed to the law, which says that women are to be subject (Gen. 3:16)."[30]

That Luther reflects the patriarchal values of that time in the passages I have quoted is clear. Bearing in mind the otherwise relentless patriarchy of his time and place, I would also say that he clearly shows some small but valuable signs of transcending those values, both in quoting Scripture in Galatians 3:28 and Genesis 1:26, and in the measures reported above by Dr Tönsing, which are clearly respectful towards women, though by far not egalitarian. Incidentally, my own first encounter with an ordained woman, as a young Anglican theology student on the visit to Lutheran relatives in Berlin in 1967 that I described above, was in the Lutheran Church.

Concerning Calvin, I turn here to a recent paper by Nico Vorster in the prestigious *Journal of Theological Studies*.[31] He wrote that for Calvin, women are equal to men in the spiritual realm but not in the world, whose God-created natural order has men possessing power over them. Citing Genesis 1:26, Vorster points out that male domination is in contradiction

---

29. Luther, *Luther's Works*, volume 30, 54–55.
30. Luther, *Luther's Works*, volume 36, 152.
31. Vorster, "John Calvin," 178-211.

to the doctrine that humankind is created in the image and likeness of God, not just men. (On women in church, contrast Galatians 3:25—28, with 1 Timothy 2:11—12). Calvin, contends Vorster, held to women's subordination in church. He grounded their subordination in Creation, not in the Fall and was neither a misogynist nor a proto-feminist. Overall, Vorster finds that the great Genevan reformer's perspective about women was mostly in accord with the patriarchy of that time. According to the *Cambridge Companion to John Calvin,* Calvin did however call for primary schooling for girls as well as boys separately, regarded wife-beating as an offence, and allowed for women to be part of the diaconate by caring for the sick. These are modest but still important gender-positive measures.[32]

What of my own Anglican tradition? If the signs of a move in the direction of gender justice in church and society were slight in both Luther and Calvin, signs wholly absent then and now in the official pronouncements and practice of the Catholic Church about the priesthood, they were also totally absent in the Anglican Reformation. This is scarcely surprising, for two reasons. The first one, of course, is the English King Henry VIII. As the head of the new Church of England following his breach with Rome in 1533, this much-married and murderous monarch is perhaps the ultimate archetype of patriarchy of the worst kind, notwithstanding his interest in Luther and his theological literacy. Under such a leader the subordinate position of women in church and society was not likely to receive even the slightest relief.

The second reason added its own great weight to the first, namely the strong organizational continuity between Catholicism and the new Church of England. Among the members of the latter there was plenty of interest in and support for Luther, and in Scotland for Calvin, but the inherited male hierarchy of priests and bishops in England under the headship of the monarch meant that women's emancipation in church and society would be a very long time coming. Not even the spirited and powerful reign of Henry's daughter, Elizabeth I, and centuries later of Queen Victoria, could change that reality. In the Anglican world of my background, for instance, the first woman priest in South Africa, Nancy Charton, was only ordained as recently as 1992.[33]

Moral action is part of the task of the churches and a passion for justice runs deep in the Jewish and Christian prophetic traditions, so it is distressing that the subordination of women has taken so long to be reduced and

---

32. See also McKim, *Cambridge Companion.*

33. Charton, *The Calling;* see also Elton, *England under the Tudors,* and MacCulloch, *Reformation.*

overcome in societies where the churches of the Reformation have been, and to some extent still are, important players. Why is this the case? Here are some possible answers. Firstly, patriarchal cultures may well be a lot more powerful in preserving male privilege and power than we egalitarians tend to believe. Secondly, the biblical sources about the status of women do not speak with one voice, with Paul in Galatians declaring that gender distinctions no longer count for Christians, but other Pauline passages saying the opposite. Given the enormous authority of Scripture in the Protestant churches, that would suggest ambivalence about women's liberation, and thus delay it. Thirdly, I want to suggest that the pre-Enlightenment world that includes the Reformation exhibits what could be called an obedience ethic of deference to authority, whether of the Bible, of traditional culture or of the Popes, rather than a critical ethic capable of questioning and judging inherited norms, as shown so well by Immanuel Kant's words near the beginning of his *Critique of Pure Reason* of 1781, about ours being an age of criticism, to which he held that everything must bend.

So, half a millennium after the start of the Protestant Reformation, I end this excursus into the heritage of patriarchy that still plagues important parts of Christianity by suggesting that the great Reformation principle of *semper reformanda*, or ongoing reformation, means the same as Kant's dictum about comprehensive critical evaluation, and indeed the same as the great prophetic principle of speaking truth to power that goes back to the Hebrew prophets, and beyond them to the Exodus accounts of Moses confronting the Pharaoh.

Campaigning for a constitutionally secular state

By the late 1980s it was clear to many of us that the apartheid state was in terminal crisis, making it essential to prepare for a new South Africa. For me this meant working on two closely related issues, both with ethical implications of great importance for the future: a new constitution and a secular state. Both were to bear fruit for the country after apartheid. My departmental colleagues and I cooperated to produce a contribution to an official Law Commission report about the views of human rights in the most widely followed faiths and in secular philosophies like western liberalism and Marxism.

For me the more important issue of the two was to determine the appropriate status of religion in a future, democratic and egalitarian South Africa. It soon became clear that if justice and equality, as two of the main constituent values of goodness, were to be the governing values of the future, then the country should become constitutionally secular, with freedom of religion and belief for all. Apartheid South Africa gave Christianity a constitutionally privileged status which made our Hindu, Muslim, Jewish, African Traditional and secularist citizens, and others, second-class citizens. That clearly violated those two core values. I therefore began a public campaign for a constitutionally secular state, writing a press article that found its way, so I was later told by a high-ranking member of the African National Congress—now the governing party of the country's national government and most of its provincial and local governments—into that organization's thinking, and eventually helped lead to our present constitutional dispensation.

It was published in the *Sunday Tribune* in Durban on May 20, 1990. I contended that both politics and religion would benefit by separating the apparatus of the state from all religious activities, and by replacing state support for Christianity with neutrality towards all belief-systems, which would all have equal freedom to operate. This would put an end to the existing injustice whereby members of a privileged group of churches used the apparatus of the state, like public education and broadcasting, to impose their beliefs and values on the country. I went on to warn against the domination of certain Calvinist churches being replaced by a new alliance of more liberal Christians, as that would merely be a new way of unjustly discriminating against people of other faiths. Then I added that a constitutionally secular state was also necessary on religious grounds. It would free religion from pressure to conform, and from the pretences and hypocrisy such pressure fosters, encouraging "spiritual flabbiness rather than true dedication, inquisitors rather than saints." The article ended by saying that believers "should be the first to welcome that arrangement and none more so than Christians: far from enjoying state support the founder of their faith was tortured and crucified by it."[34]

Some years later influential, conservative Christian voices began to condemn the secular state, alleging that it was responsible for the serious moral problems manifesting themselves in the country, and in others with similar constitutions. In response I delivered a paper defending the secular state on ethical and spiritual grounds at the 2009 conference of the Association for the Study of Religion in Southern Africa, held that year in Stellenbosch. It was later published in the academic journal *Alternation*. Here is a slightly edited extract from that paper. It relates to my earlier campaign for a secular state and is included here because of the way it deals with the power of moral goodness at a national level:

---

34. Prozesky, "After the Hegemony."

"The ANC supported the call for a secular state in the new South Africa. The faith communities were, however, divided. My own activities revealed strong support from liberal Christians and from leading Jewish, Muslim and Hindu figures. It also revealed opposition from others, mostly from conservative parts of Christianity, who relied heavily on the fact that Christians were and remain a large majority in the country. This was held by such people to justify making the new South Africa a constitutionally Christian state. I cannot recall any of those who wanted a Christian state admitting that there are in fact many Christianities, ranging from extremely conservative fundamentalists to extremely radical people, with many intermediate positions. How fair and honest was it for anybody to claim to speak for all our Christians, given such divisions, I often wondered. In any event, the upshot was the 1996 constitution which ushered in our present secular state, which is now under fire from some as the alleged source of our moral problems.

"It will be apparent that I appealed mostly to ethical values to justify my advocacy of a secular state. The first one is to problematize imposition and domination. While I did not then analyze these two evils further, I do so now. They are evils because they violate the right of people to equality of treatment and therefore to respect. When somebody or some organization presumes to impose a view on others, that is an offence against the dignity of the recipients of the imposition, and therefore unethical.

"The second ethical value is social justice. I was saying that we needed an arrangement that was fair and just to everybody, and that this could not be achieved by giving any religion (or non-religious philosophy) legal status above that of all others, but that a secular state could provide that justice because it treated all faiths and philosophies even-handedly. Indeed it would treat everybody as first-class citizens. That made it just.

"In the third place, I appealed to the principle of inclusivity, by calling for first-class status for everybody. These were and remain the main ethical grounds in favour of a secular state, except for a further one to which I now turn, by drawing attention to the nature of such a state as indicated in my original press article and later enacted in the country's Bill of Rights, which occurs in Chapter 2 of the 1996 constitution. Clauses 9 and 15 deal with equality and freedom of belief.

"The operative contentions in my original press article are that a secular state is neutral with regard to religion (or any non-religious belief-system), that it is even-handed towards them all, that it favours none, and that it provides freedom of operation for them all. The terms 'neutral' and 'even-handed' express two features of how a secular state relates to religion, and both of them reveal that it does so justly and thus ethically. The third term, freedom of operation, takes us from the state to religion itself, and is ethically crucial. It means that in a secular state all religions have full scope to operate, which includes teaching their ethical values, obtaining radio and television time, building great new places of worship, and so forth. That cannot happen in a secularistic state, or is made extremely difficult. How many new cathedrals were built in the USSR under Stalin, for example?

"By giving all religions the same right to freedom of operation, a secular state acts justly and ethically, unlike a religiously defined state (or a secularistic state) in a country with a diversity of faiths, which cannot do justice even-handedly towards them all because it privileges one of them for no objectively good and just reason."[35]

An important spiritual and ethical lesson emerged from the campaign for a secular state, its adoption, and subsequent religious objections to it. As presented in this book, spirituality is centered on the experience of a surpassing goodness that summons all who feel its beauty and power to align their lives and faiths to it in every way possible, leading to ethical action. Sometimes deeply held religious convictions can reduce rather than enhance our ability to do this and to recognize what really is the greatest good in any situation, including the way a nation organizes itself.

Saved from acute pain and anxiety

An emotionally charged medical experience happened to me some years later. I was flying from South Africa to a conference in Mexico City in 1995 when I began to feel the flare up of a now-gone, extremely painful problem for which I carried antibiotics when travelling. I looked for the container in my hand luggage and remembered to my dismay that I had thoughtlessly packed it in my checked baggage, which I would only get after landing at my destination after a change of planes at Miami and a stop at Dallas-Fort Worth. The pain had considerably worsened by the time we reached Mexico City, but relief eluded me when to my added dismay I found my checked luggage missing.

35. Prozesky, "Is the Secular State?" 246-48.

I reported it and was assured by the officials that my baggage would follow, so I gave them my name and hotel number and gratefully accepted the help of uniformed conference staff at the airport in getting to the minibus that took me to the Hotel Majestic in the middle of that vast and fascinating city. There I lost no time in getting directions to a nearby pharmacy where my luck again ran out. Nobody could speak enough English to understand what I was asking, and the best I could get was a pack of over-the-counter pain-killers. By nightfall no message had come from the airport for me to collect my baggage and the searing pain was worse.

After a shower I went to bed but the pain was too bad for me to sleep despite another round of pain-killers. Besides, the condition required frequent visits to the bathroom. And then, after once more hurrying to the bathroom, I found there that I was bleeding quite copiously, something that had never happened to me before. Not since the motorbike event when I believed I was about to be killed had I ever again felt the sheer desperation of the moment, alone in a huge, foreign city where I knew nobody and no Spanish, in the middle of the night and without the medication that had always cleared the problem.

When the passing of blood stopped I returned to my bed, lay down, turned the light off and, at the end of my tether, simply said, "Help me God" and fell asleep. I woke up early next morning completely free of any pain and any need to hurry to the bathroom and no trace of blood. When my baggage finally arrived I had no need for the antibiotic and have never needed it again; though I still travel with a new supply in case things change, O me of little faith!

What explains this further experience of baffling deliverance? After returning home I told my medical practitioner what had happened and asked for his opinion. He listened carefully, reflected for a while and said simply that sometimes healings happen that we can't explain, and left it there. By then long past believing in the deity of my early years but still open-minded, I recalled the opening words, already quoted in this book, of a book by my brilliant Oxford theology tutor, David Jenkins, later to be a celebrated but also controversial Bishop of Durham. He wrote, "God is either a gift or a delusion."[36] Very much a liberal, David Jenkins no more believed in that deity than I did. What kind of a God, if any, we can still embrace with integrity is something I did not understand in Mexico City in 1995, but I understood what it can be to receive a gift of healing that was certainly no delusion.

---

36. Jenkins, *Living with Questions*, 1.

Working full-time on ethics at the university

Suspending the exciting life of an academic with such richly powerful scholars as Hick, Geering and Cobb to guide and inspire me for the life of a university dean with its endless paper work and meetings is not what I sought, but when it was my turn to accept the four-year position as Dean of Humanities, I knew I had a duty to do so. What I didn't know when I exchanged the lecture room for the administrative office in 1991 was that it would lead to the ethically most valuable part of my career, in which I could work full-time at seeking to further the good. Here is what happened.

My deanship coincided with South Africa's unforgettable transition from apartheid to a fledgling, non-racial democracy, so it was a highly fertile time to lead the Faculty of Humanities. It had to think deeply about the future when the doors of learning opened to our black majority. That was a challenge I, too, had to face. What should my role be in a new South Africa? I was sure that it should be academic as I had no desire to climb the administrative ladder. My deanship brought me into contact with the national academic situation and it was soon clear to me that the country's most pressing single need from the humanities was ethical strength, both as an academic field and especially as the practice of what is right and good. Apartheid was a viciously relentless departure from goodness that did immense damage to people. That was obvious. What was not widely grasped was that it had systematically damaged and sometimes destroyed the three most important ways in which moral character is built for vast numbers of our people: family life, the school and even religion. South Africa has a very large Christian majority and the white community was overwhelmingly Christian in membership or orientation. Yet it had created and enforced a shameful evil. How could its moral credibility not be in question, as I had earlier pointed out in the College Lecture described above, which some of my critics considered blasphemous?

So I resolved to devote myself to making what contribution I could to rebuilding the gravely damaged moral fabric of South African society, by starting an ethics center at my university. In yet another instance of the remarkable way goodness can happen, our Vice-Chancellor, Professor Brenda Gourley, later to be the Vice-Chancellor of Britain's Open University, was also passionate about ethics. She gave me her complete support, which included helping to find very generous donor funding from the Unilever Foundation, and by 1997 the ethics center was a reality.

The Ethics Center 1997–2007

Excellent work was already being done in ethics by the country's philosophers and theologians, so I wanted an approach that would complement that work in three ways. It would be multi-disciplinary, multi-cultural, and practical. It would pursue the kind of inclusivity that apartheid had rejected. My experiences and research over the years had made me reject as mistaken and even unethical the notion that there are only two doors to knock on if you want ethical guidance: western philosophy and western religion in the form of Christianity. This does not to deny their value but it does see their limits. As I explain in the next chapter, my work in ethics owes much to western philosophy, but its complexity and abstraction render it highly vulnerable to Karl Marx's famous statement in the last of his famous *Theses on Feuerbach* of 1845, that the "philosophers have only *interpreted* the world in various ways; the point, however, is to *change* it."[37]

What I was seeking, and am still seeking, is an ethic that could help change harmful structures and practices in the world or at least in my own country. As is surely clear already, my moral debt to Christianity is even greater than to western philosophy but this faith has no monopoly over goodness nor any moral superiority, for saintliness happens in the other belief-systems too. So we decided that the ethics center would call its subject matter Comparative and Applied Ethics, and be handled by a small, interdisciplinary team.

Its work had four aspects. Firstly, in response to Vice-Chancellor Brenda Gourley's wish for an ethics course for students in all faculties, we started a new semester course for undergraduate students called Ethics Studies 101. It provided an introduction to a multi-disciplinary and multi-cultural understanding of ethics and grew rapidly into a successful major subject with postgraduate follow-up options. Secondly, we embarked on fresh research; thirdly, we helped develop resources to aid ethical practice in the university, and the fourth aspect was community service in response to many requests for ethics inputs from the wider society. In my case that included a regular, new press column for *The Witness* newspaper in Pietermaritzburg called "Right Angles."

My research involved two areas: the ethical critique of religions and global ethics,[38] which led to the appearance of my 2007 book *Conscience: Ethical Intelligence for Global Well-Being*. The method I followed in order to identify values that are shared by all people was to use research into hu-

---

37. Marx, *On Religion*, 65.
38. See Kidder, *Shared Values*: and Küng, *Global Ethic*.

man nature as its foundation, arguing that as a single species, members of modern *Homo sapiens* possess a shared biology which gives rise to certain shared, basic values, no matter what we subsequently learn from our cultures, as explained in the next chapter.

A great privilege during those years was being part of a small team set up by the country's Moral Regeneration Movement or MRM to draft a code of ethics for South Africa. Led by Professor Paulus Zulu in Durban, it laid the conceptual foundations for a consultative process around the country about the draft we produced, which led to certain modifications and finally to its ceremonial adoption under the title, *Charter of Positive Values*. The drafting team was culturally diverse and worked consciously to identify the main values shared by all of our cultures. The end result is as close to a national code of ethics as the country now possesses.[39]

Best of all at the ethics center was our initiative to promote awareness and appreciation of African traditional ethics by including it in our ethics courses and by facilitating the research of a new generation of African ethics scholars. Here we were generously supported by funding from the Atlantic Philanthropies to finance three outstanding young black students' doctoral studies. All three now hold academic positions and from two of them important books about African ethics have now been published.[40]

My Liberal Christianity and its end

My move from conservative, traditional beliefs to Liberal Christianity was a gradual one. As I look back I recognize the underlying influence of my youthful experience of an Anglican Church in which there was no trace of biblical fundamentalism and evangelical fervor in our parish, in some contrast with what I initially had at home, but rather a concern for regular worship and social justice. I recall no doubts or questions then about Christianity's beliefs or the status of Scripture. It was my early university experiences, as recounted earlier, that challenged and changed those certainties, starting with my exposure to critical biblical studies.

The university context is very significant because it opened me to a much wider world of important realities, chiefly other faiths, atheism, historical methods and much more philosophy than just Descartes. So I moved into a typical, liberal Christian orientation. It was marked by a universalist view of salvation and by increasingly serious doubts about the so-called nature miracles of Jesus; also by doubts about the virgin birth and the

---

39. MRM Charter of Positive Values.
40. Murove, *African Ethics*, and *African Moral Consciousness*; Matolino, *Personhood*.

empty tomb; and by rejection of biblical literalism, especially concerning the creation narratives and a biblical cosmology with a heaven above us to which Jesus supposedly ascended. What didn't change was my passion for the moral force of a love-based faith and its historical founder; that passion increased in strength.

My move into an ever more liberal faith was for a while arrested by the ascendency in those years of Karl Barth's neo-orthodox theology, with its radical exclusivism about a supposed revelation by an utterly transcendent, trinitarian God revealed to us in Christ, the Bible, and the preaching of the church. Barth's exemplary moral courage against Nazism certainly won my admiration, but the attraction I felt for a while to his theology soon gave way to what I had learnt from Schleiermacher at Oxford and in my doctoral research, as explained in some detail earlier in this book.

Having to lecture to students about comparative religion, the philosophy of religion and process theology from 1971 onwards further strengthened my liberalism, as did the research that led to the explanatory theory of religion in my 1984 book, *Religion and Ultimate Well-Being*, but they also undermined it in a sceptical direction. The strongest intellectual factors in making me explore radical Christianity and move away from any lingering Liberal Christianity came from the work on ethics that marked the last decade of my academic career, and in the years since then, strongly supported by studies of the new quest for the historical Jesus by scholars like Marcus Borg and John Dominic Crossan.

There was also a spiritual side to the end of my Liberal Christianity, ironically enough provided by the church itself. I was a regular Anglican worshipper during the years from about 1975 to the early 1980s as I moved ever more into the world of liberal theology, stimulated by the friendship of ordained colleagues and mentors in the churches and at the universities. But as I worked on my 1984 book with its inclusive approach to and naturalistic account of the world's religions, I began to experience a growing sense of alienation from worship and from the sermons I was hearing, theologically liberal though they were. Then, after completing the book and returning to South Africa from sabbatical at the end of 1982, an experience in Pietermaritzburg's former Anglican cathedral of St Peter brought my churchgoing days to a sudden end.

Here is what happened. Soon after returning from sabbatical I went to the service of Evensong, which I loved, but knew at once that I was no longer part of that world of belief and ritual practice. The words of the service, the hymns and especially the sermon were, naturally, the familiar ones, but I was no longer responsive to them. My mind and soul had opened to a far wider spiritual world of other faiths, philosophies and scientific discoveries, making me miss any appreciative mention of that wider and, for me, spiritually much richer world. What had been alive and warm for me in those lovely church interiors now felt remote, narrow and lacking in vitality, and I left at the end of the service knowing that even liberal church worship and belief had ended for me. Ahead lay years of exploring a new world of what I came to call, for a while, religious humanism; religious because the appeal of spirituality never left me and humanist in the sense that its focus was on the human condition, the evils besetting it and the yearning for ways to defeat them.

The knowledge that I could no longer find spiritual and theological nourishment, even in a liberal church that totally rejected apartheid, was deepened and furthered by times at the beautiful Buddhist Retreat Centre in the southern part of our province. I came to love the meditation sessions we were taught, both seated and walking, and admired greatly the philosophical and moral depth of Buddhist teaching, above all its message of universal compassion and the example of the Buddha himself in this regard.

Entering this new, inclusive world of post-ecclesial faith, ethical values and understanding, of which the historical Jesus being re-discovered in the new quest about him was a central but not exclusive part, was wonderfully exciting and enriching, so I later wrote about it in one of my 1992 press columns for *The Natal Witness*, as it was then called, which I quote here.

"When Great Rivers Converge

"Our present culture can be likened to a lake fed by a number of rivers. One of them flows from traditional Africa, giving us, for example, the idea that we can only be truly human in and through other people. Another comes from ancient Greece and Rome, providing parts of our systems of laws and philosophy, the beginnings of science and much else. A third draws its waters from the mountains of the ancient middle-east, which produced some of our most powerful moral teachings and religious beliefs, while a fourth rises in the Indian sub-continent, enriching us with Gandhi and the Gita. Then there are the shorter, fast-flowing streams that have given us our business world, modern science and medicine, and much else besides.

"The waters of these streams mingle in the lake of daily experience, but their sources are mostly far separated from one another. As a result Rome, Athens, Jerusalem, Mecca and Benares have all existed in mutual separation, so that prophets and philosophers have mostly been different people. But now and then things have been otherwise in the form of those rare individuals in whom several great streams come together.

"One such was Alfred North Whitehead, in whom philosophy, science, mathematics, poetic expression and deep spiritual insight formed a rare and powerful blend of ideas. Born in England in 1861, he spent the last part of a distinguished career at Harvard where he died in 1947. In the past few years I have been exploring his writings and their relevance for a country like ours. While doing so I found many striking passages to challenge our thinking and spur us to fresh insight, and therefore I use the rest of this article to quote a few of them, taken from his 1933 book *Adventures of Ideas*.

"The first one goes as follows: 'The progress of religion is defined by the denunciation of gods. The keynote of idolatry is contentment with the prevalent gods.' If we look at history it is striking how many of the great religious leaders attacked existing beliefs and proposed new ones, just as Whitehead says.

"Elsewhere he discusses Plato, seeing him as perhaps the deepest spiritual thinker of the western tradition and not just as a great philosopher, an unusual idea in a culture where people think just of the various Scriptures as the place to find religious inspiration. Here are Whitehead's own words: 'The religion of Plato is founded on his conception of what a God can be, with gaze fixed upon forms of eternal beauty.' What Whitehead was driving at is that the greatest power in the universe is chiefly characterized by beauty—without which the deepest joy and fulfilment are impossible.

"Concerning Christianity, he provocatively wrote that in conflict with its own best teachings it retained from the culture where it arose 'the concept of a Divine Despot and a slavish universe, each with the morals of its kind.' This is a reference to the idea of a deity more interested in obedience than love. For Whitehead and many others, such a preference is out of line with the basic teachings of both Jesus and Plato. And lastly, commenting on the element of persecution present in some faiths, he wrote that 'wherever there is a Creed, there is a heretic around the corner or in his grave.'

"At first sight ideas like these might seem rather hostile to religion as most of us know it. But because the word 'spirit' can validly be taken to mean freedom and creativity, Whitehead in fact offers a deeply spiritual vision based on the idea that the greatest power is the power of persuasion and not compulsion, and that there is such a power working in the universe, luring us to experience it for ourselves by its sheer beauty, and setting us free by encouraging us to be fulfilled, whole, and beautiful beings rather than docile servants."[41]

Stimulating though this new chapter of my ethical, spiritual and intellectual pilgrimage was, it was also a lonely one, for it lacked the kind of supportiveness that churches, mosques, temples and synagogues give their members. Despite the nostalgia for that supportiveness and for the beauties of church music and stained glass windows, my personal exodus from a world where I felt constrained and even claustrophobic has continued except for the rarest of return experiences, invariably because of the presence of a spiritually deep and serene priest or bishop. One such involved Archbishop Emeritus Desmond Tutu and was so meaningful to me that I wrote about it in the press column that follows, slightly edited, which also expresses my questing ways in matters spiritual.

"The return of the comet

It is still dark on a chilly winter morning in Cape Town as I hurry down Wale Street to St George's Cathedral for the early Friday Eucharist, which Archbishop Tutu celebrates. Even though I am not a regular church-goer, being more drawn to ethical spirituality than to ritual spirituality, I feel at home as he conducts the service with grace and dignity in a small side chapel for a congregation of about thirty.

"Halfway through he stops to welcome everybody, asking all who are visitors to introduce themselves. There is a group of university students from America on a study tour. A man from Ireland confesses that he is in Cape Town mainly for a rugby test and isn't even an Anglican. The Arch chuckles and welcomes him warmly none the less. Where I am standing makes me the last to introduce myself. The Arch welcomes me and a friend of his near me tells the group that I do ethics work. They clap their hands and I am touched.

"Months later another morning dawns, and it is sunny and warm in my home village of Hilton. Friends have invited us to attend a service of blessing at their lovely new home. I remember from my boyhood that our curate held a short service of blessing for my father's new car. We happily accept the invitation. The officiating priest is gracious and friendly, like everybody else. We are fascinated by the way he blesses the rooms. While

41. Prozesky, "When Great Rivers."

outsiders to such rituals, we feel at home because of the warmth and kindness we experience.

"Reflecting afterwards on these experiences, I recall what I wrote many years ago in *Shalom*, the magazine of Pietermaritzburg's new Anglican cathedral, then just open for worship. I wrote that I hoped it could be a home to any and all. Being since boyhood fascinated by the night skies with their planets and stars, I used the solar system as a model for this idea. I hoped the new cathedral would be a home, like the sun, not just to the spiritual planets which circle it in their regular, faithful orbits, but also a home to those starry travellers, the comets, who journey far away from the sun, way beyond Pluto, returning only, if ever, at long intervals to their home in the heavens.

"Where really is home for spiritual comets like these? As I reflect on that winter morning in St George's Cathedral and later back in Hilton, I liken myself to a comet returning to the sun and enjoying its warmth, but not staying there for long as my journey continues. It goes outward now, away from the sun, to those distant zones which only comets and NASA probes are privileged to encounter directly.

"Where then is home for people like this? It is everywhere. It is where I pass Mars, it is where I pass mighty Jupiter and gorgeous Saturn with its stunning rings. It is also out there far beyond the furthest planet, where the immensely distant sun is just another bright star, another diamond on the beautiful ebony skin of the heavens, and I remember Daniel 12:3 which my father marked for me in my first Bible, about those who could shine like the stars forever.

"Home is everywhere because the force of gravity that holds us all, like goodness itself, is everywhere. Out there the sun's light is very faint and its warmth all but gone, but the view of the stars, both physical and spiritual, is magnificent beyond anything you can see from close to the sun, and the void holds no terrors, for gravity, like goodness, is everywhere."[42]

Another mystical experience

Never in the spiritual experiences I had so far undergone did I ever have an apparition of a being of any kind, nor heard a voice, until that quite unexpectedly changed in mid-2006. Here is my record of what I experienced

---

42. Prozesky, "The Return."

in one of my early morning meditations, written shortly afterwards and slightly edited for the present context.

> "It was very early in the morning of Sunday, June 4, 2006. I sat in silence, meditating and seeking guidance about what to do next with my life, half expecting it to be one of the projects open to me at my university. But as clearly as if spoken aloud, a set of words came to my mind and I 'heard' the words 'Save my church,' followed by a strong sense of the deep meaning of a love that enfolds the world, a love that lets others love, lets others be whole but only with others, for solitary love is not love but longing. And I 'heard' the message to all Christians and to me that as we are all on the road of faith and not yet home, so we must all expect to grow into greater, loving, wholeness. For while we can be sure of the love in our hearts and the love we receive, we cannot know the full picture of reality with our finite minds, only that we believe we come from love, live in love and are led by love."

What, or who, was I hearing in those words in my mind but not with my physical hearing? I had absolutely no belief that I was being divinely addressed the way some of the biblical figures were according to Scripture. Was a lifetime of engaging with Christian belief and with a missionary family history, mostly as a scholar but also spiritually, generating in my brain an unconscious sense of mission and converting it into words, yet another unexpected but wondrous gift? Was it something else that I had perhaps become too self-assured to accept? Or was it yet another powerful reminder that the workings of the universe hold many surprises for us, even now in our age of information, so that the informed spiritual path will always be a journey into a mystery that passes all understanding? I cannot say and am content to live with the mystery in a spirit of open-minded and open-hearted wonder.

In the decade since that early morning spiritual experience I have sought its practical meaning by exploring what it might be that the churches need most. From what and for what might they need to be saved or helped by concerned people like me? This book gives the answers I have found. Perhaps not surprisingly, they center on ethics, on goodness and the doing of all the good we can here in this life. What has surprised and inspired me is encountering, through research into the best scholarship and through personal contacts, that this passion for the good *in this life* is the heart of what Jesus of Nazareth initiated, transforming for me an improbable heavenly savior into an ethical revolutionary and pioneer of magnificent courage and unsurpassed power.

As I reflect now on that experience in 2006, I recall another event which has also richly influenced my life and work. I was in the cemetery outside Grahamstown to visit a sister's grave. After finding it and remembering her with love and sadness, I found the grave of my philosophy professor and friend at Rhodes and Oxford, Daantjie Oosthuizen, whose great influence I have already acknowledged. The grave was planted with succulents and carried a bronze plaque mounted on a small, rounded rock. On the plaque were written these words from John 16:13: "When the Spirit of Truth comes he will lead you into all truth." The word "lead" is very important, making us ask just how a God of perfect goodness would lead us. In the chapter in part III about an alternative understanding of God I give my answer, but for now let it be said that such a God would lead us only by means of pure goodness and therefore in the direction of ever-greater love and truth, by the hand and not by the nose.

ETHICS TRAINING AND WRITING FOR THE WIDER SOCIETY FROM 2008 ONWARD

The response to the Unilever Ethics Centre's work in the wider society led to my early retirement at the end of 2007 in order to give all my time to applied ethics training, together with a team of outstanding colleagues, and to voluntary ethics work. For this I set up an agency called Compass Ethics. At no time over the preceding decade had we advertised our availability for ethics training. Instead we responded to calls for such training, and in that way did plenty of it, mainly for professional bodies and for me also in sports ethics. We found that there was, and is, a great need for a deepening and strengthening of moral standards in a way that involved all the most widely followed cultures of the country and which placed the main emphasis on ways of *doing* greater good and not on theory. What proved very effective was doing this work in a way that explicitly acknowledged and respected the moral strengths and experiences of the attendees, and by offering ways to help them extend and enhance it, so breaking with the religious approaches that create the impression that most people are morally deficient and in need of an injection of ethical strength from us or somebody else.

An exceptionally enriching opportunity for voluntary ethics work came to me from the Hospice organization in Pietermaritzburg. I had already experienced the loving care its members and volunteers give, when a younger sister needed it in her brave struggle with cancer, so I immediately accepted a request to be part of, and later chair, its new ethics committee. That gave me an inspiring insight into what can be done when people with caring hearts have organizational power to enhance what they so willingly do, a lesson that relates to what I propose in chapter 15.

Early retirement from my academic position in Pietermaritzburg did not mean the end of my academic work. First the University of KwaZulu-Natal, and then some years later the University of the Free State, appointed me to honorary research positions so that I could continue my research and publications about religion and ethics within their respective structures, to my great benefit. At the University of the Free State in the city of Bloemfontein the invitation came from the Faculty of Theology and Religion. The friendly and ever-helpful reception there from the theologians and biblical scholars, and their interest in my work on religion and ethics opened the way to a return to my erstwhile focus on Christianity, this time in critical, ethical perspective. The present book owes a great deal to that facilitative reception in Bloemfontein, for which I will always be grateful.

My other research in the years after taking early retirement concentrated on two issues affecting Christianity which I continue to see as vital to a better future: the use and misuse of the Bible and the new movement called Progressive Christianity. As well as preparing for the present book and my 2017 novel *Warring Souls*, I wrote articles for local and national newspapers on both of these issues, articles which were not always welcomed by certain readers. I quoted these two articles in part III.

As I look back today over my life and especially over my academic career, I see it is a steady and at times also dramatic process of being drawn into the service of goodness by its ubiquitous, attractive power, also feeling the summons to discern and oppose what is wrong. The words of Daniel 12:3 have seldom been far from my sense of self as this process has unfolded. Universities might think of themselves as citadels of truth-building; for me the academic life has had a deeper meaning as I moved from a primary concern with religion to a more fundamental concern with goodness. Research findings in related disciplines over the years that deepened and enriched my knowledge have added great value to this process. In the next chapter I present the most relevant and important of these.

Chapter 5

Themes and Thinkers from Multi-Disciplinary Research

WHO WE ARE: UNDERSTANDING OUR HUMAN NATURE

WHEN I BEGAN TO ponder how best to explain the phenomenon of religion, which has been part of human existence for as long as 50,000 years and perhaps as long as 70,000 years,[1] I focused my research and reflections on the only feature of religion that has been constant: the humanness involved. Down the ages and across the world, from the religions of the Australian Aborigines and the Aztecs to Zen Buddhists and Zulus, the worshipping, praying and believing agents have all been members of the single species we call *Homo sapiens*. It follows that an understanding of human nature based on what we now know about our species could enable us better to understand religion in general and Christianity in particular.

As has already been indicated, my research into this issue had begun by 1978 in connection with religion and more recently in connection with morality.[2] It has been updated and extended ever since, culminating in a journal article in 2014 which provides a convenient account of the results. From it I now use the relevant section, suitably updated and edited, in order to offer an account of the ethical and religious dimensions of our human existence.[3]

1. Lewis-Williams, *Conceiving God*, 11; Schellenberg, *Evolutionary Religion*, 3.
2. Prozesky, *Religion and Ultimate Well-Being*, 99-152; and *Conscience*, 32-60.
3. Prozesky, "Homo Ethicus," 283-301.

My view of human nature summarized

In summary the account is as follows: *all human beings are fundamentally and uniquely constituted, as vulnerable, inter-related, sentient, valorizing, highly intelligent, but always fallible and finite beings, with a drive to imagine, conceptualize, express in language, and creatively bring about maximum well-being.* This assertion contains an echo of process philosophy's central emphasis on both creativity and relationality that was not present in the original research referred to above. It also reflects the earliest available evidence of human activities, like tool making, ritual burial, and organized hunting, until the present.[4]

Specifically, the account entails the following more detailed contentions. It is based on a vital difference between people on one hand and all other intelligent species on the other. We are genetically very close to bonobos and chimpanzees. They too are intelligent and able to understand, and respond to a fair number of words, though vastly fewer than we are, but cannot speak. They too feel pain and pleasure, and desire the latter; they too are capable of walking on two legs and have opposable thumbs.[5] But there is nonetheless a crucial difference: on their own all such species can survive only in or near a native habitat, whereas *Homo sapiens* has repeatedly created and re-created the means of surviving and thriving in a range of enormously different habitats. I think this indicates a human capacity for mental and physical creativity which is unique: the ability to imagine safer and more enjoyable ways of living and then bring them about. So our species has moved from the African forests of some 200,000 years ago to the savannah, the deserts, the ice fields, the river banks, the tilled fields, the temples, mosques and cathedrals, the industrial suburbs, the Moon, and fairly soon, it seems, the planet Mars.

Experience as empirical evidence

Next, the account about what it means to be human is *empirical and experiential*. It purports to assert a truth about people in the concrete actualities of their existence as they themselves experience it, a matter that I have tested again and again in ethical training workshops and found repeatedly confirmed by attendees.[6] As such it has a biological dimension, because it implies that human beings are physically equipped for the pursuit of the

---

4. McCarthy and Rubidge, *Story of Earth*, 275-295.
5. Fernandez-Armesto, *So You Think*, 9-54.
6. Prozesky, *Conscience*, 32-36.

increased well-being that they are also biologically equipped to imagine and desire. The hypothesis additionally has a social-scientific dimension because it implies that a wide range of phenomena of the kind studied by social scientists all have their common foundation in, and bring to expression, the drive to imagine and maximize well-being. These disciplines are collective human behavior and institutions (the field of sociology), individual human behavior (psychology), the pursuit of power and wealth (political economy), the diversities of culture (social anthropology), the diversities of transcendental orientation (religion studies, theology and some forms of philosophy), and of course humanity's value-systems. Thus the hypothesis is in principle open to falsification by the biological and social sciences, and indeed by common experience. Whether or not it is consistent with this or that philosophical or theological theory about morality is irrelevant in the present context, where experiential and empirical justifications are what count.

Next, the hypothesis is an empirical *generalization* in that it purports to identify a basic truth about *all* human beings. As such its validity depends on the hypothesis being applicable to all known human cultures past and present. Any attested pattern of human activity that cannot be plausibly subsumed within its logic would therefore refute or at least seriously modify the hypothesis.

By asserting that the inter-related drive to maximize well-being is a fundamental human characteristic, the hypothesis implies that all other aspects of what it means to be human depend upon or arise from this characteristic. An inability to demonstrate a plausible dependency-relationship between any of those other aspects and this drive to imagine and maximize well-being would thus count against its being genuinely fundamental.

Well-being and other terms defined

Some of the terms used in formulating the hypothesis must now be clarified. The basic term is "well-being" and signifies *an experienced condition of satisfaction which the subject of the experience would not want to lose but could wish to enhance.* There is nothing essential about the choice of the term "well-being"; the words "flourishing" or "thriving" could also serve, but not happiness, This is because well-being or flourishing can refer without distortion to both the subject's experience of enjoyment, satisfaction, and the like, and—crucially—also to the conditions around him or her that make that experience possible, like friendship, employment, peace and social justice. Happiness is too subjective to cover that essential, broader, contextual reality.

Thus I assert that people experience well-being whenever their consciousness is free, or largely free, in whatever their circumstances, of a sense of uneasiness, discomfort, dissatisfaction, misery or pain, whether in relation to themselves personally, to their circumstances, or to both. Positively, well-being is the experience of equanimity, calm, satisfaction, contentedness, pleasure or happiness, either in oneself personally, in one's circumstances, or both.

Accordingly, the most important experiential or sensory indicator of well-being and its absence is a felt impulse to maintain or change one's present conditions: if the impulse is towards maintenance or increase, then well-being is present; if the impulse is towards change, then well-being is deficient or even absent. It will be noticed that this most basic of my terms is defined ostensively; in other words, it is given meaning by pointing to an experienced reality open to all people alike. This is the meaning of the words "sentient" and especially the word "valorizing" in my understanding of what it means to be a member of our species. Sentience is the ability to feel and valorizing is the ability to assign positive and negative value—or importance—to what we feel and to the situations that give rise to it, desiring the one and seeking to avoid or diminish the other. As Rolston puts it: "A minimally sentient awareness is required for value."[7]

It is worth repeating here that when I first began to formulate this account of human nature, I was seeking an inclusive, unified way of accounting for the world's religions, and thereby to refute conceptually a core tenet of apartheid thinking, namely that human differences are more basic than any similarities. I wanted to see if something as hugely varied as religion could be subsumed under a single logic and I believed that I found a way to do so, but that is another story. An underlying motivation for that research was therefore ethical in nature.

The term "vulnerable" is closely connected with what I am calling our desire for well-being and the drive to achieve it lastingly. To be vulnerable is to be capable of being harmed, as we and all living things are. It is not something any being with feelings enjoys, made worse for a being with the intelligence to know that it is vulnerable and anxiously fear it, so measures are sought and used to minimize that vulnerability and achieve the well-being we all desire.

The next set of terms is "imagine," "conceptualize" and "express in language." As the previous paragraphs imply, I contend that people are

---

7. Rolston, *Genes*, 38.

consciously aware of well-being or its absence and when it is felt to be absent or insufficient, they are able to envisage a preferred, more satisfying condition. Much more is thus involved than a blind or subconscious process built into us. While not denying that it may have important subconscious aspects, I nonetheless wish to place the main emphasis on well-being as a *conscious* experience that involves a range of important cognitive dimensions. It involves imagining the elimination of particular discomforts, often using metaphoric modes of expression like speaking of "a heavenly experience"; it involves knowledge about proven avenues of satisfaction and dissatisfaction; and it involves critical awareness of potential and real threats to human well-being.

Another expression requiring elucidation is "creatively realize." By asserting that human existence is governed by a drive to conceptualize and *creatively realize* maximum well-being, the hypothesis extends from the intra-personal to the extra-personal; it contends that people act in myriads of ways in order to implement imagined, new scenarios of satisfaction, so converting the expectations of human consciousness, albeit incompletely, into empirical reality. Thus the worlds of other people, of nature and of human cultural creation are changed, and ourselves as well. Here again the hypothesis has strong affinities with Whitehead's philosophy, especially his celebrated statement that creativity is "the universal of universals" whereby "the many become one and are increased by one."[8]

Relatedness

The next term that needs comment is "inter-related." My use of it has a strong affinity with the African concept of *Ubuntu*,[9] and also with process philosophy. Given the simple fact that for every individual there are countless other selves and even more non-human objects which greatly affect every individual, so that reality is always, objectively, more constituted by that preponderant externality than by its individual subjects on their own, it is obvious that any adequate account of human existence must pay particularly careful attention to the drive to maximize well-being *in relation to the total context of human existence*, as shaped by natural forces and, perhaps especially, by the innumerable actions of other people. We are indeed a social species, living in an inter-related totality with other beings and nature.

Just how crucially this contextual reality bears on the nature of the ethical and spiritual dimensions of our existence will be shown in part III

---

8. Whitehead, *Process and Reality*, 21.
9. Murove, *African Moral Consciousness*, 172-219; Shutte, *Ubuntu*, 21-33.

of this book. It also shows that these aspects of our human performance cannot be adequately understood without an understanding of our total context of existence, which is provided in the coming section. As Laszlow has said, "We are natural systems first, living things second, human beings third, members of society and culture fourth, and particular individuals fifth."[10]

Inter-relatedness has important implications for our understanding of freedom, as Laszlow further points out. "There is freedom in choosing one's paths of progress, yet this freedom is bounded by the limits of compatibility with the dynamic structure of the whole."[11]

What Whitehead and others in the process philosophical tradition speak of as our relatedness is more frequently termed our social nature by social scientists and philosophers like Peter Singer, arguably the most influential practical ethics thinker of recent times. He rejects the idea advocated by Enlightenment thinkers such as Rousseau, Hobbes and others that we humans are essentially individualistic beings; contending instead that we are social animals.[12] He also rejects the idea, current in the behaviorist psychology of B.F. Skinner[13] and others that was highly influential a generation or two ago, and for different reasons also in Marxist thought, that our human make-up is so fluid as to be capable of being shaped into whatever we wish by means of education, social influence and especially by rewards and punishments. Some Marxist thinkers went so far as to reject the concept of a human nature altogether as false.[14] They contended that the concept of a human "nature" means something so biologically fixed in us as to be unalterable, citing as a prime example our allegedly innate selfishness, which if indeed were the case would make genuinely co-operative and considerate behavior impossible. Singer's own view, shared by the present author, is that human nature is both fixed in certain respects, for example genetically, but also flexible, as is so clearly attested by our manifest and often spectacular creativity, adding that human nature "cannot be made to flow uphill, but its direction can be altered."[15]

To be inter-related with others as we are, means being affected while we grow up from earliest infancy by whatever culture we are born into.

---

10. Laszlow, *Systems View*, 25.

11. Laszlow, *Systems View*, 75; see also Cupitt, *Nature of Man*, De Beer, "Being Human," also Lilley and Pedersen, *Human Origins*, 113–30.

12. Singer, *Expanding Circle*, 3.

13. Skinner, *Beyond Freedom*.

14. Geras, *Marx and Human Nature*, 11, 107.

15. Singer, *Expanding Circle*, 156.

Culture is the totality of human creations that are passed on by means of education. It centrally involves language but also much else: customs, mores, beliefs, laws, art and so forth. It is here that the exceptional intelligence of our species in comparison with all other primates is most evident, for it is the endowment that permits not just the discovery of knowledge but also the means of preserving and transferring it to others, and their ability to receive and understand it. Of very great importance for establishing the truth about religion is the fact that cultural variation is the rule, notwithstanding some cross-cultural continuities, a matter that is addressed in parts II and III.

The term "drive," means that the ability to desire well-being is behaviorally constituted so as to direct the flow of human energy *powerfully* towards its satisfaction. The hypothesis thus means that our inner sensory equipment for experiencing well-being and its opposite, which we may call discomfort, acts like a trigger for the discharge of directed energy in the form of mental and muscular activity. If we feel cold, we take steps to obtain warmth; if warm, we deploy our energy into a maintenance mode, and so forth. The term drive also means that the phenomenon it names is a persistent and powerful part of our make-up as human beings, not something incidental or insignificant, and that it is both innate and beyond our ability to neutralize through any act of will, though this does not mean that the drive in question cannot be directed to various ends on the basis of human choice.

The remaining term is "maximize." It is present in my account in order to reflect an important, empirical reality. As already noted, human history can be seen as a record of restlessness, of persistent efforts to change sociocultural, environmental and personal reality. It is not a record of contentment or stasis, except in relatively short-term periods when cultures and individuals achieve a degree of stable satisfaction. To account for this fact, my account proposes that people are not merely equipped for a drive to satisfy their desire for well-being in its many forms, but for ever-greater satisfactions of that desire, imaginatively probing the entire texture of their existence for anything that generates a sense of dissatisfaction or discomfort in order to obviate it by the realization of yet more well-being. The single word that best captures this is "maximize."

The account being set forth here about what it means to be human holds that the inter-related, contextually located drive to imagine and maximize well-being operates as a directed flow of creative energy in all societies, producing human behaviors and cultures in all their aspects, from saintliness to crime, agriculture to acupuncture, and of course the diversities of good and evil, the diversity being a consequence of varied environmental resources coupled with genuine, creative novelty. The cathedral of Notre

Dame, the massive motor assembly plant at Wolfsburg in Germany, Soweto, the Kremlin past and present and all other human creations thus have, I argue, a common source in humanity's species-wide drive to conceive of and maximize well-being in whatever geographical, social, cultural and historical situation it finds itself.

Such is my account, needing, like all such proposals, critical testing and if need be modification and even abandonment, if found to be empirically or logically too flawed to be capable of illuminating the nature of *Homo sapiens* in relation to our moral and spiritual experience. If correct, it must illuminate human reality on this planet successfully; it must account better than its rivals for the fact already noted that while even the most intelligent of non-human creatures, the higher primates and the dolphins, have existed in a condition of behavioral stasis throughout their species history, endlessly repeating the same profiles of behavior in the same narrow band of environments, human beings have changed theirs in that immensely long and diversified process that leads from the ape-like forest agilities of our most distant forebears to Manhattan, Mecca—and also to Auschwitz, Sharpeville, Chernobyl and the Twin Towers.

Freedom

Among the experiences we humans desire most for our well-being is freedom. The present account explains it in terms of our creativity, which is our power to bring about something new. We could not do this if we were machines, for machines endlessly repeat the same actions for which they are designed, with no room for variation other than breakdown. As Australian ethics consultant and former business leader Ted Scott points out in an unpublished paper, freedom is real but limited, defining it as the ability to exercise our choice over how we live within the constraints of nature and society.[16] Of great relevance for this book is what Scott regards as our most important exercise of freedom, seeing it as "whether to relate to the universe in fear or out of love."[17] He adds that love "comes about as a result of making a fundamental paradigm shift at the core of one's being." The shift is to make love, understood as active concern for the good of others, the foundation of our lives.[18]

Among the most valuable insights into the nature of freedom was the one I heard from the German theologian Jürgen Moltmann at a lecture he

---

16. Scott, *Ethics*, 6.
17. Scott, *Ethics*, 1.
18. Scott, *Ethics*, 15.

gave in Pietermaritzburg during a visit to South Africa in the late 1970s. He defined freedom as acceptance, indicating that what really liberates people is the experience of being accepted by others. Moltmann was reminding his audience that freedom is poorly understood in the strongly individualistic way of western liberalism, where it is typically seen as an individual right. Instead, he said, it is first and foremost the social reality of a caring, accepting community. That makes genuine freedom the gift of the surrounding goodness that is the focus of this book, at work in our communities when they are kind and welcoming.

The account of human nature offered in this book includes sentience. Feelings and emotions are a powerful part of how our brains work, alerting us through feelings of discomfort and pain to whatever threatens our wellbeing, and through feelings of contentment and happiness to situations we need to preserve. In these ways they affect what we think we know and what we come to believe. They can and do cloud our judgment; they can make us cling to comfortable illusions and flinch from facing disturbing truths. This part of our human nature can thus seriously undermine the achievement of genuine knowledge and sound beliefs. Metaphysical beliefs, so the comparative history of ideas shows, vary enormously, most of all when they purport to give us the ultimate truth about reality, whereas scientific knowledge is far more uniform. This should make the rigorous truth-seeker extremely cautious about being dogmatic concerning metaphysical contentions about ultimate reality.

Our spiritual nature

One more contention about our human nature remains to be made, following a lead given first by William James and then by Sir Alister Hardy when he was a professor of zoology at Oxford, and more recently confirmed by David Lewis-Williams and J.E. Schellenberg. Noting the evidence from all over the world and in all periods of which we have evidence, that religion of some kind has been a significant part of all known cultures, Hardy advanced the concept of the "spiritual nature" of humankind, even using those two words in the title of one of his books. He and James before him gathered a large number of personal reports of what their informants saw as religious experiences. Here is an example from James: "as I was walking in a thick grove, unspeakable glory seemed to open to the apprehension of my soul. I do not mean any external brightness, nor any imagination of a body of light, but it was a new inward apprehension or view that I had of God, such as I never had before."¹⁹ Noting that the reports he had received generally tended to say that whatever was experienced was benign, and referring to Christianity, James wrote that in "the Christian consciousness this sense of the enveloping friendliness becomes most personal and definite."²⁰

Working in Britain much more recently, Hardy gathered a large amount of such material for his study of what he called our spiritual nature, wisely referring to experiences of a power rather than specifically to a deity. He did so by appealing in 1970 to readers of the influential Sunday newspaper, *The Observer*, for records from all "who have been conscious of, and perhaps influenced by, some such power, whether they call it the power of God or not," to send their records to him. A subsequent appeal was directed to all who "feel they have been conscious of, and perhaps influence by, some Power, whether they call it God or not, which may either appear to be beyond their individual selves or partly, or even entirely, within their being" to submit an account of the experience.²¹

He concluded from his research that even today in a heavily secularized society like his, a large number of people "possess a deep awareness of a benevolent power which appears to be partly or wholly beyond, and far greater than, the individual self."²² My own spiritual experiences agree with this; more importantly, the work of geneticist Dean Hamer in the USA also supports Hardy's notion that there is a spiritual dimension to human nature. He does so without seeking to either affirm or reject the existence of God in his 2004 book *The God Gene: How Faith is Hardwired into our Genes*.

The forgoing account of what it means to be human is fairly complex, so I want to conclude with a concise statement that captures the heart of it in relation to goodness, ethics and religion, as follows. To be human is to share a biology that makes us want the greatest, inclusive, lasting well-being; and as intelligent beings we understand that nothing can matter more to us than knowing what it is that could yield *ultimate* well-being, the well-being that would be unsurpassably valuable.

WHERE WE ARE: COSMOS AND EARTH

The cosmos is taken in this book to be the totality of all that is real and not just what the empirical methods of the sciences reveal.²³ We as vulner-

19. James, *Varieties*, 213.
20. James, *Varieties*, 275.
21. Hardy, *Spiritual Nature*, 20.
22. Hardy, *Spiritual Nature*, 1.
23. Murphy and Ellis, *Moral Nature*; see also Smuts, *Holism and Evolution*, and

able, thinking, feeling, valorizing, loving, fallible, conscious beings are just as much part of it as quarks and electrons, rocks and trees, microbes and galaxies. Thus understood, the cosmos is not only blind matter/energy following impersonal laws, but just as much the cradle and home of consciousness, truth-seeking, morality and spirituality. The only alternative to such a holistic cosmology is dualism, the view that reality comprises two entirely distinct kinds of reality, matter and mind, body and spirit, but this is a discredited view because it generates the acute problem of explaining how such wholly different types of reality can interact, as they do; after all, our minds or thoughts make our bodies do things like type these words on a computer. So I contend that interaction and inter-relatedness are experienced realities that point better to a holistic account of the cosmos than dualism.

Conservative Christianity includes the biblical cosmology of the first chapters of Genesis and elsewhere. Since the time the biblical texts were composed, cosmology has undergone a revolution through the work of science, work which involves important questions of truth for any attempt at rigorous truth-finding. These questions will be faced in part II; for the moment what is needed is an account of the essentials of what we now know about the cosmos and our own planet within it, not only because that knowledge is important in its own right but also because we cannot further understand human nature without that knowledge, given our inter-relatedness with the settings in which we exist.

Whitehead and Laszlow on cosmology

The philosopher who has done most to expound systematically our new knowledge and experience of the cosmos is Whitehead, so what follows is partly based on his work. The cosmology that emerges in this way has the following set of characteristics: it is creative, forever generating new realities; it is therefore in continual processes of change, evolving over a period now of at least thirteen billion years in ways that are orderly rather than chaotic; it forms an inter-related totality of which we humans are part; and it is unimaginably vast with its billions of galaxies each containing billions of stars, planets and other heavenly bodies, all in constant motion and operating according to the laws that physics has discovered, like Newton's laws of gravitation and Kepler's laws of planetary motion. It is an account of the cosmos that is strongly endorsed by a recent scientific writer whose work we will encounter in the next chapter, the eminent South African archeologist David Lewis-Williams.

Balcomb, "Of Iron Cages," 358–79.

Arguably Whitehead's most significant contention about the cosmos is the following, cited by Lucien Price: "There is a general tendency in the universe to produce worthwhile things, and moments come when we can work with it and it can work through us. But that tendency in the universe to produce worthwhile things is by no means omnipotent. Other forces work against it."[24] The existence of forces working against what Whitehead called "worthwhile things" is precisely what makes our existence a challenge that calls for resolve, courage and effort, leading to John Hick's verbal comment that "the world is structured not for comfort but for growth." These contentions by Whitehead and Hick exactly match the experiences of the power of goodness that have directed my own life, and continue to do so.

Following the work of Erwin Laszlow, we can therefore conceptualize the cosmos as a mega-system, with no unrelated parts.[25] A necessary consequence of these features is that no state of affair is ever final. This means that existence is at heart a journey, not a domicile, in a cosmos where there is both order and freedom, stability and change, and where we have the power to make choices that make a real difference. Hence it is an environment that is structured for significant freedom and for the possibility of good, in the sense of beneficial influence on other entities and not just those that are equipped to understand goodness. This is a marvel—that there is such a creative, dynamic context for us, and not otherwise.

A knowledge of the history of science reveals that its picture of the cosmos itself evolves as new discoveries extend and even sometimes undermine earlier paradigms. At present the consensus is that the cosmos began with the so-called Big Bang and has been expanding and cooling ever since. What lies ahead after further discoveries we cannot know, any more than we can be dogmatic about cosmic beginnings. This means that we must accept a very real element of mystery about the cosmos and not behave like the cellar mice in an amusing but telling parable reportedly created by the French thinker Pierre Bayle (1647—1706). He invited people to imagine a colony of cellar mice in a huge palace, from which cellar none of them had ever left. Undaunted, they nonetheless pronounced grandly upon the nature and qualities of the palace and its architect.

Cosmos, earth and time

Planet earth shares the cosmic properties given above though on an utterly minute scale in terms of size and for much less time, having been formed

---

24. Whitehead, *Dialogues*, 296-97.
25. Laszlow, *Systems View*, 80-84.

only some 4.6 billion years ago. Life on this planet also shares those properties, though lasting now some billion years less than the planet itself. Humanity, which means all species belonging to the genus *Homo*, has been here for far less time than that, since about 2.5 million years before the present, while our own species of *Homo sapiens* is a late-comer with an existence now of a mere 200,000 years.[26] The first indications of what could be seen as religious awareness are much more recent, dating back only about 50,000 years, or somewhat more, as we have already noted.

The philosopher of religion J.E. Schellenberg has in recent work introduced the study of religion and human nature to the concept of deep time. This means developing a greatly extended view of time than is usual from our knowledge of human civilization and written history, which go back only about six thousand years. In particular, we need to think of deep time as also applying to the future. When we do that, and when we heed what science is telling us about the slowly increasing temperature of the sun and therefore the greater heat it radiates, we come to see that the earth can be expected, barring unforeseeable catastrophes, to carry life for another billion years, by when conditions will be too hot for life to continue on it. That immense stretch of future time makes it possible for our own species to evolve into far greater capabilities in future, including intelligence.[27] That deep time has very significant implications for Christianity and for religion in general, which mostly work with very much shorter time-scales, especially regarding the future, will be clear. These implications mean that we can expect religion itself to undergo great change in the world of the future.

From physics to metaphysics, mystery, and good news

Is the cosmos a brute fact? Can it be ultimate, or does it point to something more fundamental to explain it, like a Creator? Here we enter a final mystery about which the present book offers an answer in part III. For now the following can be ventured. The cosmos of scientific discovery, philosophical insight and our own critical experience can be interpreted as a cosmos of radical generosity because it is has the root ethical property of freely giving, freely generating new actualizations like life and culture. Superficial generosity is like a parent who gives a child pleasures without challenges. Radical generosity gives something deeper and far better: that which has true, rich and lasting value, and the ability to appreciate it.

---

26. McCarthy and Rubidge, *Story of Earth*, 276.
27. Schellenberg, *Evolutionary Religion*, 8–33.

What then is the home to which we belong and to which we are adapted? Guided by modern knowledge and our own thoughtful experience, we might reply that we are part of a dynamic cosmic process or evolving stream that can make consciousness, unselfish creativity, conscience and spirituality emerge and prevail, as well as their opposites; perhaps the gift of a mysteriously beneficent giver or source, of which—or whom—we can have but the most fleeting mental grasp, but whose invitation to do that which is right and good can make our spirits soar and leap into action to build a better world.

To summarize: what emerges from the foregoing is the following understanding of reality. It is ultimately mysterious but also has much that is intelligible. It is richly enabling yet also severely demanding and at times very harsh; a blend of creative opportunity and rigid constraints, offering scope but no guarantee of profound well-being. It is structured for the emergence of experience, knowledge, morality and spirituality. Overall, it is reasonable to see these features of our shared experience as evidence of a deep but ultimately mysterious generosity, its very mystery being why it is so deeply generous: it leaves us free to engage, explore, experiment, probe, grow endlessly, sensing, perhaps, the presence of a sublime and surpassing mentality or rationality, like the logos of ancient Greek philosophy and the Fourth Gospel, more wonderful than we have hitherto been taught by the churches. It also enables us to recover the saving truth and practice of Christianity that Jesus pioneered, now buried under centuries of well-meaning but inward-looking piety.

There is, thus, a flow of energy in the cosmos that is creative, liberating, radically generous and mysterious, an energy we can all tap into and share—a true "wind of heaven" as the Japanese say—that invites our freely given allegiance and action. It is the source of our deepest fulfilment and joy. To experience it is to be energised, inspired, set going and to have soul. This is what it means to be spiritual and ethical at the same time. It is a call to create and cherish holistic, inclusive well-being. Such is the gift of the cosmos as defined in this book, and of whatever divine being or beings might indeed be its empowering and foundational reality.

HOW WE THINK, KNOW, AND BELIEVE

Knowledge can be defined as publicly confirmed, true belief, while believing means accepting something as the truth, which it might not be, like slave owners who thought they enjoyed some sort of inalienable right to own other people, or Robert Mugabe's belief that he had the permanent support of most Zimbabweans. Knowledge is essential if we and our planet are to survive and thrive because we need reliable information about what helps and what threatens our existence. A persistent cough may not be serious but it could signal the presence of a malignant tumour in the lung or throat. If it is misdiagnosed as a mere infection, in other words, if the truth isn't found, that could be a death sentence, as happened tragically to a long-standing friend of mine. Conservative Christianity teaches that humanity has the worst of fatal diseases and therefore, rightly, urges people to accept the freely available remedy. The question that today's knowledge about how we think, know and believe forces all rigorous truth-seekers to face is whether Conservative Christianity has correctly diagnosed our predicament and whether the cure it speaks of with such admirable conviction is in fact the right one. This vital question is addressed in part II and an answer given. In preparation for that, the following paragraphs present the essentials of reliable truth-finding about any issue, religion included.

The most important point to understand is that our minds work *sub specie humanitatis,* meaning under the influence of our finite, fallible, culturally conditioned human nature, which therefore significantly affects how we think, know and believe. We just are imperfect, fallible beings and our fallibility sets limits to what we can know. For us there is no God's eye view of things. Some might say that divine revelation gives us certainty about central religious beliefs. Logically there is no problem about the concept of a perfect divine mind possessing complete and infallible knowledge, but there is no way that such perfection can be transmitted intact into our human minds without over-riding our minds and giving them god-like abilities. It is difficult to see that a perfectly good and wise Creator would do that and if it did happen, the recipient would no longer be human but mentally divine. None of the theistic faiths I have studied and encountered teaches that, and as far I can see, Conservative Christianity does not even teach that about Jesus as the incarnate Son of God. If he thirsted, as he did because of the limitations of bodily existence, then his brain was also subject to the limitations of bodily existence.

Happily, our level of intelligence is such that we know we err and sometimes lie; it is also such as to enable us to work out methods of minimizing and, at times, even overcoming our proneness to delusion, confusion, plain error and moral lapse. So we humans have come to prize both criticality of mind and the value of competent corroboration of whatever we suggest might be the truth.

As previously mentioned, the great German philosopher Immanuel Kant (1724–1803) stated the principle of critical thinking memorably in the preface to the first edition of his celebrated *Critique of Pure Reason*: "Our age is pre-eminently an age of criticism, and to criticism everything must bend." Shrewdly, he singled out religion and government as especially in need of critical appraisal. Both give their leaders power over others, and power, as Lord Acton's famous dictum reminds us, has a tendency to corrupt, often by seeking to influence other people's ideas in ways that serve the leaders' own interests. Political leaders sometimes do this cynically, religious leaders generally do so devoutly, but both prefer their followers to believe what they hear. That is not a good way to minimize the rise and spread of mistaken beliefs.

As social beings our thoughts, knowledge and beliefs are greatly shaped by what we learn from others, and through them by our cultures and also by the historical period in which we live. That makes it vital for us to seek reliable confirmation of what we believe, in order for it to rank as knowledge. Psalm 23 praises the Lord as a protective shepherd, which is a powerful metaphor in a culture that kept sheep, but unlikely on the lips of an Inuit psalmist living in the frozen north of Alaska, or a San hunter-gatherer in the Kalahari Desert.

Before he became a bishop in the Church of England, John Austin Baker was, as I mentioned above, one of my tutors at Oxford. He was then writing the book that contains the beautiful celebration of goodness that was quoted at the start of chapter 1. He did not read that passage to us during our tutorials but he did teach me another lesson that has richly influenced my spiritual and theological path. He taught me just how deeply the projections of our own minds affect what we come to believe and even what we are able to understand. We think of things under the shaping influence of what we already know, so that we can identify regular, three-sided shapes that meet at three points as triangles only if we've already learnt some geometry. We love because we were first loved. We speak because we were first spoken to, and we embrace the good because we first experienced its blessing in our own lives.

The philosopher Baruch Spinoza (1632–1677) is reported to have provided a witty illustration of our tendency to project what we know of ourselves on to external reality, though I have been unable to verify the source. Here, anyway, is his supposed comment: "I believe that a triangle, if only it had the power of speech, would say that God is eminently triangular, and a circle would say that the Divine Nature is eminently circular, and in this way each thing would ascribe its own attributes to God." By way of confirmation, J.Z. Young has written that our brain programmes "are so highly organized around concepts of persons that gods (whether many or one) are nearly always personified."[28]

John Baker also urged us to read a book that contains a vivid example from Ancient Egypt of the way our minds use what we know to make some sense of the unfamiliar. It is Henri Frankfort's *Before Philosophy: The Intellectual Adventure of Ancient Man*. The ancient Egyptians, with their rainless climate, spoke of rain as "Nile-in-the sky," the familiar being the model for describing the unfamiliar. They also used the same words, wrote Frankfort, for northwards and downstream, and for southwards and upstream, the Nile again being their model. So when they encountered the Euphrates which flows southwards for part of its course, they used from their Egyptian experience the delightfully illustrative but also delightfully inept term for it as "the river that goes downstream upstream, or northwards southwards."[29]

On page *v* of his 1957 book *Faith and Knowledge* John Hick makes the same epistemological point in a different way, reporting that he got from the eminent Kant scholar Norman Kemp Smith the insight that "the mind plays an active part in its own apprehension of reality." The same point was made by the philosopher Ludwig Wittgenstein in his discussion of the epistemological phenomenon of "seeing-as," which makes us see something new in the form of something already familiar to us.[30]

A devout, doctrinally traditional Christian friend of mine might therefore see my astonishing escape from being hit by a car as an act of God. Exactly the same event would not be seen that way by a Shinto friend if it had happened in the middle of Tokyo, because the Shinto faith does not have the concept of God of the Abrahamic traditions. Which of the two friends, who are equally intelligent and upright in their behavior, is correct? Hick elsewhere contends that the test is whether their respective beliefs are confirmed in practice. Do they engender lasting happiness? Do they truly benefit humankind, he asks, giving us a crucial insight that the test of a faith is its overall ethical quality, as I will show in part II.[31]

It is important to note that neither my Christian nor my Shinto friend is compelled to see my escape as they do, even though their interpretations probably came automatically to their minds from their prior conditioning, but other interpretations could come to mind like "very good luck," as a third friend put it. This shows that there is a measure of freedom in our believing, whereas very little freedom is present in direct sense experience like

---

28. Young, *Introduction*, 254.
29. Frankfort, *Intellectual Adventure*, 45-46.
30. Wittgenstein, *Culture and Value*, 194e.
31. Hick, *Philosophy of Religion*, 63.

feeling the heat of an open fire. A God of perfect goodness who desires that we live ethical lives will, logically, allow such freedom of believing, because moral responsibility depends on freedom. Hick therefore quotes Samuel Taylor Coleridge approvingly as saying that God "could not be intellectually more evident without becoming morally less effective."[32]

In conversation during his time in Pietermaritzburg, Hick mentioned that St Thomas Aquinas made the same point very effectively with the following short statement: "The thing known is present in the mind in the mode of the knower." So my Christian friend, who is the knower in this example, on coming to hear about my amazing escape from being hit by a car—which is the thing known—and who already has the Christian concept of a miracle-working God in his mind, sees it as a divine intervention—"in the mode of the knower," in St Thomas's terms.

Beyond doubt then, one of the ways our minds work is by unconsciously projecting what we are already familiar with on to the unknown and mysterious. Since the supposedly supernatural and transcendent beings of much religious belief will, by definition, be mysterious, none more so than a Deity who is believed to be the ultimate reality and even wholly other than everything else, projection will inevitably operate in the formation of religious beliefs. No thinker recognized this more clearly and forcefully than the nineteenth century German philosopher Ludwig Feuerbach (1804—72), in his landmark book of 1841, translated into English later as *The Essence of Christianity*. He contended that God is our projection of our nature. Accordingly for him, theology must be transformed into anthropology, or at least connected with it.

As Lloyd Geering and Alistair Kee have shown, Feuerbach's influence on subsequent religious thought has been immense,[33] but the clear evidence of projection in theism, such as calling God our "Heavenly Father," does not necessarily mean that such projections of our human nature and experience cannot refer to anything real, as Gottlob Frege's important work, which is discussed next, enables us to see.

As explained by one of my philosophy teachers, Frege (1848—1925) enabled us to distinguish between the meaning or sense of a word and its reference.in a paper with the title "On Sense and Meaning."[34] Consider the example of the word "angel." As used by religious people it *means* a winged, supernatural being. Most of these people believe that the word *refers* to actual beings of this kind who are thought to exist in heaven and who carry

---

32. Hick, *Philosophy of Religion*, 141.
33. Geering, *Faith's New Age*, 132-48; Kee, *Way of Transcendence*, 148-60.
34. Frege, *Collected Papers*, 156-77.

messages from God to the world. Others might say that there are no such beings; instead it refers metaphorically to the insights and inspirations they believe God directly gives to those he wishes to guide. Secularists would say the word "angel" refers literally to nothing at all and should simply be dropped. Another example is the word "unicorn," which means a horse-like animal with a single horn on its forehead. Most of us today would say it refers to nothing other than a purely imaginary animal, or perhaps to a very garbled idea of a rhinoceros.

Frege's distinction, as explained by my philosophy teacher, is especially helpful in connection with the word "God." In the sense used by Christian believers it means a personal, supreme being with the qualities of a perfectly loving father and noble king, and it refers to the Holy Trinity of Father, Son and Holy Spirit. Muslims and Jews use it with the same sense but deny that it refers to any such being as the alleged Trinity, for, according to them, God is a strictly unitary being. I will be using Frege's insight in my account of the concept of God in part III.

The underlying research for this section was guided mostly by philosophers and philosophers of religion. For this last part of the section, I include something from the work of the eminent Swiss educational psychologist, Jean Piaget (1896—1980).[35] He discerned four stages of mental development in children, which have implications for how we believe in religion. Here, in summary form, is what he offered. The first stage, sensory motor thinking, comes in earliest childhood, up to about eighteen months and is governed by the child's sensory experience. From then to the seventh year Piaget discerned what he called pre-operational thinking. The third stage, from seven to twelve years of age, is the one that is of greatest interest for religious thinking. Piaget called it the stage of concrete operations, where thinking is dominated by concrete reality like the objects of perception and the vividly imagined characters in stories.

For many Christian believers who were raised in a religious home, these are the years when vivid Bible stories like those about David and Goliath are told, and trust in Jesus is inculcated, drawing on the young child's implicit trust in parents and older siblings. This kind of thinking and believing may dominate the mind for the rest of the child's life. From around adolescence comes the fourth or formal operational stage of mental development, bringing the ability to think with abstract concepts. In mathematics education, this is when arithmetic gives way to the abstractions of algebra and geometry, and when religious stories can connect with abstract religious doctrine. However, it will be clear that the mental image of a God

---

35. Piaget, *Origin*.

in the form of a king on a throne, or a protective shepherd, is easier to grasp than the concept of a sovereign, transcendent, prevenient being. Piaget's findings and, somewhat controversially, those of the American psychologist Lawrence Kohlberg, which will be discussed in the next section of this chapter, have important implications for the development of moral judgment and also for religious consciousness, as we will see in chapter 6.

ETHICS

Honest to Goodness explores what it means to be a Christian when governed by ethical values. The most important of the academic factors in my long journey to the answer I give in parts II and III is therefore what I have discovered about ethics itself, along with my research about religion. The present section brings together the most important and relevant parts of those ethics discoveries.

Understanding the concept of values

It is essential to distinguish between a general and a specific concept of values. In general a value is anything that is important to us and upon which we base our actions. A lifestyle is therefore "the sum total of values acted upon."[36] An example would be the way a despot values control over others, usually to their detriment, or the way a Nelson Mandela valued justice. This means that our values can be both harmful and helpful to others, and perhaps somewhere in between, the way capitalist values benefit some but not always the workers or environments when they are exploited in a relentless pursuit of profit. That in turn means that we need guidance about how to distinguish reliably between beneficial and harmful values. Ethics provides that guidance, giving rise to the specific sense of the concept.

In the specific sense, values are *ethical* values. These are the values that help others and ourselves to greater well-being, and counter harmfulness. Having such values and living by them is the way to counter the tendency to value things that damage others and even ourselves, like over-eating or dominating people. To base life and faith on ethical values therefore means two basic strategies: firstly it means identifying, prioritizing and practicing genuinely *beneficial* values, those that are lastingly good for others and ourselves, and secondly identifying and countering unethical ones—the ones that cause harm and even evil when very serious—in society, religion and

---

36. Freudenberger, *Gift of Land*, 31.

personal life. Hans Joas therefore defines a value in the ethical sense as what is *worth* desiring or a preference that is *worth* desiring.[37] An ethical value is not merely a preference or a desire, as the word "worth" shows; there must be something *about it* that renders it worth accepting. In this book that is seen as the goodness we humans desire in order to experience well-being. Joas therefore correctly adds the important clarification that "there is attached to the concept of 'value' an ineradicable reference to the valuing subject."[38]

Some values stem from our biological make-up, like prizing food, safety and sexual expression. Others are the products of our cultures and thus of human creativity, a culture being what we create and pass on through education. This in turn means that we can change some of our values, including how we choose to handle those that are biologically based, like controlling the high value we necessarily place on nourishment and safety, which, if uncontrolled, can cause problems like over-eating or oppressing others when we believe they might threaten us and our interests.

Religions, in so far as we human beings produce them, are cultural products, and values shape cultures, along with the constraints of our biological natures. "Cultures are, in the final analysis, value-guided systems" and "values are goals which behavior strives to realize."[39]

What, then, are the core values of our existence as environmentally embedded beings? The work of Dean Freudenberger a generation ago remains highly pertinent to this question. He provides a most helpful guide about changing problematic values. We can identify and change values we regard as most important if they involve too much self-interest. We can check our level of moral judgment, asking whether it is sufficiently inclusive; we can become more aware of options and their consequences for ourselves and others; and we can ask if our religious values are sufficiently universal.[40] In relation to Christianity in our time, Freudenberger asserts that it "is first and foremost a call to repentance, to radical change in our thinking about what we value, in our lifestyle, in our whole way of being towards God in Christ, towards our fellow human beings and to all beings (animate and inanimate) of creation."[41] With these clarifications about the word "values" in mind we can now focus attention on ethics itself.

---

37. Joas, *Genesis of Values*, 17, emphasis added.
38. Joas, *Genesis of Values*, 21.
39. Laszlow, *Systems View*, 101, 105.
40. Freudenberger, *Gift of Land*, 38.
41. Freudenberger, *Gift of Land*, 49.

Ethics defined

My research about ethics has led me to understand it at its richest as *choosing* to live caringly, generously and truthfully, and by the specific moral values these core values entail, which are set out below. Ethical living also means wanting not to live selfishly, heartlessly and dishonestly, but rather seeking to turn selfishness into healthy and necessary self-concern. Such a view of ethics does not deny the importance of what might be called habitual ethics, which is the daily practice of helpful values that were implanted in us from earliest childhood and that have become an intuitive part of how we live, rather than a deliberate choice, but ethical living achieves its greatest power when a person *chooses* to live that way. This is because the act of choosing brings our conscious, creative potential into our minds and actions, giving them greater power than habitual goodness. Such, in essence, is what it means to be *homo ethicus*, the ethical being.

The next matter is the specific moral values entailed by the core values mentioned above, and the vices that are opposed to them. I present these below in tabular form from page 131 of my book *Conscience: Ethical Intelligence for Global Well-Being*, adapted to include the vices. Prior to my own work on this issue for that book, Hans Küng and Rushworth Kidder had produced their own conclusions. Küng confined himself to values shared by the most widely followed religious traditions, which I consider too narrow to serve as a foundation for ethics world-wide.[42]

Kidder's work struck me as methodologically more reliable because he used surveys of respondents' views from a range of cultures.[43] My method was to work by logical deductions from a bio-cultural view of human nature, based on the drive to maximize well-being, and deduce from that the virtues that are required for its fulfilment. For convenience these are grouped in the following tables into two clusters, and their opposite vices: those involving beneficence, meaning that which brings benefit, and an integrity cluster for the virtues based on and flowing from truth, integrity being the moral quality of consistent, principled truthfulness.

---

42. Küng, *Global Ethic*.
43. Kidder, *Shared Values*, and *How Good People*.

Beneficence virtues	Corresponding vices
Generosity	Selfishness
Respect	Contempt
Fairness, justice	Bias, hurtful discrimination
Inclusivity	Exclusion, neglect
Beneficial effort	Harmful effort, laziness
Beneficial freedom	Harmful freedom, captivity
Created beauty	Avoidable ugliness

Integrity virtues	Corresponding vices
Truthfulness	Dishonesty
Reliability	Shirking,
Trustworthiness	Dissembling
Self-knowledge	Self-deception
Open-mindedness	Bigotry, dogmatism
Judicious criticality	Gullibility, nasty criticism
Wisdom	Folly, rashness

Ethics and our setting in the evolving cosmos

There are implications for ethics in the holistic view of the evolving cosmos, and these must now be noted. The cosmos makes possible the emergence of brains that are capable of developing a moral sense of good and evil, right and wrong; of understanding what they mean, and of creating the words that express that knowledge, like "goodness." The cosmos also has the power to act beneficially, and it also makes harm and destruction possible. As our abiding environment the cosmos is where, in our form of existence, there is both beauty and ugliness, love and hatred, understanding and confusion, truth and falsehood, life and death, and where the difference between those opposing realities matters enormously to us; and because it is an interrelated cosmos, Ted Scott can say that "Everything I give to another I give to myself,"[44] and Murphy and Ellis can call their important 1996 book *The Moral Nature of the Universe*.

---

44. Scott and Harker, *Humanity at Work*, 55.

Character and context

From the reality that *homo ethicus* is an inter-related part of the cosmos comes the crucial insight that ethical living is a matter of both individual moral character and morally supportive contexts. Few of us are so morally advanced that we will always resist temptation to do wrong, so we need the support of an ethical culture in our families, communities, workplaces, organizations, nations and indeed the wider, globalizing world. Our religions play a significant part in helping humanity to create these morally supportive contexts, perhaps the most significant part, as long as they accept that religion does not own or control moral goodness, as explained next, and that what they create may be morally deficient.

While every layer or level of context is ethically important, there is supreme importance in the widest, most encompassing and most powerful context of all, for that, whatever it may prove to be, is what concerns us ultimately, in Paul Tillich's important words.[45] Religion and some secular philosophies all seek to tell us what the ultimate reality is, their declarations ranging from the Kingdom of God and the domain of Allah's will to a Marxist brute-fact material universe, and others. Within their communities these answers enjoy acceptance but the disturbing reality is that there are so many incompatible answers to the same, crucial question. Claims to be able to say with complete certainty what is ultimate take us into the realm of metaphysics, and we have already seen that this is an area of mind and spirit where, remembering Bayle's parable of the cellar mice, we need to tread very carefully and accept a policy of humility, not dogmatism. Could it be that our ability to settle this question is less adequate than we believe? Part III offers my perspective on this question.

Homo sapiens as homo ethicus before being homo religiosus

Perhaps the most important single point about ethics in a book about religion is that ethical living, not religious faith as we know it, has been and is the foundation of survival and well-being. As I have already emphasized in the section on human nature, we humans are a social species, not a random collection of sovereign individuals. We survive and thrive by developing cooperative ways of existing that compensate for our individual vulnerabilities. Ethical living is our term for living that way, and not allowing individual self-concern and especially selfishness to dominate. It follows logically that *homo ethicus* is as old as *Homo sapiens*; the two are in fact

---

45. Tillich, *Dynamics of Faith*, 96.

one in the sense that our species has moral capacity and cannot survive or lastingly thrive without it, not that we always do what is right and good. By contrast, the earliest signs of what can be interpreted as a religious sense—of some or other transcendent being or power—are much more recent, going back about 50,000 years or somewhat more, as we have already noted. So important is this fact that I will use it in the next chapter and part III to show that religion owes its very existence to our moral nature as a species. *Homo religious* is the offspring of *homo ethicus*, not the other way around.

My account of ethics

A strong interest in the concept of values was present in the research on the nature of religion that yielded my 1984 book, *Religion and Ultimate Well-Being: An Explanatory Theory*. It continued thereafter, growing into a focus on ethics that has characterized the rest of my work. A useful introduction to my 2014 account of ethics was included in the article in the *Journal for the Study of Religion*, to which I have already alluded, so I reproduce part of it here, again suitably edited and revised for the present context. I began by writing that my understanding of ethics differs in some important ways from that of both philosophical ethicists and religious ethicists, so it must now be explained. This can be done by means of five statements:

> "Firstly, in common with others I see the good as the central concept in ethics, while not neglecting its opposite terms like bad, wrong and evil. Accepting the usual understanding of this word, as our most general term of approval, I further understand it to refer to whatever is beneficial to its recipients, in all the countless ways that can happen, like acts of generosity, the beauty of a spring morning, birdsong, friendship, telling the truth and acts of courage. Evil accordingly means that which involves harm in all the dreadful ways that can happen, especially when such harm is intended and very serious.
>
> "Secondly, my approach is grounded in direct, repeated, personal experiences of the good as a beneficial force operative in the world, indeed in the whole cosmos, at least in so far as it affects us. It is therefore not grounded in philosophical theories or religious teachings. The goodness I have in mind can thus be experienced by anyone, anywhere and at any time. It does not require a philosophical training or membership of a religion to be felt.
>
> "Thirdly, ethics is a bio-cultural reality. We now know enough about human brain science to know that the capacity

for moral choice involves structures of the brain analogous to but also distinct from our neurological equipment for language.[46] The brain stem, nicknamed the 'reptilian brain' because it first evolved in the reptiles that dominated animal life until the extinction of the dinosaurs about 65 million years ago, is a very powerful structure that drives our survival needs for safety, food, water and reproduction. Uncontrolled, it generates selfish behaviors like greed and other kinds of immediate self-gratification.

"Mid-brain structures in the mammal brain involving the limbic system enable us to counter its power by providing us with feelings and memory, which make co-operative behaviors possible. This is the biological seat of our sentience, our ability to feel and experience emotions. We remember who made us feel pain by hurting us, and we avoid them, just as we remember those whose help and support made us feel good, and we seek to be with them. In that way this mammalian brain structure works as a bonding structure.

"Dominating the human brain is our very large neo-cortex which gives us advanced intelligence, language and the ability to *understand* that there are things to value and others to avoid, and that we have choices about how we will live, whether selfishly or co-operatively, so taking us into the moral domain by enabling the development of the moral sense of good and evil, right and wrong. Here we become consciously valorizing beings.

"Like language, however, this biological ethical equipment must be activated from our earliest childhood by the influence and teaching of parents, siblings and others as they pass on to us their own ethical values. This brings culture, in the broadest sense of that word, into the picture; another indication that ethical living requires morally supportive contexts and not just moral individuals.

"In the fourth place, I have consciously sought both personally and academically to move beyond the narrow moral worlds of my own initial ethical formation, the worlds of Christian ethics and western moral philosophy, in quest of a vision of the good informed and inspired by as many of the world's value-systems as I could personally experience and explore. These value-systems run now from African and Australian Aboriginal to Zen and Zulu, with special attention to the first-named

---

46. Ashbrook, *Humanizing Brain*; van der Walt, "Limbic system," 23–39; Hick, *New Frontier*. See also the special edition about recent work on human brain science in *Scientific American*, Summer 2017.

because science tells us that Africa is humanity's historical home continent.

"The key lessons of this exploration of comparative ethics are twofold: on one hand there are very many issues about whose rightness or wrongness the various cultures differ, sometimes very greatly, as we see in connection with abortion and sexual orientation. The other key lesson is, I would argue, more important. It is the very widespread, cross-cultural consensus about core moral values like the importance of truth and concern for others, or the danger of selfishness, evidenced in the work of Hans Küng and Rushworth Kidder to which I have already referred.

"Fifthly, I believe that ethics as theory is only worth supporting if it serves the more important purpose of effectively enriching ethics as practice. I have great respect for the intellectual power of the great moral philosophers like Aristotle and Kant, but I remain convinced that Marx put his finger on a crucial proviso that applies also to philosophical ethics when he wrote the following in his famous eleventh thesis on Feuerbach: 'The philosophers have only *interpreted* the world in various ways; the point, however, is to *change* it,'[47] as already mentioned in this book."[48]

So I hold that for ethics to make a greater difference for the good today and in the future, personally, nationally and globally, it must be multi-disciplinary and multi-cultural. In a globalizing world the moral silos of the past and present are simply unacceptable if they are seen as all we need, rather than as ingredients in a truly inclusive morality.

Peter Singer's insights

From this account of ethics I turn now to additional ethics insights from my research. Available evidence confirms that there are both cross-culturally common ethical values but also important divergences. Peter Singer discerns this in connection with the worldwide acceptance of the principle of human equality, yielding "the principle of equal consideration of interests," though I consider the use here of the term "interests" too broad, since it would include the interests of those who harm others. I would rather qualify Singer's wording to "interests that involve no harm." What is important here

---

47. Marx, *Theses on Feuerbach*. 65.
48. Prozesky, "Homo Ethicus," 287–88.

is that ethics is a human universal. In the words of Singer, "[the] core of ethics runs deep in our species and is common to human being everywhere."[49]

Altruism, which is behavior that benefits others at some cost to oneself, and is motivated by the desire to benefit others, is not just an ideal but a reality, for it is well documented in some animals, such as wild dogs attacking a cheetah to save a pup, or birds that give warning calls, thereby drawing attention to themselves when hawks are spotted.[50] Of great importance is the way Singer extends altruism to "the point at which all whose welfare can be affected by our actions are included within the circle of altruism."[51] That means far more than just all other people and their possessions; it includes all living things and indeed the whole of nature.

Against those who hold that we are genetically predisposed to selfishness, like Richard Dawkins—at least according to Singer—he cites altruistic, voluntary blood donations and contraception to regulate and control reproduction as showing that "reasoning beings are not bound to do what makes evolutionary sense . . . reasons can master our genes."[52] As Holmes Rolston comments, "One doesn't have to have . . . Jesus's genes to be a Christian."[53]

Another valuable point made by Singer is the importance of approaching ethics rationally, so that we think logically about ethical issues, but at the same time understand the limited power of reason in human life. "Alone and unaided, reason cannot give rise to action. There must be some desire, some want or aversion, some pro or con feeling with which reason can combine to generate an action."[54] The argument of this book is that the experience of goodness in its many forms provides the necessary feeling, which, combined with adequate knowledge and clear, logical reasoning, can give rise to highly effective ethical action. Here too we can see the way the human brain is involved in ethical living, in this instance the mid-brain structures that enable us to have feelings, and the reasoning powers of the neo-cortex.

Lloyd Geering and stages in the history of ethical development.

The next scholar who has enriched my understanding of ethics is Lloyd Geering. He has shown that there have been three great historical stages in the development of morality, basing his account on his earlier work about

49. Singer, *Practical Ethics*, 21; see also Singer, *Expanding Circle*, 27.
50. Singer, *Expanding Circle*, 7.
51. Singer, *Expanding Circle*, 120.
52. Singer, *Expanding Circle*, 131.
53. Rolston, *Genes*, 136.
54. Singer, *Expanding Circle*, 142.

the same stages in the history of religions, which are explained in chapter 6.[55] These stages are not to be confused with James Fowler's stages of personal spiritual growth that are also discussed in chapter 6, but like them are of the greatest importance for the way we can now understand the world's religions.

Geering calls the first of these the ethnic stage because identity was based on kinship, and with it a shared language, customs and ancestry. It was common to all the world's cultures until about 2,500 years ago, all of them being ethnic in nature, most of them separated by distance and terrain from others in a world where travel was mostly on foot. The Maori people of New Zealand before contact with Europeans are an example, as are traditional African ethnic communities. These ethnic moralities were resistant to innovation. As Geering says, "In the ethnic stage of moral development the moral person is the one who conforms to established custom."[56]

From about 2,500 years ago ethnic cultures in Asia began to experience the challenging rise of a new stage of moral development. The German philosopher Karl Jaspers reportedly saw the few centuries before and after that date as the most significant turning point in history, and coined the term "Axial Period" for it as a result.[57] From China westwards towards Greece a set of highly influential spiritual, ethical and philosophical luminaries emerged, people such as Confucius, Lao Tzu, the Buddha, the classical Hebrew prophets and the first Greek philosophers. Their teachings about transcendence as a universal reality gave rise to the second stage, which Geering therefore calls trans-ethnic morality, many of whose features are revealingly presented in the last chapters of Robert Bellah's important 2011 book about the development of religion in ancient times.[58] In time these Axial cultures, as they are often called, provided a foundation for the rise of both Christianity and Islam. Where people in ethnic moralities believed that their values derived from the ancestors, now the belief was that they had a universal, transcendent source of some kind, and were not exclusive to particular cultures and their beliefs, as can be seen in the writing of the classical Hebrew prophets of the Axial period, where a universalism of outlook appears. It is conceivable that the Axial, post-ethnic sense of the transcendent arose from the discovered ability to generalize and universalize that marks the human ability to think in abstract terms, once childhood is behind us.

---

55. Geering, *Faith's New Age*, 29–48, 66–91. See also Barrett, "Emergence," 29–45.

56. Geering, *Creating the New Ethic*, 8.

57. Jaspers, *Origin and Goal*, 1–21. See Geering, *Faith's New Age*, 32; Bellah and Joas, *Axial Age*, 9–29.

58. Bellah, *Religion in Human Evolution*, 573–87.

Among the changes brought about by the new, vastly more inclusive moralities was the conviction that moral purity was more important than ritual purity or adherence to traditional customs. This meant that kinship was no longer relevant to morality, which enabled these second stage moralities to spread far beyond the societies in which they arose, as we see very clearly in Buddhism, Christianity and Islam, in particular. In time most of the world's ethnic cultures came under the influence of trans-ethnic moralities and were absorbed into them, but without entirely losing their earlier character. An excellent example is the way the morality of the ancient Israelites continues to be part of traditional Christian morality. A striking feature of second-stage, Axial age morality is thus the lure of inclusivity, of widening our circles of concern, so memorably expressed by Paul in Galatians 3:28 (ESV): "There is neither Jew nor Greek, there is neither slave nor free, there is no male and female, for you are all one in Christ Jesus."

Geering's third stage is much more recent, having begun to develop in the eighteenth century with the European Enlightenment. It has since then spread to most of the world, transforming and at times undermining the ethnic and trans-ethnic moralities it encountered. What happened was the rise of critical, historical and scientific ways of thinking, directing their powers of insight at traditional beliefs and values. Human experience and reason, and the new ways of obtaining knowledge, were seen as the basis of morality, not a supposed supernatural source. Since human reason and the new knowledge are equally and freely available to all people alike, this third stage enables the emergence of a global sense of values to take place. The already nearly worldwide acceptance by people in all cultures of human rights is a good example, as Peter Singer noted above, like the growing global conviction that this-worldly problems like poverty and global warming demand priority of attention in the interests of all. As a result, Geering speaks of the third stage as secular, global morality, the word "secular" here meaning that which relates to this present life.[59] It also signifies independence from religious control and not necessarily any hostility to it, though that is certainly present among some who embrace the third stage of ethics. We shall see in part III just how momentous this stage is for Christianity as a force for good in the world.

A real-life example from South Africa will help bring Geering's stages of ethical development to life. It took place soon after the end of apartheid with the passing of new, progressive legislation, based on a new constitution with a Bill of Rights guaranteeing freedom, dignity and equality for all. This encouraged a young woman to make public that, while attending an

---

59. Geering, *Christian Faith*, 9–13.

independent, multi-racial, high school in a rural part of the country, with a strong, conservative Christian ethos and an excellent academic record, she and others had suffered corporal punishment. The school responded by saying that corporal punishment had indeed been used because it was biblical and thus, in its view, God-given, but had been discontinued because of the new law against it in post-apartheid South Africa. Then a public figure from the traditional African ethnic culture of the area was reported as wondering what the problem was, since corporal punishment had always been part of their culture.

He was judging the issue from within Geering's ethnic stage of morality, where traditional custom specifies what is acceptable and what is not; the school had been following what it understood as Christian practice based on a belief in divine authority, which is part of trans-ethnic morality stemming from the Axial age, while the young woman exemplifies Geering's third ethical stage, that of secular, global morality, based on acceptance of global human rights. All three were sincere about their views but all three understood right and wrong in different ways because of significant differences in their convictions about the source of our values.

From micro-ethics to mega-ethics

In Deon Rossouw's ethics work and that of others I found my next insight into the nature of morality, also highly significant for my appraisal of Christianity as a force for good. It is his distinction between what he calls micro-, meso- and macro-ethics.[60] Micro-ethics refers to the practice of individuals; meso-ethics means ethics in and among organizations and institutions, while macro-ethics is about large-scale ethical issues like those determined by national professional associations, governments and international structures and instruments such as the Universal Declaration of Human Rights. To these three dimensions we could perhaps add a fourth that I would call the mega-ethical dimension, following Murphy and Ellis on the moral nature of the universe, involving forces affecting morality that operate in the cosmos, for example the scope it gives for creativity without sacrificing order, giving rise to the myriad pathways of the good and, alas, also of evil.[61] These four dimensions will be applied in the ethical discussions of Christianity in parts II and III.

---

60. Rossouw, *Business Ethics*, 2.
61. Murphy and Ellis, *Moral Nature*.

Personal ethical development

The next insight into ethics that requires attention is the finding of both research and personal moral experience, which show that the development of the moral sense involves successive stages. They are related to Piaget's discoveries about the way our mental skills develop, which we have already encountered, and, more controversially, to the work of Lawrence Kohlberg, which has been criticized for gender bias by Carol Gilligan and others.[62]

Ted Scott and Phil Harker provide a helpful account of the stages of moral development, as follows. The initial stage involves the first six years of life and is dominated by the child's physical senses and feelings. In ethical terms, it is a stage where, as they put it, "my self matters."[63] Rewards and punishments define right and wrong. Then, between the years six and twelve, the ability of the brain to think in concrete terms allows the developing moral sense to move from the earlier, natural egocentricity to where the moral sense is defined by what Scott and Harker call ethnocentricity, meaning the values of the groups to which the child belongs. Here, as they say, "our selves matter," and morality is conventional.[64]

From about age twelve the brain becomes capable of abstract thinking, so enabling a potential further stage of the moral sense to develop by means of abstract thinking. This makes it possible to think of realities beyond those of sense perception, moving from the objects of concrete experience, like one's own family or ethnic community, to an understanding that there are others far beyond direct experience who also matter. Morality can now become post-conventional and the recognition can form that all selves matter, and indeed even that all selves matter equally.

A yet further stage can be reached. Here the mental capacity for self-transcendence, or becoming aware of one's thinking, including its limitations, can give rise to awareness of transcendence as a reality in its own right. Scott and Harker call this a spiritual level of consciousness as it is free of the constraints of material reality, and morality can take on a universal, all-pervading quality.[65]

It is important to understand that not everybody moves from conventional to post-conventional morality and to a transcendent moral sense; some may stay at the conventional and even at the first level all their lives, depending on the culture, the education available to them and, crucially, on

---

62. Kohlberg, *Psychology*; Gilligan, *In a Different Voice*.
63. Scott and Harker, *Myth*, 44.
64. Scott and Harker, *Myth*, 45.
65. Scott and Harker, *Myth*, 44-45.

how strongly the control mechanisms on them were applied at each stage. Thus, too many enjoyable rewards and too few constraints in the early years can limit that person to a strongly self-centered, even selfish orientation, and thus to an under-developed moral sense for life; or too much social control can tie people into the values of the family, ethnic community or religious affiliation. In terms of human brain science, this means too much activation of the powers of the brain stem and the mid-brain, respectively, and too little liberation of the immense potential of the neo-cortex for abstract thinking of the highest order.

At the same time, Scott and Harker point out that the brain never loses the influences of the earlier stages of development. Even a Mahatma Gandhi, with his undoubted ability for a transcendent moral vision, remains prone to the pull of physical feelings and the impact of the conventional morality of his youthful, Axial age Hindu morality, even as he transcends their potential to control his behavior.

It will be clear that the stages of mental and moral development have very important implications for religious experiences, as will be shown in the next chapter when the findings of research into the nature of faith are presented.

Investigating evil

The word "evil" is commonly understood to mean the strongest form of moral badness or wrong; as something grimly destructive and harmful that undermines and attacks all that is good, bringing suffering, misery and even terror in its wake to those it affects, and ultimate downfall to those who embrace it for whatever reason, often this being plain selfishness. It can be thought of as a menacing force that is capable of becoming a reality in our lives and even being welcomed there, causing great harm, suffering and misery to others and poisoning its human hosts. In the Abrahamic faiths it is held, ultimately, to have a supreme host in the person of a powerful evil being called Satan or by variants of that name.

No approach to goodness and ethical living can be adequate that fails to pay very careful attention to its opposite, evil, so part of my research has been directed at seeking greater understanding of that grim and deadly reality, starting with *how* we should understand it. Philosophical works about ethics that I consulted were generally of little help, some even failing to list it in the index of subjects covered, but the *Stanford Encyclopedia of Philosophy* has an excellent survey article on the subject,[66] and a conspicuous philo-

---

66. Calder, "Evil."

sophical exception to the neglect I mentioned is Friedrich Nietzsche.[67] In some of the social sciences the very concept of evil is, I have found, completely missing in favor of terms like anti-social behavior, which strike me as being far too polite and even effete for so terrible a reality.

Theological works, by contrast, face evil head on, but understandably treat it from within a theistic perspective, which is too narrow for my purposes, for non-theistic faiths like Buddhism are just as aware as any theism that goodness is opposed and harmed by a contrary reality. Within this limitation the best theological account that I have found remains John Hick's 1977 book *Evil and the God of Love*, while Theodore Plantinga's 1982 book *Learning to Live with Evil* is a helpful contribution from a more conservative Christian perspective.

Not finding the insights I wanted from these disciplines, I therefore adopted an empirical approach as a starting point and set about identifying the sorts of phenomena people have in mind when using the word evil. Slavery would be high on most people's lists, as would the systematic lies and mass murders of Nazi Germany, all genocides, and Stalin's Gulag; so too would treating people cruelly as inferiors because of characteristics they cannot change like their skin colour, gender and basic sexual orientation. Attempts to find out for myself empirically what Satanism is all about proved totally unsuccessful, besides producing serious warnings to keep well away from it by an ex-insider who heard of my interest in this alleged phenomenon.

From instances of commonly recognized evil I could then derive the qualities that make these phenomena so profoundly wicked. Depriving people of their freedom and dignity, treating them like draught animals, good only for their labour; cruelty and even just the threat of it; murder, brutality, injustice of every kind; lies, deceptions, exploitation, hypocrisy and cowardice all come to mind as specific instances of moral wickedness. These vices correspond very closely to the set of specific evils I identified in my book *Conscience: Ethical Intelligence for Global Well-Being*[68] and presented earlier in this chapter.

Lest this discussion of evil risks being drawn into too much detail and losing sharp focus, it may be helpful now to identify the core vices that afflict our existences. I propose that they are falsehood and the lovelessness of the outrightly selfish in all their specific forms; these being the destructive opposites of honesty and love as the main facets of goodness. To them I would add the ugliness that accompanies the absence of love and honesty,

---

67. Coplestone, *History of Philosophy*, VII:II, 174-180.
68. Prozesky, *Conscience*, 109-30.

for beauty is surely a key feature of goodness. Related to these are the harmful and at times deadly mega-ethical structures of society like racism, sexism, exploitative economies, aggressive nationalisms, and more.

Another approach in this investigation was to study the lives of people we would see as responsible for gross evil. I chose Hitler and Stalin, and by finding Gitta Sereny's haunting study of the man who became commandant of Hitler's extermination camp at Treblinka, I studied a third one in the person of Commandant Franz Stangl.[69] Two vitally important lessons emerged: harmful early childhood experiences of violence and neglect can provide the emotional foundations for later wrong-doing of a very deadly kind; and, just as goodness involves both personal moral character and a supportive moral context comprising families, neighbourhoods, institutions and so forth, so too does evil have both an individual and a structural face. Slavery was not just a large collection of brutal individuals who were prepared to capture, chain and buy or sell fellow human beings like cattle; it was also an accepted *system* involving a justifying belief or philosophy, institutions like slave markets and ships, and also handsome profits and financial institutions willing, even eager, to look after and increase those profits. In the same way apartheid was not merely a population of white South Africans bent on subjugating and controlling the country's black majority; it was also, much more importantly, a carefully organized system involving a quasi-religious, ideological self-justification, plus institutions, laws and enforcement measures of a relentless kind, making it an organized system that partly mirrors those of Stalin's Soviet Union and Nazi Germany. These systems have great power over those who come to support them, shaping their minds and values by perverting proper education and treating those who refuse to believe their lies with unforgiving severity. They know how to reward their supporters and how to use fear to counter their opponents. In short, no understanding of evil will be adequate that fails to include its structural aspect.

At this point in the quest for a deeper understanding of evil, ethicist Deon Rossouw's distinction between the micro, meso and macro dimensions, already introduced, offers important further insights. Applying it to evil enables us to see the harm that *individuals* can cause one another, through lies, exploitation, sexual assault and so forth, as evils on the small scale or dimension of inter-personal harm, which in no way implies that it is not serious, for it most certainly is. When entire institutions, like a corrupt police force, are responsible for evils like turning a blind eye to the crimes of friends or favored politicians, thereby encouraging them to continue with

---

69. Sereny, *Into that Darkness*. See also Kershaw, *Hitler,* and Service, *Stalin*.

their wrongdoing, we can speak of a middle scale of moral harm, thus of meso-evil.

The scope for damage to all that is good becomes massive when an entire country comes under the control of racist or financially corrupt leaders who introduce and enforce systems that favor their views and policies. Here the scope for profound wickedness becomes truly great, qualifying such systems for designation as macro-evils. I would argue that things can get even worse in our age of globalization, for example in the planetary outreach of broadcast media with their ability to influence the minds and values of large parts of the world, encouraging, for instance, uncritical attitudes towards ethically suspect parts of big business or the teachings of powerful religions. I have been unable to find published research into the anatomy of evil on such immense scales of magnitude, and fervently hope it is not long coming. The cause of honesty and goodness suffers when the grim and arguably growing reality of massive evils is under-estimated or downplayed, or such research dismissed as mere theology or scare-mongering by impatient secularists.

Whether there are good grounds for contending that evil also has an even larger, deeper and more powerful dimension, which we could call mega-evil, is an important but unsettled matter. John Hick includes what he calls metaphysical evil in his typology of evil, defining it as the reality of our finitude and fallibility, which is built into us and all of the created order. Theodore Plantinga includes what he calls demonic evil in his account, interpreting it as the pervasive domain of evil beings under Satan, rather than seeing such evil symbolically as the undoubted evil that affects us.[70]

Human brain science has already been introduced in this book in connection with ethics. It also sheds valuable light on humanity's biological equipment for evil, which must now be mentioned. All three of the main brain structures are relevant. The brain stem, which can be seen as a survival structure for every individual, governs such basic drives as the instincts for nourishment, safety, flight from danger or fighting it, and sexual expression, as we have seen. It is easy to see that if not controlled it can lead to selfish and also violently selfish behavior, dominating, exploiting and controlling others for personal gratification.

The mid-brain structures, especially the limbic system, equip us and other mammals for strong feelings and the power of memory. Since the feelings that result from being harmed are unpleasant, the natural consequence is to avoid whatever caused them. Memory of who they are aids further avoidance and thereby contributes to survival. Conversely, the experience

---

70. Plantinga, *Learning to Live*, 25-33.

of being supported, helped or rescued from danger generates the very pleasant feelings of relief, attraction and gratitude, and the desire for more such; memory preserves the important knowledge of the people or other agents that caused them, making this part of the brain a powerful bonding structure, and thus a counter to the potential for selfishness that resides in the brain stem. Bonding, however, does not automatically produce noble human groups; it can just as easily lead to loyalty to harmful groups like criminal gangs, rampaging soldiers and destructive nationalisms. The potential here for evil is surely clear, made worse when aggressive individual behavior is encouraged as part of the group's desire for domination, as the world so horrifying recalls in Hitler's brutal SS and Gestapo thugs.

The highly developed human neo-cortex, giving us the power of advanced knowledge and understanding, among other competencies exclusive to the human species like choice and complex languages, can then readily be used to teach people, the young especially, to use these abilities in the service of human groups bent on controlling and exploiting others. Nazi Germany was expert at doing this through the considerable but evil talents of leaders like Josef Goebbels. There is thus a biology of evil which alerts us to ways in which it can be made to thrive, benefiting its agents while it lasts, but invariably doing great damage to others.

The ethics of power

My applied ethics colleagues at the University of KwaZulu-Natal and I introduced a course about the ethics of power in 2004. In my research for it I found important material about different kinds of power that is highly relevant to a critical study of religious ideas, also to our need for a better understanding of good and evil and how better to foster good and fight evil. Theists contend that there is an all-powerful God who governs everything, directly or indirectly, and religion itself exercises significant power over the minds, values and actions of adherents. The thinker whose work was of greatest value to me in this context was the philosopher Alfred North Whitehead, together with the process theology that his work inspired. Other thinkers are the influential economist John Kenneth Galbraith and Whitehead's erstwhile mathematics student and later academic collaborator at Cambridge, the mathematician and philosopher Bertrand Russell.[71] In chapter 14 I return to Galbraith, but for the book as a whole Whitehead is most relevant because of the way his philosophy centralizes creativity, deeming it a fundamental feature of all that is real. Creativity is the ability to

---

71. Galbraith, *Anatomy of Power*; Russell, *Power*.

produce change and novelty, and thus involves power, however slight. That being so, it follows that power, understood as the universally distributed ability to produce novelty and change, cannot be entirely monopolized.

From this follows an ethically vital distinction between coercive, controlling power and persuasive power, with the latter being morally superior because it respects the independent power and creativity of others, whereas coercive power involves domination and even violence. Process theology uses this distinction in developing what its Christian creators see as an ethically superior concept of God to that of traditional Christian theism. In process theology God is a God of persuasive power, not controlling power, the most powerful of all realities but not all-powerful, since omnipotence logically means possessing all the power there is, leaving no independent power for others.[72] I will return to this view in part II when the concept of God in Conservative Christianity is discussed critically. In the meantime I need to report on the most important parts of my long research, into religion itself, in the next chapter.

---

72. Cobb and Griffin, *Process Theology*, 49-52; Hartshorne, *Omnipotence.*.

Chapter 6

Researching Religion

THIS CHAPTER IS A bridge. It takes the reader from the formative factors already described to the conclusions about Christianity that are set out in parts II and III, by presenting the main insights of my studies of religion itself. I start with the word "religion," which has two meanings. The more familiar one is belief in supernatural beings, powers and realms. The other one signifies passionate attachment, as in the expression, "Jack's real religion is golf." This second meaning is classically illustrated in a statement attributed to Martin Luther, whose source I have been unable to find, that "whatever your heart clings to, that properly is your God." Both meanings are required for an adequate understanding of religion past and present, starting with the second one because it involves our human nature and also because it is the clue we need to the deepest understanding of spiritual reality and our experience of it, as will be shown in part III. To make this clear it is necessary to return now to the founder of modern thought about religion in general and Christianity in particular.

FRIEDRICH SCHLEIERMACHER ON RELIGION

My spiritual and theological debt to Schleiermacher is probably greater than I realize, so intensely did I study and critically appreciate his writings at Oxford and for my doctorate. All the same, there is one major respect in which I do not share his remarkable, pioneering insights, and that is his account of the transcendent object of religious experience, an account which I consider to be not so much mistaken as incomplete. There are two reasons for this incompleteness. Firstly, in Schleiermacher's day the available knowledge of the world's religions was extremely limited compared to ours, so that the much fuller understanding we now have, and of *homo religiosus*, was naturally unavailable to him. I contend that this prevented him and others from seeing that what all religions fundamentally share is the experience of a richly transforming and beneficial power that they severally call liberation, salvation and enlightenment. Secondly, the prevailing academic policy in Schleiermacher's day was to separate theology from ethics, regarding them as the two distinct academic fields of *Glaubenslehre* (the doctrine of the faith) and *Sittenlehre* (the doctrine of morals), respectively. I conclude that this further prevented a very necessary explicit integration of the two, and hindered recognition of the experience of a supreme goodness that arises from richly beneficial experience. For the rest, Schleiermacher's contentions remain highly instructive.

What follows presents the four most important of the insights about religion that I derived from those studies and from the work of other Schleiermacher scholars like Richard Niebuhr and Terrence Tice and from the excellent, more recent survey of his theology by Trevor Williams.[1] Three of Schleiermacher's works are the sources of what follows. They are his *On Religion: Speeches to its Cultured Despisers* (1799, second edition 1806), *Christmas Eve: Dialog on the Incarnation* (1806), and his mature work of systematic theology, *The Christian Faith* (1821–22, second edition 1830–31). For direct quotations from the *Speeches* I provide translations that I used in my 1981 article about Schleiermacher's early work, where I used the critical German edition by B. Pünjer of 1879, and from the 1928 English translation of the second edition of *The Christian Faith* by H.R. Mackintosh and J.S. Stewart.[2]

The first of these insights is Schleiermacher's vitally important distinction between what he called inner and outer aspects of religion, with the inner aspect the fundamental one. Here he clearly foreshadows the same distinction made with a different wording by Wilfred Cantwell Smith, between faith and the cumulative traditions of the religions, and perhaps more clearly by Chomsky's differentiation between the deep and surface structures of language, which I apply to religion. These are discussed later in the book.

Secondly, for Schleiermacher the inner aspect is the heart or essence of religion and is neither a matter of knowledge, even knowledge of God, or of moral action, but of experience and feeling, mediated above all by love, involving a sense of wholeness, as he put the point in the *Speeches*. In *The Christian Faith* he later reworded this view of religious experience,

1. Williams, "Schleiermacher," 757-64.
2. Prozesky, "Young Schleiermacher," 50-75.

famously, as "the feeling of absolute dependence" on the absolute reality which Christians call God, adding that this is the same as being in relation to God because of the redeeming impact of Christ.[3] Here too he emphasized the communal nature of the redeemed life, as he had in the *Speeches*. Since love is involved in creating religious feeling and since love involves relationships, life in community is essential to religion, not solitary faith. Long before the emergence of process theology with its great emphasis on feeling and relatedness, the same emphasis was made by Schleiermacher, who hailed Jesus as the supreme mediator of divine reality through love, but Schleiermacher held that there have been other mediators, including ones in other religions, and that there will also be more in the future.

The pioneering work of William James about humanity's religious tendency has already been mentioned. Unlike Schleiermacher, whose work on psychology was philosophical, James was an empirical psychologist, so his confirmation of Schleiermacher's contention about feeling as basic in religious experience is very important. He wrote as follows: "I do believe that feeling is the deeper source of religion, and that philosophical and theological formulations are secondary products."[4]

The third insight is Schleiermacher's contention, which I share, that the outer aspect of religion includes whatever words and actions the context makes available to express its core experience of religious feeling. Beliefs and doctrines, including the *concept* of God, use words and are therefore secondary, outer aspects of religion, which Schleiermacher contended will always change as knowledge grows and faith deepens. In his own words, "God as he is usually thought of, as a single being outside and behind the world, is not the be-all and end-all of religion, but merely a contingent and inadequate way of articulating it."[5] Nor are beliefs and doctrines the only outer component of religion. "Miracles, inspirations, revelations, supernatural experiences, one can be deeply religious without any of these concepts" he wrote in the 1806 revision of the *Speeches*[6]

A survey of the religions world-wide as we know them today confirms Schleiermacher's view. It reveals that a concept broadly akin to the Christian concept of God is indeed present in many of them, mostly closely in Judaism, Sikhism and Islam, but also recognizable in some others, but not in all others. In all of the faiths that do assert the existence of a deity, two characteristics stand out. Firstly, the word "God" is held to refer to a beneficent,

---

3. Schleiermacher, *Christian Faith*, 12.
4. James, *Varieties*, 431.
5. Prozesky, "Young Schleiermacher," 66.
6. Prozesky, "Young Schleiermacher," 66.

personal power that gives people their experiences of rich but unexplained blessing, like protection from danger, rescue, sustenance, healing, victory over enemies, and above all some kind of supreme benefit or blessing like eternal life and a happy outcome at a coming day of divine judgment.

The second shared characteristic of these theistic faiths is that they see their deity as a personal being with whom a relationship of dependence, trust and obedience is possible and supremely beneficial. What is not always known by such faiths, as I have already pointed out several times, is that the world has others which have no such concept, such as Buddhism, parts of Hinduism and the ancient faiths of China, namely Taoism and Confucianism, but are nonetheless ethically, spiritually and philosophically highly sophisticated. The human brain is structurally the same for everybody so it is very significant for any new thinking about God to understand that the concept of a personal deity is by far not universal in religion. It creates very serious problems of reconciling this reality with the belief that there is a God who is perfectly good and therefore equally accessible to the faith of all. Why hasn't this happened to about half of humanity?

In the fourth place there is Schleiermacher's view of religious pluralism, which he gave in the fifth and last of the speeches that comprise *On Religion*. He contended that diversity was inevitable because there are many ways of seeing the universe. In his discussion of Christianity he describes Jesus as "the sublime source of the most glorious things that have so far appeared in religion."[7] What is divine in Jesus, wrote Schleiermacher, "is his clear awareness that everything finite needs a higher mediator if it is to harmonize with Deity."[8] The following sections of the present chapter will show just how remarkably Schleiermacher's work on the nature of religion foreshadowed that of recent scholarship, including that of John Hick and Wilfred Cantwell Smith.

HUMAN NATURE AND RELIGION

Everything that was stated in the previous chapter about human nature is relevant to what it means to be a religious person who as *Homo sapiens* is also both *homo religious* and *homo ethicus*— a being who exists with others, in whom the cosmos evolves its ethical and spiritual potential. To summarize briefly what was presented in chapter 5 about human nature, the key characteristics are our sentient vulnerability to harm, anxiety and pain, which drives our creative, valorizing search for well-being and the desire

7. Prozesky, "Young Schleiermacher," 68.
8. Prozesky, "Young Schleiermacher," 68.

to maximize it as richly as possible; our inter-relatedness with others, especially our contemporaries who share the same culture, and with nature; our finite and fallible ways of thinking, knowing and believing; our moral sense and ability to do both right and wrong; and our hunger for connection with whatever affects us ultimately.

What stands out for me most about these human characteristics is that we humans cannot fail to respond to whatever we experience as offering us the greatest of benefits, and that our understanding of both ourselves and the perceived source of that supreme benefit, or blessing in religious terms, will perforce always be imperfect. That suggests that faith calls for the spiritual modes of first the pioneer and then the settler, for adventure and then security, and comfort. Both of these orientations shape our spiritual experience, of which faith is a central component.

RESEARCHING THE NATURE OF FAITH

What then has modern research by the best experts revealed about faith? Two such scholars stand out for me, John Hick and Wilfred Cantwell Smith. Hick's account of faith distinguishes two aspects: faith in something, for example a God, which involves trust, and faith that God is real, with the former logically depending on the latter. In other words, I would add, trusting God is obviously misplaced if there is no God of perfect goodness. From Hick I also found the vitally important clarification, presented in the previous chapter, that the mind plays an active part in its own apprehension of spiritual reality,[9] with Thomas Aquinas reportedly making the same point centuries before by pointing out that the thing known is in the knower in the mode of the knower. Hick's point is that our existing ideas and beliefs greatly affect how we understand our spiritual experiences, especially our first ones. This implies that to a very significant extent, spiritual experience can easily be captive to the misconceptions of earlier thinking. We never leave our humanity behind and our humanity is always fallible. That this undermines any claim to possess doctrinal finality and certainty is clear.

Wilfred Cantwell Smith's contribution to a deeper understanding of faith is the distinction between faith and belief, with the latter understood as the acceptance of certain propositions as true, for example that democracy benefits everybody or that God exists.[10] This corresponds to the understanding of faith in Hick's account as assent, as accepting that something is the case, but Smith shows that this is not what belief originally meant at

---

9. Hick, *Faith and Knowledge*, v, 3.
10. Smith, *Faith and Belief*, 9.

all, for the word derives from Latin and Germanic words meaning to set your heart on something.[11] Far from merely giving your assent to propositions like those in the Creeds of the church and its doctrines, faith is "to be faithful, to care, to trust, to cherish, to be loyal, to commit oneself."[12] Just as important for our understanding of what religious faith is all about, Smith finds the same meaning in the other religious traditions that he examines and not just in his own Christian tradition, deeming it a planetary reality.[13]

So important and powerful is Smith's definition of faith that it is worth quoting in full from the same book. He wrote that faith is "an orientation of the personality, to oneself, to one's neighbour, to the universe; a total response; a way of seeing whatever one sees and handling whatever one handles; a capacity to live at a more than mundane level; to see, to feel, to act in terms of, a transcendent dimension." Continuing on the same page, he added that faith "is a quality of human living. At its best it has taken the form of serenity and courage and loyalty and service: a quiet confidence and joy which enable one to feel at home in the universe, and to find meaning in the world and in one's own life, a meaning that is profound and ultimate, and is stable no matter what may happen to oneself at the level of immediate event. Men and women of this kind of faith face catastrophe and confusion, affluence and sorrow, unperturbed; face opportunity with conviction and drive; and face others with a cheerful charity."[14]

Smith's landmark account of faith convinced me not just because of his immense erudition but even more because my personal contacts with people of other faiths than my native Christian tradition made it perfectly clear that they possessed exactly the spiritual and ethical qualities that Smith describes, and that it also stemmed from their own orientation to a transcendent dimension. That we all had our own, different words for that dimension seemed to me, then and now, much less significant that what we shared.

The eminent linguistics expert Noam Chomsky's distinction between deep and surface structures in our languages enables us to extend and deepen our understanding of the difference between faith and belief as explained by Smith. It does so by identifying the shared, very longstanding human experience of a transcendent and seemingly ultimate source of the greatest blessings as the deep structure of religion, made possible, now using human brain science, by the way the brain functions in relation to

---

11. Smith, *Faith and Belief*, 76, 106.
12. Smith, *Faith and Belief*, 117.
13. Smith, *Faith and Belief*, 141.
14. Smith, *Faith and Belief*, 12.

the stimuli it receives of what is most valuable to us. The many cultures then interpret that experience as best they can; traditionally by the notion of a supernatural order of reality, as today's language expresses it, giving rise to the surface structures of religion, which Smith calls our cumulative traditions.[15] These traditions are understood in the culturally and historically diverse ways that have shaped the minds of the believers in the various cultures. The main ways are monarchy and milieu; the interpretation of the experience of an ultimate source of benefit as a heavenly sovereign whose rule is comprehensive and even universal, as we see in the theistic faiths, and the interpretation of that experience as a limitless, all-enfolding, beneficent context of existence, as in those that do not include the concept of a God, like Buddhism and parts of Hinduism.

Continuing with Chomsky's distinction, for religion an essential component of its surface structures is symbolism. Symbols in this sense are something, like a word, image or action, that stands for something else, the way the image of an olive branch symbolizes peace for many people. As such, symbols have been helpfully defined as "images with deep meanings in which we invest ourselves heavily."[16] Examples are the way people speak of the God they worship as their Heavenly Father or King of the Universe. We create and use such images to capture something of the nature of a beneficent divine reality which, or who, far transcends our ability to grasp perfectly.

The influential systematic theologian of an earlier generation, Paul Tillich, provided some instructive insights into the nature of faith in his book *The Dynamics of Faith*, describing it as the state of being grasped by an ultimate concern and warning that the "weakness of all faith is the ease with which it becomes idolatrous."[17] This happens when it takes its symbols literally or is directed at anything less than ultimate: for example, a faith whose concept of God implies that God is less than perfect in every respect.

STAGES OF SPIRITUAL DEVELOPMENT

Another important insight that my spiritual experiences and accompanying research about faith provided is that spirituality has stages of development. They relate to the work of Piaget and others that we have already encountered. I had noticed that among the Christians I was encountering there were some who dismissed other faiths, Africa's in particular, as evil,

---

15. Chomsky, *Cartesian Linguistics*, and *Language and Mind*.
16. Freudenberger, *Gift of Land*, 36.
17. Tillich, *Dynamics of Faith*, 96.

while others were respectful and accepting. James Fowler's work about stages of religious development in the believer, very neatly summarized by Ron Nicolson in a recent publication, help illuminate this disparity.[18] It is based on educational psychologist Jean Piaget's work about stages of mental development, which was summarized in the section of how we think, know and believe in the previous chapter. Fowler proposes that there are six such stages but that not everybody passes through them all. I summarized them in my little book of 1997, *Soulscapes*, based on an earlier press article of mine which used what I learnt about these stages from discussions with my American friend and colleague, Ruth Tiffany Barnhouse, a psychiatrist and theologian. I wrote as follows:

> "The journey begins in early childhood. That first stage is marked by imagination and the imitation of parents and others. The second stage sees the vivid stories of religion being accepted in a literal way. Some people never leave this stage. The next one is typical of adolescents but many adults have remained there. It is a conformist stage where faith is mainly experienced as obedience. The fourth stage is not reached by all. When it is reached a measure of critical awareness of one's beliefs arises.
>
> "The fifth stage only comes once there is a sense that life is more complex than it seemed at the previous stage. Instead of thinking on an either/or basis, the person thinks on a both/and basis . . . This stage, says Barnhouse, 'is open to the strange truth of others.' It is unusual before mid-life. The final stage is very rare. As an expert on these matters, James Fowler says that people who have reached this level have a truly holistic sense. They don't want there to be any outsiders or outcasts. Instead, their community is universal. He adds that 'such persons are ready for fellowship with persons at any of the other stages and from any other faith tradition.' Gandhi is mentioned as an example. Those at this stage reach out to all others in a spirit of love and acceptance."[19]

To my mind, people of both faith and conscience—and faith without conscience is not faith at all but dangerous delusion—must surely aspire to the highest levels of spirituality identified by Fowler and Barnhouse. What else does the great commandment of Jesus in Mark 12:30 mean, but that we must love and serve God with *all* our hearts, souls, minds and strength (emphasis added)?

---

18. Fowler, *Stages of Faith*; Nicolson, "O worship the Lord," 237-49.
19. Prozesky, *Soulscapes*, 14. See Barnhouse, *Identity*.

How might such growth be achieved? In my experience it is impossible if religious dogmatism prevails. My own attempts to achieve spiritual growth and be capable of fellowship with people at any stage of faith and from any faith tradition, have failed when faith is taken by such people to mean belief, in particular the notion that one's own beliefs and doctrines are the ultimate truth and everything else is at best mistaken. Believers of this dogmatic kind have at times treated me and others of a similar spiritual orientation with great venom, making any possibility of fellowship with them impossible. One such seemingly shackled soul even denounced me as the Anti-Christ! By contrast, when a devotion to goodness is paramount on both sides, I have found fellowship and friendship with people of various faiths, or none, to be a reality.

GANDHI'S EXAMPLE OF INCLUSIVE SPIRITUALITY

What is also clear to me is that somebody at Fowler's second or third stages is genuinely incapable of appreciating the faith of those at what Fowler sees as more advanced stages, seeing it rather as blindness to true faith and even as a betrayal of it. Reactions to Gandhi as a Hindu by new Christian friends in South Africa in 1893 and afterwards provide an excellent illustration of this unfortunate reality which, involving a great twentieth-century saint and moral activist, are worth reporting in some detail from his own account. He had qualified as an attorney in England and, before returning to India, had already begun his exploration of various faiths and also atheism, about which he later wrote that he had "already crossed the Sahara of atheism."[20]

Soon after arriving in Durban in 1893 the young lawyer from India, much influenced in his early formative years by Hinduism and India's Jain faith, went to Pretoria where he met an attorney named A.W. Baker, a keen evangelical Christian who invited him to his prayer group. According to Gandhi they prayed that the Lord should show "the path to the new brother who has come amongst us."[21] Then he was encouraged to read Christian books and commented later that "the arguments in proof of Jesus being the only incarnation of God and Mediator between God and man left me unmoved." A local Quaker tried to convince him that no matter whether there was some truth in other religions, salvation was impossible for him unless he accepted Christianity.[22] Even though Gandhi admired Jesus and the Sermon on the Mount, he saw no reason to give up his Hindu faith.

20. Gandhi, *Autobiography*, 102.
21. Gandhi, *Autobiography*, 181.
22. Gandhi, *Autobiogrqphy*, 183.

His new attorney friend A.W. Baker thereafter took him to a Christian convention in Wellington, not far from Cape Town, where he met the eminent Christian leader Andrew Murray, a descendent of the famous Reverend Andrew Murray of the town of Graaff-Reinet. Murray's efforts at conversion proved in vain, for although Gandhi appreciated them, he still saw no reason to change faiths, sensing in them not the usual perception of divergence but a deeper unity. Here are his own words: "I could accept Jesus as a martyr, an embodiment of sacrifice, and a divine teacher, but not as the most perfect man ever born . . . Philosophically, there was nothing extraordinary in Christian principles . . . It was impossible for me to regard Christianity as a perfect religion or the greatest of all religions . . . Neither was I then convinced of Hinduism being such."[23]

Thereafter his spiritual and moral growth deepened while still in South Africa. He began to study the Koran, as he called it, read Tolstoy's *The Kingdom of God is Within You*, became convinced that "God could only be realized through service," familiarized himself with the *Upanishads*, the great religious Hindu classic, and read appreciatively about the prophets Muhammad and Zarathustra. Evidently the greatest impact of these spiritual and ethical explorations came from Tolstoy, for Gandhi named his settlement near Pretoria Tolstoy Farm[24] and, after reading more of him, wrote the following: "I began to realize more and more the infinite possibilities of universal love."[25]

Underlying Gandhi's inclusive spirituality was probably the Jain influence of his early youth, kindly confirmed to me verbally by the eminent Gandhi scholar at Oxford, Judith M. Brown, and by email on August 22, 2018. She wrote that his inclusive vision "reflects the influence of Jain thinking on him as Jains believe Truth is many-faceted; and of course there were Jains in his home region of Gujarat, and one of the most profound influences on him was a Jain, Raychandbhai, as he made clear in his autobiography." According to this view, truth is like a polished diamond each of whose facets reveals something of the larger truth involved. This is the Jain doctrine of *syadyada* meaning "the way of perhaps" which expresses the insight that reality is too complex to be fully grasped in any single set of beliefs.[26]

23. Gandhi, *Autobiography*, 201-203.
24. Gandhi, *Autobiography*, 235.
25. Gandhi, *Autobiography*, 236.
26. Hutchinson, *Paths of Faith*, 164.

FLATLAND

Early in my research I found a remarkable way of expressing the way limitations of outlook can blind people to the reality of things outside their range of experience. It was a small book by Eric Abbot called *Flatland*, seemingly a treatise about geometry, for it was catalogued and filed in my university library in the mathematics section. In fact it is a symbolic, social satire on Victorian England, published in 1884, which can also be seen as a treatise on our limitations of spiritual vision. Abbot postulates an imaginary world of beings who exist in just one dimension, the straight line. Since that is all they experience, they can have no knowledge of beings in a two-dimensional world of flat surfaces where there is also sideways movement from straight lines. Those in this world of flat surfaces can, however, fully understand the world of the linelanders for they have lines in their existence. Next there is the three-dimensional world of up and down and well as straight and sideways, and so on into a four-dimensional world. The point is that those in the simpler dimensions of existence cannot even be aware of those at more complex levels, but not the other way around, much as a sensitive parent can fully appreciate the simpler reality of a small child, but not vice versa. We who live in a four-dimensional reality need to be aware that ours might not be the top storey of existence at all, with higher dimensions of which we cannot have knowledge unless whatever exists in them has ways of enabling us to sense their existence *in our own modes* of thinking and knowing.

WAYS OF BEING RELIGIOUS

As reported by C.D. Battson and W. Larry Ventiss, psychologists of religion have discerned certain important and very revealing differences of motivation among believers. For example, Gordon Allport distinguished between what he called intrinsic and extrinsic religion, the latter being more plentiful, saying that the extrinsically motivated type of person *uses* religion for ends like friendships, power, political influence, getting out of financial trouble and even making money, while the intrinsically motivated *lives* it, because it is found valuable in itself. Bernard Spilka and others were reported as distinguishing, similarly, between what they called committed and consensual religion, but it was Battson and Ventiss themselves whose work was most valuable for my investigation of the religious life. To Allport's two motivations they added a third one, of very great significance for me personally, calling it the "quest" category.[27] In the next paragraphs I summarize their findings from their empirical research.

Unlike the extrinsic believer who goes to church, synagogue, temple or mosque for ulterior motives, intrinsic believers go because of very meaningful religious experiences which provide them with final answers to which they adhere rigidly and totally. William James provided a vivid example of this reality in his great study of religious conversion experiences, mentioning "the loss of all worry, the sense that all is ultimately well with one, the peace, the harmony, the *willingness to* be, even though the outer conditions remain the same."[28] Quest religion, on the other hand, is more complex in how it arises and is also more open.

Concerning the effects of these motivations, the intrinsic type is, reportedly, liberating because it provides freedom from crises like the fear of death, and also enslaving because such believers are reportedly unable to re-examine and even reject what they believe, since the congregations they belong to exert real group pressure on them, and their beliefs provide them with important benefits, or, as they would say, blessings. As for quest religion, the minimal data then available indicated to Battson and Ventiss that it is "less enslaving but also less freeing, than an intrinsic orientation."[29]

Other consequences of the different orientations include mental health. The intrinsic type is "positively associated with reports of greater freedom from worry and guilt . . . But not with greater open-mindedness and flexibility." Quest religion is found to be "positively associated with greater open-mindedness and flexibility, greater personal competence and control . . . but not with greater freedom from worry and guilt."[30]

Most revealing of all Battson and Ventiss's findings for the present book are the moral consequences of these three motivations. They report that "there is no evidence that an extrinsic, means orientation to religion increases one's love and acceptance of others," while for the intrinsic type, concern for others seems to matter rather less than their own, personal spiritual concerns, rather like the priest and the Levite in the Parable of the Good Samaritan. By contrast, the quest orientation is linked with "reduced intolerance and increased sensitivity to the needs of others" and with more love for others. However, the intrinsically religious give greater help by

---

27. Battson and Ventiss, *Religious Experience*, 143-50.
28. James, *Varieties*, 248.
29. Battson and Ventiss, *Religious Experience*, 210.
30. Battson and Ventiss, *Religious Experience*, 249.

volume to others than the small quest group because of the greater numbers in their religious institutions.[31]

RESEARCH INTO BELIEF IN TRANSCENDENCE

Attention now focuses on belief in one or more benign, transcendent powers, and also of others that are seen as malevolent. Transcendence as a positive force is the uplifting, beneficial and transforming attractor that permeates reality, to which our desire for ultimate well-being responds, equally accessible to the religious and the secularist alike. Of many important guides to a better understanding of the world's religions, none has been as discerning, according to both my own research and my spiritual experience, as John A. Hutchinson in identifying its living heart. He showed in his book *Paths of Faith* that whatever a religion regards as transcendent is not only seen as the ultimate reality, but also as the ultimate *value*. As he puts it, "*religious experience is definable as experience of ultimate valuation.*"[32] So a religious revelation, understood as a founding inspiration, not only creates a new vision of reality but also new values and thus a new faith and a new ethic—in short, a new perception of what is truly good and what is, by contrast, evil, just as we saw in connection with Geering's account of trans-ethnic morality. Encountering Jack Hutchinson personally in Claremont, California in 1982 and in the pages of his book was a vital support for my own developing attempt in that year to explain the nature of religion, in which the understanding of humans as valorizing beings was and remains fundamental.

By definition nothing can matter more to us with our yearning for the greatest well-being, than whatever *ultimately* affect us, but being ultimate, it will always transcend our fallible, finite attempts to capture it in words and concepts. Significant stuttering, as the philosopher of religion and bishop Ian T. Ramsey memorably once said, is the best we can manage in the grip of an experience of something so vastly greater than ourselves.[33] Here the immense importance of Schleiermacher's understanding of feeling in religious experience as the heart of faith becomes especially clear, for it is in the uplifting joy of feeling the presence of a transcendent source of supreme blessing that we connect with it, not in words. They come later as the significant stutterings of which Ramsey spoke. Problems arise, therefore, when our mythological stutterings about the actions of supposedly supernatural powers are taken literally. Then their symbolic power and beauty is lost and

---

31. Battson and Ventiss, *Religious Experience*, 295-98.
32. Hutchinson, *Paths of Faith*, 4; his emphasis.
33. Ramsey, *Religious Language*.

with it the wondrous underlying reality of an ultimate good to which they point when better understood. Mythology taken literally is the religion of our human childhood, and it is time we moved on into better service of that ultimate goodness.

THE DIMENSIONS OR FACETS OF RELIGION

According to the American professor of religions Robert Ellwood in his visit to the University of Natal in 1986, the leading religion scholar Joachim Wach held that there are three basic dimensions in religion. These are the practical, the theoretical and the sociological. My own preference, however, is for Ninian Smart's original, six-dimensional model. He contended that all religions exhibit the following dimensions: ritual, mythological (meaning symbolic stories and *not* something false), doctrinal, ethical, social, and experiential.[34] My own encounters with various faiths confirm this contention and also confirm that the emphasis placed on the dimensions by and even within the different religions varies. Catholic Christianity attaches more importance to the ritual dimension than Calvinism, for example, recognizing seven sacraments and not the two of Calvinism and some other Christian traditions; Protestants in general emphasize the biblical narratives which, in Smart's technical terms, are the mythological side of their faith, together with doctrine, whereas mystics are more drawn to spiritual experiences.

Judaism, with its very powerful culture of belonging, accordingly emphasizes the social dimension more than evangelical Christianity with its prioritizing of the individual act of embracing Christ as personal friend and savior, while traditional ethnic faiths generally emphasize the social and ritual sides, showing little interest in doctrine, understood as formal, often abstract, formulations of beliefs otherwise expressed in mythological ways. In all the religions, however, the experiential element is pervasive and, as Schleiermacher so influentially showed, it can be considered the basic dimension which infuses the other five. It will be clear already that my contention in this book is that it is more specifically our *ethical* experience of the power of goodness that explains religion best, even though some religious beliefs and practices seem to be anything but truly good, as the next section so distressingly demonstrates.

---

34. Smart, *Religious Experience*, 15–25; see also the revised version of the model in Smart and Hecht, *Sacred Texts*, xiv-xv.

UNETHICAL RELIGION

Is there really such a thing as unethical religion? To propose a critique of Christianity on the basis of ethical values is to imply that there are verifiable grounds for believing that religion, or at least some parts of it, can sometimes be unethical. Violence by believers in the name of their faith, like that of the crusaders in the eleventh century, the medieval Inquisition and the murderous jihadists today, provides just such verifiable grounds.[35] So did the Christian supporters of apartheid and of Nazism, reportedly like the cleric Heinrich Grüber, Dean of Berlin in the Hitler period. According to the radical Jewish religious thinker Richard Rubenstein, Grüber maintained that it was "God's will that Hitler committed six million Jews to slaughter."[36]

Vincent J. Donovan was an American Roman Catholic missionary in East Africa and wrote from that experience about finding anew what Christianity can at times be. He reports the following about the start of mission work in combating the terrible slave trade by Arabs and then by Europeans. The missionaries bought slaves by the thousands and then baptized and Christianized them. But it was "a miserable failure," as very few real converts emerged. Donovan also regards the next method, schooling in exchange for conversion, as another failure, and rejects the kind of "winning individual souls for heaven" view of mission involved in these practices. The place at the coast from which the slaves were shipped is called Bagamoyo, from the Swahili *bwaga moyo*—"leave here your heart and hope."[37] At the end of Donovan's the book there is "An African Creed" with the following about Jesus, as he "who left his home and was always on safari doing good."[38] For Donovan, the rediscovered heart of faith, in a context where people from two great faith traditions, Islam and Christianity, had practiced slavery, is goodness encountered and goodness practiced.

Huge numbers of German Christians adulated Hitler even when it was clear that his agenda included the most vicious and ruthless ethnic cleansing of Jews and others deemed sub-human; a majority of white South African Christians accepted apartheid despite obvious evidence of its often exceedingly cruel injustice; large numbers of very conservative Christians are resolutely homophobic; and the world's biggest single religious organization, the Catholic Church, refuses to accept women into the priesthood. Then there is the horrifying violence of some who act in the name of Islam,

---

35. Sacks, *Not in God's Name*, 207-19.
36. Rubenstein, *After Auschwitz*, 46.
37. Donovan, *Christianity Rediscovered*, 5.
38. Donovan, *Christianity Rediscovered*, 163.

and the evidence provided by Israeli scholars like Ilan Pappe of the violence, at times deadly, that he reports as having accompanied the creation of their state.[39] According to South African archeologist David Lewis-Williams, Mayan religion in Central America provides shocking examples of a seemingly insatiable blood lust in the form of human sacrifice.[40]

Lest anyone in Christianity think that such violence is an aberration, let us remember that the Bible itself, all of which Christians call holy, alleges that violent ethnic cleaning by the ancient Israelites was commanded by God himself, as even a cursory reading of the opening chapters of the book of Joshua makes painfully clear, an ethical problem to which I return in part II. All of us who insist on the facts as an essential part of moral goodness must therefore take with utmost seriousness the studies of religious violence, like that of Mark Jürgensmeyer at the University of California.[41]

Just as important is to listen carefully but also critically to competent scholars who radically question the moral value of religion. Thus R.A. Sharpe shows not only that morality is possible without religion but "that in some ways morality is corrupted by religion."[42] Worship can harm morality, he contends; if we are told that our chief end is to glorify God, then other vital duties can be neglected;[43] religion encourages trust in God as a child-like thing, but that is alleged to perpetuate immaturity and even error,[44] which is to mistake intellectual gullibility for genuine trust. Sharpe also finds moral fault with religion in connection with sexual love and the teaching of immortality. This reference to Sharpe does not mean agreement with him. It is included because honesty requires that we carefully consider such objections and not simply ignore them.[45]

Another issue that is cause for ethical concern is that the different religions give different and at times contradictory accounts of issues as basic to them as ultimate reality; as what happens when we die and what we must do about it. The three main Abrahamic faiths teach that the ultimate reality is the Creator God they worship and seek to serve; Buddhism, Confucianism and parts of Hinduism disagree, as we have already seen; Hindus and others hold that after this life we are reborn in different bodies, perhaps many times, whereas the Abrahamic faiths hold that we live only once and could

---

39. Pappe, *Ethnic Cleansing*.
40. Lewis-Williams, *Conceiving God*, 15, 186.
41. Jürgensmeyer, *Terror in the Mind*, 27.
42. Sharpe, *Moral Case*, 2.
43. Sharpe, *Moral Case*, 22-35.
44. Sharpe, *Moral Case*, 36-48.
45. Sharpe, *Moral Case*, 64, 76.

face a truly terrible destiny after we die unless we embrace the salvation they generally say is exclusively available through them. Christians embrace Jesus as God incarnate; Muslim see that as blasphemy but accept Jesus as a true prophet, while for Judaism he is regarded as having tragically departed from his native Jewish faith. These are outright disagreements so they cannot all be correct.

Comparative studies of religion are a wonderful way to deepen tolerance and respect for spiritual diversity, but also an urgent wake-up call about how reliable any religion is about its teachings concerning these crucially important matters. The question then is which one is to be accepted. They cannot all be correct and our atheists assert that all are mistaken, so there is clearly a need for another way of understanding them. This book, however, is concerned only with Christianity, seen in the context of the many other religions of the world and of secularistic belief systems. Part II therefore explores the moral and intellectual credibility of Conservative and Liberal Christianity in the light of all relevant, critical considerations.

Refusal to face scientific research results as was done by the church against Galileo or Darwin is a further indication that religion can make itself guilty of unethical practice. Another problem about ethical limitations in the outlook and values of Conservative Christianity occurs in the 2016 book *Dethroning Mammon: Making Money Serve Grace*, by Justin Welby, currently Archbishop of Canterbury. While his book contains very useful questions to ponder about personal spiritual experience and wealth creation, Welby does not to my mind emphasize that macro-ethical issues like global poverty and environmental degradation are vital. None are listed in the index.[46] The present book therefore accepts the critical challenge posed by radical Christians against Conservative Christianity, that it involves ethical limitations of a very serious kind. These are set out in part II.

To round off this section on unethical religion, a new evil needs to be faced. At the most conservative and fundamentalist end of the Conservative Christian spectrum in South Africa and perhaps elsewhere, we are now seeing great growth in the phenomenon of self-appointed pastors with very little training or none at all, but great skill in attracting a following from trusting, anxious and often poor people, who are also, in perhaps most cases, minimally educated. This outreach is not in itself wrong, but it carries the clear potential for error and exploitation and therefore urgently needs attention by the great many honorable Christians with love in their hearts, to help educate the spiritually vulnerable against self-appointed pastors who sometimes seem more interested in wealth and power than in the Gospel.

---

46. Welby, *Dethroning Mammon*.

For life-saving medical treatment, who would entrust themselves or their loved ones to a practitioner with merely a year at medical school at best, when experienced, highly qualified and properly registered practitioners are available, or entrust their life's savings to somebody with no more than high school accountancy when experienced, highly qualified financial experts are available for advice? Nobody in their right mind would do that. So why do so many people entrust their souls to unqualified and underinformed religious practitioners who present themselves as Christian leaders? It is because parts of religion thrive on irrationality, dependence and ignorance of how to understand the Bible. Martin Luther, John Calvin and other reformers sought to free the Bible from priestly and papal control. It is time we freed it from well-meaning ignorance and a dangerously narrow view of morality. As the eminent South African theologian John de Gruchy has crisply and validly noted, "Bad religion is infinitely worse than no religion at all."[47]

THE CRITICS OF RELIGION

The difficulties compound when we turn to secularism, understood as the various convictions on ethical and evidential grounds that all religion is, at best, mistaken in believing there is some kind of spiritual reality, distinct from the physical universe. These world-views, nowadays chiefly secular humanism and lingering Marxism, contend that there is never openly available any clear evidence that one or more personal deities exist at all, besides contending that religion exhibits other grave failings.[48] As we have seen, the religious experiences of theists are quite well documented and tell us much about what goes on in the consciousness of believers, but that is not in itself an adequate reason for deducing that these experiences are caused by a God, or several gods, who exist independently of the workings of the brain. Centuries ago the English philosopher Thomas Hobbes (1588—1679) reportedly remarked that if somebody says God spoke to him in a dream, he replies that this person merely dreamt that God had spoken to him.

Arguably the most challenging philosophical critique of belief in supernatural beings was authored by the skeptical Scottish thinker David Hume (1711—1776) in his work *The Natural History of Religion*, published in 1757. I encountered it well after writing my 1984 book referred to above. Hume argued that we can explain religion quite adequately on the basis of

---

47. de Gruchy, *Being Human*, 100.

48. Flew, *God and Philosophy*; Dawkins, *God Delusion*; see Nürnberger, *Richard Dawkins*, and Grayling, *God Argument*.

ordinary human experiences like fear, much as I had myself contended, but unlike him I did not therefore conclude that there is no more to religious belief than purely natural factors, so I cannot agree with his dismissal of most religions as "sick men's dreams."[49]

Deeply challenging for theists are the moral objections raised by their secularistic critics. The most serious are based on a commitment to the highest standards of justice, which a perfect deity would obviously exemplify. The theistic faiths all have their own ideas about who God is and what he (always "he") does, which is invariably culturally limited to their own strand of history, like freeing Hebrew slaves from ancient Egypt, becoming incarnate in Jesus of Nazareth as the only savior according to Conservative Christianity, or inspiring the Qur'an in Arabic and no other language as the final testament. Yet these theists also insist on universal validity only for their own variant of theism, deeming others at best surpassed and at worst harmfully wrong. The critic then says that this is hopelessly contradictory. A morally perfect deity would not have favorites but would make the divine blessings freely and equally available to all.

A book dedicated to the truth-loving service of goodness is morally obliged to pay very careful attention to the critics of religion, even those whose knowledge of it is limited and at times superficial, like Richard Dawkins. For this reason David Lewis-Williams's well-informed book *Conceiving God: The Cognitive Origins and Evolution of Religion*, already mentioned, has been selected for special mention here. This is necessary even though there are places in it where the book strikes me as dogmatic rather than scientific, for example when he asserts that "faith obliterates curiosity,"[50] a notion which even a minimal knowledge of Schleiermacher, Tillich and other theologians would dispel, plus a few other assertions which strike me as unfair, like dismissing church views as "in-house propaganda," and spirituality as "religion's poor cousin."[51] Nobody who has encountered Desmond Tutu, Jonathan Sacks and the Dalai Lama, or studied the faith of Mahatma Gandhi could hold such an opinion. In the main, however, his is a remarkably well-documented study of a subject which is not his own academic speciality.

Lewis-Williams, like E. Fuller Torrey more recently,[52] uses human brain science to offer his explanation of the rise of belief in supernatural beings and contends that this makes belief in them spurious, but believers are

---

49. Cited in Hendel, *Hume*, 282.
50. Lewis-Williams, *Conceiving God*, 255.
51. Lewis-Williams, *Conceiving God*, 262, 275.
52. Torrey, *Evolving Brains*.

free to reply that the brain is what the Creator has given our species in order to be aware of him.[53] Much more disturbing are Lewis-Williams's ethical criticisms of theism and various aspects of Christianity, of which a selection is noted here: his critique of theism; his argument that two of the church's greatest thinkers, Augustine and Aquinas, had obsessed, twisted minds "that verged on madness"; that biblical literalists are dangerous because they hold "indefensible positions of belief": that circumcision and its God are morally pernicious; and, most significantly, his argument that elitism and exclusivism, the belief that one's religion is the only valid one, undermine the genuine respect for other cultures that the world sorely needs.[54]

These criticisms must be faced and evaluated carefully and fairly. I have done so and in part II will offer what I consider the most important moral and rational objections to Christianity, accepting what is sound from its critics and adding other problems. There is thus a set of important moral and intellectual lessons for believers to face in Lewis-Williams's book, even though I consider his contention that religion is a spent force to be seriously mistaken. He has western Europe in mind and there he may perhaps be correct, but the indications are very clear that Christianity is far from spent in the USA, sub-Saharan Africa, and eastern Europe after communism, however problematic its beliefs prove to be. These societies show us that God is back, the title of an important study of the phenomenon by John Micklethwaite and Adrian Wooldridge, who tellingly call their concluding chapter "Learning to live with religion."[55]

Critics from Hume to Flew, Dawkins, Lewis-Williams, Grayling, and others have argued that theism is manifestly wrong. There is no God, they flatly declare. But that is a spurious conclusion. What they and other critics have shown is that there are grave and probably fatal problems in some of what the theistic religions teach about their own *concepts* of God—about their cumulative traditions or surface structures, as Smith and Chomsky would respectively say. That is not the same as showing that there is nothing to which such concepts refer, at times with uncritical sincerity. Those who have attacked theism should have done better philosophical homework and heeded Frege's crucially important distinction between meaning and reference, and they should have studied theistic believers much more carefully. They would then know that the usual concept of God could indeed be an inadequate, even fatally inadequate, way of referring to something real, as we will see in part III.

53. Lewis-Williams, *Conceiving God*, 161, 256.
54. Lewis-Williams, *Conceiving God*, 134, 256–89; 181; 183; 203–205; 279, 286.
55. Micklethwaite and Wooldridge, *God is Back*, 352–73.

For Christianity and any other belief-system to be genuinely honest about goodness means facing its sternest critics and these especially include the secular, atheist critics who share their commitment to the highest ethical standards. Richard Robinson and Richard Rubenstein—who wrote from within radical, post-theistic Judaism—have been chosen for this purpose because of the detailed treatment Robinson gave to the question of values, as we have already seen, and because Rubenstein specifically directed his critique at the concept of God as the sovereign Lord of history.

Here now is the key part of Robinson's critique of religion. He asserts that "it buys its benefits at too high a price, namely at the price of abandoning the ideal of truth and shackling and perverting man's [sic] reason," adding that the "main irrationality of religion is preferring comfort to truth."[56] Are these criticism fair? My response is that they are too sweeping, for there are many believers who do not sacrifice truth for comfort, but at the same time it must in all honesty be admitted that there certainly are parts of Christianity, and other faiths, which are not as rigorous in their pursuit of truth, and therefore also of goodness, that the highest ethical and spiritual standards require. Dogmatic insistence on the literal interpretation of the Genesis creation narratives, thereby refusing to explore evolution with an open mind, is an example of the moral failure Robinson has in mind.

Turning now to Rubenstein, we find him offering the following declaration about the end of what could be called traditional Judeo-Christian theism, as he saw it: "God really died at Auschwitz. This does not mean that God is not the beginning and will not be the end. It does mean that nothing in human choice, decision, values, or meaning can any longer have vertical reference to transcendent standards. We are alone in a silent, unfeeling cosmos . . . Ultimately, Nothingness is Lord of all Creation."[57] His reason for this bleak and seemingly despondent verdict is that if the God he and countless others believed in, and so many still believe in, really is the controlling hand in history, then God is responsible for the Holocaust, and, one can add, for every other atrocity. That negates belief that such a God can also be perfectly good.

The position taken in this book is, let me repeat, that while the criticisms by Robinson, Rubenstein and others must be faced and taken to heart because they involve genuine ethical problems in faiths like Christianity and conservative forms of Judaism, that does not automatically mean the end of Christian theism, nor of other theistic faiths. What it does mean is the end of old, highly problematic beliefs about God. On the other hand, Rubenstein

---

56. Robinson, *Atheist's Values*, 115, 117.
57. Rubenstein, *After Auschwitz*, 224–25.

correctly points to the great difficulty that the theologian, as a believer, has in achieving a balanced, rational position about divine reality. So he writes that all theologies "are inherently subjective. They are statements about the way a theologian experiences his world."[58] This would apply to him too and indeed to all of us, including Robinson, who cannot possibly free our minds and values of the experiences that have shaped us. But we can strive to be more open-minded and balanced, and to resist the temptation to absolutize our own convictions as though we had a God's-eye view of reality. Accepting this limitation, Rubenstein comments that religion "is the way in which we share our predicament; it is never the way in which we overcome our condition."[59]

The mistake made by the atheists is therefore their failure to do sufficiently thorough research before pronouncing their negative verdict about belief in God. As a result they fail to understand the heart of the Christian faith as experienced by insiders, and for that matter the heart also of other theistic religions, which also treat the concept of God as if it were the reality about which it is merely a human concept. Theistic religion which makes that mistake and the atheism which feeds off it can therefore be seen as separated twins who desperately need to meet and work together to achieve the great goal of maximum well-being. In part III this book shows how that could be done.

THE EMERGING PICTURE OF RELIGION

On the basis of the investigations that led to my 1984 book *Religion and Ultimate Well-Being: An Explanatory Theory*, here is how I defined the world's religions, taken as a set of comparable movements.

> "The religions of the world are a set of provisional, culturally conditioned and regionally differentiated human constructs created by people themselves in order to maximize benefit through the salutary power of a transcendentally orientated system of existence, understood hitherto as involving a realm of spirit from which assistance in dealing with present problems may be obtained and in which ultimate well-being is thought by some believers to be possible, but not necessarily tied to this spiritual conceptuality or to any other; produced because finite physical beings cannot satisfy all their needs on their own or in spatio-temporal conditions; devised, maintained and modified

58. Rubenstein, *After Auschwitz*, 246.
59. Rubenstein, *After Auschwitz*. 263.

in on-going interaction with the forces of a mysterious, transcendent cosmos, often under the influence of exceptional luminaries, events and scriptures; and finding expression in locally conditioned, personally distinctive systems of belief, ritual behaviour and institution."[60]

As will by now be clear, today I would refine this conclusion in one essential way. I would contend that the experiences which lie at the heart of humanity's religious creativity are its experiences of a goodness that is greater than all those of which we can explain. I would therefore add that religion is the coming together of a transcendent gift of supreme goodness, not necessarily supernatural at all, and humanity's creative gratitude, tending to greater goodness of life, but not inevitably, because we remain fallible beings, freely capable of both good and evil.

Conviction about some or other power that seems to surpass us, and a desire for lasting connection with it is the defining part of all the cultural phenomena seen as religious, according to many scholars, of whom a few are cited here to support the elaborate definition of my own that I offered above. The influential anthropologist Melford Spiro is cited by Michael Banton as saying that belief in superhuman beings who can help or harm us "is the core variable which ought to be designated by any definition of religion." Accordingly, Spiro defines religion as "an institution consisting of culturally patterned interaction with culturally postulated superhuman beings."[61] Ninian Smart, writing from within the world of comparative studies of religion in his book *Beyond Ideology*, stated that the essential claim of what he called the great religions is "that there is a Beyond or an Unborn; and this is somehow accessible to the religious experience of the human race, and is not just a philosophical speculation or a theory about the world."[62] Lastly, William James had earlier written that believers everywhere have a consciousness of "an intercourse between themselves and higher powers with which they feel themselves to be related."[63] It can thus be taken that whatever else religion involves, at its core is experience of a reality of some kind that greatly transcends the mental and moral capacities of those who have these experiences, and which is experienced as greatly beneficial.

My own emphasis, that the believer's yearning for an assurance of ultimate well-being is directed at such a transcendent reality, was poetically expressed by the philosopher Ludwig Wittgenstein, who wrote in words that

60. Prozesky, *Religion and Ultimate Well-Being*, 234.
61. Banton, *Anthropological Approaches*, 94, 96.
62. Smart, *Beyond Ideology*, 178.
63. James, *Religious Experience*, 465.

call to mind Chomsky's distinction between deep and surface structures, that religion "is, as it were, the calm bottom of the sea at its deepest point, which remains calm however high the waves on the surface may be."[64]

While the understanding of religion just presented rests on much published research, it also reflects my changing experience of Christianity. In fact there was a reciprocal relationship between the academic and personal parts of my experiences, as the following section shows.

ENCOUNTERING AND STUDYING PROGRESSIVE CHRISTIANITY

In my preface I mentioned that I had encountered and studied the new, fledgling movement of Christian radicals called Progressive Christianity. I gave a brief introduction to it, while also indicating that more would be provided later in the book. This is done in the present section, starting with an unexpected, preparatory experience in Dallas, Texas, in 1987. I had gone there as a visiting professor at the invitation of my friend and colleague, the late Professor Fred Streng of Southern Methodist University. His wife Suzie met me at the vast Dallas-Fort Worth airport. On the drive to the Dallas campus she told me she was the president of a local Unitarian congregation, to which her husband also belonged, and invited me to attend a Sunday service with them at their church. I was already familiar with Unitarianism from other friends like Gene Reeves, then president of their Meadville Lombard theological seminary in Chicago, and from research, but had only known it at an intellectual and social level, so I gladly accepted this opportunity to experience something spiritually new to me.

What I experienced was an eye-opener for me. On the way to the church Fred said that some of the members of the church were atheists or agnostics, and added that he hoped I wouldn't find that a problem. I assured him and Suzie that I didn't. The service itself was a very striking blend of formality and informality, quite unlike the fixed liturgies of my earlier Anglican experience. There was uplifting music, spiritual readings that included but were not limited to the Christian Scriptures. Most striking of all was what replaced the sermon. The presenter, who was not one of the ministers, was informally but neatly dressed. He placed a chair on a slightly raised platform facing the congregation, sat down and began an interactive address. I have forgotten his theme but vividly recall the way he would offer thoughts to the congregants and invite their responses. These came plentifully and richly, some contesting what he had said, others supporting it from

64. Wittgenstein, *Culture and Value*, 53e.

their own experiences and reading. I found this totally absorbing, but it was the social gathering that followed the service that moved me most. Besides those having coffee, I saw people gathering in groups of varying sizes to share their thoughts and ideas informally, standing at placards on the walls identifying their concerns. There was a group for gay people, another for those concerned about people from Mexico, some of them illegally I later heard; others interested in children's needs, yet others for single parents and for gender justice. It was a wonderful demonstration of ethical concern and inclusive fellowship.

The academic part of that month-long time at Southern Methodist and the nearby Perkins School of Theology was very enriching, including as it did the start of friendship with a leading American theologian, Schubert Ogden, but it was that Sunday morning, ironically in a city I was told was the "buckle of the Bible Belt" and thus largely very conservative in its Christianity, that inspired me most about a church life in which I felt I could be at home. Sadly, none such was available to me back in my area of South Africa, though I was able to have some welcome links with the small but lively Unitarian community in Cape Town, then led by my friend Gordon Oliver, a former mayor of that great city.

These new experiences took place before I knew of the emergence of the Progressive Christianity movement as such, but nonetheless gave me an important foretaste of what was to come. Lloyd Geering first mentioned it to me, knowing that my own views would make me interested in investigating it. This I did in a research visit to libraries in Cambridge, Massachusetts and Oxford, which included the important meeting and experiences described in the next section. Afterwards I wrote the following press article, slightly edited, about this new movement, based on what I found on that research trip.

"A new home for questioning Christians

"What happens to Christians who question things they once believed? Is the Bible really infallible? Did Jesus rise physically from the dead? Is he literally the incarnate Son of God? Are non-Christians heading for hell? Can you be a Christian and an evolutionist? Such people either go into spiritual exile or stay in their churches with a growing sense of alienation, mostly keeping their doubts to themselves. For troubled clergy the situation is worse. Their livelihoods are at stake, so exile is all but impossible for them. That makes them troubled, divided insiders.

"These people often long for a deep sense of true belonging. Now, it seems, there is good news in the form of Progressive Christianity. It is not a new denomination but a support structure within some of the existing churches that focuses on Christ's example of loving compassion rather than on belief, about which it welcomes a questioning mind. The Bible is prized but not as the literal, infallible word of God. Other faiths and philosophies are respected.

"Having done my doctorate on the founding father of this kind of Christianity, Friedrich Schleiermacher, I was naturally intrigued when word of this development recently reached me from one of its leading lights, the radical Christian thinker Lloyd Geering.

"There appear to have been two founding initiatives. In 1994 an Episcopal priest in Washington DC, allegedly began the move towards an organized structure called Progressive Christianity for people who reject conservative and fundamentalist expressions of Christianity. This led two years later to the founding of the Center for Progressive Christianity in the USA. Then, in 2002, a similar initiative started in Canberra, Australia, calling itself the Center for Progressive Religious Thought. Groups in some other countries have followed suit. While the movement appears to rely heavily on electronic networking, it also has local groups and even, I gather, affiliated churches."[65]

Progressive Christianity.org has issued a statement of the nature of the movement in the form of eight points, as follows:

"By calling ourselves progressive Christians, we mean that we are Christians who . . .

1. Believe that following the path and teachings of Jesus can lead to an awareness of the Sacred and the Oneness and Unity of all life;

2. Affirm that the teachings of Jesus provide but one of many ways to experience the Sacredness and Oneness of life, and that we can draw from diverse sources of wisdom in our spiritual journey;

3. Seek community that is inclusive of ALL people, including but not limited to:

    · Conventional Christians and questioning skeptics,

    · Believers and agnostics,

---

65. Prozesky, *Witness*, September 9, 2010.

- Women and men,
- Those of all sexual orientations and gender identities,
- Those of all classes and abilities;

4. Know that the way we behave towards one another is the fullest expression of what we believe;
5. Find grace in the search for understanding and believe that there is more value in questioning than in absolutes;
6. Strive for peace and justice among all people;
7. Strive to protect and restore the integrity of our Earth; and
8. Commit to a path of life-long learning, compassion, and selfless love."[66]

During the research trip that led to my press article about Progressive Christianity I underwent the powerful spiritual experiences described in the next section, which gave great impetus to my belief that Christianity urgently needs to have a richer and much more powerful ethical impact on the world, guided and inspired by its founder.

CLIMACTIC SPIRITUAL AWAKENING

Inspired by my martyred namesakes, St Martin of Tours and Martin Luther King, I too have a dream, a dream to give back far more goodness than I have received, especially to Christianity, which has so greatly enriched my life. The dream came unforgettably to me in the crypt of St Martin-in-the Fields in London on September 22, 2011. I had gone to the basement restaurant there to meet a leader of the Progressive Christian movement in Britain and hear from him about the movement's work. Then I explored the adjacent crypt. Here is how I described the crypt in my travel diary at the time, the words and punctuation slightly edited.

> "I had just paused at the whipping post, with the blood of suffering from cruelty and injustice caused by floggings seemingly embedded in its wood when, a few steps further, a feeling came on me that I have never had before nor since. It was like a soft electrical current, vibrating in my whole body and rising gently up my back to be stronger, yet both peaceful and exhilarating, and at once I knew I had found the doorway to my dream to give something good back to the faith that had shaped me, to both

66. www.progressivechristianity.org

the new movement called Progressive Christianity and its older, bigger, conservative forerunner."

After that experience I attended a short, lunch-hour service in the church above where I loved the words of the young priest who officiated. She said, "Wisdom takes us to the heart of the universe." So much came together then: my compassionate, namesake saint, Saint Martin of Tours, generosity of spirit and action, and my love of the starry heavens that began when, as I mentioned early in this book, I first read about the wonders of the universe as a nine-year-old boy in South Africa's Little Karoo, with its clear, bright, night skies. A way opened to face the problems besetting traditional Christianity as fearlessly as any atheist, but not therefore to dismiss it the way they do, but to explore ways of helping it overcome those problems by remaining loyal to the movement of loving goodness begun by Jesus of Nazareth.

That, in humility and gratitude, is how I now understand the puzzling words that came to me from my past that early morning in 2006: "Save my church." But from what might it need to be saved? My answer is that anything falling short of the best the church could be ethically needs the help of all who can assist it with such problems. In part II, which follows, I set out what my spiritual, intellectual and ethical experiences and my research reveal as needing help in the Conservative and Liberal forms that were once my home.

PART II

Conservative and Liberal Christianity in the Light of Great Goodness

Chapter 7
Essentials of Conservative Christianity

A BELIEF-SYSTEM THAT CLAIMS to have a God of infinite power and perfect goodness as its revelatory author and guide must pass the most stringent test of its ethical quality, especially the tests of truth and equal concern for all. Conservative Christianity is precisely such a belief-system and its ethical and spiritual quality must therefore meet those tests.

In its deep structure, to use Chomsky's distinction, it certainly does, but not so in some central parts of its surface structures. Its deep structure or, to use a building metaphor, its foundation, is the sublime goodness it knows as God, together with the saving goodness it rightly sees in Jesus. This is a massively strong, richly ethical and deeply spiritual foundation, indeed the supreme foundation, but in the light of this sublime goodness, some of the defining beliefs it has built on those foundations cannot be correct when taken at face value, as its members invariably seem to do. Nor are some of its main practices, chiefly certain features of its worship and evangelism, as loving and fully truth-based as they can and should be.

In what follows it is absolutely essential to keep that highly positive verdict about Conservative Christianity's moral and spiritual foundation in mind while the difficult but unavoidable process of judging its surface structures unfolds, showing that in some central respects they are ethically wanting. Given those shortcomings, skeptics might ask why bother with Conservative Christianity any longer; why not simply abandon it, as they do. The reason is supremely important. The ethical problems, while very serious, are not its heart, which is commitment to the path pioneered by Jesus of Nazareth, and therefore commitment to love as the guiding value of life, and also to all that love implies. That certainly includes commitment to truth, without which we cannot love wisely or well. A further reason is the capacity for renewal and growth that is so clear in the history of Christianity, as will be shown below.

To these objective grounds for loyalty to what I shall call the Jesus movement, even by a nostalgic exile from church life like me, there are other grounds of a more personal nature: the many loving Christians who have so enriched my life; the beauty of much worship, music and architecture; the tradition of fellowship, friendship and care; the wonderful educational and career opportunities I owe to my Christian mentors and benefactors, including encouragement to write this book; and above all the way they first shaped my moral sense. This blend of objective and personal grounds for wanting to offer the best I can to Conservative Christianity is more than enough justification for refusing to follow the secularists, as somebody who was once part of it.

In this chapter I set forth what I mean by Conservative Christianity; in the next I present the norms of ethical judgment I use to assess its soundness, followed by my judgments about what these norms show to be unsound.

The account of Conservative Christianity in this chapter contains nothing that will be new to most of its members. It is included here not to inform people about matters they already know, but in order to meet the vital ethical requirements of fairness and truthfulness. The ethical evaluation that follows in the next two chapters can only be done fairly on the basis of an accurate account of Conservative Christianity, presenting the results with the empathy and the setting aside of personal beliefs and biases that is required by the phenomenological method of studying religion, which I describe further in part III. To achieve this two measures have been taken. The first is study of the material over many years from highly credible sources, including C.S. Lewis, Alister McGrath, N.T. Wright, Michael Green, Frances FitzGerald, and South Africa's Michael Cassidy; and second, a review of my results by experts on traditional, orthodox Christianity. Two of Alister McGrath's books have been especially helpful in confirming that my understanding of Conservative Christianity, which he would identify as its evangelical form, is accurate. They are *Evangelicalism and the Future of Christianity* (1994) and the fourth edition of his excellent textbook, *Christian Theology: An Introduction* (2007), now in a sixth edition.

No religion in its entirely can be understood in isolation, yet isolation is precisely the misfortune of all whose view of Conservative Christianity comes solely or largely from within, who see it as what they learnt from Sunday School, worship, catechisms, sermons, Bible study groups, conservative Bible colleges, seminaries and even from inward-looking university centers of Christian studies. Like most other things, a religion can only be understood and evaluated thoroughly and openly when seen in the light of information and insights such as those that were presented in part I, and especially in the light of the global and historical picture of the world's religions, along with the arguments of its atheist critics.

Seen this way, Conservative Christianity emerges as a significant part of a minority faith with just one third of the total population of planet Earth. Its teachings are not known and cannot be known by most of the world's people because of geographical, cultural and historical isolations over which nobody has any control. Comparative religion shows that Conservative Christianity shares a clear family resemblance with Judaism and Islam; the three are therefore often called the Abrahamic faiths because all three see the biblical patriarch Abraham as their main ancestor in faith. While these three faiths also have some important resemblances to other religions, chiefly a basic concern with what they accept as the supreme blessing of salvation and its equivalent terms, there are also marked differences, especially the absence, already noted several times in this book, in Buddhism, the Chinese religions and parts of Hinduism of the concept of a personal God. Furthermore, at least one other religion, Islam, like Conservative Christianity, also claims finality and therefore spiritual and ethical superiority over all others.

Seldom fully appreciated by a great many Christians outside scholarly circles is the fact that modern studies show just how greatly Christianity as a whole has evolved and changed in the two thousand years since its beginnings in and near Jerusalem. It was not born fully formed but started as the earliest group of Jesus's Jewish followers, endured the appalling horror of his death by crucifixion, was spurred to new life by the events of the first Easter, and began to spread into the Greek- and Latin-speaking Gentile world of the Mediterranean, with its very different cultural influences from those of Galilee and Jerusalem.[1]

Then early Christianity started creating a literature of its own over a period of sixty years and longer, in the form firstly of the letters of St Paul, then the narrative texts known as the Gospels and Acts, and lastly the other canonical Christian writings. The details of this process are admirably presented by Raymond E. Brown and in connection with the Creeds by J.N.D. Kelly,[2] and need not be identified here; the point to emphasize is that what is today seen as the Christian Bible only reached its present form in the

---

1. Meeks, "Social and Ecclesial life," 19-64; Brown, *Authority and the Sacred*, 3-26, and *Rise of Western Christendom*, 3-92; Freeman, *New History*.

2. Brown, *Churches*; Kelly, *Early Christian Creeds*.

fourth century, and did not exist at all in the very earliest church, whose Bible was the inherited Jewish Scriptures.

Also lengthy was the process of deciding who Jesus truly was, apart from his being the flesh and blood person who started this new movement.[3] Today's orthodox doctrine that he is none other than God the Son, the second person of the Trinity, who became flesh as Jesus of Nazareth, and is thus both truly human and truly divine, was only settled in 451 CE at the Council of Chalcedon, building on the statement of faith of 381 known as the Nicene Creed. Even then total agreement was absent, with the Greek-speaking churches not accepting the last three words in the credal statement that the Holy Spirit "proceeds from the Father and the Son." The Christians known as Monophysites rejected the belief that Jesus had both a divine and a human nature, and yet others denied that he was genuinely human but merely appeared to be so, the belief known as Docetism.

Nor did the evolution of Christianity end there. From the seventh century CE onwards it was displaced in its Palestinian homeland and from North Africa and the Iberian Peninsula (for some six centuries) by the spectacular spread of Islam. Other momentous developments were to follow. In 1054 the Greek-speaking eastern part of the church split from Rome; then in the 1500s the Roman Catholic Church was rent asunder by the protest movements of Martin Luther, John Calvin and others, giving rise to today's Protestant churches with their different view of authority in the church, replacing that of the Popes with that of Scripture,[4] and then came the rise of modern knowledge and secularism, leading to the current divergence of Christianity into the two forms, Conservative and Progressive, with which this book is mainly concerned, with the Liberal Christianity pioneered by Schleiermacher somewhere between them, to be discussed critically in chapters 9 and 10.

The challenges to traditional faith coming from new, secular developments, of which evolution is now probably the best known, help explain why today's Christianity is the faith of such very different, very sincere believers as fundamentalists and radicals, supporters of an all-male clergy against demands for gender quality, America's noisy television pastors and Desmond Tutu, and many others who also seem poles apart on important aspects of their faith and practice.

Conservative Christianity is thus the cluster of beliefs held at this time by at most a sustantial part of one-third of the world's people, who make

---

3. McGrath, *Christian Theology*, 272–324; Grillmeier, *Christ in Christian Tradition*; Kelly, *Early Christian Doctrine*.

4. Nürnberger, *Martin Luther's Message*, 77.

very strong, exclusive truth claims about God, Jesus Christ, salvation, the Bible, the church and other religions. It is, however, not a monolithic body of believers, as the differences even within its conservative side between evangelicals and fundamentalists show. Both of these conservative groupings are influential and evidently growing, especially in the USA and in some of Africa's developing countries like Nigeria.[5]

EVANGELICALS AND FUNDAMENTALISTS

It is instructive to note the main differences between evangelicals and fundamentalists, starting with the former. British and American evangelicals can serve as fairly typical of those elsewhere. In an account, accepted for America by Frances FitzGerald,[6] and confirmed in a book by Alister McGrath,[7] David Bebbington sees them as having four defining features: what he calls conversionism ("lives have to be changed"); activism; biblicism; and crucicentrism, which is "a stress on the sacrifice of Christ on the cross."[8] Turning to fundamentalism, he and his co-author David Jones write that "evangelicalism in Britain cannot simply be equated with fundamentalism," adding that some would define fundamentalism as insistence on biblical inerrancy, asserting that a fundamentalist is an evangelical who believes in a literal six-day creation.[9]

According to them and to McGrath, British evangelicals are better described as insisting on the authority of Scripture.[10] Fundamentalists also insist on separatism, evangelicals not always or even at all. Fundamentalists oppose theological construction or innovation; evangelicals sometimes innovate. Finally, fundamentalists have a "broadly negative and pessimistic view of culture" but this is not always so for evangelicals.[11] In a review of their book, Graham Gould writes interestingly that "fundamentalists are evangelicals characterized, to varying extents, by intransigence in the face of critical biblical scholarship, militancy and separatism."[12] Another helpful discussion of the differences between evangelicalism and fundamentalism

---

5. McGrath, *Evangelicalism*, 94-96.
6. FitzGerald, *Evangelicals*, 637.
7. McGrath, *Evangelicalism*.
8. Bebbington, *Evangelicalism in Modern Britain*, 16.
9. Bebbington and Jones, *Evangelicalism and Fundamentalists*, 349.
10. McGrath, *Evangelicalism*, 54.
11. Bebbington and Jones, *Evangelicalism and Fundamentalists*, 350-64.
12. Gould, "Review of Bebbington," 362.

is provided by John de Gruchy, drawing on both scholarly and personal resources.[13]

Addressing the same matter of differentiation between evangelicals and fundamentalists, Richard McDonough contends that "fundamentalism is the view that people must obey God's directives unconditionally because God is absolutely infallible." He maintains that it can be seen as a subset of evangelicalism. The term has been broadened to other religions and to non-religious beliefs. All share the character of not yielding to modern or alternative belief-systems. For religious fundamentalists the key thing is the belief that a perfect God has revealed saving truths only in the Bible that must therefore be accepted unconditionally. You can argue with a Marxist fundamentalist but you don't argue with God.[14]

Discussing evangelicalism, with particular reference to his own Church of England, Martyn Percy makes a key contention about what he regards as its ethical shortcomings. He notes that it reveals a marked individualist emphasis with no great, evident concern for grave global ethical problems like poverty.[15]

Notwithstanding internal differences of the kind just noted and those separating Protestants, Pentecostals and Catholics, and also between their liberals, all Conservative Christians known to me hold that their defining beliefs come, directly or indirectly, from God as the sole and ultimate source of truth. These beliefs are therefore no mere matters of fallible human conviction but as reliable as anything can be. The essentials of each of these tenets are presented below, after I draw attention to the prominence of belief in Conservative Christianity, based on my own studies of Christian theology and my lectures about it, and checked against the writings of contemporary Conservative Christian scholars.

CONSERVATIVE CHRISTIANITY AS A BELIEF AND RITUAL SYSTEM

It needs emphasizing that Conservative Christians generally define their religion as a system of distinctive, exclusive *beliefs*, along with ritual practices, chiefly Baptism and the Eucharist, and the spreading of the message of salvation as taught in the New Testament and the Creeds. Theologian Graham Ward contends, by contrast, that the rituals in fact give rise to and express

13. de Gruchy, *Being Human*, 19-20.

14. McDonough, "Religious Fundamentalism," 561-64; see also Harris, *Fundamentalism and Evangelicalism*.

15. Percy, *Future Shapes*, 137.

those beliefs, making doctrine a form of prayer.[16] Against his contention, however, there is the fact that the rituals and prayers he has in mind themselves contain or clearly imply the core beliefs of Conservative Christianity, so it cannot simply be the case that the rituals underlie the beliefs, though they certainly reinforce them powerfully.

This is not to deny that Conservative Christianity also has an ethic but none of its core values of love, compassion, justice and truth are exclusive to it. They are also taught by other faiths and indeed by secularists. Lest there be any doubts about portraying Conservative Christianity as primarily a belief-system, consider the fact that both as a whole and in its many denominations it calls on members to profess its Creeds and accept its statements of faith, and these mostly or even wholly contain articles of belief. The most important of these is the Nicene Creed. It confines itself entirely to the beliefs that such Christians accept as true, without any mention of the ethical practices and the rituals required of them. What follows it is therefore mainly about the central beliefs of Conservative Christianity, outlined as a basis for critical evaluation.

GOD: CONSERVATIVE CHRISTIANITY'S TRINITARIAN MONOTHEISM

Along with directly related beliefs about Jesus, discussed below, the most important Christian belief is of course not just that there is a God but that God is the Holy Trinity of Father, Son and Holy Spirt, three divine persons in one God. Additionally, Conservative Christians hold that the doctrine of the Trinity has been revealed by God and is therefore absolutely sound. They also believe that God is a perfect being, wholly and absolutely good, all-powerful, the creator of heaven and earth, and all-knowing.

John Hick has offered a helpful statement of the traditional concept of God as "the unique, infinite personal Spirit, holy, righteous, wise and loving, who has created the existing universe and who is fashioning human personalities for eternal fellowship with himself through their own free responses to the environmental challenges which he appoints."[17] These specific, divine attributes are also taught in Judaism and Islam, so while they certainly are part of Conservative Christianity they are not uniquely Christian. Much more crucial to the faith of such Christians is the belief that their faith alone has received the revelation of God's trinitarian nature in Scripture and the person of Christ. For the understanding of and belief

16. Ward, *How the Light*.
17. Hick, *Faith and Knowledge*, 3; see also McGrath, *Christian Theology*, 203-42.

in the Holy Spirit, from biblical times to the present, Anthony Thiselton provides an instructive, recent scholarly survey.[18]

JESUS CHRIST AS THE INCARNATE SECOND PERSON OF THE HOLY TRINITY AND OUR ONLY SAVIOR

As mentioned briefly above, in a complicated process lasting over four hundred years from the time of Christ, the early church arrived at the understanding of its founder that remains definitive of Conservative Christianity.[19] The result was the christology or orthodox doctrine about Christ, which declares that Jesus is the union of a divine nature and a human nature, the second person of the Trinity, who became flesh as Jesus of Nazareth for our salvation from the dreadful consequences of our sins. It is a vital part of all parts of Christianity to affirm that Jesus was a real historical figure and not a mythical being, for his life is anchored in a definite, dated period of history in both the New Testament and the Nicene Creed, with their references to named Roman authorities like Pontius Pilate, as is of course well known to all Christians.

Conservative Christianity has additional beliefs about its founder. These are the events, words, and deeds given in the New Testament, namely that he was born of the Virgin Mary, gathered a group of disciples at the start of his public ministry in Galilee when he was about thirty, performed miracles of great compassion, and taught a message about a loving God and the need for a loving life, among other teachings. Then he came into conflict with the religious authorities of Judaism and also, in the end, their Roman overlords, was arrested and tried in Jerusalem under Pontius Pilate, executed by the terrible Roman method of crucifixion, and was buried; and above all that he rose bodily from the tomb on the first Easter, never to die again; and was seen by named persons and others before ascending into heaven, from which he would return to the world in judgment.

EVIL, SIN AND ITS CONSEQUENCES

A religion that accepts Christ not only as God incarnate but especially as savior will concomitantly have a powerful sense of the reality of evil, and that indeed is true of Conservative Christianity, though this dreadful reality

---

18. Thiselton, *Holy Spirit*. See also Studebaker, "Review of Thiselton," 814-17.

19. Bockmuehl, *Cambridge Companion to Jesus*. See also Young, "Prelude," 1-34, and "Monotheism and Christology," 452-69.

is more often spoken of as sin. The account of evil given in chapter 5, as a deadly negative force involving physical pain, mental suffering and moral wickedness, is accepted by Conservative Christians, but they place these evils in the context of their concept of a holy and righteous God. According to Scripture, the first humans, endowed with free will, chose to disobey God's command, preferring material satisfaction, symbolized by the forbidden fruit, and their own wishes, to obedience to God. The fundamental meaning of sin in Christian theology is therefore transgressions of what God in his perfect goodness and holiness commands, which is uprightness of life and conduct in obedience to his will. Genesis chapter 3 tells us that the consequence of sin is dire indeed. A holy God cannot ignore or tolerate evil and must therefore punish it. This he did for the first humans by banishing them from the goodness of the original human situation, while ultimately the result of our sins is the loss of the eternal presence of the Creator, which the New Testament calls eternal life, a dreadful predicament from which humanity cannot save itself.

As a consequence of the original fall into sin, the whole subsequent human condition has been tainted, as taught in the traditional doctrine of original sin. Bruce Vawter explains that this doctrine holds that "by the very fact of birth into the human race, a person inherits a 'tainted' nature in need of regeneration and with a proclivity to sinful conduct."[20]

What this short summary of the essentials of the Conservative Christian understanding of sin clearly shows is that sin and evil are taken with utmost seriousness because they are so utterly serious. As Alister McGrath comments, citing Calvin, "the full benefit of salvation can only be known if the full seriousness of sin is first appreciated."[21] Loss of eternal life is itself a dreadful fate; far worse are the unending torments of hell that some of the most Conservative Christians believe await those whose sinfulness comes under God's holy wrath. The need for God's saving grace to avoid such a fate takes us to the way salvation is understood in Conservative Christianity.

SALVATION

Absolutely definitive of Conservative Christianity is the conviction that Jesus is the only savior, for Christianity takes as God-given the words of Peter in Acts 4:12 (NIV), where he says that "Salvation is found in no one else, for there is no other name under heaven given to mankind by which we must be saved." In a paper about Calvin's theology on the question of whether

20. Vawter, "Original Sin," 420; McGrath, *Christian Theology*, 324.
21. McGrath, *Evangelicalism*, 148.

there are other means of salvation outside Christ, South Africa's Calvinist theologian P.C. Potgieter writes that for the great Genevan reformer there definitely are not; nor can God even be known apart from Christ.[22]

Additionally, it is part of Conservative Christian belief that hell is real, for its existence is affirmed in the Gospels (for example in Matthew 25:41) and also in the Nicene Creed where it says that after his body was buried Jesus "descended into hell." Where differences of interpretation occur is about the nature of hell, for only the most fundamentalist of believers insist that it is literally a place of endless fiery torment. Thus Wayne A. Gruden, writing from a very conservative, fundamentalist standpoint, can state that hell is a "place of eternal punishment" where those who are sent there are tormented for ever with fire and sulphur.[23] By contrast, the famous words of John 3:16 in the English Standard Version make no such claim: "For God so loved the world, that he gave his only Son, that whoever believes in him should not perish but have eternal life." This verse, so loved by many evangelicals, says that those who are not saved for eternal life will "perish," which can reasonably be taken to mean that at death, or after judgment, they simply cease to exist and are thus separated for ever from God and his love. All Conservative Christians, however, agree that hell means eternal loss of the glorious presence of God as the result of our sins and of our failure to accept Christ as our only savior. Hell, though variously described, is thus accepted as the just destiny ordained by a righteous God for everybody who does not accept salvation in Christ because all have sinned, and a holy God cannot just turn a blind eye to evil.

Also affirmed in the Creed is the belief that in the future there will be a Day of Judgment where the righteous and the lost will be finally separated, but much disagreement appears to exist as to exactly how this fits the basic doctrine of salvation as summarized above. What is not doubted is that only through Christ can anybody be saved, but Catholic and Protestant Christians have different ideas about exactly what is required of people in order to be saved. The former require membership of the church and participation in its sacramental life as well as acceptance of the defining beliefs of the faith. Protestants believe that the essential requirement is acceptance in this life of Jesus Christ as savior, basing this on the words of John 3:16 quoted above.

---

22. Potgieter, "Ander Weë tot God?" 108-27. A comprehensive account of this doctrine is provided by Alister McGrath, *Christian Theology*, 326–59.

23. Grudem, *Christian Beliefs*, 132.

THE BIBLE AS GOD'S REVEALED WORD

When Conservative Christians call the Bible "the word of God" they don't mean that the Bible is merely about God. They mean that it is *from* God, who inspired human writers in their Hebrew and Greek languages to produce its constituent books. Often the words of 2 Timothy 3:16 are quoted to support this belief: "All Scripture is God-breathed." (NIV). Our modern translations are seen as the work of dedicated, believing Christian scholars with the knowledge, skills and above all trust in the guidance of the Holy Spirit that are needed to ensure that the results are trustworthy renderings of the original Hebrew and Greek. What is read or heard in church, in Bible study groups and studied individually, is therefore expressed in human words, but the content is from God and is therefore trustworthy, especially the New Testament.

The leading, critical Biblical scholars of Conservative Christianity are highly trained experts who work from within a dedicated faith. They know that the Bible did not descend from heaven ready-made but grew over a very long period of about a thousand years from the first of the Hebrew Scriptures to be written to the last of the New Testament texts, and that it was only after several more centuries that the collection of books or canon now accept by Christians as Holy Scripture was settled in 397 CE, with a fair number of other writings excluded because they were judged to be inauthentic in regard to the truths of the Gospel.[24] This background information is seldom known by many conservatives with no great exposure to academic biblical studies, but that does not matter for their faith, because Conservative Christianity believes that the whole process was guided by God the Holy Spirit in order to deliver to all believers a Bible they could trust.

For Conservative Christians, the supreme revelation of God is of course Jesus Christ as the incarnate second person of the Trinity, confirmed in the revealed documents of the New Testament. It follows that such Christians will regard the Hebrew Scriptures of the Jewish people into whom Jesus was born as pointing to and anticipating the Christ who was to come, as Bredenkamp contends about the words, "the virgin will conceive and give birth to a son, and will call him Immanuel" in Isaiah 7:14 (NIV).[25] In that way those earlier writings could be accepted by Christianity as part of Holy Scripture but not as saving truth in themselves; hence, of course, their des-

---

24. Barton, *Cambridge Companion*; Raymond E. Brown, *Church*; Peter Brown, *Authority and the Sacred*; and his *Rise of Western Christendom*; Freeman, *New History*; Meeks, *Moral World*; Mitchell, "Emergence," 177-94.

25. Bredenkamp, *What and Why?* 24.

ignation as the "Old Testament," whereas for Jewish people they are the *only* Testament. Clearly, then, the beliefs of Conservative Christians about the Bible share the element of significant exclusiveness of their beliefs about the Trinity, about Jesus as the incarnate second person of the Trinity, salvation, and the Holy Spirit as the inspiring, creative force that gave rise to the Bible as a whole, but to no other religious book.

The shared belief of Conservative Christians that the Bible is divinely inspired and thus supremely authoritative does not signify complete agreement about Scripture, for within the ranks of Conservative Christians there are marked differences about the meaning of biblical inspiration. At one extreme we find those who believe in what amounts to a mechanical process of God delivering the very words of the biblical books into the minds of the human writers, who added nothing apart from the physical act of penning them. Thus Wayne Grudem can write that "All the words in the Bible are God's words." He adds the logical implication of that fundamental conviction: the words of Scripture are the final measure by which all supposed truth is to be gauged. Therefore, that which conforms to Scripture is true, that which doesn't conform to Scripture is not true.[26]

As I said in part I in connection with my own encounter with critical biblical studies as a university student, the rise of critical biblical scholarship led to a markedly different, liberal understanding of biblical inspiration, which allows for the human realities of the writers to play a part in the creation of the Bible, including their inevitable limitations as culturally conditioned, fallible beings. Bredenkamp provides a carefully worded statement of this standpoint. Commenting on 2 Timothy 3:16, he asserts that Scripture "was written under the direction of the Holy Spirit who moved the authors to record their writings." The word "direction" does not mean dictation, and the word "authors" is not the same as "writers," for it implies an element of creativity, whereas the word "writer" can mean no more than writing down what one hears or receives from another. Interestingly, Bredenkamp illustrates this more liberal understanding of biblical inspiration by contending that just as Jesus is believed to have had two natures, divine and human, so the Bible has a divine and a human element, adding that divine inspiration "does not relieve us of the spiritual and mental effort necessary to understand and interpret it correctly."[27]

In short, within the ranks of Conservative Christianity there is considerable scope for disagreement about the meaning of certain biblical passages, such as the creation narratives in Genesis, sexual orientation and

26. Grudem, *Christian Beliefs*, 13, 14.
27. Bredenkamp, *What and Why?* 16.

Paul's assertions about the status of women, within a broad consensus that in some very real way the Bible is indeed the Word of God and therefore a holy book.

THE CHURCH AS THE BODY OF CHRIST

According to the Bible and the various statements of faith that inform what follows, such as those of the Episcopal Church in the USA, the Anglican Church of Southern Africa, and the Reformed churches, for Conservative Christians the church is no mere human institution but one that Christ himself founded and commissioned to carry his saving truths into the four corners of the earth, as required in the concluding words of Matthew's Gospel: "Go therefore and make disciples of all nations, baptizing them in the name of the Father and of the Son and of the Holy Spirit, teaching them to observe all that I have commanded you." (Matt 28:19—20, ESV).

The metaphor of the church as the body of Christ expresses this idea, reserving the headship of the church to its founder but linking its members to him in the closest way. It also provides a way of understanding the Bible as a book that was, as we have noted, physically produced during the early centuries of the fledgling church by its human writers as members of the body of Christ, while its content is believed to come from God himself, whether verbatim, as fundamentalists and many conservative evangelicals hold, or through the culturally conditioned minds of its human writers.

It follows that the church must then be seen by Conservative Christians as our supreme guide in matters of faith and morals in a way that no other institution can ever be, provided it is faithful to its founder and to Scripture itself. Thus the "Outline of the Faith" of the Episcopal Church in the USA can say of the church, among other features, that it is "the pillar and ground of truth," adding elsewhere that its mission includes the promotion of "justice, peace and love."[28] The question that must now be addressed is whether Conservative Christianity lives up to the supreme goodness it believes it truly serves, which is the subject of the next chapter.

---

28. *Book of Common Prayer*, 854.

Chapter 8

Is Conservative Christianity sufficiently ethical?

IN ORDER TO DECIDE whether Conservative Christianity is as ethical as it should be, and therefore as rich in the inspiring goodness lived, taught and pioneered by Jesus himself, it is first necessary to identify the principles and ethical norms by which that evaluation can be done, starting with the principles. These must of course themselves be ethically appropriate; of all things ethics must itself be ethical. The principles are as follows. Firstly, the evaluation must be scrupulously fair. This requires that what is under evaluation has been accurately presented and be free of factual error, bias and misrepresentation, however unintended. Every effort has been made to ensure this in the previous chapter. The next principle follows logically from fairness. It is the principle of internal criticism, which entails that the norms used must be appropriate to what is being judged. To meet this principle, what follows will use the main biblical values of Conservative Christianity itself in the first instance; but if Christianity is to be a greater force for good in the wider, secular world, due cognizance must also be taken of the ethical norms of that wider world. The third judgmental principle is that the evaluation must be done thoroughly, remembering Immanuel Kant's important statement that in our age of criticism, to criticism *everything* must bend. Genuine truth-seeking demands nothing less; anything less is evasive and even, perhaps, lacking in moral courage.

The remaining principle is respect. Conservative Christianity is a living reality in the religious life of many millions of people. It serves as the basis of their lives, their sense of meaning and their emotional well-being. It would be profoundly unethical to lose sight of that human reality when subjecting its foundational beliefs, practices and also values to rigorous criticism in a way that lacks sensitivity, concern and respect.

CRITERIA FOR ETHICAL EVALUATION FROM CHRISTIANITY ITSELF

Applying the principles given above yields firstly the specific ethical values of Conservative Christianity itself, as given in Scripture, as professed by the churches, and as practiced by believers seeking to do their best. These values are love, truth and justice, which constitute an inter-related triad. Love is of course Christianity's supreme value, but love requires truth and justice or it will be less than loving, as the following example shows. Most parents truly love their children and they know that they must love them equally, which means loving them fairly. Fairness is at the heart of justice, so it is clear that love cannot be adequate if it is unjust, favoring one child over another. Loving one's children, and indeed loving others, also means doing the best for them, and to do that we need to know them well enough to be able to offer them what is most beneficial to them. That requires truth, because knowledge, as distinct from mere opinion, must be true to count as knowledge, and to guide us reliably.

From these three core ethical values others follow logically and are specified in the Bible or implied by it. Respect is one of them. It means recognizing and appreciating the unique value of every person and the integrity of nature, and treating them in ways that reveal that appreciation. Generosity of spirit and action is another consequence of love, so that love becomes far more than just a feeling of deep attachment. Freedom must also be cherished, for love is a free gift that cannot be demanded or commanded, but freedom is not unreservedly good, for freedom is only ethical when it harms nobody and nothing. Also implied by love and justice at their best is inclusiveness, so that loving concern extends to all and not just to members of one's family, culture, religion or nation. Inclusivity, I would argue, is the moral lesson, among others, of the Parable of the Good Samaritan.

CRITERIA FROM THE WIDER WORLD

These internal norms of Conservative Christianity, while essential in the interests of fairness and respect, are however not sufficient. Christians live in and seek to be a blessing for the wider world of other faiths and secular institutions. These have their own values, and the moral value of Christianity in the wider society is judged by people in those other belief systems on the basis of their ethical values, so these must now be identified and kept in mind. In addition, commitment to the best possible truth-finding obliges Christians to be willing to deepen their ethics from any source from which they can learn. For the greatest inclusivity I return now to the results of research into global ethics by the German radical theologian Hans Küng and the American ethicist, the late Rushworth M. Kidder, which were introduced in part I. I will also refer to my own research findings about global ethics, as presented in part I.

As already noted, Küng limited himself to the ethical values that are shared by the world's most widely followed religions. The most interesting version of them was issued by the 1993 Parliament of the World's Religions in Chicago in a document called *The Declaration of a Global Ethic*. The so-called "Golden Rule," about doing to others what you would have them do to you—which is taught in various wordings by a wide range of faiths—was accepted as foundational, followed by four ethical principles: non-violence and respect for life; economic justice; tolerance and truthfulness; and, in the fourth place, equal rights and gender justice.[1] Conservative Christianity teaches the Golden Rule, as every member of the faith knows. It also values truth and economic justice; whether it also accepts non-violence, respect for life, tolerance, equal rights and gender justice as part of its ethic is a matter that is considered below.

Rushworth Kidder used a more inclusive method for his research on global ethics, again as previously noted in this book, by interviewing authoritative figures from various cultures, not just the religions, and also by using cross-cultural surveys. From these sources he produced a set of eight shared values. They are love, truthfulness, fairness, freedom, unity, tolerance, respect for life, and responsibility.[2] Conservative Christians certainly accept the first five and the eighth, but once more there are questions to be asked about how fully they all also value tolerance and respect for life. My own approach to global ethics yielded the following moral virtues, as tabulated in part I.

---

1. Küng and Kuschel, *Global Ethic*.
2. Kidder, *Shared Values*, 18.

Beneficence virtues	Integrity virtues
Generosity	Truthfulness
Respect	Reliability
Fairness, justice	Trustworthiness
Inclusivity	Self-knowledge
Beneficial effort	Open-mindedness
Beneficial freedom	Judicious criticality
Created beauty	Wisdom

In the beneficence cluster only beauty seems absent from the explicit virtues of Conservative Christianity, but those virtues are certainly not opposed to it and beauty could be seen as strongly implied by the biblical account of creation, where it is written that the Creator saw that creation was good. Instructively, the Zulu word *muhle* can mean both good and beautiful, according to my informants. Two values in the integrity cluster seem either absent or insufficiently explicit in those of Conservative Christianity, except among its more liberal members: genuine open-mindedness and really rigorous criticality.

To synthesize this account of the criteria for the ethical evaluation that follows, the following moral norms are appropriate, relevant and fair to Conservative Christianity, most of which it certainly professes: love, truth, justice, respect, generosity, active care for others, freedom without harm, inclusiveness, non-violence, respect for life, tolerance, equal rights for all, gender justice, beauty, open-mindedness and judicious criticality. These are the principal facets of goodness. While all are relevant and important, two are foundational. They are love and truth, so the main emphasis of the critique is on them. It will therefore be asked if the defining beliefs and practices of Conservative Christianity are as loving—as richly beneficent— and as rigorously truth-loving, which includes unfailing respect for factual evidence and logical consistency, as they can and must be, if they are to be true to the supreme goodness believers know as God and find in the person, work and message of Jesus. To that critique I will proceed after a crucial reassurance to Conservative Christians.

ETHICS REQUIRES CARING, SENSITIVE CRITICALITY

At the start of the critique it is vital to keep clearly in mind that what follows will be deeply disturbing to Conservative Christians, so it must be done sensitively and caringly, the way both ethics and love themselves require. To achieve this, what follows is not seen as a critique merely of beliefs and practices, but of beliefs and practices *that mean the world to huge numbers of people*. It is therefore done on the analogy of a small team of experienced, caring explorers or scouts who have come back from exploring a new and at times very challenging area, beyond which there is a beautiful new homeland for the community they want to help by guiding them there. The scouts know these people will need courage and perseverance, especially the more insecure ones. They may even want to pull out of the journey if they find it too demanding, like the children of Israel in the biblical story of the Exodus who found the memory of the food of slavery in Egypt more appetizing than the hazards and hardships of freedom; but even the more liberal ones will find some of what lies ahead very challenging.

Knowing all this, our caring scouts understand that they must offer the people something that will give them stout hearts and minds. They do this by assuring them that while much of what lies ahead will indeed be very challenging, they embark on the journey with a wondrous gift that will never fail them, the gift of a goodness that is richer, deeper, greater and more lovely than anything else in the world, the gift of what they believe is the loving presence of a God of perfect goodness. The scouts assure them that there is nothing wrong with their faith in this wondrous reality and with their loving actions, for the problem is a problem of adequate understanding and of doctrines that obscure rather than reveal the perfect goodness and love that Jesus embodied and taught. Their hearts and hands are therefore in the right place, but their understanding of the faith that governs their lives has been harmed by a system of belief which, in great sincerity, has allowed domination to surpass liberation in the way it works, as the journey ahead will enable them to see. The caring scouts then add that the difficult time ahead will take them even closer to the perfect goodness that they call God and to the Jesus who revealed it in his life and in the movement he began. Gently but with the deepest conviction, the scouts might also say that the way ahead *is* the way Jesus himself pioneered, much more so than what they will leave behind if they follow through with it. That having been said, we can now proceed to the ethical critique of Conservative Christian beliefs themselves.

INABILITY TO PRIORITIZE ACTIVE GOODNESS AND OPENNESS TO ALL TRUTH

In the light of the greatest goodness, Conservative Christianity can be seen to suffer two fundamental problems: the subordination of loving, ethical practice to belief and worship, and the culturally restricted and partly obsolete nature of some of its core beliefs, to which its members are required to declare their assent. Very early in its history Conservative Christianity transformed the revolutionary path of this-worldly ethical and spiritual practice, pioneered by Jesus, into a set of beliefs expressed in ethically inadequate and culturally restricted thought forms, which are perpetuated in its doctrines and worship. This transformation is greatly hindering Conservative Christianity from revealing the world-changing power of supreme goodness, experienced as divine, and channel it into a world in ethical trouble serious enough to threaten the future of life as we know it.

There is a reason for this ethically problematic transformation of ethical spirituality into doctrinal and ritual spirituality. Like all the religions of very long standing, Conservative Christianity emerged in great cultural isolation. At that time there was simply no other way a religion could form. The isolation was at its greatest in what Lloyd Geering termed the ethnic stage of history, elements of which Christianity inherited from its Jewish cultural motherland. The isolation was considerably less restrictive but still very real in the trans-ethnic stage of about 500 BCE onwards, which the church also inherited from ancient Israel, as developed especially by the great prophets of the Axial Age, the second Isaiah, Jeremiah and Ezekiel. That cultural matrix or motherland was itself enveloped by the much larger cultural world of the Mediterranean area, which profoundly affected its intellectual and organizational development in the first five centuries of Christianity's history, starting with Paul's conversion of a new Jewish religious movement into a Gentile one.

That was a world of imperial rule, highly sophisticated Greek and Latin philosophy and especially of Rome's way of handling power through law and political organization. Philosophy and law both typically express themselves in propositions, like Aristotle's statement that ethics requires a careful balancing of behaviors to avoid unhelpful extremes, or the way Roman law could state that slavery is permitted. The result was an assumption, natural enough to a cultural world of philosophy, imperial law and political might, that religion was also, at heart, a matter of formulating and believing the right propositions, like those of the Nicene Creed, and that the model of power by which to conceive of God was monarchical rule, benevolent but still always a matter of supreme, sovereign power.

Monarchical power involves hierarchies of domination and control, which foster dependency and obedience, often unquestioning, in those who are dominated. An independent critical quest for truth is not welcomed and as a result, problematic beliefs are accepted without much likelihood of being questioned, and are even enforced, as the history of the Inquisition so chillingly shows. What this produces is a religion with an unhealthy amount of authoritarianism and too little liberation from what Ted Scott and Phil Harker call "the dependency trap."[3] For a powerful, recent account of authoritarianism in the churches in contrast with its more humane face, see the late South African psychologist of religion Richard Oxtoby's book *The Two Faces of Christianity*.[4]

In considering the context of ideas out of which Conservative Christianity arose, it is important to remember that the Jewish world of the earliest church had known subjection to alien, imperial rule for an almost unbroken period of at least six centuries, before the church entered and was subject to the world of Roman imperial power.[5] It was a world of such pervasive, long-lasting cultural influence that its impact on the way God was understood was inevitable. In a haunting paragraph, Alfred North Whitehead, arguably the most important systematic philosopher of modern times, summarized the change from Jerusalem to Rome as follows: "When the Western world accepted Christianity, Caesar conquered; and the received text of Western theology was edited by his lawyers . . . The brief Galilean vision of humility flickered throughout the ages, uncertainly. . . .. The Church gave to God the attributes which belonged exclusively to Caesar."[6]

Today's world is very different. It is a globalizing, multi-cultural world of revolutionary scientific knowledge, equal human rights, democracy, and dethroned kings, which has radically changed the way we think and speak of our experience, including our spiritual experience. Most important of all is the emergence of a multi-disciplinary and global understanding of the nature of goodness itself. It provides the knowledge and ethical insight that show what is wrong with Conservative Christianity, the business of the rest of this chapter, and how to change it, which is the subject of part III.

The critical appraisal of Conservative Christian beliefs being pursued in this part of the book is well illustrated by Klemm and Schweiker when they write as follows: "We advocate freedom within religion . . . a way of being religious in which religious and other authorities are submitted to criticism and tested in light of actions and relations that respect and enhance the integrity of life."[7] They speak of two deadly dangers in the heritages of both religion and humanism: what they call "hypertheism" and "overhumanization." By the former they mean an exaggerated expression of the idea of all-powerful, totally controlling God as the only truth, and by secular

---

3. Scott and Harker, *Humanity at Work*, 21-25.
4. Oxtoby, *Two Faces*, 149-84; 185-279.
5. Esler, "Patterns of Political Rule," 467-70.
6. Whitehead, *Process and Reality*, 342.
7. Klemm and Schweiker, *Religion and the Human Future*, 3.

humanism's "overhumanization" they mean an equally exaggerated glorification of humanity.[8] I do my best to avoid these two dangers in part III.

JUDGING CONSERVATIVE CHRISTIANITY

The problems besetting the main beliefs of Conservative Christianity, when those beliefs are taken at face value, as traditional believers invariably do, are not merely differences of interpretation. They are very real and some of them appear to be fatal. In this part of the book that contention is substantiated in detail by means of the strongest criteria which a belief must meet if it can validly be judged to be true. Two criteria stand out from the detailed set provided above as crucial for a belief to be accepted as true. It must not be self-contradictory and it must not clash with relevant facts. It is vital to be clear at this point that these criteria are not some alien, secular notion arising from indifference to religion or hostility to it. They come from the heart of Christian ethics itself because it includes truth as a sacred value. Not only is it the ninth of the Ten Commandments; it is also central to the values of the New Testament, as can be seen from the following passages: John 1:8—9; 8:32 ("you will know the truth, and the truth will set you free" (ESV), and many others.

Two of the central beliefs of Conservative Christianity present no ethical problems at all. They are that the supreme reality is one of perfect love, justice and goodness; and that Jesus was truly human. The evidence for his historical existence as a flesh and blood person is overwhelming. Accepting his historical existence therefore in no way violates the ethical duty to cherish truth. It is certain other, orthodox, defining beliefs of Conservative Christianity that present very grave problems when taken at face value.

It is no small thing to ask Conservative Christians to take what is seriously problematic to heart, contending with powerful arguments that beliefs they have trusted as good news are mistaken. The way to act caringly towards them at this difficult moment of truth is to add immediately the re-assurance that there really is great good news, which we can now see has been obscured by the way Conservative Christianity has mistakenly made traditional *doctrines* its foundation, rather than the wondrous *reality* of a perfect goodness, seen as divine, that Jesus incarnated, directly experienced and understood anew in ways that involve no ethical problems. This is explained in part III after the critical, ethical evaluations that follow.

---

8. Klemm and Schweiker, *Religion and the Human Future*, 13.

A LESS THAN PERFECTLY LOVING DOCTRINE OF GOD

The ethical problems for Conservative Christian theism come from three further parts of its doctrine of God, all three based on Scripture and set forth in the Nicene Creed and the theology of the church. They cannot be true if they are meant to be taken literally, as they are by most traditional Christian believers, especially evangelicals, fundamentalists and conservative Catholics.

Firstly, there is the belief that a God who is perfectly good, loving, and all-powerful, wills in his perfect justice that sinful humanity cannot have eternal life in heaven after death but must suffer eternal punishment in hell or in oblivion for its sins. The second belief is that God has provided the means of salvation through the incarnation of God the Son as Jesus Christ and that only by consciously accepting him as savior in this life, becoming part of his church and participating in its sacraments can anyone be saved. Thirdly, that God has revealed the truth of his loving, all-good and saving nature in the Bible by inspiring its human writers; by way of preparation in the Hebrew Scriptures and supremely in the New Testament. Conservative Christianity does not therefore, and cannot consistently, believe that the writings of the other religions come from God, but must regard them as purely human.

The ethical problem in all three of these beliefs is both a problem of truth, for they all involve the most serious problem that can beset a contention that something is true, the problem of outright self-contradiction, and of acute ethical inadequacy. No contention that contradicts itself can be true, or even make sense. It cannot be true that I am both literally alive and dead at the same time, both male and female, unless those words are clearly meant to be taken metaphorically and not literally, and Conservative Christianity certainly teaches that these three beliefs mean what they say. The self-contradiction in all three beliefs is that a perfectly loving, just and all-powerful God could not possibly do what these Christians insist he has done.

The assertion that we humans are headed in God's sovereign will for eternal punishment for our sins contradicts the justice of a perfect God, especially if the fate of the unsaved is the fires of hell forever. Even the most elementary understanding of justice reveals that there must be a balance between wilful wrong-doing and the punishment for it. To punish people for all eternity for at most a lifetime of unremitting and total wickedness, as if anybody, even Hitler, were guilty of that, is not justice because the punishment is so horrifically out of proportion to the offence. Not only is this not justice; it is far worse. It is unspeakably cruel and vengeful, above all when certain Conservative Christians assert that the unending punishment takes place quite literally in the fires of hell. About them John Austin Baker acidly wrote that "no one can preach hell as a means to the Gospel. If he does so, he tells us nothing about God or Jesus, only about himself and his neurotic, sub-human fears."[9] To my mind, only in a dominationist belief-system which calls for unquestioning acceptance of what it teaches, coupled with the threat of dreadful punishment for all who resist, could such an appalling contradiction of belief in a God of perfect love and justice have currency.

As noted briefly in chapter 6, process theologians contend that the doctrine of divine omnipotence is also fatally problematic, for if God is truly all-powerful, that not only means he can do anything that it is logically possible to do, but that he in fact owns and controls all the power. This means that other beings, including human beings, have no genuine, independent power, but only do what they are divinely ordained or allowed to do. That would make it unethical for such a God to punish or reward them; their actions are in fact just his, for he is responsible for all their actions. At least as serious, say these Christian process theologians, divine omnipotence means that a morally perfect God in fact is immoral, about as obvious a self-contradiction is we could conceive.[10]

A HEARTLESS AND CONTRADICTORY DOCTRINE OF SALVATION AND DAMNATION

The second outright contradiction is the belief that God wills that only by believing in Jesus as the only savior and by being part of his church can people have everlasting life and be spared the unspeakably awful fate of being forever lost. Note again that Christians who make this claim intend it literally. They say it means exactly what it says. This involves the same self-contradiction as the doctrine of hell because it is appallingly unloving and unjust to most people, who through no fault of their own cannot possibly avail themselves of this lifeline supposedly thrown out by a perfectly good and all-powerful God in the person of Christ, merely because they are born in places, periods of time and cultures where the Christian message was or still is unavailable, or only available in ways that render it alien and threatening, like parts of the world that suffered invasion and conquest by Christian Europe.

If we humans really are in deadly peril of eternal damnation, and cannot save ourselves, then a morally perfect God would certainly provide a

9. Baker, *Foolishness of God*, 296.
10. Cobb and Griffin, *Process Theology*, 63–64.

lifeline for us, in fact for *all* of us, and an all-powerful God would obviously be able to do so. Being perfectly just, the lifeline that such a God would provide *must be equally available to everybody*. A lifeline requiring conscious acceptance of Christ as the only savior and becoming part of his church is manifestly *not* available, equally, to everybody, but at most only to those in the Christian stream of history. In effect, what the orthodox, Conservative Christian doctrine of salvation says is that God is both perfectly just and horrifically unjust about exactly the same thing, namely the means of salvation. That is obviously an outright self-contradiction. Taken literally it cannot be true; worse still, it cannot even make sense, like talk of square circles. If God is all-good then the doctrine must be mistaken; if the doctrine is correct, then the God it implies cannot be all-good. In this book and elsewhere in progressive circles, the doctrine is discarded as manifestly mistaken, discarded out of commitment to the perfect goodness that underlies the concept of God.

Unless it is accepted as a purely symbolic notion (and a severely misleading one at that), the Conservative Christian doctrine of salvation must therefore, if we are truly honest to goodness, be rejected as seriously mistaken. The loving God that Christ spoke of could *never* ordain such an unjust measure for the fallible creature he made. Once more, an orthodox doctrine turns out not only to be untrue but, on the part of the believer who holds it, unintentionally blasphemous, because it imputes, albeit inadvertently, the gross evil of monstrous injustice on the part of one who is perfectly good. It implies that one who is wholly loving does something supremely unloving. When the restricted vision of traditional indoctrination—note the word—is removed, any reasonable and upright person will see with a sense of profound shock that to believe this is to malign the Deity, which is what blasphemy means.

It will by now be clear that an analogously fatal flaw besets the Conservative Christian doctrine of biblical revelation, that the Bible is the only text that comes from the ultimate source of truth. Truth is a vital good, and a perfectly loving God, in whom there is utterly no falsehood, would want to give it to a humanity that is incapable of discovering it for itself, but clearly such a God would give it equally and fairly to all people, not just one minority strand of the world's cultures.

There is unfortunately even more to be faced about the traditional doctrine of exclusive revelation. Conservative Christianity asserts that its doctrine of the Trinity has been revealed exclusively to Christians by God himself, who is all-loving and all-good. That also involves the worst of self-contradictions, since it is demonstrably true that no other faith believes in a Trinitarian God. Christians regard the Hebrew Scriptures as part of the

Bible and thus as part of God's revelation, and nowhere in them is there any clear indication that God revealed his Trinitarian nature to the children of Israel. Islam rejects the doctrine outright as tantamount to polytheism and as blasphemous. Nor is there any evidence of the Trinitarian divine revelation in any of the world's other belief-systems; the Trimurti in Hinduism is something else. The clear implications of these facts is that the God believed in by Conservative Christians did not reveal the Trinitarian truth about himself to any of those other faiths. That is plainly unfair. So there seems no way to avoid the conclusion that if there is indeed a God who is perfectly good and all-loving, then he can't also be the Trinity *when that belief is understood literally and is seen, unethically, as exclusive to Christianity.*

These points of ethical criticism, made by trying as best I can to be honest to goodness, are not a proof that there is no God but they are a conclusive refutation of core, defining doctrines, literally meant, of the Conservative Christian religion, imputing to a holy and just God such appalling acts of injustice as unfairly, cruelly and lovelessly prescribing *eternal* punishment and then providing an unfair escape from punishment for a favored minority of his children. What could be more morally unacceptable and intellectually absurd? What could be a more grotesque violation of the Christian duty to love God with one's whole heart *and whole mind* than to treat such notions as the most sacred of truths?

For anyone who grew up under and was revolted by apartheid, it is dismayingly clear that the way Conservative Christian doctrine portrays the Kingdom of God is essentially the same as the apartheid state, as I pointed out over thirty years ago in a published essay called "Implications of Apartheid for Christianity in South Africa."[11]. Apartheid too, in the name of a perfect God but with gross injustice, reserved the greatest of the country's benefits for a favored minority and condemned a deeply disadvantaged majority to the worst of things through no fault of their own, in that case because of their skin colour.

A MISUNDERSTOOD JESUS

There are no ethical questions about the way Jesus of Nazareth demonstrated and taught that love and compassion were the heart of his message and practice. For believer and skeptic alike, his moral stature and influence are acknowledged and greatly admired. Nor is there any ethical or logical problem about the contention that he incarnates a supreme goodness. Where ethical difficulties arise is in some of the main beliefs that formed about

---

11. Prozesky, *Christianity Amidst Apartheid*, 122–46.

him in the earliest years of the church, and were then accepted by it and by most believers ever since as God-given truths. Once more the problem is of orthodox, biblical teachings that contradict belief in a God of perfect love and goodness, and also clash with fact. These teachings also have the grave effect of harming the moral quality of the faith.

The problematic beliefs echo those presented in the previous section. They are that Jesus and he alone decisively reveals the God of perfect goodness and love, as stated in John 14:6; that he and he alone offers salvation to those who accept him as savior and become members of his church, as stated again in John's Gospel, this time in chapter 3, verse 16; and that he taught that there is a literal hell of horrific, eternal torment for those who do not accept him, as stated in Matthew 25:41.

Each of these exclusivist beliefs contradicts the fundamental Christian belief that there is indeed an almighty God of perfect goodness and love who, being perfect, must embrace all of humanity and not make himself (note the gender here) accessible to just one strand of it. Even worse is the way they give us a Jesus who, if these beliefs were correct, would not be the magnificent, ethical and spiritual figure we have excellent historical grounds for holding that he is.

A striking and beautiful feature of Jesus's ethical teaching is that our love must extend to all, even our enemies, with special concern for the poor, the outcasts and the vulnerable. It seems impossible, logically, that he would also teach a view of revelation and salvation that does the very opposite, namely create outcasts in the form of those who cannot possibly know about him, like most of the world's people down the centuries, or believe in him because they never even hear of him through no fault of their own, or hear of him from Christian invaders of their lands who naturally then come across as brutal oppressors. Even more morally disturbing, to put it mildly, would be if he really did teach the existence of a literal, everlasting hell of terrible punishment, which is surely the very opposite of real justice and real love, as was explained above.

These three beliefs about Jesus presenting himself as the exclusively supreme revelation of divine truth, as the only savior and as an advocate of eternal damnation, fail two key criteria of truth: the avoidance of contradiction and of conflict with fact, in this case the conclusive evidence that Jesus really did teach a message of inclusive, divine love. At this point it is of the utmost importance for commitment to the Jesus of history to know that there is recent research into Christian origins that is bringing to light a message of radical, revolutionary ethical importance taught by Jesus, which the unethical beliefs just identified have long obscured by their message of exclusive and unfair salvation and damnation. In part III the essentials of this research will be presented.

A SERIOUSLY MISTAKEN VIEW OF THE BIBLE

The Bible is a cherished part of Conservative Christian faith, and rightly so. In the fifteen centuries and longer since it attained its present, canonical form, it has guided, inspired and nourished the spiritual and moral life of innumerable Christians and indeed even people of other faiths, like Gandhi. Through much of it, but not all, the light of supreme love and goodness shines with great brilliance and power, with one great proviso that is not always heeded by many Conservative Christians: it must be read and understood under the guidance of perfect goodness and the values that go with it.

This means firstly that the contentions of Scripture must be of the highest possible ethical quality if they are indeed the result of divine inspiration and qualify as truly ethical. Our minds must therefore always be open to the possibility that the limitations and moral failures of the human writers have negatively affected parts of its message. Only what is indeed loving and true can be accepted as inspired by a God of perfect goodness and love.

Secondly, the doctrine of the divine inspiration of the Bible must be most carefully and ethically understood. That rules out certain widespread ways of seeing the Bible, which must now be indicated, with great sensitivity for those involved in this mistaken view. Addressing the first of the two ethical concerns just identified, to my knowledge no Christian has done this with greater courage, competence and thoroughness than John Shelby Spong, a bishop of the Episcopal Church in the USA, now retired, in his 2005 book *The Sins of Scripture*. He showed convincingly, as one who knows his Bible backwards, that Scripture contains material that is unethical about the environment, women, homosexuality, children, Jews, and what he calls certainty, the belief that Christianity has a monopoly on religious truth. There is no need to repeat all of these. All that is needed in order to show that there really are ethical problems about parts of the Bible is to cite a few of the most serious ones. They are genocide, the subordination of women, homophobia, and rejoicing at the killing of children.

Starting with genocide, here are two passages in the Hebrew Scriptures, from the English Standard Version of the Bible (as are all the biblical passages in this section), that present acts of genocide as ones that God commanded. Deuteronomy 20:16–17 is about the time when the Israelite conquest of the land of Canaan led by Joshua was under way. This is what it presents God as saying: "But in the cities of these people that the LORD your God is giving you for an inheritance, you shall save nothing alive that breathes, but you shall devote them to complete destruction, the Hittites and the Amorites, the Canaanites and the Perizzites, the Hivites and the Jebusites, as the LORD your God has commanded."

The taking of the city of Jericho under divine direction is reported in Joshua chapter 6. It reaches a climax in the following words from verse 21 about the conquerors: "Then they devoted all in the city to destruction, both men and women, young and old, oxen, sheep, and donkeys, with the edge of the sword." (ESV). Nobody with a conscience could possibly take these passages as truthfully recording what a God of perfect goodness could command. The only alternative is to see them as purely human creations that seek to give retrospective divine support to a murderously brutal invasion.

To their great credit, there are scholars even in the more traditionalist parts of Conservative Christianity who do not shrink from honestly facing up to these genocidal passages. One such is Douglas Earl, an evangelical who does not shy from facing the violence in parts of the Old Testament and especially in Deuteronomy and Joshua. He gives a valuable discussion of the key Hebrew word here, *herem*, evidently signifying "utter destruction," but argues, to my mind puzzlingly, that it is not to be defined as genocide.[12] In a response in the same volume, Christopher J. Wright agrees with Earl's view that the book of Joshua is not about "privileged ethnicity."[13] It is however, difficult for me to see what else it is.

Murdering women and children was part of that conquest, if Scripture in these passages is to be believed, because putting everything that breathed to death, young and old, clearly includes women and children. The biblical passage that causes me, as a father and grandfather, most pain is however Psalm 137:9, the well-known lament at captive life in Babylon, centuries after the conquest of Canaan. In the ESV translation it says, "Blessed shall be he who takes your little ones and dashes them against the rock!" Not only is it inconceivable for anyone truly seeking goodness to accept such words as divinely inspired or God-breathed, whatever that might mean, but worse for Christians is the way these terrible words contradict the loving warmth of Jesus himself for children, who said "Let the children come to me . . . And he took them in his arms and blessed them, laying his hands on them." (Mark 10:14 and 16, see also Luke 18:16, ESV).

Biblical justification for the unethical treatment of women is not confined to the murders mentioned above, for it is well known that it also involves passages that portray women as inferior to men, giving those who

---

12. Earl, *Joshua Delusion?* 53–63.
13. Earl, *Joshua Delusion?* 140.

want such supposed support an allegedly divine justification for male domination. Nor are they confined to the Old Testament, for among the most influential are two from the letters of Paul. In 1 Corinthians 14:34—35, Paul stipulates that "As in all the churches of the saints, the women should keep silent in the churches. For they are not permitted to speak, but should be in submission, as the Law also says . . . For it is shameful for a woman to speak in church." Writing in 1 Timothy 2:12 in the ESV, Paul, if it is indeed he, extends this subordination of women in church to what certainly seems to be a general rule, writing that "I do not permit a woman to teach or exercise authority over a man; rather, she is to remain quiet." Paul then justifies this in the next verse by citing the Genesis story about Eve being created after Adam and being the first sinner. These biblical references are not isolated, for subordination of women is evident in many other parts of the Bible, as Bishop Spong shows in great detail.[14]

In many of the churches today, but not all, these biblical requirements about women's allegedly subordinate status have, as is well known, long been ignored and thus, by implication, rejected as having any divine source. As is also only too well known, the world's largest church, the Roman Catholic Church, remains completely resistant to gender equality in the offices of the church, from priests upward in the hierarchy to the Papacy itself.

The reason for the coming of gender justice in large parts of the Protestantism is instructive, for it followed largely, though not totally, on the movement for gender justice in the modern, secular world, with its powerful, ethical emphasis on human equality and its revulsion at the evil of discriminating against anybody for things they cannot change, like gender. This is a good illustration of why a Christianity that seeks to be true to a God of perfect justice must be open to moral inspiration from any source, including the secular world, recognizing that moral goodness is a global, universal reality and not confined in its workings to any religion.

Much slower to make itself felt in the churches as a force for good is the movement for justice in connection with sexual orientation.[15] Here too there are highly influential biblical passages which, when accepted as divinely authorized, as so many Christians do, are cited in support of discrimination against any departure from heterosexuality. What people do with their sexual nature is a matter of choice, like practicing it or being celibate or promiscuous, but their basic sexual orientation or nature is now held to be fixed, and to range from the strongly heterosexual through bisexuality in various degrees to the strongly homosexual, so any discrimination against

---

14. Spong, *Sins of Scripture*, 71-100.
15. Nicolson, *Church and Same-Sex Marriage*.

anybody because of their basic nature, provided nobody is being forced or hurt, is just as cruel and evil as all other kinds of unfair discrimination like racism and sexism.

Yet here too there are biblical passages in both Testaments that purport to deem it divinely authorized. Probably the most frequently cited in Conservative Christianity, as is well known there and elsewhere, is Leviticus 18:22, addressing men: "You shall not lie with a man as with a woman; it is an abomination" (ESV). In Leviticus 20:13 the death penalty is prescribed for homosexual acts.

Lest anybody in the churches dismisses these verses as part of what they regard, with unintended and at times deadly anti-semitism, as superseded by the New Testament, here is what Paul wrote in Romans 1:26—27, in the context of a passionate denunciation of what he saw as ungodliness and unrighteousness, directing himself at both women and men: "For this reason God gave them up to dishonorable passions. For their women exchanged natural relations for those that are contrary to nature; and the men likewise gave up natural relations with women and were consumed with passion for one another, men committing shameless acts with men and receiving in themselves the due penalty for their error." In verse 32 of the same chapter, Paul writes that God himself has decreed that those who do the things he sees as unrighteous must suffer death.[16]

Both gross physical and structural violence involving unfair discrimination and victimization therefore appear without condemnation in the passages of Scripture cited above, posing fatal ethical problems for those who insist that all of the Bible is divinely inspired. In fairness, however, it must also be acknowledged that the passages involving violence are by no means typical of Scripture, as S. Wesley Ariarajah points out in an important recent paper about religion and violence, citing the much more prominent thread of peace and non-violence in the Bible.[17]

It is surely clear that a truly loving God cannot be the author of passages involving genocide, gender injustice, cruelty to people who cannot change their sexual orientation and, most morally repulsive of all, rejoicing at the thought of brutally murdering little children. These examples of lovelessness and injustice in the Bible take us to the critical importance of ethically acceptable ways of interpreting the doctrine of divine inspiration and permanently rejecting unethical ways, which must now be discussed.

The worst way is the notion of divine dictation of every word in Scripture, for that makes a holy and morally perfect God the author of evils of the

---

16. Spong, *Sins of Scripture*, 113-42.
17. Ariarajah, "Jesus the Christ," 57-59.

worst kind. This view of Scripture in effect treats the text as God, and not just as God-breathed; that seems to me to be idolatry and thus a violation of the first and second of the Ten Commandments. It is therefore a belief that must be summarily dismissed as completely mistaken and as, unintentionally, utterly insulting to God. When that is not done the evils those passages encourage simply persist, made worse because they are then driven by the unrecognized but very real delusion that God ordains them. Another ethical problem about this way of interpreting the Bible is the authoritarianism it fosters, for it encourages readers simply to accept what they read and obey it unquestioningly. We have learnt that this is incompatible with real truth-seeking, which requires critical evaluation and not blind obedience.

An illuminating discussion of the moral and intellectual problems of fundamentalist ways of using the Bible is provided by Richard McDonough. He contends that "fundamentalism is the view that people must obey God's directives unconditionally because God is absolutely infallible."[18] He argues that it is incoherent because what is alleged as being directly from God is, and must come under, human, fallible judgment. He holds that all kinds of religious fundamentalism share the character of not yielding to modern or alternative belief-systems. For a religious fundamentalist the key characteristic is the belief that a perfect God has revealed things that must therefore be accepted unconditionally, adding that you can argue with a Marxist fundamentalist but you don't argue with God, as already mentioned in this book.

McDonough then notes that fundamentalism can have both innocuous practical outcomes, like sincerely preaching about the Parable of the Good Samaritan, and extremist ones, like killing dissidents, but he is concerned only with the logical aspect of it. He sees an insuperable problem in the belief that God communicates infallibly in a sacred book, for there are "many layers of human fallibility between contemporary Scripture and God's original infallible revelations." So he asks which version of Scripture is infallible since there are differences, and which meaning of its passages is the infallible one.[19]

What is his view about allegedly direct, God-to-human communication? McDonough rightly points out that we never get out of our human limitations in what we understand of the supposed revelation. He concludes that in the final analysis this kind of fundamentalism is deeply and extremely irreligious; it elevates what a mere human insists on as the truth to divine

---

18. McDonough, "Religious Fundamentalism," 561.
19. McDonough, "Religious Fundamentalism," 565.

status, claiming for itself a right to say what God infallibly holds as true, and thus usurps God's sovereignty and perfection for itself.[20]

Less mistaken but still problematic is the view that the Bible is in some sense divinely inspired, or as some translations express the idea, God-breathed. It is not clear what this can mean. If it means that the entire Bible has God's influence behind it in some vague sense, then that still imputes moral responsibility to God for the evils identified above, which manifestly contradicts his nature as a loving and just Deity. Therefore it cannot be true. The only way to avoid the error is to accept that there are parts of the Bible that are not in any sense God-breathed but purely human. In my experience, even many liberal Christians seem unwilling or unable to take this step, such is the hold of the traditional view that the Bible is a holy book. Certainly the way the Bible is presented in the context of worship has never, in my experience, been presented in a way that even hints at the grave ethical problem of treating as holy that which is manifestly unholy in some parts.

There is therefore a related problem to be faced. It is the way the churches often limit people's understanding of the Bible to its presentations in the context of worship, where the readings are introduced and concluded as the words of the Lord, or with similar words, so encouraging the unquestioning acceptance that prevents an honest facing of the ethical problems in parts of the biblical text. John Bowden has written about this as follows, perfectly matching my own experiences: "Problems of understanding the Bible are accentuated by the patterns of its use in the contexts where it is most prominent, in public worship or private devotion. Rather than being introduced to the Bible in a rational way, being helped to explore it, church congregations tend to suffer extremes, being over-exposed to some parts, bored to tears by others which are incomprehensible in their liturgical settings . . . and are expected to understand its significance without ever really being told much about it."[21]

An unintended but serious result of the way the Bible is mostly presented in the churches is to cause some people to have doubts about God. Thus Chuck Blaisdell can write that he is "not so sure about a God whose book seems so contradictory." He adds that he accepts that there are inconsistencies in the Bible because it is "a long-running conversation, not a book of source code, not a phone book . . . and that sometimes the biblical authors disagreed with one another." In an important further comment for the purposes of this book, he then writes that the purpose of engaging the biblical text is to make God's love for all better known. It aims at "a growing

---

20. McDonough, "Religious Fundamentalism," 568.
21. Bowden, *Voices in the Wilderness*, 40.

understanding of the universality of God's grace." He also quotes a memorable statement by Martin Luther, whose attachment to the Bible is legendary, that just as "the cradle is not like the baby, the Bible is not the Word of God but it contains the Word of God." Blaisdell's criterion of what really is the word of God echoes what has been used in this book. He writes that it is "conformity with a God of love and justice and liberation and healing and hope," quoting his wife Barbara.[22]

Emerging from this section about mistaken views of the Bible is the following overall conclusion. The root ethical problem is once again the problem of a dangerously mistaken elevation of mere *belief* to a defining status about Christianity, the God it worships, the Christ it embraces as savior and the Bible it regards as holy. Beliefs are necessarily embedded in the words and thought forms of the cultures in which they arise, shaped by their human members in all their inevitable limitations and fallibility. As such they can never carry perfectly the burden and privilege of divine infallibility and perfect goodness, and must not be treated any longer as if they could. This brings the discussion of ethical problems to the most important way in which the churches themselves almost always define what it means to be a Christian.

THE CONSERVATIVE CHRISTIAN CHURCH IN ETHICAL PERSPECTIVE

The churches of Conservative Christianity, of whatever denomination, believe themselves to have been brought into being and empowered by God through the work of the incarnate Son of God, Jesus Christ, whose message and example of love they embrace wholeheartedly. That being so, it seems entirely appropriate to expect them to see themselves first and foremost as continuing the ethical work of loving transformation begun by Jesus. In all my research and personal experience, this is not what I have found. Loving, ethical action is certainly seen as an essential feature of the Christian life in these churches but not as their main business. Worship and belief are treated as the main business of the church and as the primary duty of those who believe in and love their Lord, whatever claims may be made to the contrary. I have often been asked by Christians where I worship but never once have I been asked what humane projects I actively support. When a national or international disaster strikes it is the Islamic Gift of the Givers organization that swings into action from my country and receives my contributions, not

22. Blaisdell, "I'm not so sure," 3–7.

any church organization, though I know there are plenty of small-scale and very admirable charitable projects in many of them, maybe in all.

Of course it is valid for Christians to rejoice at and express the deepest gratitude for the blessings they experience as coming from the Lord of perfect goodness and unfailing love. Of course it is valid to celebrate these blessings in word, music, gesture and architecture, and to cherish the rituals the church provides for life's great events of birth, marriage and death, but should these things have priority in the Jesus movement, when his priority was loving service of such unforgettable power and beauty?

In attempting to understand this difference of priorities, with belief and worship having priority over ethical practice, even though such practice is always required of church members, my proposed explanation is once more that it results from the way the early church changed in basic character from a Jewish movement of loving action started by Jesus into a Gentile movement of supernaturally oriented belief and worship, based on its unfolding convictions about God, Christ and salvation. This explanation in no way ignores or under-estimates the innumerable acts of love, kindness, courage and service by vast numbers of Conservative Christians down the centuries, but it does make me deeply lament the erosion of the massive potential for world-changing good that Jesus embodied, taught, lived by and died for, a power for immense good which ensured that even his terrible death could not defeat it but gave it new life at the first Easter.

In viewing what I find in the churches in ethical perspective as fairly and thoroughly as I can, the verdict is thus a mixed one, with very great good alongside a certain important deficit of it, and, alas, some features that are surely wrong, even gravely wrong and in urgent need of correction. Ethically valuable and important are at least the following: embracing love as governing moral value, supported by justice and truth; devotion to Christ and a God of love and goodness; compassion and kindness; love of the Bible as means of inspiration and guidance; a noble record of courageous support for political justice; and beautiful music, singing, words and architecture.

Not yet ethically good enough, in my judgment, is attention to macro-ethical problems like poverty, the endangered environment, unfair discrimination, sexual abuse, tyranny and violence; insufficient open-mindedness in the quest for truth wherever it is to be found; the courage to heed the results of two centuries and more of devoted, judicious and highly informed, critical study of the Bible, and of religion in general. Related to this shortcoming is the inadequate teaching ministry of the churches, which leaves most of the faithful and even some of the clergy ignorant of vitally important new knowledge about Christianity, the Bible and the other faiths; also uncritical adherence to the wording of Creeds that never even mention the ethical duties of a follower of Christ, or even love itself, let alone prioritizing them as he did. Also ethically problematic are Creeds that perpetuate the totally obsolete cosmology of a heaven somewhere above and a hell somewhere below, besides encouraging continued acceptance by some believers of the horrific and unethical doctrine of eternal torment in hell.

Morally wrong and deeply harmful as judged by ethical values that Christianity itself enjoins are the following wherever they still occur in the churches: imputing to Christ and to God anything that is unloving, unfair, untrue and cruel; a cruelly and unjustly exclusive doctrine of revelation and salvation; dogmatic insistence on any belief which cannot be true; authoritarianism and its consequence of dependency, which prevents the fullness of life for all people that the Gospel itself promises; in effect declaring that what the church or the Pope say the Bible says is what God says; and lastly every trace of unfair discrimination, above all that which victimizes anybody for things they cannot help or change like their gender, skin colour, basic sexual nature and religious heritage. In short, we have in the churches of Conservative Christianity a faith tradition that is in some very important respects blinkered and at times even blind, that is not living up enough to the potential for global good of its founder's message, example and way, but is also to be cherished and valued for so much in it that is ethically and spiritually good.

Arising from this and the previous chapter there is an important question that must now be put and then answered as best I can. It is based on my first-hand knowledge of the fine ethical qualities of all the evangelicals and fundamentalists I have known. They are women and men of strong moral principle, honest, caring and deeply sincere. Some of them are intellectually brilliant and highly educated in theology and biblical studies. Why, then, do they hold so strongly to beliefs and practices we have now seen to be so deeply, and at times fatally, ethically flawed? People like these want to be just as honest to goodness as I do, some much more so.

In facing this question and especially in offering my answer to it, I am aware that I might seem to be claiming some sort of moral and intellectual superiority. This I am most certainly not claiming or assuming. What I offer in the following pages comes from part 1 of this book, where it is made abundantly clear that I am the recipient and presenter, and not the author of that material. What I manifest here is not conceit or arrogance, but gratitude for what I have been given by others over most of my life, combined with a deep sense that I have a moral responsibility to goodness and to all Christians to offer an answer to the question presented in the paragraph above. Moreover, in putting the question and offering an answer, I do so with my own involvement in Conservative Christianity in my younger days foremost in my mind.

WHY DEEPLY ETHICAL CONSERVATIVE CHRISTIANS HOLD UNETHICAL BELIEFS

It is just not possible to be dishonest to goodness, but it is possible to be entirely and sincerely unaware that what one believes is, in fact, not the truth at all, and is neither fair nor loving. I know this from my dreadful boyhood judgment of gay people. From my peers I had absorbed the shameful notion that gay men—I had never then heard of lesbian women—were dangerous and wicked, apt to prey on little boys. When later contacts with people who knew better rescued me from that deeply unethical prejudice, I could shake off every vestige of it. So I know that a poorly informed, uncritical context can make otherwise good people, and I really was trying to be a good person, believe things that are just not so, and continue to believe them until they are exposed to the truth by a different context and rescued from the unkind and unjust results of their unwitting error.

In the next pages I offer material that shows a parallel between my early wrong beliefs about gay people and especially the context that caused them, and—though far less disturbing—the beliefs of Conservative Christians, like my younger self, and the context that makes them continue to believe them with great but, so the evidence shows, sometimes misplaced sincerity.

The new knowledge about religion and ethics that was presented in chapters 5 and 6 lets those who take it to heart understand what it is about Conservative Christianity that keeps its adherents, deeply sincere and good people that they are, unaware of the serious ethical problems identified earlier in this chapter. That material concerns the understanding of the world's religious and moral traditions that is now available. In my personal experience of Conservative Christians, their worship and their studies, and in my research into their writings, I have found very little real understanding of that new knowledge, and even less evidence of sustained, personal contact with people of other faiths and none.

The first part of this new knowledge comes from the great stages in the history of religion and ethics, which Lloyd Geering has helpfully called the ethnic, trans-ethnic and global types, as we saw in part I. Two insights from this source are relevant here. First, Conservative Christianity is post-ethnic, but it is not global in the consciousness it inculcates. Its conceptual horizons are far broader than those of ethnic faiths, past and present, but they are also much narrower than the multi-cultural world-view of Liberal Christianity and especially narrower than the kind of all-encompassing, global consciousness encouraged by Progressive Christianity, and by open-minded, informed secularists.

When the trans-ethnic faiths arose it was impossible for any of their members to be well informed about, let alone appreciate, the other faiths of that kind, with the exception of those in China, namely Taoism, Confucianism and Buddhism, which were accessible to one another in that land. Real awareness of other trans-ethnic faiths like Hinduism was otherwise just not possible for people like the classical Hebrew prophets, because of the immense geographical, political and cultural separations involved. Nor was it possible for Jesus and Muhammad to be knowledgeable about Buddhism and Taoism, or Plato and Aristotle, for the same reason.

The second way in which our new understanding of the trans-ethnic faiths explains the problem being addressed in this section flows from the first one. Nothing could be more natural and contextually justified than for each of these faiths to be convinced of its ethical and spiritual superiority over other belief-systems, given that the only ones known to the founders and members of these faiths were ethnic, and as such were seen as ethically too restricted. No wonder St Paul could declare that in Christ there is neither Jew nor Greek, and so on. In short, a sense that one's own faith tradition, and it alone, provides the truth about reality and our human destiny, is exactly what is to be expected in a trans-ethnic faith.

Eric Abbot's *Flatland*, together with what we now know about trans-ethnic faiths, and about the stages of personal ethical and spiritual development, is the next source of illumination about why Conservative Christians, like my younger self, remain so unaware of, or at least unperturbed by, the ethical problems in their beliefs that others perceive. Those problems are simply not visible to them. Because of the naturally limited nature of their consciousness, Abbot's work enables us to see ethnic faiths as Lineland faiths because of their confinement to single cultures, and to see a trans-ethnic faith like Conservative Christianity as a Flatland faith, because its naturally limited vision prevents an awareness of the realities that Liberal Christians have come to recognize and accept. These would qualify Liberal Christianity as three-dimensional in Abbot's terms. By definition, limitations in the range of our awareness prevent us from knowing and understanding the bigger picture beyond that range.

The connection between what has just been explained and the stages of personal ethical and spiritual growth is easy to make. Trans-ethnic faiths are by their nature conformist and they require trusting obedience by the faithful. That is what we would logically expect of a faith that is understandably sure of its own rightness and of what it sees as its superior knowledge of ultimate truths. The natural response to convictions of this kind is to accept and conform to them, giving such a faith a strongly cohesive character.

We can see this accepting character most clearly in biblical fundamentalists and in conservative evangelicals. So convinced are they that, without belief in Jesus as the only savior, people are eternally lost, that they will devote their lives to mission and evangelism, never questioning whether such a belief could really be true and ethical.

James Fowler defines this as the third stage of personal spiritual development. Among many other evangelicals who respond positively to developments like the rise of science and human rights movements, we can discern the beginnings of the presence of Fowler's fourth stage, which is marked by a more questioning orientation. An example would be sophisticated evangelical biblical scholars who reject the notion that the New Testament requires that women be subservient to men. This leads to a lessening, but not a loss, of the conformist character of trans-ethnic faiths.

Much the same is to be seen in connection with the ethics of trans-ethnic faiths, whose moral teachings, like the Ten Commandments and the Sermon on the Mount, are embraced and practiced with great personal integrity. As we saw earlier in these chapters about Conservative Christianity, such an ethic, valuable though it is, tends to focus on inter-personal ethics, or micro-ethics, in Deon Rossouw's terms. This is especially evident among the most conservative of such believers, but a concern for structural ethics among evangelicals moving to, or towards, stage four, is evident in their meso-ethical questioning and probing of issues regarded as fixed and sacrosanct by stage-three believers. Accepting the equality of women and men has already been mentioned as an example.

An equal or even greater concern with macro-ethical problems, like the moral status of contemporary capitalism, the environment, or the need to work with people of any faith or none on these problems, strikes me as requiring Scott and Harker's fifth level of moral growth, and that is not easy to achieve in a trans-ethnic faith because its very nature is to be very inward-looking, sure that what it deeply believes is the supreme truth which has been given to it. When you believe that all the ethical guidance you need is to be found in the Ten Commandments and Jesus's command to love your neighbor as yourself, it can very easily follow that structural evils and issues like animal rights will not even be recognized as evils by good people in trans-ethnic faiths.

The naturally inward-looking character of these faiths also means that there is unlikely to be much great concern with what the outside world is revealing about religion and ethics. Here we have a further source of illumination about why such morally admirable and often also highly educated and brilliant conservatives are so deeply committed to beliefs we have seen to be unethical. The illumination comes from Wilfred Cantwell Smith, Noam Chomsky and Gottlob Frege. My contact over the past few decades with Conservative Christianity has consistently shown me little and even no awareness of the work of Smith about the difference between faith and Christianity's cumulative tradition of beliefs, doctrines, Scriptures, and Creeds; and I have never found any awareness of what we can learn from Frege about the difference between the meaning and reference of the word "God," or from Chomsky about deep and surface structures. The result is a spiritual and ethical condition of too much acceptance and too little critical and creative thinking about what it means to be a Christian in our time.

Then there is what Battson and Ventiss show us about the three types of religious orientation, calling them the intrinsic, extrinsic and quest orientations, as presented in chapter 6. I think it is clear that a trans-ethnic faith is not an ideal place for the quest orientation, with its persistent probing and questioning of received ideas. But it is fertile ground for the intrinsic believer who finds there the joyous assurance of salvation, and also for the extrinsic member who is drawn by the fellowship, and sometimes by the prospect of financial support or a marriage partner.

The remaining source of insight into why Conservative Christians, fundamentalists most of all, continue to believe as they do is the most important one. It relates directly to the immense love of the Bible that is such a defining feature of their faith. This source of insight is today's revolutionary knowledge of the extent to which the Bible is indeed a human book. No matter how much we may still discern a divine influence in and behind Scripture, it was subject in its creation to cultural and historical conditioning, as well as to the natural limitations to which all of us are subject. I have repeatedly found insufficient or even no knowledge of this hugely important development in their circles and writings, even in the work of scholars for whose moral quality and immense erudition I have the greatest respect. Even there I find a seeming inability to see that a deeply ethical, biblical revolution has happened; an inability that is a barrier to greater ethical discernment of the ethics of the Bible and of traditional Christianity, and is preventing these wonderfully good people from experiencing the marvellous liberation of this revolution.

The conclusion to which this section points is that by its nature as a trans-ethnic faith, Conservative Christianity's basic character is inward-looking in a self-perpetuating way, most strongly so among biblical fundamentalists, but still strong among even the most educated and more liberal evangelicals. This gives it great durability, but denies it the larger, critical and creative consciousness needed since the rise of science and the European Enlightenment, which is absolutely essential today. The result is unawareness, through no personal fault, of the serious ethical problems I presented earlier in this chapter.

Evaluated as fairly as I can on the basis of widely shared, appropriate ethical norms, and above all by the norm of perfect goodness, too many of the very influential beliefs and practices of Conservative Christianity prove too flawed to merit continued acceptance by those of us who commit ourselves to those norms. This judgment is what has given rise to the gradual emergence of Liberal Christianity over the past few centuries. Conservatives and liberals share faith in a God of love but understand the divine very differently in some fundamental respects; they share a commitment to Jesus of Nazareth but differ in what they regard as the facts about him, apart from agreeing about when and where he lived, that he was crucified as a young man, and that a new religious movement grew from his impact after and because of the first Easter. These two parts of Christianity obviously also share the same Bible, though Roman Catholics accept in their form of the Old Testament the collection of books known by other churches as the Apocrypha, but the two understand its nature and use it differently. Also shared is a set of central ethical values, above all love, compassion, justice and truth, but the two forms of Christianity do not always agree about how these values must be practiced. With these contrasts in mind we can now assess the liberal side.

Chapter 9

Essentials of Liberal Christianity

LIBERAL CHRISTIANITY GAVE ME a spiritual home when I could no longer accept the conservative beliefs of my youth, until it too became a problematic part of my spiritual history. So I look back on and study it today with a mixture of gratitude, sadness and great admiration for its important qualities and achievements. The present chapter gives an account of what I see as nine defining liberal characteristics, based on that erstwhile experience as a liberal and on well-known authorities about it. All nine of the characteristics of the movement match my own liberalism, more or less closely. Then in the next chapter I consider its strengths and weakness, just as I did for Conservative Christianity, ending with my judgment about it both as a source of religious truth and as a force for good in the world.

The first of my nine characteristics concerns the words liberal and liberation, signifying freedom from the grip of tradition that is applied to the beliefs, doctrines, ethics and practices of Conservative Christianity and the wider society. A revealing fact about Liberal Christianity is that it emerged in the revolutionary, new world of free thinking, new knowledge, modern philosophy, political revolutions in France and America, literary and artistic freedom of expression, new methods of enquiry, and somewhat later also the important liberation movements from racial, gender and other oppressions.

These intellectual and political revolutions have roots in the Renaissance, gained impetus from the Protestant Reformation, and achieved their fullest expression from about 1700 in the Enlightenment, and afterwards.[1]

---

1. Geering, *Faith's New Age*, 66–91; Miller, *Case for Liberal Christianity*, and "Liberalism," 324–25.

Among the specific developments that had the greatest influence in giving rise to Liberal Christianity were the new cosmology and methods of scientific and historical enquiry; Kant's highly influential arguments against the belief that metaphysical certainties are possible, a belief vital to all religions that claim to furnish knowledge of a supernatural order of realities; geological discoveries indicating a very old earth; and of course evolution.

Turning now from the historical context to Liberal Christianity itself, in the churches, especially the Protestant ones, there emerged from about the late 1700s thinkers who responded positively to these liberating developments, revealing an openness of mind and great moral courage in doing so amidst a powerful ecclesial world of faithfulness to tradition that did not look with much favor on challenges to its beliefs and authority. Foremost among them remains Friedrich Schleiermacher who has already been extensively discussed in this book; others in the German liberal tradition include Albrecht Ritschl, Albert Schweitzer, Dietrich Bonhoeffer, Hans Küng, and in some aspects of his work the important Catholic theologian Karl Rahner. Those in the English-speaking world include Paul Tillich, who moved to America from his native Germany before World War II, John Cobb and Schubert Ogden in process theology; the earlier John Hick, Keith Ward, Ursula King, and Bishop David Jenkins in England; and in South Africa, John de Gruchy, Ron Nicolson, Wentzel van Huysteen, and others. John Robinson, the later John Hick, Rosemary Radford Ruether, Don Cupitt, Lloyd Geering, and arguably also the later Keith Ward, could be seen as having moved from an earlier liberalism to radical Christian thinking.

As I experienced and studied Liberal Christianity, it arises when the experience of the Christian life as a truly liberated life engages positively with the revolutionary developments of the period since about 1600, chiefly science, of which Whitehead's book *Science in the Modern World,* first published in 1926, gives a superb account. Loving and serving the God of love in Christ is then experienced above all not as submission to an almighty ruler but as perfect freedom, in the words of a well-known prayer; freedom from alienation and for love and fellowship, from unconcern and even hardness of heart to generosity of spirit and action; from self-centeredness to concern for others; from a sense of discontent to the deepest sense of well-being; and certainly also as liberty to think afresh about the meaning of Christian faith in a world very unlike that of pre-modern and especially biblical times.

In my own days as a liberal Christian I once described it to a troubled, conservative theology student as an experience of grace in search of a conceptuality worthy of itself, revealing thereby the influence of Schleiermacher, in whose systematic theology grace is a central conceptual and spiritual reality.² I found in Liberal Christianity a freedom of spirit and mind to create new understandings of the teachings of Scripture and the Creeds, coupled with membership of the church and respect for tradition but not subservience to them.

In the work and lives of prominent exponents, eight further characteristics of Liberal Christianity can be detected, noting that there is also considerable variation among liberals in how far they go in questioning traditional doctrinal understandings and church practices. The first of these further characteristics, the second one of my total of nine, is rejection of dogmatism, especially exclusivist dogma, in favor of the conviction that doctrines cannot be final statements of something as mysterious and transcendent as the divine. I would even contend that the very logic of the liberal orientation, with its sense of freedom and creative opportunity, militates against doctrinal fixity.³ For example, while there is no need for further work about the date of the Council of Constantinople which formulated the Nicene Creed, which is about as settled as anything in church history, for liberals things are very different with anything that is found to be as endlessly rich and important as the divine. The impact of Kant's critique in the late 1700s of claims to possess metaphysical knowledge has struck liberal Christian thinkers as spelling the end of metaphysical dogmatism, just as it helped Schleiermacher move the basis of faith from religious thought to religious experience.

The third characteristic is thus the importance liberals attach to personal experience and feeling in their faith, provided it is informed by and subject to rational scrutiny. Behind Schleiermacher in this regard is the influence of Romanticism, much in the air when he wrote the first edition of the *Speeches* in 1799. Foreshadowed in the work of Jean Jacques Rousseau and Blaise Pascal with their emphasis on feeling, in Germany and elsewhere at the time of Schleiermacher, Romanticism numbered some of its greatest writers, like Schiller and Goethe.⁴ To prize feeling in their way is also to prize critically informed experience as a guide to truth and values, an abiding feature of liberal Christian theologians, philosophers and church leaders, none perhaps more influential in deepening our understanding of religion as feeling than William James, as we saw in part I.

The fourth characteristic is creativity in developing new lines of thinking about the nature and content of faith. Even today, over two centuries since he first published his understanding of religion in the *Speeches*,

---

2. Schleiermacher, *Christian Faith*, 355-737.
3. Richmond, "Liberal Protestantism," 325-28.
4. Burkill, *Evolution*, 328-29.

Schleiermacher's work has about it a novelty of vision and expression that has scarcely been equalled. Other eminent examples of creative intellectual power are the systematic theology and related work of Paul Tillich with his interpretation of Christ as the bearer of the New Being, and that of John Hick, as revealed in his liberal years, about the problem of evil and the need to respond in new ways to the reality of religious pluralism.

Perhaps the most widely noted feature of liberal Christian thinkers, and the one that seems to trouble conservatives most, is the fifth one in my list of characteristics. This is their reinterpretation of traditional church teachings. A universalist view of salvation is an important indicator of the liberal position, as is the belief that the Bible is in significant measure human in its creation, and with this a non-propositional view of divine revelation. Instead of viewing divine revelation as something given in the propositions of Scripture, the non-propositional view holds that the biblical writers saw certain landmark *events*, like the Exodus and the crucifixion of Christ, as acts of God.[5] Other re-interpretations are a much larger concept of sin and evil than just its interpersonal, micro-ethical forms, coupled with serious misgivings and at times rejections of the doctrine of original sin and guilt; total dismissal of a literal hell; views of salvation that focused as much and even more on combatting the evils of this present life than on an afterlife; and most important of all, new interpretations of Christ and the God he proclaimed. To cite a well-known example of such attempts at theological creativity, in *Honest to God* over half a century ago John Robinson explored Paul Tillich's ideas about the divine as not "another Being at all," but rather as "the infinite and inexhaustible depth and ground of all being," and proposed the concept of Jesus as "the man for others."[6]

In the sixth place I mention the practical importance attached by liberals to the ethical dimension of religion.[7] In Schleiermacher's religious and theological works this is not as evident as it is in that of later liberals like William Temple, Dietrich Bonhoeffer, and John A.T. Robinson,[8] but it was extremely important as part of his total output from his earliest writings onward, though treated separately from doctrinal writings, as I explained earlier in this book.

I judge the emergence of long suppressed women's voices in theology and some of the churches as the most important example of this liberal

---

5. Hick, *Philosophy of Religion*, 64–67.
6. Robinson, *Honest to God*, 46, 64.
7. Miller, *Case for Liberal Christianity*, 324–25.
8. See Craig, *Social Concern*; Bonhoeffer, *Ethics*; Robinson, *Christian Morals Today*.

concern with social ethics and liberation from domination, now certainly shared by many evangelicals. Such a liberation is in itself a huge ethical achievement, and so are the highly creative and critical works of women theologians like those mentioned in part I, not least in exposing patriarchy in the church's traditional, masculinist concepts of God but in church life as well.

In the seventh place, a movement with liberation from all that stifles and suppresses as a hallmark cannot fail to challenge and overcome problems like sexism, racism and homophobia in church and society. While all three outrages continue to plague our existence, parts of church life included, racism in the apartheid period and before the civil rights movement in the USA has probably been the most vicious. All of us who fought apartheid as Christians know that the lead was mostly taken by liberals in many denominations, with conservative and especially fundamentalist Christians slow to join the struggle. How often in those dark years we heard the conservative mantra that the business of the church was saving souls, not "meddling" in politics!

Not surprisingly, the eighth characteristic of the liberal trend is its support for practical changes in church life, like acceptance of divorce and the re-marriage of divorced people in church; the equal place of women and men in church life and in its ministries; rejection of ecclesial segregation; also acceptance of differences in sexual orientation and practice, same-sex marriage, and liturgical renewal.

One small but telling example of changes in worship concerns the well-known hymn, "All things bright and beautiful." In my boyhood it included a verse saying, "The rich man in his garden, the poor man at his gate, God made them high and lowly, and gave them their estate," as I recall. Recent versions rightly omit that verse because it is incompatible with divine love and justice. One can only wonder what harm generations of worshippers suffered by being encouraged to believe that disparities, at times gross, between wealth and poverty are the will of God and thus not to be challenged.

The ninth and last of my characterizations is the positive view of liberals about other faiths, a far cry from the exclusivist, conservative view of them as unable to lead to salvation in their own right, and therefore to be opposed and their members won lovingly for Christ. There are both milder and more radical forms of this positive view of the other faiths. The milder view affirms all that is good and true in them but holds that salvation is still made possible only because of Christ. This has been called an inclusivist view, in the sense that Christ's saving work is held to include all cultures and to be able to work through them, even though their members are not aware of it. The radical view regards all of them as valid pathways to the greatest good that religions variously offer, probably best known now in John Hick's pluralist interpretation of religion.[9]

In my student days and early academic career liberal theology and practice were a powerful presence in the church, probably the most powerful in the so-called mainline Protestant orientations. Now it is much less of a force, overshadowed in many parts of the church by conservatism, particularly in the USA. Why has this happened? I very much doubt that many theological liberals become evangelicals and certainly not fundamentalists. Something else is therefore at work. The critique in the next chapter will reveal a possible answer, with my personal experience of the problem reserved for part III.

---

9. Hick, *Problems of Religious Pluralism*, 28-45; see also D'Costa, *Christian Uniqueness*.

Chapter 10

An Ethical Critique of Liberal Christianity

ETHICAL STRENGTHS

IN THIS CHAPTER I first offer my judgment of what I found lastingly valuable about my liberal faith and that of others when assessed ethically, and then I identify what I see as ethically problematic.

The typical liberal willingness to be critically open to truth wherever it can be found, both inside the Christian tradition and outside, and to counter authoritarianism in religion and elsewhere, strikes me as ethically outstanding because it betokens a commitment to truth-finding that is richer and more fruitful than the adherence to tradition so evident in Conservative Christianity. So too is the creativity of seeking and proposing new and at times very radical interpretations of the faith, like Hick's pluralistic affirmation of the other religions, in what I have called the Eighth Day of Creation.

The moral courage that such openness of mind at times requires is another great good. After publishing the *Speeches* in 1799, Schleiermacher earned the wrath of his church authorities in the person of Court Preacher Sack, who wrote him an acid letter accusing him of pantheism and of associating with people "of dubious principles and morality."[1] John Hick and Lloyd Geering both faced and fortunately survived heresy charges and even trials for their views.[2] The first Anglican bishop of my home diocese, John William Colenso (1814–1883), was not so fortunate, for his church drove

1. Prozesky, "Young Schleiermacher," 6.
2. Geering, *Wrestling with God*, 157-74.

him into exclusion for views about the Bible that would today be commonplace even in the ranks of some evangelical theologians and biblical scholars, like disputing the Mosaic authorship of the Pentateuch.[3] Nearer our own time Hans Küng was severely punished by his Catholic church for questioning papal infallibility.[4]

Next, and in my view supremely important, is the acceptance by liberals of the unbounded nature of the good, if often implicitly rather than explicitly. This principle means that literally nothing is exempt from the light and power of goodness, leading where necessary to changes for the better. What else is rejection of gender discrimination and denouncing the attempt to defend racism on biblical grounds but a denunciation of injustice, and therefore the appeal to ethical values as having higher authority than church teaching and practice, indeed as having the highest authority? My question here is whether Liberal Christianity takes this critical and creative challenge far enough, and my answer is given in my identification of Christian liberalism's shortcomings in the next section.

Also admirable is the theological creativity of Christian liberals. When questions arise for them about the adequacy of traditional beliefs, their typical response is to explore new and more credible alternatives, giving liberalism a distinctly positive character. Paul Tillich's ideas about God as the ground of being, and of faith as the state of being grasped by an ultimate concern is well-known, as are the immensely important feminist theologies that challenge patriarchy in Christian belief and practice. A minor example from my own work as a liberal is my advocacy of a relativist view of doctrine in the christology conference during John Hick's visit to the former University of Natal, which I mentioned in part I.

All the liberal theologians I have known or studied are loyal to their churches, even those who have had to suffer official steps to counter them, like heresy trials. Loyalty of this kind is a moral virtue, so it must also be admired. But loyalty can be problematic. That happens when it gets in the way of ethical progress or involves support for anything that is morally questionable, or worse. I know of and have a few times encountered conservative Christians who were steadfast in their loyalty to churches that defended and even commended apartheid; I know of no liberal who knowingly remained loyal to churches whose beliefs and practices involved ethical shortcomings like that.

Here I feel obliged to pose a sensitive question: is liberal theology sufficiently aware of the problems identified in part II, and if so, sufficiently

---

3. Guy, *Heretic*.
4. Küng, *Infallible?*

An Ethical Critique of Liberal Christianity

committed to take up the prophetic duty to challenge and change them in their churches? I must confess that in my own liberal days I was not sufficiently aware of them, which brings me to my judgment about what I see as ethically problematic in the liberal movement, with myself as a liberal believer as my main example.

ETHICAL PROBLEMS IN LIBERAL CHRISTIANITY

My answer to the question just posed is that the admirable ethical and intellectual commitment of liberalism does not go far enough in response to certain very important realities of the wider, contemporary world. These realities were either absent in the world in which the movement began and gathered momentum, or so remote as to have little or no effect, until that changed in the mid-twentieth century. The recent, new realities I have in mind are direct, sustained contact with people of other faiths, ethical secularism, and new knowledge about religion and ethics globally, of the kind outlined in chapters 5 and 6.

Turning first to religious pluralism, my criticism here is directed at the inclusivist view evidently held by a good many liberals and certainly by me in my years as a liberal believer. While always respectful of what is judged good and true in other belief-systems and asserting, admirably, that salvation is universal, inclusivism still asserts or at least logically implies that in some way Christian truth is salvifically truer than theirs, with Jesus Christ indeed the only savior, whose atoning work somehow brings about the salvation of those outside the Christian faith, even though they do not know it. As I became directly aware of the deep faith and fine values of Buddhist, Hindu and Muslim friends and colleagues in other faiths, and in people like Gandhi, a direct awareness which apartheid had made difficult and even impossible earlier in my life, it became clear to me that there was something very wrong with the inclusivist view. It implied that their beliefs were in fact flawed and inadequate in themselves because they did not include Christ and his saving work, seen by these Christians as God-given. The unintended patronizing and subtle disrespect involved became obvious and must count as falling short of the best ethical standards. While the inclusivist view of other faiths is less morally flawed than the exclusivist doctrine of most conservatives, it still involves the grave problem of believing in a God of perfect goodness and love who bestows the precious knowledge of saving truth in Christ on just one strand of the world's people. It is thus not in the least surprising that John Hick once told me that his own adoption of a pluralist view of the religions, as all having salvific power, came with and from his direct experience in Birmingham of people of other faiths, such as people of the Sikh faith, which he describes in one of his books.[5]

I would extend this living encounter with people outside Christianity to secularism and the reality of its very rich ethic, its sophisticated philosophies and often devastating critique of the theism of conservative Christianity, as discussed in part I. Great goodness is not the preserve of theistic religion or of any religion, a verifiable reality that, to my mind, must drive the liberal willingness to re-think the concept of God much more radically than anything I have seen hitherto, among liberals, as I propose in part III.

Chapters 5 and 6 set out the new knowledge that has become available about the nature of who we are, where we are, how we think, know and believe, what ethics is all about and how best to understand religion as a global phenomenon. In my liberal days I had not yet discovered, and thus not yet taken these discoveries to heart, as I was to do when researching my first book. This new knowledge shows, when faced openly and without religious pre-suppositions or by setting them aside, that religion in its entirety can be explained naturalistically as a human, cultural creation that does not require, or even strongly imply, the existence of spiritual beings, or just one supreme spiritual being, to account for its presence on earth. The mere possibility, let alone reality, of a valid, naturalistic account of religion seems to me to make unavoidable the conclusion that being honest to goodness calls for a post-liberal interpretation of what Jesus pioneered and what the concept of God means.

Overall then, the evidence available to me makes me see Liberal Christianity as very valuable both ethically and spiritually in freeing Christianity of the doctrinal restrictiveness of its older, bigger, conservative sibling, and also for moving significantly away from the fatal ethical and conceptual shortcomings of that sibling, but still as an incomplete liberation from the ethical problems in question. To my mind its very liberating tendency, when placed explicitly and forthrightly under the spotlight, or better still, the searchlight, of great goodness, drives it to the spiritual and ethical radicalism that the world badly needs, a contention that generates a question I must now put.

WHY DOES LIBERAL CHRISTIANITY ENDURE?

The question addressed in this last section of the chapter is why so many Liberal Christians remain liberals, when some of us former liberals, perhaps many of us, have moved to a radical spiritual vision and practice, like that

---

5. Hick, *God Has Many Names*, 4–5.

of Progressive Christianity, or into what I call religious humanism, and even into secularism. Why, then, does Liberal Christianity endure, and may even be growing, as Martyn Percy has contended,[6] when even its reformulated beliefs like universal salvation and gender-inclusive ways of thinking about God are ethically and logically flawed, as this chapter has shown? This question is similar to my question at the end of chapter 8, about why such morally good people as the Conservative Christians I have known continue with beliefs I showed in that chapter to be fatally problematic. The liberals I have known are also deeply ethical people, highly intelligent and probably even more academically sophisticated than most conservatives.

Locating Liberal Christianity historically helps us to the answer. It emerged from the older belief-system of traditional Christianity during and following the rise of modern knowledge and the European Enlightenment. From these revolutionary developments in the surrounding culture of Europe, pioneering liberals like Schleiermacher saw the need to adapt some of their inherited teachings, most notably their view of Scripture and how to interpret it. Other beliefs were retained largely unchanged: Christ remains the savior but saves everybody, even using other religions; God is still the God of the Abrahamic tradition but as revealed by Christ, and is not Allah and certainly not Brahman; and atheism has little that is doctrinally important to teach Christians.

This means that while Liberal Christianity is not classifiable as what Geering calls a secular, global ethic and spirituality, mostly because it does not adequately confront the problems of its concept of God, it has nonetheless moved well away from its trans-ethnic roots, and it is those roots that explain why it endures and may even be growing.

Three features of that inheritance are operative. The most powerful is the loving community of fellow Christians that liberals experience, with its strong ethic, micro-ethical though it tends largely to be. We humans have a deep need to belong to something where we can feel at home and accepted; religious communities of all kinds do that, winning and keeping the loyalty of those who experience that blessing. It is a blessing that I remember with great nostalgia myself, so I understand its appeal only too well.

Next, there is the appeal and beauty of worship. Ritual is very powerful in itself, even when it is an almost solitary thing, as in sacramental confession before a priest. Congregational worship, with its prayers, music, candles, flowers, singing and instructive sermons, conducted in imposing church buildings, is thus another powerful factor in retaining the membership of

---

6. Percy, *Why Liberal Churches*.

liberals, even those who may listen somewhat skeptically to the sermons and Bible readings they hear in church.

The third factor to bear in mind applies more to liberal priests and ministers than to lay people. Few congregations are made up mostly of fellow liberals. Many and at times most members are conservatives and some are fundamentalists. In my experience they do not take kindly to signs that their leaders believe differently. I recall being angrily challenged by such people after delivering a course about Christianity today, with plenty of liberalism in it, done at the invitation of a former dean of the cathedral I was then attending. I was discussing the humanity of Jesus and ventured the thought that as a person of his time, and being truly human, he would not have known about cancer and certainly not how to treat it. One of those who was angered by what I was saying leapt up and loudly denounced it with the words, "But he was God!"

I was an academic and faced no possibility of serious consequences for my utterances in that course. A serving priest or minister of liberal views is in a very different position. Disgruntled conservative members of the congregation can gather support to oppose and even get rid of them, calling on the authority and power of their church leaders to act against what they see as a betrayal of the faith. I mentioned this reality above in connection with Hick, Geering and Colenso.

These three factors are enough to explain why churches that continue, in so many ways of belief, worship and organization, to be trans-ethnic, nonetheless retain the loyalty of their liberal members, whose minds and values have moved beyond that kind of faith. The result is too little exposure to the newer developments that have made former liberals like me and others move away to seek a Christianity that is truly global. The most powerful of these new developments, in my experience, are personal encounters with people of other faiths and secularists, and global ethics.

It is of course the case that Conservative and Liberal Christians also have contact with Hindus, Buddhists, atheists and others, but do not find the experience a challenge to their beliefs. So the question here is why some of us react so differently. I see here a need for further research into the psychology of religion, so all I have now is a few suggestions based on the research reported in chapters 5 and 6 and on my own experience.

One suggestion is that it takes the quest orientation identified by Battson and Ventiss to lead to the conviction that religious pluralism means the end of any remaining religious exclusivism.[7] By their very nature, people with this kind of mind are searchers, forever asking questions and seek-

---

7. Battson and Ventiss, *Religious Experience*.

ing new horizons of faith. More, however, is involved, and certainly was for me. It is the discovery that ethics must govern belief and not the other way around. I was led to this conviction by studies of global ethics and especially by direct, sustained encounters with people of other faiths and none. Great goodness just is a human, global universal. It is not the gift of Christianity or any other religion, or of all the religions. Knowing atheists of immense moral goodness and courage, as I do, ends forever for me any idea that religion is somehow inherently morally and philosophically superior to secularism. It is a discovery that opens the way to Fowler's fifth stage of spirituality, which was summarized in chapter 6 as a stage that only comes once there is a sense that life is more complex than it seemed at the previous stage. Instead of thinking on an either/or basis, the person thinks on a both/and basis and is open to the often very different views of other people. To my mind it must change your understanding of your Christian faith if you are indeed seeking to be honest to goodness. My understanding of that great change is set out in part III, which follows.

PART III

Progressive Christianity as an Ethical Faith and Practice

Chapter 11

Overview of a Goodness-based Faith

This third part of *Honest to Goodness* sets out a dream of what the Jesus movement can be as a force for immense good in the world. It does so on the basis of a prior question: what does goodness itself now require of all of us for whom it is our ultimate concern? My answer is that it requires every effort we can make to protect and enhance all that is already good in the world, and to transform all that is not good. That is what I believe it means to further the project begun by Jesus himself in our own time. For the traditional church, the resultant question now is whether it can serve this project rather than retard and even harm it, given the serious ethical problems identified in part II.

Part III is written with a powerful sense of being in the uplifting presence of an inexhaustible goodness, or blessing, in the idiom of religion, seeking to be as open as possible to its creative power, the self-same blessing that I now believe has encompassed my entire spiritual and ethical journey since boyhood. This final part of the book therefore rests upon and follows from all that was presented in parts I and II. It begins in this chapter with introductory considerations, building on them, in the next chapters, my proposals for an understanding of the great reality believers call God, of the other faiths, Jesus, salvation, the progressive church and the Bible.

The most important contention of this book must now be stated. *Supreme goodness is the only true foundation for faith and practice, and everything in Christianity, and every other faith and philosophy, must align with and serve it or lose moral depth, spiritual credibility, and power.* We saw earlier in this book that the deep structure of Conservative Christianity, which is its sense of and faith in the presence of an ultimate goodness that both transcends and envelopes us, is sound, but that some of its most important surface structures of belief and related practice are too gravely flawed to be retained. Therefore pioneering Christians, with a questing love of Jesus, of others and of truth in their hearts and minds, must now move onward in faith and informed creativity, through the doorway that is now open to an ever richer and deeper experience of this greatest blessing and the beliefs and practices it requires.

In this way, by centralizing and prioritizing its ethical dimension, serving and celebrating goodness, I believe that Christianity expresses its true identity. I want to assert with all the passion and evidence I can muster that what Jesus began is a superb, lived faith, strongly concerned with the needs of the present world and its people. But it needs to recover that beginning and find in it a way to a return from exile for people who are alienated by Conservative Christianity and left wanting by what is incomplete in Liberal Christianity. My own exile from church life has been a long and often lonely one. It was only when I moved, at about the turn of the millennium, from the study of comparative religion to comparative ethics, and then to a re-appraisal of religions as comprehensive value-systems first and foremost rather than belief-systems, that the first glimmer of a sunrise of possible return began to appear on the horizon.

As I pursued this changed angle of approach, a coherent, integrated pattern emerged, centered in a glowing, summoning reality that, in the words of a prayer I loved in my pre-exilic days and still cherish in memory, passes all understanding; and as I wrote these words the memory of a hymn came back for the first time in very many years: "The King of Love my Shepherd is, His goodness faileth never."

To qualify as Christian a movement must be Christ-filled; to be Christ-filled it must be God-filled in Christ's way; and to be God-filled in Christ's way it must know and cherish the experience of a sublime and all-surpassing goodness as the *ultimate context of our human existence*. No longer can we think and believe on the small scales of the Christian tradition hitherto, as if the ultimate meaning of things is to be found in just one cultural and historical strand, from just one of the world's regions, on one of the planets in the universe. Instead we must think and believe on a cosmic scale the way pioneered by Teilhard de Chardin in the previous century,[1] and recently by J.E. Schellenberg in his vision of evolutionary religion.[2]

Conservative Christianity understands the supreme goodness at its heart in the thought-forms of the eastern Mediterranean world of 2,000 and

---

1. King, *Spirit of Fire*; and "Teilhard de Chardin's Vision."
2. Schellenberg, *Evolutionary Religion*.

more years ago; it is time for a massive refreshment of vision and spirit, for transformation from bemusement by belief back to the values-based vision and practice of its founder. Part III seeks to meet these requirements in the following chapters fully and faithfully. The world with its many avoidable evils needs a far better activation of the reality Jesus reveals than it has ever had, a force for good more powerful and durable than ever the Kremlin and Washington DC, and certainly more powerful than the richest corporations. In such a situation, faith's chief concern must not be for comfort and security but for helping to save the world and its people from those avoidable evils in the power of the greatest goodness, on which we must now reflect in preparation for the chapters that follow.

REFLECTING AGAIN ON GOODNESS

The word "good" is our central term of approval for whatever we find fulfilling, meaningful and enjoyable, which we therefore seek to perpetuate because it has the greatest value for us. The enjoyment is at first purely physical, but in time we learn that there are other enjoyments of an intellectual, moral, aesthetic, social and spiritual kind, and so we extend and deepen our sense of the good. This is the subjective or personal justification of my appeal to this supreme reality as the basis of religion and of all other aspects of human culture. Such experiences can of course be delusional, so the cosmological or objective justification of basic religious experience is absolutely vital. My contention is that the cosmos, in my expanded, holistic conception of it, brings about developments that we humans, given our valorizing nature and our restless hunger for ever greater fulfilment, will find beneficial and call good, as set out in detail in chapter 5's section on the cosmos.

Illnesses and injuries heal, at least for those who survive them; droughts end sooner or later, at least for those they do not destroy; crops grow, rescues happen, friendships form, love quickens, goals are achieved, battles won. Much of these we now explain on the basis of science but for most of humanity's existence they were not understood at all, giving such beneficial happenings a profoundly mysterious character. As such, these events, and above all the power at work in them, would initially have no names. That is always the case with genuine novelty. So new ways have to be found of giving them expression in order to remember and communicate them. Improvisation and creativity are just as much part of our human nature as our sentience, though less basic, and they enable us to find words for the unknown on the model of whatever is similar in the things we do know and have already named.

Given the habit of the mind to project, nothing is more surprising than the rise of personal analogues for whatever makes animals multiply, rains fall, crops grow, injuries heal, and so on. As long as the purely provisional, metaphorical character of such naming is remembered, there is no problem. As the late I.T. Ramsey, the British philosopher of religion and bishop of half a century ago, so aptly remarked, God-talk is significant stuttering, but always just stuttering, as all acts of naming anything so deeply mysterious must be. They are never an identikit in words with exact similarity to the reality to which they refer.

A provident, beneficial environment or history is indeed mother-like, father-like or benignly king-like for those who benefit from it, and those who perish pen no hymns of praise. Trouble comes when we lose sight of the poetry of the deep, rich, strange beneficence we encounter, and take the metaphors too literally. That is a handy step for those who desire conformity and control but it is soul-destroying for many others.

There are of course countless experiences of goodness that hold no mystery for us any longer. We know why cold fronts arrive or welcome rains come. This in no way makes such beneficial events less valuable, but it can blind us to the fact that for most of humanity's existence on this planet, such events were the amazing, welcome arrivals of an unknown, mysterious, beneficial power, causing feelings of awe and wonder, and also immense relief and gratitude. And even now with our vastly expanded knowledge, we still ponder with awe and fascination just why the cosmos is what it is, its ultimate workings as tantalizing as ever, but not so mysterious that we cannot experience the blessings it brings.

For me with my love of astronomy, a similar, perhaps even richer, sense of wordless awe arises when I contemplate the starry heavens. It is not in the least diminished because science has revealed so much about the universe, or told us things like the fine-tuning of the Big Bang, black holes and the existence of earth-like exoplanets. The sheer, mind-baffling size of the cosmos and the marvellous beauty of the galaxies, the Horse Head nebula in Orion, or Saturn's gorgeous rings through my telescope, cause in me an experience that is mystical in the classic sense. I am speechless, marvelling at the ultimate good that there is this reality at all, and that I and all others are alive to glimpse it. How can we fail to be drawn speechlessly to something so wondrous? For some of us such events are so powerful that only silence and tears can do even minimal justice to them.

There is a very good reason why words fail us all at times like these. Caught into the experience, we are in touch with something that hugely surpasses our ability to fathom or put adequately or precisely into words. We are here in the domain of the soul, the innermost part of us which seeks meaning, depth, and the richest of values. In its encounter with that which causes wonder and awe, the soul's mother tongue is not philosophical or theological prose, or any literal use of words, but metaphor, poetry and song. These are the natural expressions of experiencing such great goodness, whatever forms it takes, but, as I have already emphasized, when it hardens into literal expressions and, worst of all, dogmas and cast-iron Creeds, its life drains away.

And that is the clue to the way Christianity must now understand its central theological beliefs and be free of the strangling effect of outdated doctrines. All but one of its theological beliefs belong at heart to the realm of poetry, metaphor and symbolism, not literal truths. The one exception is this: *there truly is a rich, ultimate reality, pervasively present and available in the universe and in human life, and it is truly, literally, supremely good.*

The convinced insider to Conservative Christianity and the hostile outsider are therefore both right and both wrong. Insiders are right to be convinced that their faith connects them with a genuine and wonderful reality, but wrong to insist that it is truly described by their concept of God and his supposedly saving actions, and by none other. The outsiders are right in their critique of that insistence, but wrong to assert that they have thereby put an end to Christianity or other such religions. Their true achievement is to help free the living heart of religious faith, in whatever tradition, for an effective, saving presence in our latest stage of faith.

Can the now dominantly conservative church, accepting this help from what Schleiermacher memorably called its cultured despisers, still serve Jesus, his magnificent project and the divine reality he embodied, or is too much of it, but by no means all, now a vast collection of Sunday gatherings of the kindly but also the fearful, the blinkered, the sometimes noisy and even blind? I believe it can so serve, because those gatherings too have in their hearts the presence of a goodness that surpasses everything else; and, admiring their loving ways, there are those progressive and liberal others who can perhaps be regarded as missionaries from their future.

So it is that I have come to dream of Christianity as goodness-based, Jesus-inspired, fallibly attested in human terms in Scripture, community-creating, ethically committed and action-orientated. Being a Christian is also the certainty, bequeathed by Jesus and his ongoing influence, and confirmed by our own experience, that our lives are enfolded, enhanced and enriched by a transforming power that we find inexhaustible in the many blessings it brings to our existence: inspiration, direction, help, protection, compassion, justice, truth, knowledge, moral wisdom, beauty and much, much more.

Conservative Christians see this goodness as the gift and presence of a supreme being they call God, who is perfectly loving and all-powerful, a God revealed and embodied, for most of them, exclusively, by Jesus Christ, and reliably testified in Scripture. The study of the various faiths shows that there are other ways of seeing that goodness. So long as it is treated for what it is, a poetic human way *among other valid ways* of trying to fathom something profoundly rich and mysterious, including wholly naturalistic ways, I see no problem about the belief that goodness has a personal character and power that far transcends our own.

There are other views of what it means to be a Christian than the one summarized above. Some say it is a matter of believing the teachings of the Bible. Some say it means belonging to a church and taking part in its rituals such as Baptism and Holy Communion. But when one asks those who give these answers why they believe what the Bible says, or practice the rituals of their churches, ultimately their response is that in or through them they encounter the loving impact of God in Christ, experiencing it in many kinds of beneficial effects, such as comfort, support, guidance, and hope. In other words, these answers rest on something else, something more basic, which I am calling the experience of a surpassing goodness, so those answers can hardly be the heart of the matter. This practical, life-changing power is a reality that a world disfigured by greed, violence, bigotry and needless suffering urgently needs, for goodness always enlightens, never misleads or deceives; it never diminishes but always invites and attracts by its power. And it never discriminates unfairly.

We are living through a revolution in Christianity. It can liberate people from the servitudes of the past for ethical and spiritual service. It transforms the concept of God from moral inadequacy into inspirational credibility. It frees Jesus and his project of loving service from exclusivist dogma, and the Bible from idolatrous misuse. It can free many millions of good Christians from bemusement by a non-Gospel for the really good news of a far richer Jesus-based faith. In doing so it can change believers from faith in obedience-mode to responsible spiritual and ethical creativity, and from a dependence epistemology to one that understands the modes and limits of our knowing. The revolution of faith we are undergoing gives us a Christianity that can indeed help save the world.

The deeply personal metatheology of this book is therefore what emerges from long, questing experiences of goodness, illuminated by rigorous engagement with all relevant and available new knowledge about the world's religions and Christianity in particular. What emerges is far too rich for any final definition and certainly too rich for any one person's interpretation, so it cries out for cooperative exploration and statement. What comes next in this book is therefore a gift to others with pioneer souls. It involves a highly creative conception of the role of the theologian and religious thinker, a view strongly endorsed by British theologian Martyn Percy when he writes that "theologians dig and excavate; they look for meanings below the obvious surfaces we encounter."[3] With these foundational considerations of my perspective on a future Christianity behind us, we can now engage with its most important conviction, the transcendent reality that embraces and shapes our existence.

---

3. Percy, *Future Shapes*, 131.

Chapter 12

Ultimacy, Perfect Goodness and the Concept of God

GROUNDWORK

THE WHOLLY HUMAN CONCEPT of a Heavenly Father or Sovereign Lord of the Universe comes from three sources: the widespread experience of a mysterious, profoundly beneficial power that continues to be known by countless numbers of people; secondly from the concepts already available in the cultures where it is current, and thirdly from the way the human brain projects the familiar to make sense of the mysterious by means of personal models, like Lord, King, Father and Mother. In Gottlob Frege's terms the word "God" *means* those personal models; while its *reference* is to the reality of what I am calling goodness, especially the richest and most powerful kind that comes to us unbidden in countless ways beyond our control or understanding.

In my opening chapter I explained that *Honest to Goodness* follows the medieval soteriology of Peter Abelard by accepting the view attributed to him that Christ saves through his moral influence. I contend that this means that moral goodness must be the principle that governs faith and indeed all else. *Honest to Goodness* also draws on a second medieval theologian, Anselm of Canterbury (c.1033–1109), taking up the principle in his famous *Proslogion* of 1079 that God must be "that than which no greater can even be conceived"—the ultimate, absolute pinnacle of reality and, Abelard would rightly add, of goodness.[1]

---

1. McGrath, *Christian Theology*, 34, 184.

My proposal is therefore that the most important and thus valuable of all realities be seen, fundamentally, as none other than *the creatively saving power of goodness that encompasses and can indwell all things*, embraced as the foundational reality of our existence; and further spoken of with whatever symbols and metaphors our cultures offer to deepen and enrich our sense of this evidently inexhaustible reality. The proposal certainly has behind it the long process of personal experience and research presented in part I but it also rests, objectively, on the massive, global evidence of humanity's moral experience of goodness, and indeed also of the evils that oppose it.

Whatever the three Abrahamic religions teach about our knowledge of God as coming from his acts of self-revelation, the experience involved always happens, like all our experience, *sub specie humanitatis*—under the conditioning influence of our make-up as human beings; and the most powerful factor in our make-up is our innate concern with lasting well-being, especially the most deeply satisfying and enjoyable kind. Therefore our fundamental concern will always be with whatever most promotes or hinders that innate desire, above all concern with whatever affects that desire unbidden, in ways beyond our control and understanding.

We humans also have the gift of high intelligence, so we do our best to reduce the mystery of whatever encompassing power affects us. That takes us into metaphysics. There our powers of comprehension are small in comparison with the magnitude of the unknown that seems beyond human investigation. The historical record shows that this limitation has not prevented humanity from proceeding undaunted, in the form of the many answers we find in the world's cultures, like the Kaggen of the San in the Kalahari Desert, Hinduism's Brahman, China's Tao, the Dreaming of Australia's First People, Mwari in Zimbabwe, and the personal God of the Abrahamic faiths.

As all Conservative Christians know, their faith teaches that the ultimate good is the gift of the Trinitarian God of perfect goodness who, they believe and declare, has supremely, uniquely and finally revealed himself in the incarnation of God the Son in Jesus of Nazareth, and in the gift of the Holy Spirit, as uniquely attested in Scripture. We have already seen that this doctrine cannot be correct on decisive ethical grounds of inclusive love and justice, because a God of perfect goodness would not bestow the priceless gift of saving knowledge, of such unsurpassable importance, on just one, favored strand of humanity, that of the Hebrew, Aramaic and Christian cultures.

Would a radically changed, Jesus-based concept of God be ethically acceptable, one that recognizes as human error all traces of unfair discrimination anywhere, theology included, understandable in conditions of cultural isolation and complete ignorance of the global map of faiths, but now untenable if ethical commitment is to govern faith? Let us explore an answer by proceeding step by step, starting with an analysis of the formal characteristics of the concept of a personal God. After that we shall consider whether such a radically changed concept of God can be affirmed and embraced as the truth.

According to my understanding, philosophical theology in Christianity specifies five formal attributes of the concept of God. A being or reality can only be a God if that being is the ultimate, supreme reality, as Anselm showed in his *Proslogion*; morally perfect; more important than anything else; the most valuable of realities; and perfectly loving the way Christ taught. This is however a very minimalist statement, so I want to enhance it with a much fuller one. In my book *A New Guide to the Debate about God*, I wrote the following about the Christian concept of God. That was before I moved the focus of my quest from religion to applied ethics, but even so, more than twenty years later, I have no reason to change it, so here it is, very slightly edited for the present context. It clearly expresses the belief that God is nothing if not perfect goodness, creative and infinitely loving, but it also expresses other, traditional Christian beliefs about God that were shown in part II to be ethically unacceptable. These are written in italics.

"A Christian understanding of the divine

"In order to understand the Conservative Christian world-view more fully we must now take note of the wider implications of the belief that there truly exists a God whose power is limitlessly and unfailingly loving. When we do so we find something that is undeniably impressive. The first of these implications is what Christians call the grace of God, meaning his gift of himself. As the loving source and basis of reality, God's nature expresses itself, say Christians, in a boundless giving of life, bringing the multitude of created things into being so that they can receive his love and return it and relate to one another in a loving way. Love cannot exist in solitude. It must express itself in the giving and receiving of love—as David Jenkins said, God is either a gift or a delusion. Therefore creativity is one of the hallmarks of genuine love, meaning the act of bringing into being new occasions of love. And an infinite love does so in an endlessly rich way.

"To put the matter slightly differently, a God of perfect love cannot have planned a universe that would function, at heart, in a way that contradicts his own nature. And since the universe gets its own essential nature wholly from God, who alone is almighty, it cannot ultimately thwart his fundamental intention as creator. Accordingly, everything is as it is and operates as it does because of God's loving charter for the entire cosmos, *either through his direct, second-by-second control as some Christians think*, or because he gives it a range of possibilities, a sufficiency of energy and a degree of real freedom to unfold on its own within the ultimate framework of his loving intention . . .

"But the grace of God is not spent by the act of originating the universe. Being perfect and without limit, God ceaselessly pours forth the abundance of his love, an unfailing cascade of life-giving water in the dry lands of the cosmos. Conservative Christians receive from Judaism and accept the belief that this can be seen in *the history of ancient Israel, interpreting the history of Abraham, the liberation of the Hebrew slaves under Moses, their conquest of the land of Canaan under Joshua and the words of the Hebrew prophets* as instances of God's continuing care.

"But above all they see it continued and confirmed *uniquely and supremely* in Jesus of Nazareth, declaring his entire existence to be the *ultimate* demonstration of God's unfailing love, continuing beyond his bodily presence as the power of the Holy Spirit bringing renewed life and love to believers . . . And as a logical extension of these ideas they believe that in the end the future will see the final triumph of God's love. Death cannot have the last word. Beyond the grave, therefore awaits life made whole by God's love for all who open their lives to him. As Luther reportedly once remarked, that which God touches is certainly made immortal. How could it be otherwise if God is eternally and almightily loving?

"The next implication of this view of God is that there is no getting away from his presence. If the kind of God believed in by Christians really exists then it follows that everything else that exists—absolutely everything—always does so in the invisible presence of this infinite love. The writing or reading of these words, the rain and the winds, the births and deaths of all things, every human venture or effort including all debates about God and quite literally everything else that has ever happened or ever will, they all happened within the endless depths and range of that divine love. Obviously God does not desire sin or evil, but that does not mean that people who commit evil somehow enter an area where God's loving presence is excluded. Moreover, the divine love that Christianity says enfolds us is rich and complete, in contrast with the uneven and faltering love which is the best we humans can manage. Similarly, it is unfailingly constant; it never wavers or lapses into anything harsh, mean-spirited or unloving, even when it encounters things like cruelty and oppression which run counter to it. Obviously a perfectly loving God cannot approve of such things or will them to happen. But that does not mean that he lapses into hatred and rejection when relating to people who act cruelly or hatefully.

"Another implication of God's love is that our lives, along with absolutely everything else in creation, are irreplaceably precious to God, being the objects of his love. Our individual natures which make us unique are also therefore infinitely dear to him. We humans might find some people repulsive, but not so God except for evil, as distinct from those who commit evil; all things whatsoever are the receivers of his inexhaustible and all-powerful love, including those who reject him or give their lives over to evil. And because he is perfect, his love knows no favorites. All alike are infinitely and everlastingly dear to him. Therefore whoever hurts or destroys anything in the universe, harms that which God, with all the endless resources of his being, cherishes without reservation, and is thus in outright conflict with him, the greatest power of all.

"But in no way could God ever relate to those who inflict such harm or destruction in anything but a supremely loving manner. Love's way is to promote—selflessly if need be—the well-being of those it loves, to long for their safety, fulfilment and happiness, and do all that is possible to enable them to achieve those things. Infinite, perfect love must therefore do these things in an infinite, perfect and everlasting way, overflowing with love and concern for even the littlest of things, the ants, the very grains of sand, the most fleeting of sub-atomic particles, and even for the vilest of things, morally speaking. All alike, great or small, saintly or wicked, belong ultimately to him and their greatest well-being is his eternal will for them.

"Their love for him in return and their flourishing in a framework of love must thus be his supreme desire, and their rejection or hatred must be his supreme challenge to overcome by means of love alone and the things it can do . . . Thus a theology with perfect love as its hallmark translates into a cosmology and an anthropology—a world-view and a view of humanity—with love as their hallmark as well, and there can be no denying the inspiring power and beauty of such a faith, with its vision of all things arising from and existing in the invisible, eternal presence of the God in whom Christians believe."[2]

We see here very clearly the ethical ambivalence of Conservative Christianity's concept of God, but also the foundation of a Progressive Christian concept. Nothing that fails to measure up to the highest conceivable goodness can be accepted if faith is to be consonant with that goodness. A progressive, ethics-based Christianity must therefore reject all doctrines about God that involve even a hint of divine favoritism or, far worse, divine instructions to anyone, and not just the Israelites under Joshua, to perpetrate the horrifying evil of wholesale genocide, an evil that echoes the words in Genesis where God is said to tell Abraham to go to the promised but already occupied land of Canaan (Genesis 12:1-6). Worst of all is the belief that God has ordained the ultimate cruelty and injustice of eternal punishment to those who do not embrace Christ as the only savior, for most people cannot avail themselves of such a method of salvation through no fault of their own, as I have already emphasized.

Conservative Christianity therefore faces a critical choice: unethically retain those traditional doctrines and thereby betray the God of perfect goodness and love and also the historical Jesus who embodied such supreme goodness, or truly embrace anew both Jesus and his God, thereby committing itself, at the very least, to a universalist view of salvation. But can even such an ethically enhanced concept of God command acceptance on ethical grounds? Let me first give an answer from my own immediate experience.

It is extremely important for readers to understand that I do not write this as an academic exercise in a detached sort of way; I do so intensely aware that I exist and think within an encompassing goodness of whose presence, power and beauty I am keenly and at times even breathlessly aware. And as I look back over the many experiences recounted in the first part of this book, I ask whether they, and indeed all experiences of the power of the good, and all religious experiences of the kind reported by William James and Alister Hardy, can credibly be seen as the gift of a *personal*, morally perfect God, even though I have never had any experience that would clearly and unambiguously indicate the presence of such a God, with no possibility of illusion, experiences like the call of Samuel as told of in the Hebrew Scriptures in First Samuel, chapter 1.

My *initial* reply is that such experiences can plausibly be seen as God-given, because influencing people to practice ever greater goodness, especially love and truth, is exactly what such a deity can be expected to do for us, with our propensity to do wrong, and because there is no logical

2. Prozesky, *New Guide*, 23-26.

contradiction involved in the belief that there is a perfect, personal God who influences *all of us in every culture and period of history* towards greater goodness in our lives. People all over the world have indeed felt the many positive, ethical influences I have had, so universal moral influence is exactly what such a God would exert. Let it be noticed here that the experiences under consideration are *influences*, not direct manifestations of a divine presence of the kind that happened, according to the Hebrew Scriptures, to Samuel and especially to Moses at the Burning Bush and on Mount Sinai.

Loving us all equally, such a God would surely also want us to understand the source and foundation of the blessings we receive, and return his love in overflowing gratitude and awe, just as Conservative Christian theology asserts, by pointing to the kind of divine self-revelations mentioned above, supremely in Jesus Christ. And then the critical questions come to mind if we really are being honest and determined to leave no stone unturned in our commitment to truth. So we must now ask why a personal God of such supreme goodness would bestow the most precious and important knowledge of his existence and nature on just the religious tradition of ancient Israel, Christianity and, according to only the more liberal of Christians, on aspects of Islam, like its profound sense of a compassionate and beneficent Allah, and parts of Hinduism, but not on the majority of the human family outside that Abrahamic tradition, who need it just as much.

Is there an ethically credible explanation of why such a God has not made himself known to all the world's people past and present? How can this critically important question be credibly answered? Keenly aware that such questions and any answers we might give take us into the realm of metaphysics, I recall with relief the parable of the mice in the cellar of a vast palace, already introduced in this book, who pronounce grandly about the nature and merits of the place and its architect. So I accept the reality of our human ineptitude about metaphysics, my own certainly included, and accept also that our only option is to proceed with great humility, knowing that all who care greatly about Jesus of Nazareth and what he pioneered must work together with loving hearts and open minds, ready to be led by goodness itself at its greatest and best into ever richer approximations of its nature.

In that spirit let me say that so far as I can see there are three answers Christians and others can give to the question before us, since they are not going to embrace materialistic atheism, the belief that the universe of matter and energy that science studies is the only reality, which makes religious faith in transcendence just a delusion.

The first and most radical answer is that the cosmos is the ultimate reality. The word cosmos here refers, as set forth in chapter 5, to everything that is real, including everything we experience, especially morality and spirituality, and not just everything we can perceive empirically. Within such a cosmos there is the emergence of the moral domain, which is the reality of discerning the good and freely committing to it, and our sense of the existence of a highest good at work in the cosmos. If I understand them correctly, this would be the view of Don Cupitt and Lloyd Geering. Reza Aslan evidently offers a pantheistic version of this option, arriving it after a long spiritual journey back to his original Islamic nurture and culminating in Sufi experience.[3]

Turning now to the second answer, it suggests that the personal, perfectly good and loving God of the Bible definitely exists and is correctly understood as such, but that since goodness is what such a God most desires in us, he (or she) isn't primarily interested in beliefs, doctrines and creeds at all, and doesn't mind what kind we produce as long as they are based on goodness, love and concern for truth, and are always ready to abandon anything that falls short of those great values. Keith Ward's account of the divine is perhaps an example.[4]

The third answer is that the Abrahamic concept of God as a supreme, personal being is simply too restrictive to do justice to a goodness that is too rich and deep to be adequately contained in *any* of the models and metaphors we may employ. What we do, however, know is that goodness transforms both the individuals who embrace it and the contexts and structures of our various cultures, making it plausible to suppose that, whatever else a highest, Eternal Good, in John Hick's words, might be, it must have two basic characteristics. It cannot be less than personal in some sense, about which we must not be dogmatic, while also being able to encompass our existence in the way of an uplifting domain or milieu, rather like the way the force of gravity is present and operative in the whole physical cosmos. Perhaps a mysterious source of goodness somehow underlies or enfolds and animates the cosmos, the way the spirit of adventure animates the explorer and a passion for beauty the artist. Could that be the reality that most concerns us?

How well do these three answers meet the ethical requirements of goodness and truth? To my mind the first answer offers an admittedly very radical, even revolutionary, way forward on the God question, as I see no ethical problem in it. Besides, metaphysical humility rightly creates space for such views. The second answer, unfortunately for its proponents, fails the test of truth. It might seem generous-spirited to declare that God welcomes

---

3. Aslan, *God: Human History*, 165-71.
4. Ward, *Vision to Pursue*, 71-102.

any goodness-based concept of the ultimate, even though this view believes that concepts using personal models like Father, Mother and King are truer than those of faiths that do not. A God of perfect goodness must surely be very much concerned about truth, which makes a notion of benign, divine indifference to what would then be inadequate models untenable. The plain fact of the matter is that while all the religions share a basic concern with a fundamentally important benefit like deliverance, salvation, liberation and enlightenment, they also have other beliefs that are incompatible with those of Christianity, such as the absence of the concepts of God and Hell, and the belief of the Indian faiths in reincarnation. The second answer cannot therefore be ethically valid because of its superficiality about something as important as truth.

That leaves my third option, which I must now discuss further, noting that it has very far-reaching implications for what can ethically be accepted by Christians about other religions, which I present later in this chapter, and about Christ, the Bible, and the church, as we shall see in the next two chapters. My discussion starts by noting a few supportive views by a selection of progressive religious thinkers who have also explored new ways of re-imagining God, to use the title of a book by Lloyd Geering for such explorations.[5] After that I return to my own understanding of the third of the options set out above.

Corroborations

From process theology comes the strongest support for my perspective, especially its panentheistic conception of God. This means that the creative divine reality enfolds everything else, which therefore exists within the divine reality.[6] Next, zoologist Alister Hardy concluded his study of the spiritual nature of our species with his own, radical conception of God, as follows: "I do not . . . believe in God as an old gentleman up there or out there, but I do believe that there is a Power which *appears* to be transcendental, and outside the conscious self, and which we may call God."[7] John Dominic Crossan asks if the biblical God is not "a personified process rather than a person?"[8] Ken Miller points out that evolution opens our thinking to the search for richer understandings of what I am calling an ultimate goodness,

---

5. Geering, *Reimagining God*.
6. Cobb, *Christian Natural Theology*; Cobb and Griffin, *Process Theology*, 41–62.
7. Hardy, *Spiritual Nature*, 227.
8. Crossan, *How to Read the Bible*, 124.

writing that "to a believer, even in the most traditional sense, evolutionary biology is not at all the obstacle we often believe it to be."[9]

Perhaps the most visionary Christian thinker to go through the conceptual and spiritual doorway of evolution is Teilhard de Chardin, with his sweeping view of an evolving, spiritual universe. These examples of theistic pioneers strongly underline the importance of being open to the fullest possible, multi-disciplinary range of knowledge. As Andrew Steane, a professor of physics at Oxford says, pursuing science is "part of what loving God with all your mind entails."[10]

David Klemm and William Schweiker write as follows: "Religion is the human longing for and awareness of the divine (what is taken to be unsurpassable in importance and reality) experienced and expressed within the concrete cultural life of particular historical traditions." They also give a very good review of the changing understandings of God in chapter 3 of their book.[11]

Don Cupitt provides a fascinating account of what he calls the rise and departure of God, adding that "*God* is a master word that comprehends the whole scheme of things within which we live, personifying it in a way that we will often want to worship and sometimes to reproach."[12] Most interesting for me is part III of his book, carrying the title "Religion after the gods." There he writes that in the future "we will see our religion not as supernatural doctrine but as an experiment in selfhood."[13] Cupitt then provocatively adds that true religion is "religion that makes you smarter than your god," and that "the traditional religions of humankind can now survive only as fundamentalisms—which is what they have largely become." What remains, he writes, is "thoroughgoing permissive pluralism."[14]

Here Cupitt echoes my own contentions, shared by J.E. Schellenberg in his book *Evolutionary Religion*, where he advocates a minimalist account of what he calls ultimacy in his discussion of what he sees as "religion for pioneers," recognizing that our human incompetence in metaphysics should lead to a shared, cooperative, pioneering quest for ever richer understandings of transcendence, with no end point either possible or desirable.[15] The

9. Miller, *Finding Darwin's God*, 291.

10. Steane, *Faithful to Science*, 37; see also Holder, "Review," and Bruggemann, *Excess of Divine Fidelity*, and Lilley and Pedersen, *Human Origins*.

11. Klemm and Schweiker, *Religion and the Human Future*, 52, 38-56.

12. Cupitt, *After God*, 41-48, 49-51.

13. Cupitt, *After God*, 82.

14. Cupitt, *After God*, 82, 85, 123, 125.

15. Schellenberg, *Evolutionary Religion*, 136-56.

unfathomable, seemingly infinite richness of an ultimate good surely means that we can never understand or speak of it with the kind of exhaustive precision that is possible with finite things like a plant or piece of metal.

Although he is a religious sceptic and atheist, Schellenberg advocates a religious view that he calls ultimism. It holds that there is a reality that is triply ultimate, metaphysically, axiologically and soteriologically, asserting that this is a religious proposition because of its soteriological nature. He also asserts the following: "Skeptical religion can be spiritually authentic and fulfilling," and that a skeptical, ultimistic faith is the only faith capable of being justified.[16] Noting the amazing persistence of religion, Schellenberg concludes with a comment about religion that admirably expresses a central contention of *Honest to Goodness*: "If so culturally powerful a force could be more fully directed to pragmatic ends, such as widening love of wisdom, the eradication of war and poverty, and pre-emptive treatments for environmental maladies, surely this would be a cause for rational rejoicing. It is time to make religion work *for* us. In a new evolutionary instantiation it can do so."[17]

GOODNESS AS GODHEAD

In continuing this chapter in a deeply personal way, I now give as best I can what, for me, comes after the God of Conservative and Liberal Christianity, which I speak of ethically as supreme goodness and spiritually as Godhead, involving a quantum shift from traditional theism to an alternative spiritual and ethical philosophy and practice. To do so I quote a very slightly edited, short statement that I sent some years ago to a group of Christian friends, several of them church leaders, others senior theologians. In it I wrote the following:

> "God is a word in the English language. It is not the self-given name of a being in the heavens. It is our purely human name, in merely one human language, for the most important, most beautiful and, for us, unsurpassable reality—an inexhaustible goodness that is everywhere transforming our lives if we embrace its gracious power. It is creatively at work in the universe, closer than a heartbeat, yet also too rich, deep and wondrous for us to fathom or define with our words, experienced by many as lovingly father-like and mother-like and by means of other suggestive human images; evoking in us awe, gratitude,

---

16. Schellenberg, *Evolutionary Religion*, 145-48.
17. Schellenberg, *Evolutionary Religion*, 150.

commitment and joy, most richly in poetry and song, not the prose of philosophy or theology, though these have their place; inviting our freely given partnership in the ongoing work of extending the domain of the good; and our unfailing ally and support in the struggle against evil. To experience this most surpassing but invisible of realities is to know the reality to which the word God refers and not merely to believe that there is a God."

Such a Godhead, as supreme goodness, cannot be the source of anything cruel, unjust, untruthful, unloving; nor a patriarchal overlord who has all the power; nor one who programs all that happens and so makes moral goodness meaningless; and least of all a sadist who sends even a single person to eternal torture in hell for not obeying him, even out of total ignorance.

Jesus taught that God is love. Could the view of Godhead that I am setting forth here retain that great and vital teaching, since it seeks something even richer than an individual, personal being? If love necessarily requires someone who loves, then there may well be a problem here for a Jesus-based concept of Godhead, but is that necessarily the case? Love can refer without strain to a set of wonderful realities: the power to bring people closely together and never alienate; that seeks the good of all it touches; that safeguards, supports and liberates; that creates and enhances well-being; that requires of us the truth in order to be most effective in its work of person-making. This being so, the cosmos, in a holistic view of it, can indeed be seen as deeply loving.

Godhead therefore refers, for me, to the radically generous, enabling and mysteriously loving power of goodness which I experience both in my ordinary, everyday life and in the deepest reaches of my consciousness, always as a spur to greater generosity of effort, a sense of deep assurance that in any hardship an option for good exists, and an awareness of being truly at home when my life harmonizes with this ever-present power. It is this ceaseless outpouring of goodness, of radically enabling goodness, that, I believe, Jesus, Muhammad, the Buddha and all other spiritual luminaries experienced with such exceptional, world-changing and life-changing richness, depth and power. Godhead is thus a religious name for the mysterious, inspirational generosity that upholds and infuses all things; the creativity that fosters everything good, beautiful and true; the truth that enlightens and directs all thinking beings who open their hearts and minds to all that is truly noble.

I have just proposed that Godhead is sheer goodness. I have also argued for great mental modesty about ultimate issues, so all I can add is to propose a minimalist account of what I understand by "ultimate goodness." Following Anselm, I contend that it must be the goodness than which a greater goodness cannot even be conceived. Hence it must always be totally free of any imperfection or wrong; the purest truth, and always maximally beneficial in the way it operates and how it touches everything.

Unlike the more conservative theologies of Christianity, the present metatheology is not in the least troubled by the existence of many other religions, and does not dismiss them as incapable of opening the doors of the greatest blessing to their adherents. On the contrary, it welcomes the plurality of faiths as precisely what we should expect and celebrate on a planet that exists, like the entire cosmos, in the uplifting power of the supreme goodness that I am calling Godhead in spiritual mode. Why this is so is explained in the following section.

Having had the exhilarating flood of insights and words of the previous passages, I closed my eyes and heard the bells of the Church of the Ascension in my home village of Hilton, just as I had once heard the beautiful Muslim call to prayer over the Old City of Jerusalem and the lovely chanting of a cantor in a Jewish synagogue, and I felt greatly uplifted.

GODHEAD AND RELIGIOUS PLURALISM

The shared, sentient and valorizing nature of all the world's people gives us our common concern with the many kinds of encompassing and indwelling good that nourish and enrich our desire for fulfilment and flourishing. It does not and cannot lead to sameness of cultures, because we are also the product of particular, local influences that develop in relation to many different physical and historical environments. That is just the way of the world, and it gives us the blessing of variety, novelty, appreciation and fascination, even though it also gives rise to misunderstandings, hostilities and conflicts.

What the many cultures past and present share is thus the enveloping presence of goodness. Beset as we all, always, are by the disturbing knowledge that our well-being is a fragile thing, easily damaged and even lost through disease, injury, misfortune and the enmity of others, our concern will perforce be to connect with whatever powers of goodness there might be to help us, like an unseen world of supposed spiritual beings, or just one such being. A worldwide concern with what we now call ethics is thus entirely to be expected, with none having a monopoly on morality and none perfect at it either, given our human fallibility and weaknesses.

Ethical and spiritual individuals of exceptional ability to discern more inspiringly than others the sources of protection and assistance emerged from a range of cultures in the Axial period. This is a matter of historical record, as we saw earlier in this book. Again, the reality is a pluralistic one, though why this remarkable development happened when it did is still unclear. What is clear is that our human abilities are unevenly distributed. Very few of us can be Olympic athletes, literary prodigies like Shakespeare or scientific geniuses like Einstein. That a few individuals in history have been to morality and spirituality what Mozart is to music is thus entirely to be expected.

The point to grasp, then, is that the way goodness works in a multicultural, historically changing world means that there will naturally be different perceptions of it, giving rise to different religious traditions of belief. Goodness is experienced everywhere because it is present everywhere. Some experience it under the influence of culturally dominantly personal models, others more as an encompassing context or milieu. All religions therefore give rise to faith, in Wilfred Cantwell Smith's vitally important explanation of it, as a basic orientation of the self to a transcendent good, and all have their particular, differing, cumulative traditions as secondary, culturally relative aspects.

Using Smith's great insight, we can see, for example, that for devout Muslims, faith means being oriented to the Holy Qur'an as the very word of Allah's supreme goodness, transcendent yet graciously made accessible in Arabic; how they develop the Islamic cumulative tradition, from the architecture of mosques and the development of theology and jurisprudence to the founding of Islamic republics like Pakistan, remains human, according to this perspective.

Our various human *understandings* of ultimate goodness can never be more than tentative. They are unfinished products that can still be effective channels of that goodness, but when, as I have now often emphasized, they harden their symbolic ways of understanding it into dogmas claiming validity and finality only for themselves, they fall into error and even into the evils of exclusion, persecution and witch-hunts, besides understandably and inevitably giving rise to atheism and secularism.

The concept of ethical spaces proposed by David Cheetham is a helpful basis for a view of religions that can pass the most stringent ethical evaluation. Chapter 6 of his book *Ways of Meeting and the Theology of Religions* is about these ethical spaces for meeting people of other beliefs. An ethical space is "a space—of responsibility and obligation—characterized by meeting and encounter: a social space."[18] Earlier on that same page he quotes Zygmunt Baumann as seeing ethical space as a space defined by "a recognition and engagement with other people."

Since all religions offer ways of enhancing the good and resisting evil, all are morally salvific, but none perfectly or exclusively, suggesting the possibility of a world federation of faiths to help drive global moral salvation. In that way a positive, progressive view of religions can give rise to a shared project of effective moral action against the evils besetting the world and its people, about which I have suggestions in my final chapter. Such a shared development seems exceedingly unlikely from Conservative Christianity, and even impossible because of its elitist sense of identity, but is certainly capable of winning the support of liberals. It is just such an inclusive faith and ethic that Jesus pioneered, as we see in the next chapter.

---

18. Cheetham, *Ways of Meeting*, 149.

Chapter 13

Jesus and his Revolution

IN THE LANGUAGE OF theology, Jesus of Nazareth is Godhead incarnate, to the fullest extent our fallible, limited human nature can embody such supreme goodness. I see him this way, not as taught by the Prologue of John's Gospel and traditional Christianity, but in a much more ethically meaningful way. I contend that like all of us but much more richly, Jesus felt the uplifting presence and power of goodness, opening his very being to it, drawing on it and radiating its depths and warmth with unsurpassed power and authority, while always also subject to the influences of his culture and times. The most illuminating and indeed inspiring account of this fundamental part of who Jesus was that I have found is given by Albert Nolan in his 2006 book *Jesus Today: A Spirituality of Radical Freedom*. While Nolan naturally writes from within the world of his Catholic Christian practice, what he discerns about Jesus's experience of the divine has much wider value and relevance, and is of very great value for my own views.

Jesus's own resultant moral and spiritual goodness was so deep, rich and noble, in both word and deed, that it enabled the movement he pioneered to continue and grow despite his terrible death. Hands that healed and fed, a heart overflowing with generosity, a voice that spoke movingly of boundless love, all make it abundantly clear that he can quite literally be said to be supreme goodness incarnate. In him and the movement he created, Godhead, wrongly thought by others to be wholly other in a remote heaven, is shown to include bodily and social presence on earth. To substantiate this summary of Jesus in ethical perspective, I turn next to the sources and methods I have used in reaching it.

CONCERNING SOURCES, METHODS AND CRITERIA

My interpretation comes from two principal sources. The first is of course my own decades of research in theology, history, religious studies and especially comparative, applied ethics, into the nature, rise and persistence of religions and into the Jesus of history. The second is the work of leading scholars in the various quests into the historical Jesus. I turned to them as I am not myself a New Testament scholar or specialist historian, though I did include both fields in my first degrees at Rhodes and Oxford. In alphabetical order these scholars are Marcus Borg, Humphrey Carpenter, John Dominic Crossan, Robert Funk, Richard Horsley, Peter G. Kirchschlaeger, Albert Nolan, Mark Allan Powell, E.P. Sanders, Albert Schweitzer, and N.T. Wright.

My approach to historical method is to see it first and foremost as a form of applied ethics, in which concern for truth is a basic value. The world needs all the saving goodness it can get. That can only happen in partnership with the deepest commitment to truth—the truth about the evils afflicting it, about what can counter and overcome them and about Jesus of Nazareth. The only account of him that can be of value is therefore one that rests first and foremost on the historical facts about him, not the inherited doctrines and Creeds of Christianity as usually understood, for we have already seen that they contain defining beliefs that reflect later views of him that cannot be squared with his inclusive concern for others. Nor can evil be overcome by a wishful picture of Jesus that has little to do with confirmed evidence, as N.T. Wright has emphasized.[1] Instead, a method of securing the greatest historical reliability must be followed.

All top biblical scholars know that the Gospel accounts about Jesus cannot simply be accepted as historical fact because of the difficulties identified in part II and summarized later in this chapter. There are simply too many discrepancies in that material. This means that the search for historical fact must be equipped with reliable criteria, an issue to which I have given much thought and to which the scholars I have studied pay careful attention. A valuable account of their criteria is given by Mark Allan Powell in his book *Jesus as a Figure in History: How Modern Historians View the Man from Galilee*.[2]

For me the best evidence is direct, first-hand testimony by a morally trustworthy and mentally competent eyewitness, independently confirmed by other such witnesses. For highly unusual events two independent witnesses of that calibre who agree will not be enough, which is the criterion

---

1. Wright, *Jesus and the Victory*; Borg and Wright, *Meaning of Jesus*, 24.
2. Powell, *Jesus as a Figure*, 46–50.

known as multiple attestation. It means that the more there is agreed, competent, morally trustworthy, first-hand evidence, the more we are justified in accepting its claims. Another important criterion is coherence. It is met when what the sources say fits or coheres with existing knowledge of events, places and people relevant to it. In his review of the scholars who in recent decades have sought the historical Jesus behind the Gospel accounts, Powell lists several other criteria, such as memorable form and content of a kind that indicates ease of memory in cultures where evidence is passed on orally, as certainly happened with the Gospels.[3] None of these criteria present problems for my account of Jesus.

What is the reliable evidence to support my contention that Jesus felt the presence of great goodness with exceptional depth and power? First there is the evidence of human nature, which is the same for every member of our species, and we all experience goodness, which at times can be very rich. Next, all people live in a world that both benefits and harms our shared desire for lasting well-being. So although we have no direct access to the experience of the historical Jesus, it follows logically from the fact that he was a human being that he felt the presence of goodness, just like the rest of us, but very much more powerfully, as the discussions that follow confirm.

The evidence that his experience of it was exceptionally rich and powerful, and about his time and place, comes from the documentary evidence about him in the Gospels, for Paul's letters give us almost nothing about his life. In the interests of the greatest factual accuracy, it is necessary to proceed here with great care. To seek this I first use the phenomenological method that is followed with great success in the study of religions, as most helpfully explained early in my time at the former University of Natal by my late departmental colleague and friend, Patrick Maxwell, following its advocacy there by Professor Vic Bredenkamp.

It involves two strategies, of which the first is especially important for anyone, like me, who is steeped in the Christian tradition but wants only the facts about Jesus. It is called bracketing, and means setting aside from the enquiry one's personal interests and biases, which we all have to a greater or lesser extent. To do this we must of course understand ourselves very well, and so be able to identify the things we favor and the things we do not, and then consciously remove them from our enquiry. In the present case this means setting aside the doctrinal beliefs of Christianity about Jesus and approaching the Gospels the way a balanced secular historian would. The enquiry is not about justifying those beliefs and assuming that the Gospel evidence is sound, but rigorously testing that evidence for reliability.

---

3. Powell, *Jesus as a Figure*, 48–49.

The second strategy is empathy, an imaginative effort based on the best evidence to understand the object of the enquiry. An example may be helpful. Suppose I am studying Buddhism as a living faith. I need to understand what it is like to be a Buddhist, so I gather all the information I can about that faith from some of its members and books, and then use my informed imagination to sense what it feels like to be such a person. With careful practice these two strategies can be very effective. An ordained Anglican academic colleague of mine was asked after a public lecture how long he had been a Buddhist, and I was once asked how long I'd been a Catholic. Bearing these methodological clarifications in mind we can now evaluate the available documentary evidence about Jesus in the Gospels, with an understanding of what the best evidence would be as yardstick.

The Gospel evidence is invaluable but it falls well short of this highest standard. What we have is a fourth-century collection of texts, which is in the first instance direct evidence of the interests of those who created the canon of the New Testament at that time. They included the four Gospels but not others like the Gospel of Thomas and the early Christian text called the *Didache*, also called *The Teaching of the Twelve Apostles*. They worked not with originals but with copies of copies, whose exact number we do not know, but they are copies. The originals are the so-called lost autographs, and being lost, we can have no sure way of checking how closely the texts of the oldest manuscripts of the Gospels are to the originals.

Given the immense value of these texts in the early Christian movement, it is likely, even highly likely, that the copying was done with great care, but they remain human copies, not originals. So what we have is somewhat attenuated evidence for Jesus and the very earliest movement of his followers in their time and place. Apart from the certainty that Jesus is a figure of history in his time and place and that he was crucified, the evidence gives us probabilities, at times very strong ones, rather than certainties. This reduces their evidentiary value but it certainly does not eliminate it, for the picture the Gospels give us of Jesus and his context fits well what we know with considerable, though not absolute, assurance from independent Jewish and Roman historians. I will summarize that information later in this chapter.

There are other problems about the Gospel evidence. As all careful readers know, the three synoptic Gospels give us a broadly similar picture of the activities and many of the teachings of Jesus, but there are important differences too; while John's Gospel gives a markedly different picture in some striking ways. According to John, for example, Jesus's ministry lasted much longer than the time implied in the other three, and Jesus is presented as having given his followers lengthy discourses rather than the mostly shorter teachings of the synoptic Gospels. Again, these differences reduce but certainly do not eliminate the Gospels as historical sources for the facts about Jesus, as preserved by the earliest Jesus movement in the decades after his time. In other words, even if we had the lost autographs and could be sure who wrote them, they are primary evidence of the beliefs of their authors, not of Jesus himself, who left no first-hand records of his own, unlike Paul.

These considerations are well known to all New Testament scholars and academic theologians, but their implications for our knowledge of Jesus are not, to my mind, sufficiently recognized in Conservative Christianity. My own judgment about them is as follows. The Gospels cannot be accepted as sufficiently strong, as historical evidence, to give us much reliable detail about Jesus of Nazareth's activities, teachings and context, *but together with Acts they are certainly strong enough to give us a trustworthy account of the earliest Jesus movement and the essentials of what it understood about Jesus*.[4] We can identify those essentials by discerning the most prominent parts of their view of Jesus and his time and place, which I outline in the next section of the chapter.

JESUS IN HIS TIME AND PLACE

The political and economic situation confronting Jesus and all others in the poorer parts of Galilean and Judean society, in the early decades of the first century CE, was characterized by a number of serious evils. I am not referring the usual, small-scale evils that beset any community, like jealousy, harshness, lies and minor acts of violence, damaging though these are for the individuals involved. I am referring to three forms of large-scale, structural evil affecting the whole society. They were firstly subjection to the ruthlessly violent domination of Roman imperialism, supported by local accomplices like the Herodian royal house, parts of the Jewish wealthy class in Jerusalem and elsewhere, and by Jews who worked for this system, such as tax gatherers and other minor officials. Next there was severe economic exploitation by the powerful, creating great hardship for the poor; and a sometimes stifling, legalistic religious presence in the form of those whose faith in the Torah was interpreted as rigid conformity to its laws, of which I was taught there are 613 in all.[5]

No oppressive situation is entirely free of healthy influences. For Jesus and his contemporaries these included the prophetic and wisdom traditions

---

4. Young, "Prelude," 1-4.

5. Freyne, "Galilee and Judaea," 37-51; Harvey, "Jesus as a Historical Figure," 446-54; Horsley, *Jesus in Context*, 26; Wright, *Jesus and the Victory*, 150-60.

of Israel, known to us in the Hebrew Scriptures from books like those of Isaiah, Jeremiah and Proverbs, and also from the ethical values of the Torah. It is distinctly possible, even probable, that Hellenistic culture, with its philosophical wisdom, may have influenced the minds of some Palestinian Jewish people during the period of Hellenistic control before Roman imperialism took over, and continued thus in Jesus's time. Additional sources of encouragement came from the memory of brave Jewish resistance to imperialism in recent times, one example of it successful for a while; the solidarity of the great religious festivals of Jewish faith, then and now, and the important, daily reality of ordinary human goodness in families and communities like those of Nazareth, manifesting itself as kindness, support and friendship. An excellent account of the most important ethical features of Jewish life in the time of Jesus is given by Wayne Meeks in his book *The Moral World of the First Christians*.[6]

Turning now, with goodness as my paramount concern, to the kind of person Jesus was, I am seeking reliable evidence about the figure behind the movement that followed him and created the cumulative tradition of beliefs and writings about a risen, heavenly Savior that emerged from those earliest beginnings. The answer is to be found in two ways. The first is a discernment from the available evidence of the main emphases *in the memories about Jesus that the earliest church preserved* and which ended up in the Gospels. Any careful reader of the sources who sees the broad patterns in them can do this. The second way is to use the discoveries in recent New Testament scholarship of the highest competence, and that is sufficiently free of the controlling influence of traditional Christian doctrine, as required by the phenomenological method. Here is what these two ways of recovering the real, historical Jesus are yielding for my purposes, so far as that is possible.

The evidence, let us bear in mind always, is first and foremost evidence about the early Jesus movement, not Jesus himself. He is to be sought indirectly in that evidence by asking what kind of person would give rise to a devoted movement despite opposition by influential Jewish religious leaders that was strong enough to lead to his crucifixion by the Roman authorities, a movement that attributed its existence and purpose to him? What would create both this dedicated following and such fatal opposition?

An analogy from the study of our solar system may be helpful here. Careful observations in the early nineteenth century by Sir William Herschel (1738—1822) of the orbit of the planet Uranus revealed departures from where it should be, according to Newton's law of gravity and Kepler's laws of planetary motion. It was theorized by others that the departures

---

6. Meeks, *Moral World*, 91-96.

could be the result of the gravitational pull on Uranus of an undiscovered, large planet beyond its orbit, and a few interested astronomers set about telescopic observations of the heavens in the suggested regions, seeking a planet of the required mass and distance. There it was duly found at the Berlin observatory on 24 September 1846, as the large planet we call Neptune.

The puzzling, observed orbit of Uranus was the direct evidence, which was correctly interpreted as the result of an undiscovered cause in the form of a planet even further from the sun, exerting its gravitational effect on Uranus. In connection with my interest in using objective, non-theological methods to establish what kind of person Jesus was, the analogy is this: the earliest movement of Jesus's followers is Uranus, and Jesus himself is Neptune. So the question is just what kind of person would evoke such passionate support and deadly opposition.

Great goodness is the most powerful human attractor, especially goodness that manifests itself as a truly loving and practical concern for others, coupled with strong leadership skills and great moral courage. Such a person in my own experience is Desmond Tutu. People touched by such a person do more than admire him or her; they respond with love and commitment, and when the qualities of such a person are exceptionally noble, the person who has them attracts a truly devoted following. The existence and persistence of the Jesus movement is the evidence that Jesus did exactly that. So it follows that he possessed the necessary noble qualities, exactly as the Gospel texts say. They depict an exceptionally compassionate person, deeply concerned for the bodily, emotional, spiritual, and social needs of the poor, the ill, the hungry, the marginalized and the despised, with an exceptional capacity for inclusive friendships that extended to what polite society saw as sinfully disreputable types.[7] The inference is therefore clear: Jesus was indeed a person of truly great goodness, just as the factual content of the Gospel tradition about him asserts. Some vital details about him can also be established with great historical credibility, as noted below.

What must be brought into the discussion at this point is the deadly opposition Jesus caused for himself and his following. The clue to it is the fact that his moral greatness was spiritually based in a truly revolutionary way that could not fail to inspire the needy but also alienate some of the powerful, on both religious and ethical grounds. This was his teaching about what I am calling Godhead and its meaning for lordship, messiahship and himself.

---

7. Meeks, *Moral World*, 97-123 and 138-40; Nolan, *Jesus Today*, 50-59, 77-88; van Asselt and Sarot, "Human Friendship," 185-86.

To be a theist is not merely to assert that there is a God. It is to experience a goodness so great that it wins your freely given commitment, which then takes over your very being and inspires you to transform your entire life by and in its beautiful power. A person whose words and behavior reveal a truly outstanding quality, as those of Jesus did, is therefore a person in whom the supreme goodness I am calling Godhead was, quite literally, bodily present, and who had the kind of creative powers of deep understanding to know that this was so. So Jesus of Nazareth changes the traditional concept of God, then and now, from remote, heavenly existence to a universal and earthly presence that can enter and uplift a human life, here and now. Not to see this is, as N.T. Wright has commented, to fail to take seriously Jesus's "stark prayer for the kingdom to come, and God's will be done, on earth as it is in heaven."[8]

While this experiential transformation of the concept of deity by and in Jesus is truly revolutionary, it does not in any way limit Godhead, for an infinite goodness cannot be wholly contained in anything finite. Wright can therefore end his massive study of Jesus movingly by saying that the portrait of Jesus he has set out suggests "not a terrifying God from whose immediate, embodied presence we would shrink, but one whose glory is strangely revealed in the welcome and the warning, the symbol and the story, the threat to the Temple, the celebration in the upper room, and the dark night at noon on Calvary."[9]

Among the details in the Gospel about which there is a very high probability of historical accuracy is the tradition that Jesus spoke of Godhead with the metaphor of Father. Given the long and deeply harmful tradition of male domination and patriarchy in the Christian tradition, and in most others, this requires consideration from an ethical angle. Was Jesus here echoing the patriarchy of his own culture in a way that might be normal for that time and place, but is still ethically problematic, or is there a deeper, ethical truth to be discerned here? I contend that there is, as follows.

Apart from his brief time in and near Jerusalem, Jesus's activities took place among and were addressed largely to the people of Galilee, both rural and in its small towns, all of them under the burden of Roman domination and economic hardship, and most of them belonging to the poorer part of society, as is well shown in scholarly work about that situation.[10] I contend that if we can be sure of anything about Jesus, it is his compassion for those

---

8. Wright, *Jesus and the Victory*, 659.

9. Wright, *Jesus and the Victory*, 662.

10. Freyne, "Galilee and Judaea," 37–51; Harvey, "Jesus as a Historical Figure," 446–54; Horsley, *Jesus in Context*, 26; Klauck, "Roman Empire," 69–83; Wright, *Jesus and the Victory*, 150–60.

who suffer hardship of whatever kind. Someone of his great goodness would address himself to their situation, invoking the power of the God he spoke of as their Father. What would the deeper meaning of such a message be, but one of a caring, protecting love and goodness that was present to them then and there, more powerful than Rome and its proxies. And in a situation where serious violence from the occupying Roman soldiers was an ever-present threat and periodic reality, what Jesus needed was a symbolic expression of Godhead as a strong, reassuring, protective, love-filled presence. Caring fatherhood would express that message better than other metaphors in such a cultural and political context, so that its use by Jesus does not have to be seen as endorsing male domination, in much the same way that Jesus's choice of his closest followers could hardly have been made up mostly of women in that culture.

One of the most wonderful effects of embracing such great goodness is how Godhead becomes part of our very being and liberates us for ever greater love of others and of truth. It shows just how wrong it is to bear grudges and therefore how vital it is to forgive. This enabled Jesus to say to people trapped in crippling feelings of guilt and righteous rejection that they were forgiven, as the Gospels say he did. C.S. Lewis was correct in *Mere Christianity* to write that in doing so Jesus was divine, by exercising a divine prerogative, since he was obviously neither mad or bad, but Lewis missed just how radically Jesus was revolutionizing the concept of God by revealing that Godhead is far too great a reality to be the exclusive truth of one faith tradition, let alone one conservative strand in it, no matter how appealing it may be to its members.[11] As an African proverb is said to point out, those who never travel think their mother is the only good cook.

I want to contend that the reason why Jesus was able to experience Godhead in this inspiring, creative way is to be found in the nature of goodness itself, above all in supreme goodness. By its nature goodness *shares* itself and the greater the good, the more abundantly it shares itself and all its capacities with others. Godhead does just that in super-abundance, so Jesus showed and so our own experience of great goodness confirms, without a trace of delusion or conceit.

Empowered by what Jesus experienced and taught, we can share his revolutionary vision that Godhead can be a loving, flesh-and-blood presence, a gift for ever greater goodness in this life to all who welcome it, while always also being a power that pervades and enfolds the cosmos and all cultures with goodness in ways too wonderfully mysterious for us to comprehend fully and finally.

---

11. Lewis, *Mere Christianity*, 51–52.

Such a knowledge of Godhead must also change the meaning of lordship and messiahship. To conceive of these titles on the model of an earthly monarch of Jesus's time, place and history, like Caesar, Herod and even King David, is to misconceive those titles when they come under the power and presence of Godhead. Monarchs in the Jewish and Roman worlds were men—or almost always men—of great and at times dictatorial power, enabling them to lord it over the rest of the people, as the familiar expression so tellingly says. Knowing in his own being the reality of the greatest goodness, Jesus understood that true lordship and true messiahship meant using power with practical, active concern for the benefit of others, and thus with love and service, not to dominate and, least of all, to exploit the vulnerable.[12]

So when Jesus is seen as Lord and Son of God, it means that Imperial Caesar and his ilk are not Lord and not the Son of God, and the political implications are clear: this is deeply subversive of all forms of political and religious domination. Thus Marcus Borg can describe Jesus as a social prophet and movement initiator who challenged the domination system of his day that involved politics, the economy, the temple system in Jerusalem and those who controlled it.[13] Commenting on the kind of transformational wisdom that Jesus taught, Leslie Houlden writes that it would "be foolish to doubt that Jesus's teaching had a radical and startling character that caused a stir at the time and has continued to disturb."[14]

Once alerted to what Jesus was doing, the empire struck back; that is what empires do to those who defy them. In the short term Caesar won by crucifying Jesus, which we know to be an exclusively Roman method of extremely cruel execution, not the permitted Jewish method of death by stoning, however much Jesus's elitist, fellow Jewish opponents may have invited Imperial Rome's intervention. N.T. Wright is thus correct when he contests what he calls the "older liberal picture of 'Jesus the teacher' who . . . would be shocked to think of himself as, for instance, messiah."[15] Messiahship is exactly what he needed to claim and transform.

Thus the inspiring goodness of Jesus finds its climax in his willingness to risk and sacrifice his own life for what he embodied, taught and practiced. The cross is both the historic reality of that moral greatness and also its most powerful symbol, ethically and spiritually. The point has again been memorably made by N.T. Wright when he writes of the cross as follows: "It

---

12. Nolan, *Jesus Today*, 59-61.
13. Borg, *Meeting Jesus*, 70-73.
14. Houlden, *Jesus in History*, 446.
15. Borg and Wright, *Meaning of Jesus*, 24.

was to become the symbol of victory, but not of the victory of Caesar, nor of those who would oppose Caesar with Caesar's methods. It was to become the symbol, because it would be the means, of the victory of God."[16] Or, as I would prefer to say, it is the victory of Godhead as goodness at its most powerful.

For all who follow Jesus the great question is who Caesar is today, a question I also address in the next chapter: who or what ruthlessly dominates our existence, caring little or nothing for most of us and our planet. I suggest that it is the dictatorship of the market, the heartless, greedy economic system that affects everybody's life, creating mass poverty, environmental destruction and a host of other evils, while amassing phenomenal wealth for a small minority. To follow Jesus, by radical contrast, is to live by the lordship of love, truth and all the other moral and spiritual qualities that Godhead involves, and not kneel before the lordship of the market. And it *must* mean the unfinished business of carrying his vision and values onto the global economic and political systems of today. Caesar has not gone, just morphed into an even worse tyrant.[17] What we can do about changing it is suggested in the next chapter.

Similarly, when Jesus, in the closest consciousness of the personal, indwelling presence of Godhead, acted with complete freedom from the demands of the Law of Moses when it reduced rather than enhanced people's well-being, he scandalized, threatened and undermined the authority of those religious leaders for whom strict observance was God's cherished gift to Israel. Of these, none were more powerful than the elite associated with the Temple in Jerusalem.[18] In opposing Jesus these figures were not bad people, as genuine empathy for them and their deeply sincere convictions demonstrates; they were normal human beings guided by such light as they had. Christians must be very careful here not to fall into the terrible trap of anti-semitism by misjudging the religious opposition to Jesus as evil, a trap that into which their tradition has repeatedly fallen with the most appalling results for Jewish people, and a painful revelation of how far the Christian cumulative tradition has in some ways fallen short of its own best ethical standards.

It is thus not difficult to see that Jesus would evoke implacable hostility from those who were threatened by his message and example, whose effect is to empower the powerless politically, economically, ethically and above all spiritually. It is an ethical tragedy of the greatest proportions, in

16. Wright, *Jesus and the Victory*, 210.
17. Nolan, *Jesus Today*, 30–35.
18. Green, "Crucifixion," 93–101.

a world with so much avoidable evil, that what he began so bravely and powerfully, was so soon changed into the business, as somebody once said, of shipping souls to heaven, and of thinking that Godhead was like a benign, all-powerful Caesar, a contradiction in terms if ever there was one, all done in the name of the one who cared so greatly for the ill and the distressed in this world, and who entered Jerusalem on a donkey, not a horse, and most of all not on a chariot, there to demonstrate for all time that not even the worst of executions can kill a movement based on the greatest goodness. Embodying such goodness himself, Jesus had radiated it into the lives of those who embraced it and underwent the change of heart and mind signified by the Greek word *metanoia* (much too narrowly translated as repentance), showing that Godhead is an unstoppable force for good when we live out its implications, which brings me to the nature and meaning of Easter.

THE MEANING OF THE RESURRECTION OF CHRIST

Something of great spiritual and ethical power happened very shortly after Jesus was crucified and his body buried. That is abundantly clear on the basis of sound historical evidence and logical inferences from it.[19] For me the ethical meaning of the resurrection is that goodness, and especially great goodness, sooner or later defeats evil, and the deepest spiritual meaning is that supreme goodness defeats *any* evil, though that may take time because Godhead does not use Caesar's methods of coercion to impose instant salvation on the world, least of all violently.

In my book *A New Guide to the Debate about God* I presented and evaluated the evidence for the resurrection as carefully and thoroughly as I could. Except in one important way, I have no reason now to change my conclusion that the New Testament evidence for the bodily resurrection of Christ is too problematic to be accepted as proving that it really happened, but also too strong to be rejected out of hand.[20] The one important difference today is that in my 1992 book I did not include the lateness of our documentary evidence in the oldest manuscripts we have of it, compared to the reported event itself. This weakens the case for holding that something utterly remarkable happened to Jesus's body shortly after it was buried, leaving an empty tomb, as I substantiate later in this section. That said, let me now briefly summarize the evidence, bearing in mind that it is first and

---

19. Bockmuehl, "Resurrection," 102-18.
20. Prozesky, *New Guide*, 36-42.

foremost evidence of the *belief* that Jesus rose from the dead, not of that event itself.[21]

From as early as Paul's work for the Jesus movement and from the later, copied, New Testament Gospels, we have evidence that the earliest Christians were convinced that Jesus was still in some way alive, as Paul indicates in 1 Thessalonians 1:9-10 (NIV). It has to be accepted, all the same, that the most reliable evidence for this conviction, the original of the letter of Paul where he wrote that he had seen Christ and that Christ had appeared to him, in I Corinthians 9:1 and 15:8, has not survived, as I have already emphasized about all the originals. What we have is copies of copies, the earliest manuscripts of which date to centuries later than the originals. The same applies to the Gospel narratives about encountering the risen Jesus on and after that first Easter Sunday, and none of them can be ascertained as the work of any of the reported eye witnesses in those narratives, but come from later writers using the oral traditions about what was believed to have happened. Of this belief in the early church, that Jesus was in some way still alive, the subsequent, cumulative evidence is as good as any about him apart from the crucifixion itself, for which there is evidence independent of the New Testament, unlike that about the resurrection.

We can know about the crucifixion with as much historical assurance as is possible, from the New Testament texts themselves and also from the Jewish historian Josephus, in his work *Antiquities of the Jews* (c. 93 CE), and from his Roman counterpart Tacitus, who refers to it in his *Annals* somewhat later.[22]

We must, however, also be very clear at this point in the search for historical fact that the more unusual and especially unique an alleged event is, like a purported resurrection of a dead body, the stronger and more plentiful the first-hand, morally and intellectually credible the evidence for it must be. We do not have such evidence for the empty tomb of which the Gospels speak. Their accounts of it are not the reports of independent, verified eye witnesses but the product of an oral tradition that claims to go back to such witnesses, written at least a generation afterwards. Maybe they do go back like that, but we have no way of verifying it.

Our best evidence that Jesus somehow overcame death is Paul's statement that he had seen Christ after his crucifixion, never having encountered Jesus in the flesh, but this same evidence also hints at problems of interpreting what the resurrection tradition really means. Paul and others he mentions as witnesses in the New Testament, some by name, all had what

---

21. Bockmuehl, "Resurrection," 102-18.
22. Horsley, *Jesus in Context*, 22; Green, "Crucifixion," 89.

might be called visionary and auditory experiences of Christ after his death and burial. Many Christians accept the accounts of them as fact, believing that these experiences reveal the real, heavenly existence of God the Son, making his risen glory known to his followers. But this reasoning is at best dubious because a purported historical event isn't verified by a later theological interpretation of it.

If we think really rigorously, opening our minds not just to the methods of a dispassionate quest for facts, but also to as wide a range of information as possible along the interdisciplinary lines set out for theology by scholars like Wentzel van Huysteen,[23] we are obliged in all honesty to concede that those powerful experiences of Paul and others could be telling us something else that is factually, ethically and spiritually much more valuable: not about a heavenly, ascended Christ but about how the brain works in a situation that is very highly charged emotionally and in which claims that Jesus did not remain dead and buried were already present. It tells us that great goodness overcomes even horrifying evil and that Godhead as revealed by Jesus is an encompassing, indwelling and inspiring reality, here and now, that uses whatever it needs to generate ever greater goodness, like giving hope and direction to people's lives.

So I find myself agreeing with Marcus Borg's metaphorical interpretation of the empty tomb part of the resurrection tradition. He writes that "the truth of Easter itself, does not depend upon . . . the tomb being empty or on something happening to the corpse of Jesus. For me, the historical ground of Easter is very simple: the followers of Jesus, both then and now, continued to experience Jesus as a living reality after his death."[24]

A generation earlier Lloyd Geering had written an independently critical study of the resurrection in his book *Resurrection: A Symbol of Hope* (not listed, I see, by N.T. Wright in his very imposing 1996 book *Jesus and the Victory of God*), where Geering reached a similar conclusion. Here are his own words: "Jesus had left with his disciples such a vivid impression of the quality of life to be found in him, that when they were confronted with his death on the cross, they came to believe that death could not overpower a life of this quality . . . Since men had already been ready to believe that Moses and Elijah had been raised to heaven, how much more would those who had been Jesus's intimate disciples, and who had recognized in him one greater than Moses, come to the conviction that God had raised *him* from the dead!"[25]

---

23. van Huysteen et al., *In Search of Self*, 95–109.
24. Borg and Wright, *Meaning of Jesus*, 134–35.
25. Geering, *Resurrection*, 139.

The conclusion I find myself driven to by fidelity to the quest for facts and not by traditional beliefs about the resurrection, is once again that the New Testament accounts are not sufficiently strong as evidence to give us proven details about what happened but strong enough to justify the conclusion that something truly remarkable indeed happened to the Jesus movement after his death.[26] As for the empty tomb tradition, it is best to keep an open mind about what happened to the body of Jesus. We cannot know everything about the workings of the cosmos or the power that could come from people of truly great goodness and spiritual stature. There are claims, for example, that highly advanced Hindu ascetics can survive in icy mountain cave retreats with no warm clothing or fires. One yogi has even written a vivid account claiming to describe the bodily resurrection of his own spiritual master, Sri Yukteswar.[27]

Ethically, what counts is the triumph of good over evil. That happened in the Jesus movement despite the attempt to kill it by executing its leader in a particularly cruel way. Whatever else happened on that first Easter morning, goodness prevailed and lives on in the Jesus movement. Like Borg, I therefore interpret the New Testament narratives and Paul's letters about the resurrection as wonderful, symbolic accounts of what is perhaps history's greatest example of the power of very great goodness.

It might be contended, against this conclusion, that the sheer strength of the belief in Christ's bodily resurrection in the church down the centuries counts for its truth, but that ignores a very important psychological and emotional factor. Fear of death and grief at bereavement are very real experiences for most people. To be taught by those you trust, especially in childhood, that death is not the end because everlasting life with God and your loved ones awaits you, is to hear the greatest good news and to welcome it with joy. I have no doubt that the earliest belief in a bodily resurrection arose honestly and understandably, even if, in that literalist version of resurrection faith, it was mistaken, but once current it is easy to see how gladly it would be embraced.

Another contention in Conservative Christianity that I have encountered is that the shocking death of Jesus must have been a devastating blow to his closest and most devoted followers, spelling the defeat and end of the Jesus movement. What we know, of course, is that the movement was not defeated but thrived, despite determined and at times deadly opposition. Therefore, so the argument goes, Jesus could not have ended in death but triumphed over it by the power of God, being raised bodily on the third day.

26. Bockmuehl, "Resurrection," 107.
27. Yogananda, *Autobiography*, 336.

This argument is, however, based on a mistaken assumption about the nature of Jesus's leadership, as was explained earlier in this chapter. He *shared* his goodness and thereby enabled his movement to exist and thrive without his physical presence, once the dreadful shock of his crucifixion had been overcome by precisely the inspiration of that goodness.

Things were different with John the Baptist. His once-vigorous movement lost its momentum and died out after his beheading because it was too dependent on his personal, physical presence.[28] An analogy from recent South African history helps make the point. Steve Biko's Black Consciousness movement involved the same kind of leadership that I see in Jesus, namely sharing the leader's vison in ways that empower others, this time being proud of being black and taking responsibility for their own liberation. Biko, as is well known in South Africa and is well documented, was brutally murdered by agents of the apartheid state, and many of us remember vividly the shock of that news, but it did not mean the end of what he pioneered; in fact it gained great determination and strength from it.[29]

To conclude this exploration of the ethical and spiritual meaning of the resurrection tradition, I want to contend that the death of Jesus by crucifixion completely freed Jesus's followers from the possible dependency trap of believing they had always to look to him for leadership, while Easter freed them for new life in the unstoppable power of such great goodness to *be* his living presence for the ages to come. The resurrection is his closest followers' discovery in themselves of what he had already shown: that great goodness once shared and made into a movement cannot be defeated even by the untimely and appalling death of its founder. I therefore resonate with some words in Rowan Williams's book *God With Us: The Meaning of the Cross and Resurrection, Then and Now*: "Believing in the resurrection is believing that the new age has been inaugurated, the new world has begun." When Williams adds that the resurrection is final and the last word, and that nothing can go beyond it, I believe he is referring to the crowning truth that dawned on Jesus's followers that first Easter, that goodness will prevail over the worst evil even if it sometimes takes time, and provided we keep faith.[30]

SCHOLARLY CORROBORATIONS ABOUT JESUS

What I now wish to show is that there is no shortage of scholarly support for my conclusions about Jesus, of which I mention a few important examples.

28. Chilton, "Friends and Enemies," 72–76.
29. Pityana et al., *Bounds of Possibility*; Macqueen, *Black Consciousness*, 201.
30. Williams, *God With Us*, 62–63.

These include, but are not confined to, scholars associated with the well-known Jesus Seminar, started by Robert Funk and the Westar Institute, who worked from 1985 onwards on what we can know about the historical Jesus. In the following paragraphs I mention some of the work I have found especially valuable.

The scholar who most sparked my interest in Jesus primarily as an ethical figure is the South African Catholic theologian Albert Nolan, whose book *Jesus before Christianity: The Gospel of Liberation* came into my hands in the late 1970s. Especially in chapters 3, 4, and 5 Nolan greatly encouraged my existing conviction that if the church is to be true to its founder it must engage far more effectively with the problems facing the world, also giving what I found convincing academic grounds for distinguishing the historical Jesus from the Christ figure of church doctrine in some key respects, like the strongly this-worldly ethical passion to be discerned in the Jesus of history.[31] Thirty years after that book appeared, Nolan wrote one about the spirituality of Jesus, already mentioned, covering in it some ethically and spiritually significant developments during the interval between the two books. Those relating to my views of the cosmos and human nature were indicated in part I, while those relevant to my understanding of Godhead and Jesus appear in this third part of the book.

Soon after encountering Albert Nolan both in print and in person, I discovered the study of Jesus by British biographer Humphrey Carpenter, especially the fourth chapter of his short book simply called *Jesus*. He concluded it with the following words: "Jesus was not just a moral teacher. This book has tried to emphasize that fact. His appeal was just as much charismatic as intellectual. But in the field of moral teaching his forcefulness has had no equal."[32]

Turning now to more recent Jesus scholarship, John Dominic Crossan has written that Christianity requires "a theology founded and grounded on the historical Jesus." He adds that "if the biblical Christ is the norm, criterion, and discriminant of the Christian Bible, then the *historical* Jesus is the norm, criterion, and discriminant of the biblical Christ."[33] As far back as my boyhood, Jesus as an inspiring ethical leader appealed to me more than Jesus as the supposed, heavenly savior of the Nicene Creed. Many years later a visiting lecture on Pietermaritzburg's university campus by the eminent scholar James Barr on the subject of "The Centrality of the Historical Jesus" strongly supported this outlook. He told us that doctrine must give space to

---

31. Nolan, *Jesus before Christianity*, 20–42.
32. Carpenter, *Jesus*, 95.
33. Crossan, *How to Read the Bible*, 171, 185, emphasis added.

the Jesus of history and to the differences between that Jesus and the beliefs of mature Christianity.[34]

The next influential scholar from whose studies I draw support is Geza Vermes. Noting the differing portrayals of Jesus even in the New Testament in his book *The Changing Faces of Jesus*, he identifies the following faces: the "Stranger from heaven"; Paul's "Son of God and universal Redeemer of mankind,"[35] "Prophet, Lord and Christ" in Acts;[36] and the "Charismatic healer and teacher and eschatological enthusiast" in the Synoptic Gospels.[37] He further adds the following highly pertinent comment: "By the end of the first century Christianity had lost sight of the real Jesus and of the original meaning of his message. Paul, John and their churches replaced him by the otherworldly Christ of faith."[38] About the meaning of the concept of the resurrection in the New Testament, Vermes writes in his more recent work called *Jesus: Nativity, Passion, Resurrection* that it did not have a major effect on the Gospel, a comment that might surprise many Conservative Christians.[39]

Another influential scholar who offers general support for progressive accounts of Jesus is Marcus Borg in his books *Jesus, a New Vision: Spirit, Culture and the Life of Scholarship*, followed by *Meeting Jesus for the First Time* and by *Jesus in Contemporary Scholarship*.[40] Underlining the way Jesus showed great compassion for those who suffer, Borg wrote that he was a healer and exorcist who taught "a path of transformation centered in the sacred."[41] Lastly, a valuable scholarly account of radical scholarship about the historical Jesus is provided by Lloyd Geering in the chapters "Excavating Jesus" and "The Recovery of Jesus's Teaching" in his book *Coming Back to Earth: From Gods, to God, to Gaia*.[42]

My reading of the work of other leading Jesus scholars also provides support for important parts of the interpretation I have just offered, though none of them apart from Peter G. Kirchschlaeger[43] centralizes the ethical

---

34. Personal notes dated October 7, 1986.
35. Vermes, *Changing Faces*, 76–115.
36. Vermes, *Changing Faces*, 116–46.
37. Vermes, *Changing Faces*, 147–221.
38. Vermes, *Changing Faces*, 263.
39. Vermes, *Jesus*.
40. Borg, *Jesus, a New Vision*; see also his *Meeting Jesus*, and *Jesus in Contemporary Scholarship*.
41. Borg, *Meeting Jesus*, 68, 70.
42. Geering, *Coming Back to Earth*, 7–63.
43. Kirchschlaeger, "The Moral-Theological Dimension," 196–216.

dimension of the liberating message, practice and influence of Jesus the way Albert Nolan did from within the perspective of Christian belief, unlike my own, independently ethical perspective.

From these scholars, or at least some of them as indicated, there is support for the following aspects of my interpretation of Jesus: that the most important of Jesus's teachings and actions can be reliably established as historical fact; that his identity was strongly Jewish, as affirmed mainly by Sanders, Vermes and Wright; that he expressed marked socio-ethical concerns which Borg and Horsley confirm; that he was baptized by John but moved away from him to launch his own movement; that he was a gifted healer and teacher who evoked both a dedicated following and also deadly opposition; that he taught his followers the Lord's Prayer; that he spoke of what I am calling Godhead with the greatest sense of divine closeness; that he went from his native Galilee to Jerusalem for Passover, causing an upset in the Temple area and meeting the subsequent events that culminated in his crucifixion on the authority of Pontius Pilate; and that from the first Easter a profound conviction arose and remained among his followers that his mission had not ended in defeat on the cross.

The points just listed do not imply that there is overall unanimity among the scholars in question. On the contrary, perhaps the most striking impression their work creates is how divergent some of their most important interpretations of Jesus are. Wright, for example, finds more Gospel material to be historical than Crossan finds, while Geering and Crossan find Jesus to be more akin to the Greek Cynics as a wisdom teacher than Vermes, Wright and others, who see him as much more Jewish. These divergences are not trivial and evoke from me the question why this is so, given the great stature of all the scholars in question. Albert Schweitzer long ago warned about a tendency for scholars to see Jesus in their own image, with subjective concerns proving stronger than objective scholarship.[44] This could be the case, up to a point, for we never completely escape our own conditioning, but my own explanation is different. I think the evidence revels a Jesus of such immense ethical and spiritual depth and richness that he surpasses even our best scholarly ability and skill to capture. If so, we shall never arrive at a final, definitive, accepted picture of Jesus, beyond a reliable core centered on the inspiring goodness that he embodied, and should rejoice about that as part of the meaning of salvation, to which I now turn.

---

44. Powell, *Jesus as a Figure*, 16.

SALVATION

Salvation and its equivalents like atonement, liberation, deliverance and enlightenment, is the most important feature common to all religions, especially the Axial ones. In the ethical and spiritual perspective of this book, salvation at a personal, micro-ethical level means being enabled to participate in and practice the transforming power of the greatest, shared goodness; it means understanding this wondrous blessing as being drawn into Godhead's own goodness, which the Gospels present Jesus speaking of as the Kingdom of Heaven and the Kingdom of God.

Being universal, that goodness can be experienced and embraced anywhere and at any time. It is not the exclusive gift of any single culture or religion, which explains why saintliness is to be found in all traditions, as John Hick has shown in his landmark book *An Interpretation of Religion*.[45] Making the same point even more bluntly from an Indian Christian perspective, M. Thomas Thangaraj writes that Jesus is one of humanity's "windows through which to see God" and thus not the only one.[46] Similarly, he reports that S. Mark Heim sees salvation as a Christian view of the destination and end of human existence, among others.[47] What these examples sufficiently show is that there are scholarly Christian thinkers for whom the exclusivism of traditional, Conservative Christian doctrine is simply unacceptable.

Salvation does not end with morally transformed individuals. It also transforms contexts, systems and structures, so proving effective also at meso- and macro-ethical levels, or it should do if it genuinely carries the spirit and power of Godhead as revealed for Christianity by Jesus and by his movement at its moral best. In other words, salvation means the growing reality of holistic, lasting well-being. It starts with the radical change of heart and mind signified by *metanoia*. This certainly requires an honest acceptance of one's wrongs, but even more important is embracing with all one's heart, mind and strength the greatest goodness understood spiritually in Christianity as Godhead and as incarnated in Jesus.

Negatively, salvation means people and the structures that affect them being drawn away from every form of moral wrong, extending to the greatest evils afflicting our existence like violent exploitation and cruelty. John Dominic Crossan and Marcus Borg, among others, have shown in a film series about the historical Jesus that his message of salvation included a very

---

45. Hick, *Interpretation of Religion*, 299–342.
46. Thangaraj, "Jesus the Christ," 45.
47. Heim, *Salvations*.

powerful focus on contesting the political and economic evils of his time and place.[48]

In the popular language of human brain science, salvation can therefore be seen as people and their societies being drawn away from the grip of reptilian selfhood, reptilian systems and reptilian structures. In the language of theology, salvation means being drawn away from personal and societal sin, defined as anything that harms the love-filled goodness of Godhead.

Seen in the light of this progressive understanding of Christian salvation, the traditional theories of atonement in Conservative Christianity, excellently presented by Alister McGrath in his textbook of Christian theology,[49] are, I contend, no more than outdated, symbolic attempts to explain how Jesus saves, when he is seen as a heavenly redeemer who rescues us from an allegedly terrible fate after we die, provided we accept him as such in this one. Except for Abelard's very different view, these theories of atonement place virtually all the emphasis on the cross in the achievement of salvation, rather than on Jesus's ministry and message with their power to transform lives and societies here and now. Moreover, some of these traditional views of how salvation works strike me and others as crude, unloving and morally repugnant, like contending that God, the loving heavenly Father, sent his Son into the world to suffer and die bloodily and unjustly, in order to save us from an alleged post-mortem fate that itself seems utterly immoral, as I argued in part II.

In addition, for a progressive Christian, there are no adequate grounds for believing that there is a real being called Satan who is the basic cause of all evil and from whose power we need to be saved. That notion belongs to an obsolete, mythological mind-set which deeply thinking, ethically driven people must outgrow, which does not mean that evil isn't all too real, for it surely is. Such people also see all too clearly the very dangerous dependency trap of a belief that the devil and his alleged minions make us do bad things, in the famous but tragic words of the South African sports star, Hansie Cronje, when confronted with his corrupt, match-fixing misdeeds.[50] Moral depth means that we must have the moral courage to accept the responsibility of defeating evil ourselves in the power of Godhead.

For a Christian faith based as fully as possible on the Godhead of supreme goodness, salvation also means being saved from anything in our Christian heritage that falls short of that standard. This would include all the validly identified ethical problems noted in part II, from morally dubious

---

48. Crossan and Borg, *First Light*.
49. McGrath, *Christian Theology*, 337–50.
50. Wilde, *Caught*, 16.

and mistaken doctrines about God, salvation and hell to mistaken views and uses of the Bible and of other faiths, no matter how sincerely these are held or how firmly embedded they may be in the cumulative tradition of Conservative Christianity.

Of these the belief that strikes me as most in conflict with the reality of a Godhead of the greatest possible goodness is the notion that such a God has instituted a literal and terrifying hell of eternal torment. Here is how one influential conservative puts this notion. "When people who have rejected the claims of Christ die, their souls go immediately to eternal punishment . . . Scripture teaches that hell is real, eternal and unspeakably terrible."[51] The Progressive Christianity envisaged in this book would add that we also need to be saved from churches more interested in power, money and ritual than in defeating evil in the world and in its own ranks, like sheltering pedophile priests, harming women and gay people, or dignifying genocide with the word "holy."

It is sometimes said that we live now in a post-secular world because of the undoubted resurgence of conservative expressions of religion in parts of the globe, though not all, of the kind well described by Micklethwaite and Wooldridge in their 2009 book *God is Back: How the Global Rise of Faiths is Changing the World*. This is, however, only partly true. Along with a morally governed spirituality, the most powerful forces in our world are the democratic vision, contemporary capitalism, science, and the technology that comes from it. These are through-and-through secular forces that operate independently of religious belief, and especially of religious control. There is nothing post-secular about them.

Such a secular world not only needs the powerful, this-worldly salvation shown by Jesus in the Christian strand of history but also relevant to all other strands; it is also ready to embrace it, once it is freed of everything in its cumulative tradition that makes it merely provincial when it can and should be global. Ethically governed spiritual power can do that, not doctrines, Creeds and beliefs that are intelligible and credible only within a particular religious and cultural tradition. As for the question of what happens when we die, apart from our bodily dissolution, in honesty to goodness we can safely leave that to Godhead and the future. There is a world to save right now.

---

51. Grudem, *Christian Beliefs*, 115, citing the following New Testament passages: Matt 25:41, Mark 9:48, Luke 16:28, Rev 14:13 and especially Rev 14:11, all seemingly taken literally.

JESUS, THE SPIRITUAL AND ETHICAL PIONEER

I see Jesus as a creative, spiritual and ethical pioneer of unsurpassed significance and courage for a world that needs all the moral help it can get. Ethically he is for me supreme goodness incarnate, unique in his way but not the only embodiment of supreme goodness, opening that reality to all who embrace it as he did. As such he is globally relevant because goodness is an unbounded, holistic, global reality. The way his ethical practice was united with his spirituality makes him the incarnation of Godhead in the language of his movement, using the symbolic words of his Jewish culture for that supremely uplifting power: God, Father, and heavenly King. He applied the prophetic principle of challenging unjust power from his Jewish heritage with unsurpassed authority to start the Jesus movement, yet was also supremely free of any constraints on boundless goodness in that heritage, like trusting the minutiae of religious law for divine blessing. This made him free of what the influential scholar of world religions, Ninian Smart, once called "the dictatorship of the dead" in my hearing. The best historical evidence leaves me in no doubt that he understood with exceptional clarity that love and truth are what truly saves, and that the only truly great leadership is love- and truth-filled leadership that shares its goodness with others.

Earlier in this book I quoted a haunting passage from Whitehead where he wrote that the early church, too much influenced and even governed by Rome's imperial ethos, gave God the attributes that belong to Caesar. Now, at the end of my perspective on Jesus, I return to that quotation to complete it. The words "not of this world" in it must not be understood to mean anything dualistic or supernatural. That would contradict the whole tenor of Whitehead's thought. What they mean is that the kingdom Jesus shares with us is a present and future commonwealth, in this world yet not of its pervasive oppressions:

"There is, however, in the Galilean origin of Christianity yet another suggestion . . . It does not emphasize the ruling Caesar . . . It dwells upon the tender elements in the world, which slowly and in quietness operate by love; and it finds its purpose in the present immediacy of a kingdom not of this world."[52]

---

52. Whitehead, *Process and Reality*, 343.

Chapter 14

The Jesus Movement Today and a Global Goodness Project

It is not enough to dream of a world without needless suffering. The dream alone is mere day-dreaming if it does not inspire action. So this last chapter of *Honest to Goodness* gives what I believe must now be done if, to use religious language, the inexhaustibly generous power and dream of Godhead for a world of lasting, shared well-being for all, and for the planet itself, is at last truly to come on earth—"a *counterimperial ecology of love*" in Catherine Keller's wonderful phrase.[1]

This culminating chapter has six sections after these opening paragraphs. First it outlines what I mean by a global goodness project, followed by a short account of what the world's religions can contribute to the project. Then there is a longer account about what I believe Christians can do for it, including some brief suggestions for Anglicans and Episcopalians, given my long connection with them. The section following it is addressed to Roman Catholics, their church being the largest and most powerful religious organization in the world, followed by what I see as the contribution of higher education to the proposed goodness project. I include academia because of the immense value many universities have given to independent Christian scholarship, both critical and creative, and because of their related significance for the furthering of the good. The chapter ends with a very short section about the critically important issue of saving the environment.

What does the greatest goodness, and therefore also the moral perfection of Godhead and the Jesus movement that incarnates it, now require for the world? They require a safe and healthy planet; they require contexts of

---

1. Keller, "The Love of Postcolonialism," 224.

justice and peace in which lasting human well-being becomes the rule, not the exception as it is now, marked by health, clean water, adequate nourishment, respect, good education and other requirements for people to thrive together.

Vital will also be the identifications and transformation of all that undermines the integrity of nature and human well-being. In the language of the earliest Jesus movement, we must now identify who, what and where Caesar is, understanding that Caesar means both individual and especially structural evils like monopolies, dictatorships and cultures of gender and other discriminations, to which our religions are by no means immune. Here I recall with admiration just how well Bishop John Robinson understood this situation over fifty years ago, writing as follows in *The New Reformation*, that "the movement of re-formation will come, in Colin Williams's words, by the Church 'allowing the *forms* of her renewed life to grow around *the shapes of worldly need'*—provided, I would add, that 'need' is understood to cover the world in its strength as well as the world in its weakness."[2]

Three great forces are already available to pursue this project in the service of greater goodness on earth: conscience, provided it is given the support it needs, as I explain below; the goodness in our religions worldwide; and morally committed systems of higher education. The following pages set out what I see as their respective contributions.

THE GLOBAL GOODNESS PROJECT

Humanity now has an historic opportunity to help promote a global initiative for the greatest possible good, which I passionately believe Christians and also others should see as a vital part of today's Jesus movement. I allude here to an important point made by the influential economist John Kenneth Galbraith in his study of the nature of power.[3] He pointed out that the most effective form of power in today's world is organizational power. On reading it I was struck immediately that alone of humanity's most important activities, goodness has no such support devoted just to promoting it. Faith has religious organizations; trade has the World Trade Organization; knowledge has educational institutions; research has universities and research institutes; injury has the Red Cross and similar organizations; but ethics has nothing of the kind, and it will never achieve its potential to promote the greatest possible inclusive well-being without it. So it must be created. Some years ago I began to explore this idea further in a cooperative way by

---

2. Robinson, *New Reformation*, 91.
3. Galbraith, *Anatomy of Power*.

consulting others. Here is what I wrote to them, somewhat shortened and edited:

> "Dear Colleagues
>
> I am sending this email to a group of friends and colleagues in various countries whose insights into ethical matters have greatly enriched my own work, to request their views about a question that has increasingly occupied my mind over the past year. Here it is: Is there a need for some sort of support structure for the many but often isolated ethical individuals and groups in our societies, and even globally?
>
> "The question arose as follows. I introduced a course at my university a few years ago called 'The Ethics of Power.' As I developed it, I became more and more interested in a point made in one of the books I used, namely that the single most powerful locus of power in today's world is the organization. In reflecting on this and on the way organized structures bring such massive power to various aspects of life and work, it hit me that there is no such organizational or institutional support specifically for ethical effort, at least not in parts of the world known to me.
>
> "In the past, where largely mono-cultural societies were the norm, religious institutions traditionally provided moral guidance and support for individuals. But that has greatly changed, though not in some parts of the world, like many Muslim countries. Where religious diversity has grown and religious influence declined, and where secular societies have emerged, this religious framework of support for moral practice is no longer there for many people, and there is nothing else to encourage them except for pockets of academic support, usually with very little financial resourcing, plus some individuals with resources of their own and, very occasionally, corporates and sympathetic politicians. There seems to be nothing with any on-going organizational coherence, capacity and, crucially, with no other agenda.
>
> "Since moral strength does not take care of itself but has to be nurtured, and since brave, conscientious individuals who resist the evils of their societies, whether in South Africa, Zimbabwe, Tibet, China or the USA, are often at risk, sometimes greatly so, and are often isolated and opposed by powerful agencies, I arrived at the question above.
>
> "I recently approached an internationally eminent and highly ethical mentor about this and the reply was positive, asking me to explore it further with others and come back with some suggestions about next steps. Hence this email to you,

asking if you think that in our globalizing world, with so many destructive forces, the human conscience needs some kind of support structure, and if so, what key functions it could best provide, and what form these might most effectively take. I have developed some answers of my own but think it is best to hold them back for now."

The response was highly encouraging. All but one, who was only initially doubtful, strongly supported the idea, but none had any practical suggestions. I am therefore now including this project in the present book, only this time I am calling it the global goodness project and seeing it as what the Jesus movement must now embrace and share together with people of all faiths and philosophies. It cannot be confined to or an extension of just the religions as it needs to be global and open to all equally, but the faith communities and also academia can help support it in ways like those I suggest in the remaining sections of this chapter, in an equal partnership with people of any faith, or none, who see the huge need to promote greater goodness effectively in the world.

In setting out my suggestions, I do so as an already committed participant in the goodness project who sees the Jesus movement in progressive perspective, and I understand very clearly that my participation must express and be subject to their ethical values. It must be done caringly, sensitively, respectfully, fairly, and accurately.

THE RELIGIONS AND THE GOODNESS PROJECT

In chapter 6 the section on the dimensions of religion drew attention to the ways in which the various religions typically express their experiences of faith ritually, verbally in symbolically powerful stories, in doctrines, and also practically in their ethics and social formations. My studies of a wide range of religions have shown that the ritual dimension tends to be prominent, even paramount; for example, the way theists focus on praising and thanking the God they believe in, or non-theistic believers focus on meditation to open their minds to what they see as ultimate. The ethical dimension is always there but does not strike me as paramount in and of itself in what I have observed, studied and experienced.

The question that a secularist, mindful of this reality, might want to put at this point is whether religion really does have any part to play in a global goodness project, where ethics is absolutely paramount. Such a secularist might add that the concern of religion is with what it sees as another world altogether, a world of the spirit, and is therefore greatly concerned with how people can attain it both now and in the afterlife they believe awaits us, making it a seemingly dubious candidate for a this-worldly global goodness project.

My reply is that the religions nonetheless most definitely do have a contribution, in fact a vital one, because it is their experience of a supreme goodness that gave rise to and sustains them in the first place, as I have tried to show elsewhere in this book, and demonstrated in detail in my book *Religion and Ultimate Well-Being*.[4] To cite just a few examples of this reality, what else but a very great goodness was involved in Confucius's project of humane education as a civilizing force in ancient China, or the Buddha's message of the enlightened path to overcome suffering, or the repeated emphasis in the Qur'an on the compassion and beneficence of Allah? So although a primary concern with ritual and the belief that there is another level of reality, beyond and far more important than this present one, do strike me as outweighing the explicitly ethical, this-worldly concerns of much religion, the goodness has always been there, working through the rituals and the institutions, though less than maximally powerful.

Strong theological support for this contention that religion indeed can contribute to the goodness project comes from Keith Ward. In *A Vision to Pursue* he wrote that religion "encourages a turning away from selfishness by relating individuals to a supreme objective value which is their ultimate goal," adding that the different faiths are engaged in a common pursuit of a supreme value, though they conceive this in diverse ways.[5]

There is, however, an essential proviso that must be met by all faith traditions that seek to be part of the goodness project, which I feel ethically bound to raise, doing so with great gratitude for the abundant good in them and their members, and very respectfully. They need to face honestly, openly, bravely and exhaustively the ethical criticisms that religion's critics, and indeed believers themselves, raise about aspects of them, no matter how painful that will be, and then, drawing on the great goodness that is their foundation, overcome whatever is less than good. This is a task for insiders. But even though I am an outsider to all but one faith tradition, my encounters and friendships with people of other faiths, and none, make me believe that the rich ethics in each of them will prevail, and that the necessary self-criticism will happen.

That more than justifies my belief that the world's religions have a very important contribution to make to the goodness project. What is essential here is that they see their role as a supportive, contributory one, not one of

4. Prozesky, *Religion and Ultimate Well-Being*, 18–46.
5. Ward, *Vision to Pursue*, 188.

ownership and least of all one of control, for two reasons. Firstly, the project must be global. It must be open to all equally, believers and secularists alike, from any and every culture. No religion and no group of religions can do that alone in a world where very many people of conscience no longer accept any religion. The other reason is that so long as certain religions define themselves primarily as what they see as the true faith, which Conservative Christianity and some other powerful faiths certainly do, they will continue to divide humanity, whereas the global goodness project must be a genuinely uniting force, or a failure.

Since my own personal connection is with Christianity, I cannot even begin to say what kind of contribution the other faiths and secularists can make to the project. All I can do is respectfully invite and welcome their involvement as equals in whatever way they feel able and willing to do, adding that I reject completely the exclusivist notion that the faith that has so deeply influenced my life is truer and more ethical than others.

CHRISTIANITY AND THE GOODNESS PROJECT

What was stated above about all the religions naturally applies fully to Christianity. To be part of the goodness project and to recognize it as a great doorway of opportunity for today's Jesus movement, it too must accept goodness as its foundation, actively seeking and transforming in itself all that falls short of or even harms that foundation. That means recognizing and embracing the wondrous good news of the power of great goodness, understood as none other than Godhead and thus as the voice of Jesus for our time and world. As Archbishop Emeritus Desmond Tutu has so memorably said, "Without God we can't; without us God won't," cited by Marcus Borg, and echoed by John Dominic Crossan's description of what Jesus launched as the "collaborate eschaton."[6]

Not only must ethical soundness therefore characterize Christianity's every feature; the ethics must be multi-levelled, comprising each of the micro-, meso- and macro-levels, both in relation to itself and in its critique of the wider world. This applies especially to the now numerically dominant conservative part of the churches, most of all to our fundamentalists, but also, though in my view much less extensively, to their liberal and radical members and structures. The practice of the conservatives and some liberals may indeed be very other-worldly and evangelistic in its focus; they and arguably most liberal church members may indeed prize worship more than meso- and macro-ethics, but in all of them the ethical power that Jesus

6. Crossan and Borg, *First Light*.

infused into and continues to give to his movement remains present and ready to redeem whatever needs redemption. So I have no doubt that Christianity can and should be part of the goodness project.

Progressive Christianity and the rediscovered Jesus movement

Absolutely fundamental for the role of Progressive Christianity in the global goodness project is its foregrounding of ethics and complete openness to truth and inspiration from any source. This is made clear in its eight core points, which were cited in chapter 6. That in turn enables Progressive Christians to be pioneers in developing new ways of carrying the Jesus movement into the world and in the churches themselves. This includes the highly important ethical and spiritual challenge of identifying any Caesars within Christianity itself.

Jesus of Nazareth left the gift of his ongoing, organizational presence to the future as the Jesus movement, mostly seen as the church, but such great goodness as he motivated cannot be monopolized by any particular institution. His own flesh and blood presence has of course been very long gone, and the written traditions about him are not strong enough as historical evidence to give us much assured detail about that presence, as I have tried to show, though it does give us enough to justify commitment to him and his goodness. What we do have today is his movement of loving, truth-filled commitment as his abiding, physical presence.[7] This is the community of those who accept the Jesus way of salvation from the evils in the world, and join his movement of transformative ethical action. Jesus-focused and Jesus-inspired, it is his living presence through time, more committed to serving the good and deepening our experience and understanding of the meaning of Godhead, than to be too often praising God or asking for his mercy, least of all as supposedly filthy rags beneath his feet, as I once heard a conservative preacher say.

To be truly Jesus-filled, his movement therefore has to shed every remaining vestige of Caesar. Only so will its people be genuinely liberated from the dependency trap in their faith, worship and practice.[8] However much the Jesus movement strives to be true to its founder, it remains a movement of human beings, and is therefore subject to all the frailty and fallibility of everything human, itself in need of salvation from everything

---

7. Marcus, "Jewish Christianity," 87–102; see also Meeks, "Social and Ecclesial Life," 145–73.

8. Scott and Harker, *Humanity at Work*, 24–28 and *Myth*; 21–26; see also Tillich, *Dynamics of Faith* and Schlesinger, "Schleiermacher on the Necessity," 235–44.

that falls short of great goodness, always reforming itself, in the brilliant insight of the Protestant Reformation. What follows is my initial, personal contribution to the great creative challenge of the progressive Jesus movement to do that, to serve also as an invitation to others to do the same, for only together can we meet this challenge.

To achieve its fullest potential for goodness, the Jesus movement must be crystal-clear about its core mission, which I contend is to work always for the triumph of good over evil in the world by whatever means are both needed and consonant with the highest standards of love and truth. At heart these will be the spiritual, educational and practical forms of the goodness project. Given the deadly presence of macro-evils like organized greed, violence, exploitation, poverty, systematic untruth and environmental damage, I contend that its work of world moral salvation must chiefly focus on the macro-level of ethical transformation. Conservative Christianity tends to focus attention mainly on the micro-ethical level, with its emphasis on personal sin, repentance and forgiveness. There is no denying the importance of this level because it is where we mostly experience love and its opposite, and learn the imperative of truthfulness, but it cannot be enough. The prophetic principle of speaking truth to power must never be neglected, and it includes the moral duty of the churches to examine themselves and their leadership honestly and rigorously for everything that needs to be corrected.

In my novel *Warring Souls*, Sarah, the main character and on the radical side of Christianity, spoke of the need in the churches for what she called "five salvations."[9] They are the Bible, Jesus, the concept of God, the traditional, exclusivist Christian view of other religions, and of salvation. In chapters 12 and 13 of this book I gave my account of what it is, for me at least, to see God as supreme goodness, and as Godhead in theological terms, Jesus as the incarnation of Godhead's supreme goodness, religions inclusively, and salvation itself. There is no need therefore to repeat that here; what is needed is a goodness-based view of the Bible, for no spiritual task is more urgently needed within Christianity at this time than to confront and change the damaging reality of widespread Bible misuse, sincere and uncomprehending though it is.

The Bible in the light of supreme goodness, not of tradition

The Bible is a brilliant jewel. Even the moral and factual imperfections that are visible when we look closely enough in the light of ethical reason cannot dim the spiritual and ethical light that shines in and through it, provided it

9. Prozesky, *Warring Souls*, 90–92.

is accepted for what it is, the collected words of human authors expressing their experiences of the power and presence of the supreme goodness they trusted as Godhead, a reality their minds refracted like convex lenses, some better bevelled and polished than others. Their words have given meaning and direction to lives for over three thousand years since the earliest ones were spoken and written, just as Daniel, chapter 12:3 has given meaning and direction to my life.

One of the greatest blessings of critical biblical scholarship has been to give us this understanding of Scripture and save it from misuse and abuse. That in itself is a massive contribution to what Christianity can do for the contemporary Jesus movement and through it to the global goodness project. Progressive Christians salute this achievement, as do liberals and some conservatives, for its results are nothing less than revolutionary. They change our understanding of the Bible's origins, formation, authorship, authority and purported factual assertions, and enable us to face up to its occasional moral shortcomings when read under the controlling principle of supreme goodness, which frees us to emphasize its preponderant goodness. Many Conservative Christians, fundamentalists especially, seem unwilling or unable to face those biblical problems, giving rise to much moral and spiritual misdirection about its teachings.

The eminent South Africa biblical scholar Gerald West is thus entirely justified in presenting Scripture as itself "a site of struggle," and in asserting forthrightly that it is "both a resource for life and an agent of death," brave, prophetic words that many traditional believers will doubtless find deeply disturbing, but urgently need to understand and take to heart.[10] An example of how to do so is given in a recent journal article by Robert Stegmann and Marilyn Faure where they advocate a metaphorical interpretation of the term "Word of God" for the Bible, so rejecting the widespread literalization of it, and contend that we need a post-critical hermeneutic and post-colonial kind of biblical criticism, exactly what I advocate for Progressive Christianity because the concept of post-coloniality means liberation from all forms of hegemony like locking our reading of Scripture into obedience mode.[11]

Nobody who has even a modest knowledge of Scripture needs to be persuaded about its glories. For any reader who still needs convincing about what is morally problematic in it, here are a few examples of the type of difficulty giving rise to West's comment, some of them already mentioned in this book. I present them as questions.

---

10. West, "The Co-optation of the Bible," 197.
11. Stegmann and Faure, "Reading Scripture," 228, 232.

Why are there two differing accounts of creation in the first chapters of Genesis, in which, among other differences, different Hebrew divine names are used? Why do the Gospels according to Matthew, Mark and Luke have a strong family resemblance but also some important differences about the same thing, like the narratives about Jesus's birth in Matthew and Luke, in strong contrast to John's Gospel? Why do the Gospels give different accounts of who first saw the risen Christ? Why do some of the letters attributed to Paul differ from others about the same issue, like the position of women and slavery? Even more serious are the moral problems we find in a number of parts of the Bible, but these have already been presented in part II and do not need to be repeated here. It is an enormous ethical achievement by critical scholars to have enabled us to recognize these and the many other difficulties in Scripture and interpret them in ways that no longer treat as sacred passages that are clearly ungodly.

The next section of this chapter sets out my understanding of Scripture from a progressive perspective. After that I have things to say about the Bible in the hands and lives of its more traditional, conservative readers, especially fundamentalist Christians. To set the scene, I reproduce here, again very slightly edited, a press article of mine that appeared in my daily newspaper, starting with its title:

"Reading and misreading the Bible

"The Bible is vital for Christians and a powerful, indirect influence on others, especially about ethics, but sometimes its readers give us conflicting messages. Thus there are Christians who quote biblical passages that say gay practice is sinful. They take them as final simply because they are in the Bible, and they believe that what the Bible says, God says, and He cannot err.

"Such Christians believe that theirs is the only way to interpret the Bible. While the term 'fundamentalist' is not scholarly, it has stuck, so I will use it for them. I do so with much sympathy as I myself once read the Bible their way, before wise and loving Christians showed me another way that has been a spiritual and ethical liberation. These Christians regard some Biblical passages like the ones about gays as invalid. They include some evangelicals and moderates as well as liberals and radicals. For them it is not true that everything in scripture comes from God.

"Which group is right and why is there this difference about the Bible? I am not a biblical scholar and have no mandate to speak for Christianity. Nor am I now a liberal theologian.

My field is religion and ethics. So I turn to Christians who are experts on biblical matters. We go to trustworthy experts about bodily health, so why not also about spiritual health? I particularly recommend Keith Ward, a top Oxford theologian.

"Mindful that all Christians seek to live by a God of perfect goodness and love, embodied in Christ, my questions to these experts are why there is this difference about how to read the Bible and why so many committed Christians reject certain biblical passages like the ones about gays. Overall, they answer that Scripture itself shows that fundamentalists are inadvertently misreading the Bible. I give three details of this verdict.

"Firstly, they point to passages they say cannot come from a God of perfect goodness. Here is one example. Deuteronomy 20:16-17 (NIV) says that the ancient Israelites were told that 'in the cities of the nations the LORD your God is giving you as an inheritance, do not leave anything alive that breathes. Completely destroy them—the Hittites, Amorites, Canaanites, Perizzites, Hivites and Jebusites—as the LORD your God has commanded you.' Could a God of perfect goodness and love demand genocide, these Christians (and others) ask?

"Those who say God could never do that have identified a biblical passage which most of us would surely deem utterly ungodly and unethical. You don't have to be unbiblical to reach that conclusion, just a caring and reasonably thoughtful person, especially if you also try to live by a loving and just God.

"Secondly, the Christian experts tell us that the Bible itself shows that some of its teachings are superseded by others. Here is one example. The Law of Moses says that God requires male circumcision of all Abraham's descendants. Christians regard Abraham's descendants as all who have his kind of deep faith and not as just his ethnic, Jewish descendants. The New Testament makes it clear that the earliest Christians, being Jewish, naturally accepted circumcision as binding. Then Gentiles began to convert to Christianity. Did they have to undergo circumcision? Some said they should be circumcised. But as Acts in chapter 15 makes clear, the leading apostles Peter and Paul both ruled otherwise, in effect saying that there are some Biblical laws that no longer hold for Christians.

"Thirdly, Keith Ward contends that fundamentalism inadvertently fails to follow the central rule of biblical interpretation for Christians. This is to ask of any passage whether it is fully in line with the perfect, unconditional love of God revealed above all in Christ, the core Christian belief. If a passage isn't, like the one about genocide and anything involving injustice towards women, gay people and anybody else, it cannot be from God, say Christians like Ward.

"There are ways of reading the Bible in conformity with divine love and there are ways of misreading it which can have devastatingly cruel consequences. This is all too clear from our own South Africa history when certain Christians read, or rather misread, the Bible as sanctioning apartheid."[12]

To this press article I now add an invitation that combines the valid concerns of critical interpretation with the valid concerns of our yearning for the richest spiritual and ethical nourishment. This is to make it an unfailing practice to precede the reading and study of the Bible with a meditation in which one becomes keenly aware of the enveloping presence of what I am calling Godhead. A simple way of doing this, based on the meditation from my novel that I quote fully below, is to let oneself become quietly aware of whatever goodness is immediately present, like close friends, a quiet place and especially the ever-present opportunities for even the smallest acts of kindness or honesty. From these can then come an awareness of other, greater blessings like the progress of justice and knowledge in much of the world, themselves part of the divine reality. In that way we open our minds and hearts for the presence of Godhead, giving both light and warmth to whatever biblical passages we then proceed to study, and the only reliable norm for its interpretation.

The Bible in a progressive Christian perspective

Many years of study, reflection and questioning have led me to conclude that the Bible is indeed, through and through, a fallible human creation, the product of three great factors. The first and most important is goodness itself, with the goodness I am calling Godhead paramount. Experience shows that, at the very least, Godhead is a surrounding, ever-available presence making for good. It also shows that there are times when its goodly power makes itself so clearly felt, though always persuasively and never coercively, in a manner that suggests that we are being directly addressed, as if personally. The biblical writers were just like the rest of us in this regard, except for an important differentiating factor, which is the second of the three I am proposing.

The time, place and main events in which we live greatly affect our religious convictions. For example, there are Christians in South Africa for whom the dramatic end of apartheid without predicted bloodshed was

12. Prozesky, "Reading and Misreading."

a divine miracle. One such was the influential South African evangelist Michael Cassidy in his book *Witness Forever*.[13] This phenomenon is very evident in connection with the biblical writers and by inference, also those who shaped the oral traditions with which the writers worked. The ancient Israelite heritage involved the trials and tribulations of a small people caught between powerful empires and yet surviving, surely the very stuff of believing in the guiding, saving hand of a great, benevolent power.

It is not just such historical events that play a key part in the biblical epic, it is also the fact that they happened in a culture already theistic in its world-view. We saw in part I how we intuitively see events affecting us in the shape of what is already in our minds, so there is nothing odd about the biblical writers seeing the great events of their history and experience as the saving hand of Yahweh. This shows that we do not need the notion of a supernatural world to explain religion. Instead, the supernatural just is the natural, holistically understood and experienced.

The third factor that gave rise to the Scriptures is already implicit in the second, namely our make-up as human beings, also introduced in part I. With our natural desire for well-being and to avoid suffering, we cannot but be attracted to whatever favors those basic human interests, none more so than the beneficent power that we see as protecting and guiding our nation and ourselves, and believe in as our God.

We thus have at work, in this intuitive capacity to interpret experience theistically, the way the human brain works, as previously explained, giving us our valorizing response to whatever touches us; we have our membership of a particular culture whose world-view is imprinted on our minds from our earliest years; and most powerful of all, we have the reality of goodness in its many forms, some of them proving particularly attractive because of their value to us, like those that deliver us from peril or great suffering. Together these three great factors are sufficient to explain the rise and formation of the inspiring account of a wondrous, saving goodness that so characterizes most of the biblical texts, without theories of divine dictation or special revelations vouchsafed to a favored tradition, but also without dismissing the Jewish and Christian concepts of God, and others, as outright delusions with nothing real to back them. Great goodness is what backs them, and it is real indeed.

So the Bible and also the other great spiritual literatures of the world, except, so our Muslims would say, for the Qur'an, emerge as culturally and historically conditioned creations, produced by human authors in response to profound experiences of good and evil, which explains why the biblical

---

13. Cassidy, *Witness Forever*, 149–90, 213.

content is of such greatly varying spiritual and ethical quality. Pure, direct divine authorship simply cannot do that without God thereby being the author of the blemishes. It is hard to see what could be more irreligious than asserting this about a God of perfect goodness, or more blasphemous, in the idiom of Conservative Christianity.

A single example of the greatly varying moral quality to be found in the Bible will suffice to justify the statement that it is present, if any still be needed. Of sublime goodness is Paul's account of love in 1 Corinthians 13, known and cherished by every Christian and by many others. Opposed most shockingly to it is the terrible celebration of brutal infanticide of Psalm 137:9, which is not love, least of all divine love. It is sheer barbarism, and it means that the practice of calling the Bible as a whole the "Holy Bible" must surely stop. It does immense damage to moral goodness by making vast numbers of trusting Christians treat as God-given things in Scripture that cannot possibly be holy. Instead, calling Scripture the "Christian Bible" would, I contend, at least be honest.

In Wilfred Cantwell Smith's terms, Scripture is part of Christianity's cumulative tradition, a part, for Christians, which emerged creatively from faith in Christ as the embodiment of Godhead. It is not the heart of faith itself, which is the orientation of the self to what he, John Hick and others call the Transcendent.[14] Another way to make this clear is to point out that the Bible is not at all what the Qur'an is in Islamic belief, a text revealed word for word through angelic delivery from the very mind of Allah to one human recipient, Muhammad, over a short period of time and promptly written down. The Bible, on the other hand, comes from many writers and an oral tradition spanning as long as a thousand years, maybe more, in greatly varying contexts.

It must therefore also be asked, in view of the Bible's very different provenance and formation, whether it is appropriate to call it "the Word of God" when the prologue of John's Gospels tells us that Jesus is the Word of God.

Another progressive way of understanding the Bible as a whole is, I want to propose, to think of it as a sacrament. Christianity recognizes two sacraments initiated by Jesus himself, Baptism and Holy Communion, and defines a sacrament as an outward and visible sign of an invisible grace. The abundant biblical material that is so rich in goodness can certainly be seen as expressing, in written words, the grace of the abiding presence of Godhead; and just as Baptism uses ordinary water and Holy Communion ordinary wheat for its bread, and the fermented juice of ordinary grapes

---

14. Smith, *Faith and Belief*; Hick, *Interpretation of Religion*.

for its wine—visible signs, in other words—so the ordinary human words, ordinary ink and ordinary paper of the Bible, mediating messages of the greatest goodness, show that it meets the definition of a sacrament.

Progressive Christianity thus adopts a discerning, critically informed and always deeply respectful approach to the Bible because progressives, and indeed liberals, so highly prize ethical values and rational knowledge, and because the Bible's depths of meaning, ethically, spiritually and historically, cannot be accessed in any other way. Discerning those wonderfully rich meanings depends on the expertise that comes from years of advanced academic study, and from the guidance of those who have it for those of us without such knowledge. This approach accepts the view of David Stacey that "no religious group that values learning can be satisfied with the ploughman's understandings."[15] It also agrees with him when he wrote that the "Bible cannot speak for itself. Someone must open it, select a passage, read and draw conclusions."[16] Even those who open the Bible randomly and let their eyes fall wherever they might, draw their conclusions from what they read under the influence of the needs, beliefs and orientations of their own humanity.

Such an approach to Scripture does not mean that Progressive Christianity ignores the concept of inspiration, but it does understand it, recalling David Jenkins's statement that God is either a gift or a delusion, as something creative and not passive, as "what happens when an exceptionally gifted person has moments of supreme insight."[17] So the Bible is the work of people over many centuries in all their personal and cultural limitations, who felt moved by their experiences of great good, sometimes unforgettably, occasionally very mistakenly, as they wrote of them.

My favorite analogy for this way of understanding the origins of the biblical texts comes from my love of beautiful, stained glass church windows. They are the creations of people who wanted to express something of their spiritual experience in this medium. When the sun shines through those windows and you see them from inside, some can be wonderfully inspiring, while others may not move you at all and even be off-putting, but without the sunlight shining through them, they are all lifeless. So I see the biblical texts as so many stained glass windows, of varying aesthetic, ethical and spiritual quality, but they are not the sun that shines through them. They are human creations that attempt to say something powerful,

---

15. Stacey, *Interpreting the Bible*, 8.
16. Stacey, *Interpreting the Bible*, 9.
17. Stacey, *Interpreting the Bible*, 45; Thomasson-Rosingh, et al., *Re-imagining the Bible*.

true, beautiful and good about the faith of their creators, and sometimes they fail to do that, even failing very badly on the few occasions presented in this book.[18]

What the Bible cannot be

As will by now be abundantly clear, Scripture is not a scientific or historical manual and where it says things of this kind that clash with modern knowledge, like the origins of the cosmos and how life came about, the latter will be a better source of knowledge. Lest its ethical and spiritual value be harmed, it must not be treated as if it were a source of ready-made facts, like an encyclopedia or telephone directory. This does not detract from its paramount value as a source for critically discerning the history of ancient Israel and the historical Jesus, as I have shown in my chapter about Jesus.

In addition, the norm of goodness makes it entirely clear that the following contention by Wayne A. Grudem about the Bible, in words which vast numbers of very Conservative Christians would endorse, cannot be correct: "All the words in the Bible are God's words." Shortly after that he adds the following: "As God's very words, the words of Scripture are more than simply true, they are truth itself." Even less credible is his comment that the Bible is "the final measure by which all supposed truth is to be gauged."[19] Nor can the belief be correct that the Bible is infallible, inerrant, divinely dictated, and totally reliable about whatever it says, in view of the problems identified in this book and by others like Spong. So there really must be an end to this kind of sincere but very real misconception, in the interests of the goodness and truth that Jesus pioneered, of Godhead, and of loving service for a world with so much avoidable wrong.

What Progressive Christians need to do about the Bible

The first task of Progressive Christians regarding the Bible is the positive one of trying caringly and respectfully to encourage Conservative Christians to form a new and ethically sounder view of biblical authority. They need to be persuaded that Scripture is not intrinsically authoritative, even about Christ, just as it is not intrinsically holy, even in its finest passages, as was argued above. It acquires authority from conformity with the supreme goodness of Godhead, revealed for them in and by Jesus. As Keith Ward

---

18. Bauckham, *Bible in the Contemporary World*.
19. Grudem, *Christian Beliefs*, 13, 15.

has said, "scripture gives us, not a final revelation of truth, but a mysterious signpost towards an unfolding understanding that is still in progress."[20] Fundamentalists in particular need to be urged caringly to see that their beliefs about and use of the Bible verge on idolatry, which is expressly forbidden by the second of the Ten Commandments.

In pointing this out about idolatry, Progressive Christians must not, of course, fall into the trap of using the very belief that they are seeking to correct, namely that whatever the Bible says must be accepted just because it says so. Idolatry is spiritually and ethically wrong because it severely diminishes the idolater's sense of Godhead, while elevating that which is not divine to divine status. Then we get sincere believers justifying unfair discrimination and other evils merely by citing Scripture. That Progressive biblical scholars are making a crucial contribution to overcoming this situation of widespread misuse and even abuse of Scripture, and thereby serving the Jesus movement, will be clear.

In concluding this section about the Bible, I return to Schleiermacher and to my section in part I about how we think, know and believe. Although known primarily as a theologian, he was also a pioneering, early New Testament scholar and did highly influential work about the psychology of interpreting texts. He knew that we see new realities under the mentally and emotionally conditioning influence of what we already know and believe. This enabled him to make the point that those who first encountered Jesus were not ideally equipped to perceive his radically new and revolutionary character and message.[21]

There is, I would contend, an excellent example of this phenomenon in Mark 8:27-33. We read that Jesus asks his disciples who they think he is, and Peter replies that he is the Messiah, the Christ. But when Jesus tells them that he must suffer and be killed, Peter objects strongly, only for Jesus to rebuke him sharply. Jews of that time understandably had a longing for a warrior king like David to arise and lead them against Roman overlordship, and the rite of king-making in their culture was that of anointing with oil, which is what the Hebrew title Messiah, and Christ in Greek, mean in that context. Peter was seeing Jesus under the conditioning influence of that background of beliefs, which naturally blinded him then to the very different kind of kingship Jesus was revealing. So fundamentally wrong was that preconception that Peter and perhaps others among the disciples needed the very sharp mental and spiritual corrective Peter received from Jesus.

20. Ward, *Vision to Pursue*, 153.
21. Palmer, *Hermeneutics*.

The implication Schleiermacher saw, correctly in my view, was that Christians must be cautious about taking for granted that those earliest followers, including Paul, whose views of Jesus are held to have influenced the Gospel tradition, were in the best position to appreciate what he really was. Only with time would a deeper and truer perception be able to form. A late date for John's Gospel, which many but not all New Testament scholars accept, would fit this psychological phenomenon perfectly, for in that Gospel we find extensive and often very beautiful and profound discourses on the lips of Jesus as well as a sophisticated prologue, which are absent in the other three canonical gospels. This can readily be seen as the result of mature, later insight, though Schleiermacher himself argued that the Fourth Gospel was in fact the earliest, interpreting the lengthy discourses in question as Jesus's own words, remembered by John, the disciple who heard them, and not an interpretation by a later follower of Christ.

The lesson to be learnt from Schleiermacher's insight is that the New Testament gives us an irreplaceably important example of the *start and direction* of the process of growing understanding about Christ in the human minds of his earliest followers. But it does not end the process. I find in this a breathtakingly wonderful doorway to ever-deeper understandings of the ways Godhead operated in and through Jesus of Nazareth, for all who yearn to go through that doorway into ever-richer understanding of Jesus, and ever more abundant life, honesty, goodness and service.

Progressives and worship

The Jesus movement will always need the power of inspiring ritual to energize its mission, but the extent to which much of the church prioritizes worship as its main business must be questioned. It cannot be right to devote so much of its limited resources to praising the Godhead who invites loving service from us, above all for those who suffer from the world's evils and who desperately need those resources. It is sobering to note that John Robinson, then still a bishop in the Church of England, could make this very point over fifty years ago, with so little effect.[22] The service I attended as a guest at a Dallas Unitarian church and described earlier in this book, with its striking change in the balance of Sunday worship towards greater ethical activity, is an example of what can be done elsewhere.

We also need new ways of deepening our understanding of Godhead as supreme goodness through enhanced teaching ministries, as well as celebrating, in a flood of gratitude, that so beautiful a power encompasses us,

---

22. Robinson, *New Reformation*, 82–88.

in order to be effective instruments of its transforming effects in the world. Both John Hick and Keith Ward have provided valuable, convergent, interfaith examples of what can be done.[23] In such ways the church can be a bastion of very great and highly effective goodness and a great contributor to the goodness project, even in its ritual occasions.

From Lloyd Geering during a short visit of mine to New Zealand some years ago I found an inspiring demonstration of a Christian church that has understood what the greatest goodness means, and has taken the essential step of practicing it, reminding me of what I experienced in Dallas at the Unitarian service already described. He took me to see St Andrew's on the Terrace, the Presbyterian church he attends in central Wellington. It has a sign which says that on December 8, 1991, it was declared to be an inclusive church, adding these words: "Including all people of every creed, race, class and sexual orientation." At the bottom of the sign there is a depiction of the rainbow, adopted as a symbol of a spiritual inclusivity within which a rich diversity can be present.

At this point I want to offer readers my own way of meditating inclusively, anticipated earlier in this chapter about a way of preparing for Bible study, in the hope that it will have some value for them, as it certainly has for me. It can be practiced alone or in groups and in congregational settings with gentle and skilled guidance. I used it for the main character in my novel, *Warring Souls*, called Sarah, a university lecturer in Christian ethics. It has seven steps. Here it is now, edited to fit the present context. It is intended to bring about a deep sense of the presence of what I am calling Godhead:

A meditation on goodness

"First Sarah let herself become aware of the many goodnesses affecting her right there, not just thinking about them but focusing on the feelings these realities stirred in her, starting with present experience. She did so and became deeply aware of the peace and quiet of where she was sitting, the nearby mountains with their line of peaks beautifully outlined by the setting sun. She was healthy and had exciting, wonderful work. A feeling of intense gratitude arose in her, as it always did when she practiced the meditation, to have received so many blessings. Her spiritual adviser had told her to see herself as a meeting point where countless goodnesses, some little, some rich and powerful, came together and always would. 'Let yourself feel the

---

23. Hick, *Rainbow of Faiths*, 139-47, Ward, *Vision to Pursue*, 197-210.

goodness,' he had said, 'and you will feel both a deep joy and an equally deep gratitude because most by far of what's good comes from outside us.'

"A wordless sense of deep thanks came over her as it always did when she let her mind be aware of the many blessings she had received from other people, from nature, especially when in the mountains, and others from whence she simply did not know. These were those sudden experiences of elation that made her tremble when she read a favorite poem or heard cherished music, like Jerusalem. They made her feel that she had been lifted into another, wondrous reality too rich, deep and mysteriously lovely for words.

"The second step in the meditation was to call to mind the good she had done to others, like her trusting respect for her Bishop or the help she so willingly gave her students. She acknowledged these humbly but never lost sight of the far greater good she had received from others all her life. So she became intensely aware of herself and all others as being part of the rich flow of all these goodnesses into each person's life and also from them to others, even in such seemingly little ways as a friendly greeting or smile.

"From there Sarah's meditation moved in the third stage to the bad side of life. She knew that a faith that flinched from hard truths was shallow and shakey. So she called to mind hurts she had suffered herself, gratefully aware that none now were serious, unlike the daily humiliations she and countless others had experienced under apartheid, or still experienced because of things they couldn't change like gender, sexual nature and culture.

"As she reflected on these ugly realities, a deeply distressing picture of the world's daily pain through countless acts of hurt and harm formed in her mind, eating away at the good. She could see with her mind's eye hungry little children, the destitute, the homeless and hopeless, the uncaring rich in their obscenely luxurious mansions and expensive holiday resorts, the bleeding and distraught victims of rape and brutality, the skies dirty with smoke, streams choked with filth, rhinos killed so that their horns could be hacked off, and virgin forests falling to the chainsaws of the powerful and the greedy. Feelings of anguish and anger welled up in her at those images.

"In the next stage of her meditation Sarah passed from the pain these images caused her and called to mind the wrongs she had done to others. A quiet prayer for forgiveness followed, for she had never forgotten how her spiritual adviser had emphasized the need to seek and freely give forgiveness for even the smallest wrongs. Even such small wrongs, he had gently said, are part of God's sorrow. They too damaged the flow of goodness and had to be healed.

"Sarah loved the fifth stage of her meditation, where she could move from an honest facing of her own weaknesses and errors and from the great truth of how forgiveness had such amazing healing power, to seeing the world's many and often terrible wrongs as a doorway to corrective action. Here, above all, her passion for ethics flowed seemlessly from her spirituality. This, too, was proof of the goodness at work in the universe and in everyday life, this open doorway of opportunity to be, in the words of one of her professors, God's only hands. And once more Sarah felt a quiet but very deep gratitude that reality was not like concrete, immovably set and rigid, but alive with creative possibility and opportunities for change, provided people like her acted.

"In the sixth stage Sarah became intensely aware again, despite all that was wrong and wicked in the world, of the immense wealth of goodness present in it, inexhaustible, available yet also so deeply mysterious. At once the reaction she always had at this stage of her meditation came to consciousness. The very incompleteness of the good in life was a summons to caring action on her part in acts of caring love that were rooted in the wondrous power of goodness, at once as physical as the earth beneath her feet and yet also a soaring thing of the spirit, bringing life and love.

"The climax of the meditation was to see, in the seventh stage, that what she had been experiencing was the Kingdom of Heaven of which Jesus had spoken. 'Never think,' her adviser had told her, 'that God is remote and distant like an absentee landlord. That is not the way of perfect love, which pours forth its care and goodness unceasingly. God's is an available, ever-present goodness.'"[24]

As well as encouraging such acts of goodness-focused meditation, Progressive Christianity can pioneer new ways of seeing and celebrating the Eucharist. One way to do this is to add to its primary reference to the Last Supper the strong Gospel evidence that Jesus deeply understood the importance of sharing a meal in a society with great poverty and hunger. Not only was this about shared physical nourishment, essential as that was; it was also about loving acceptance of others, including social outcasts, so drawing

---

24. Prozesky, *Warring Souls*, 55–57.

them into the movement he was creating—the "collaborative eschaton" of which John Dominic Crossan has spoken.²⁵

When I found that Progressive Christianity uses small home groups of friends for discussion and fellowship, some years ago I invited a group of my friends, some of us Christians but others not, and all of us liberal or radical in our views of religion, to form such a group. The monthly meetings start with an input by one of us, followed by lively discussion. Then we move to a dining table for a shared, simple supper where the discussion widens into whatever issues in the nation and wider world arise. Ethical issues are the backbone of these meetings, both in what is discussed and in what happens through the sharing of ideas, values and of course, the soup, cheese, fruit, bread, and wine. None of us has ever called these sessions Holy Communion, but I have often experienced them as a way of doing to our minds and spirits what that most important act of Christian worship does for those who receive it as a sacrament.

Episcopalians and Anglicans

It is here that I want to address Episcopalians and Anglicans especially in connection with the Eucharist. As well as the problems about the Creeds that I describe below, I find another obstruction to participation in the Eucharistic liturgies that are known to me in South Africa, England and the USA. The obstruction is both ethical and theological. It is the frequent calls for God to have mercy on us, also present in the beautifully worded prayer that declares that we are not worthy so much as the gather up the crumbs under the Lord's table, perhaps going back to Thomas Cranmer (1489–1556), who evidently gave Anglicanism its first *Book of Common Prayer*.

Finding immense spiritual and ethical depth in Jesus's vision of Godhead, metaphorically addressed as the perfectly loving father, I ask, as gently as I can, whether such a being really would be a punitive one who has to be humbly and even self-abasingly asked for mercy, again and again, even with full acknowledgement that we humans are sinners, in theological terms. This does not in the least match what I have been privileged to experience of loving parenthood. Deeply caring fathers and mothers are of course anxiously concerned when their children do wrong, and they yearn to help them overcome the wrong. Trying to do so by instilling fear of painful punishment, leading to pleas for mercy as distinct from forgiveness and help, strikes me as a failure of love, not an expression of it. So I sadly find that the liturgy containing those expressions gets between me and Godhead

25. Crossan and Borg, *First Light*.

in Christ, preventing communion, and I have therefore long not been able to attend them, least of all as a communicant.

And let me now admit that I even wonder if behind these liturgical expressions there lingers a serious misconception of the Godhead shown in and by Jesus, like the admittedly worse one I found years ago in a book by a very conservative believer, who will remain nameless. He dismissed liberal conceptions of God with the adamant declaration that God in fact has "the eyes of an eagle, the memory of an elephant and the rage of a tiger," or words to that effect. To my mind and soul, that is bullying masquerading as faith, enormously harmful to both the Jesus movement and indirectly to the goodness project. No wonder those whose concept of God is even mildly like that think they need to ask again and again for mercy, rather than for inspiration and guidance.

The practical implication of this confession about liturgical expressions that hurt my spirit and my values, is to appeal for another time of liturgical renewal, this time much further reaching than the one I recall from the 1960s, which Bishop John Robinson correctly predicted would not go far enough,[26] and much more like the one implied by Keith Ward's vision of a convergent spirituality at the end of *A Vision to Pursue*.[27]

Progressive Christians, evangelicals and fundamentalists

The relationship of a renewed, progressive, Jesus movement with evangelicals is an important issue. I see it as a matter of deeply appreciative but limited continuity, respectful critical engagement and perhaps also a measure of reluctant discontinuity. To help me approach the relationship in a way that expresses the values of both the Jesus movement and the goodness project, as best I can, I do so by imagining that I am addressing the evangelicals I know or have known, respected and loved. Above all, I will imagine that I could address my own great-grandfather, who left a promising career as an artist and interior decorator in Lutheran East Prussia in the 1860s to train for and move to South Africa to save souls as a missionary of the Berlin Missionary Society. While I do not share his and others' belief that souls are lost without hearing and accepting the Gospel, I have the greatest respect for their loving concern, and in his case, courage in leaving hearth and home, family and culture, for a remote corner of what was then the British colony of Natal with a Zulu kingdom powerful enough to inflict a massive defeat on the British at the Battle of Isandhlwana in 1879.

26. Robinson, *New Reformation*, 82-88.
27. Ward, *Vision to Pursue*, 192-217.

In addressing such deeply committed, conservative Christians and through them the vast number of others like them, I would start by emphasizing that the progressive perspective admires their deep faith and love of Christ and the Bible, and their concern to save what they believe with utmost sincerity are lost souls; and that we want to support and continue everything that is loving, true and authentically Jesus-oriented in Conservative Christianity. Then, both honesty to goodness and loving concern obliges us, as progressives and radicals, to explain that everything that we are finding ethically troublesome in traditional Christianity, of the kind I identified in part II, requires caring and respectful but also frank, critical engagement, leading to whatever action goodness requires. That said, we must leave it to the power of Godhead, already in their lives and able to infuse and renew them, where needed, to do its work of persuasion, helped by the commitment to truth and the power of reason and scholarship I have found in some evangelical academics.

It might help this process, which we all need in one way or another, to invite evangelicals like my great-grandfather to take part in the opportunities of the eighth day of creation, there to redefine evangelism and mission for the world of today and the future in ways that harmonize beautifully with the Godhead of supreme goodness as given to us by Jesus himself, and as humanly echoed in Scripture, going out into that world to share the great good news of our new vision of worldly salvation.

Of all that is clearly and unrepentantly unethical there must, as a very last resort and in the interests of goodness itself, and after every effort of caring, informed persuasion, be a firm but kindly rejection of the offending views when confronted with a recalcitrant refusal to accept the implications of the greatest goodness. Most importantly, the rejection is never of the people involved but of beliefs that cannot harmonize with Godhead, and of a persistent attachment to those beliefs, that seems stronger than devotion to Godhead's supreme goodness.

As I see this sensitive but vital matter, the Jesus movement and the goodness project are harmed by everything that falls short of their noble values, not just in the wider, secular world, but within Christianity itself. And lest Progressive Christianity itself falls victim to the evil of pride and elitism, it must demand of itself the same self-scrutiny and willingness to accept the need for self-correction that it asks of conservatives.

All that was said in relation to evangelicals applies to biblical fundamentalism, but even more so because of its literalist handling of the Bible. Any movement that insists on treating the ethical problems about Scripture and about how it is read and applied that have been identified in this book and elsewhere, is harming the goodness project and with it the Jesus movement, and this must be explained, again in ways that are loving, kind and sensitive. Positively, I want to suggest that Progressive Christians can also appeal to their fundamentalist fellow Christians to use the creatively redemptive opportunities of the eighth day of creation to redefine fundamentalism itself, as basing life and faith not on the words of Scripture but on the great and wonderful goodness of a Godhead universally present and certainly as embodied in Jesus, to whom the Bible points, but is never itself divine.

A progressive appeal to liberal Christians

As ecclesiastical insiders, Liberal Christians and the scholars and ministers among them are in a highly favorable position to help reactivate the moral power of the Jesus movement and thereby support the goodness project. Being inside the churches gives them credibility and access to ecclesial power. As a movement that engages creatively with and welcomes the revolution of recent centuries about how knowledge is created and what it yields for any sphere of existence, much more so than Conservative Christianity, liberalism is especially well-equipped for the essential task of ensuring that Christianity frees itself of anything in its beliefs that cannot be true, or seems improbable.

As with progressives, the service liberals can give to goodness in our time is of course also subject to the proviso mentioned above about any religious contribution to the goodness project. This requires diligent alertness to, and overcoming anything in itself that could harm rather than help the project. What can be a problem here, as I found as a liberal, is a depth of attachment to Christian tradition precisely as an insider that can count against discerning problems there. Critical distance is an essential part of growth into greater truth, and too close an attachment to whatever we belong to can make it difficult and even impossible. Intense religious affiliation here is not unlike nationalism and excessive patriotism, as we white South Africans know from our own past under and as beneficiaries, however reluctant, of apartheid. In conversations with some of my Jewish friends I sense that there may be a similar difficulty for them in relation to Israel and the Palestinians.

Another beneficial factor for liberals as a presence inside the churches is their access to conservatives, including conservative church leaders. They can use the creativity that has always been well developed in their movement to promote the kind of critical self-appraisal in the church and by conservatives that both a renewed Jesus movement, with its collaborative eschaton, and the goodness project itself need. They can also apply the very criticality that has been such a powerful factor in giving rise to Christian liberalism as a means of ethical self-appraisal, asking in particular whether liberal proposals hitherto about the concept of God go far enough in the light of goodness and of religious pluralism. This is a question that arises for me about Keith Ward's admirably brave insights in his chapters about God in *A Vision to Pursue*,[28] making me see that inspiring book as somewhere between liberalism and a radical view of Christianity, if I have understood Ward's theism correctly.

Progressive Christians and the historic Creeds

For Progressive Christians there can be no avoiding the problems raised by the Apostle's and Nicene Creeds. Recited solemnly and ritually in frequent acts of worship by countless faithful Christians, they have long been taken for granted by vast numbers, as an unquestioned part of what it means to be Christian. Scrutiny in the light of goodness nonetheless reveals ethical and spiritual problems of such seriousness as to require a new beginning. Here is why I make this assertion, fully aware of how greatly it will disturb many good, caring Christians. I see five problems of belief and practice in these Creeds, with the fifth the one that troubles me most. Their presence in the Creeds has prevented me for a long time now from being able to join in reciting the Creeds, so shutting me and others known to me out of Christian worship.

The first is the antiquated thought forms that are used, for example the view of Christ as being of one substance with the Father, or One Being with the Father in the words of America's Episcopal Church.[29] These thought forms were doubtless meaningful in the cultural and philosophical world of the early Christian centuries but it is extremely doubtful that they mean much now, especially to those without a good deal of theological study. Related culturally to this first problem is the second one, the obsolete cosmology embedded in the Creeds in their references to coming down from and ascending into heaven, and going down to hell. This cosmology of a three-decker universe has of course long ceased to be credible, so I have to ask why the church retains it. Even if believers are told that it is just a symbolic way of saying things, it is far from clear what the symbols could be about in non-symbolic language.

---

28. Ward, *Vision to Pursue*, 71–117.
29. *Book of Common Prayer*, 326.

This brings me thirdly to the presence in the Creeds of the belief in hell. Although the Creeds do not specify what is meant by hell, some and perhaps even many traditional believers interpret it as the supposed place of eternal punishment and even torment of which there is clear mention in Scripture. It has already been shown in this book just how such a concept violates the foundational Christian belief in a God of perfect love and justice. There are far better ways of expressing the very serious consequences of turning away from goodness. One is by receiving gratefully and using the great Hindu ethical principle of karma, which reveals that our actions have very real consequences. Good deeds help others but evil harms them, and given the interrelatedness of all things, they also benefit and harm ourselves as agents.

The fourth problem is also one that has already been introduced in this book. It is that any hint of divine injustice contradicts the nature of Godhead. An exclusivist doctrine of salvation, strongly implied though not explicit in the Creeds, does just that and should never remain part of what a faith founded on supreme goodness professes. Recent rewordings of the Creeds have stopped saying that Christ was incarnate "for us men and our salvation," dropping the word "men" because it is offensively sexist, so there is nothing to stop Christianity from making other, ethically necessary changes, which brings me to my fifth and biggest problem with the Creeds.

The Creeds declare that Christianity is primarily a matter of what it wants people to *believe*, so perpetuating the assumption that what Jesus began is primarily a new system of beliefs, rather than a revolutionary new and loving way of existing. Even if every article in the Creeds avoided the four problems just identified, they would still make that declaration, for there is nothing in them about the most fundamental feature of Christianity, which is love and with it all the forms of moral goodness. It is not in the least surprising, as a result, that the church down the centuries and today has mostly not made absolutely central the practice of great goodness at all three levels, already described, that is at the heart of the example of Jesus himself, in the closest harmony with the heart of Godhead.

An explicitly ethical Creed for today

One of the university leaders under whom I served as a dean at the old University of Natal used to tell us deans that we were not to come to him with a problem unless we also had a solution to propose. In that spirit I shall now offer a short Christian Creed of my own devising, hoping that it will encourage others to do the same and perhaps induce the churches to confront the problems identified in the preceding paragraphs, and then give the Jesus movement something more ethically and spiritually believable.

What follows is a Creed in the truest sense of the word, namely an affirmation of what I hold dearest in my personal orientation to the transcendent, mysterious, yet ever-present Godhead of supreme goodness, as experienced in the stream of history defined by Jesus himself. Therefore it avoids the obscure, technical concepts of the early church, the obsolete cosmology of that time, gender specific terms and any hint of unfairness. And it is explicitly about goodness. Here it is:

> United in our commitment to love, justice and truth,
> We gather in the presence of Godhead, the inexhaustible, creative goodness that we embrace, serve and worship.
> We gather also in faithfulness to Jesus of Nazareth as our Lord, who embodied the divine love in care, service, healing and friendship.
> He did not shirk the horror of death on the cross, showing us the saving power of love in the name of the Godhead he taught us to understand and embrace as we would a most loving parent, and death could not defeat him.
> We gather also in the presence of the divine spirit promised by Jesus, which empowers, inspires and guides us.
> In this threefold presence we embrace and support one another as the body of Christ that continues his presence and work on earth.

New kinds of leadership

Also in need of new thinking and innovation in a renewed, progressive Jesus movement is leadership, about which some liberal bishops and other church leaders known to me have already set important examples.[30] Their predecessor as a bishop, John Robinson, therefore aptly asked whether "there may not be *heretical structures* in the life of the Church which do as much as—if not more than—any conceptual heresies to distort its message and frustrate its mission."[31]

Since earliest times the church seems to have believed that Jesus bequeathed to it a hierarchical structure with a dominant head, despite what seems to have been, by the end of Jesus's ministry, a more egalitarian one

30. Tutu, *God is not a Christian*; Nuttall, *Number Two to Tutu*; Jenkins, *Calling of a Cuckoo*. See also Boon, *African Way*.
31. Robinson, *New Reformation*, 88.

based on his shared goodness and shared responsibility. While strongly top-down leadership of the kind that seems to have been the rule in the early church would be understandable in a monarchical culture, it is seriously problematic in our own, increasingly egalitarian and democratic times. All organizations require effective leadership but it does not have to be such that others are unable to achieve their potential as Christian leaders, so one of the challenges of a Jesus movement that embraces goodness as its core value will now be to create leaderships that promote that more effectively. I contend that Jesus showed how to achieve this by means of his quite remarkable capacity for friendships, which is so important that it requires further explanation.

Friendship as ethical spirituality

Friendships have enriched my life immensely. They have included men and women from different faiths and none, and from different nationalities, occupations, mother tongues and cultures. Most enriching of all is the friendship of my long and deeply happy marriage. From friends I have experienced loyalty without loss of the freedom to speak freely about sensitive issues affecting me, great generosity, and acceptance of me for what I am. I hope I have succeeded in showing these qualities to my friends, too many of whom, alas, are no longer there for me to phone, email, visit and welcome to our home. Not surprisingly, therefore, I have always found special depth and direction in the words of John's Gospel, chapter 15, verse 15, where we are told that Jesus speaks of his closest followers as his friends.

That friendships are a very great good has thus always been clear to me, but it was only in the last session of library research for this book, in the Sasol Library of the University of the Free State, where I am an honorary research fellow, that my eyes were opened to their spiritual character as revelations of Godhead. I was there, let me add, thanks to my ever-supportive and friendly colleagues in the Faculty of Theology and Religion.

It was there that I found an immensely important recent journal article about the spiritual and theological importance of friendship. In it the co-authors explore a friendship-based religious epistemology to conclude, rightly in my view, that friendship can yield knowledge of God, or, as I would express this reality, yield an experience of the saving presence of Godhead.[32] They trace the analysis of what friendship means back to Cicero, citing him as saying that it "is nothing but agreement on all divine and

---

32. van Asselt and Sarot, "Can Human Friendship," 195.

human things coupled with benevolence and love";[33] they present Bonhoeffer as the first theologian to reveal its theological significance and state that Jürgen Moltmann used his martyred predecessor's work to criticize "models of domination and master-servant relationships in modern society and church."[34] Concluding that friendship "is the soul of a free and just society without masters and servants," their article shows the value of friendship for creating richer kinds of egalitarian leadership and for the institutions of society.[35] The further relevance of their article for the nature of goodness, for the goodness project and for the Godhead that is, in the reported words of the Qur'an, nearer than the vein of my neck while also being awesomely greater, is surely also clear.

THE ROMAN CATHOLIC CHURCH

Early in this book I mentioned that my knowledge of the Roman Catholic world was not extensive and deep enough for me to address it also to them, adding that my many contacts with dear and loving Catholics have always been happy and enriching. They began in my boyhood with music lessons from a Franciscan nun at the local convent, extended later to many contacts with Jesuit fathers and to the privilege of meeting two archbishops, one of them a cardinal, who both gave my ethics work their support, and it involves friends today, both ordained and lay. All I feel able to do, given this limitation but also encouraged by reports of the actions of Pope Francis at this time, is hope that this book may be found not just challenging but also helpful in their world. Catholicism, as the largest and most powerful religious organization in the world, is already a very great force for good for many millions around the world, but is its goodness, I ask as respectfully and caringly as I can, as good as it should be for women Catholics who cannot hold priestly office in it. And as recent revelations show, is it always as safe and caring for the sexually vulnerable as it should be, or as decisive in countering those few who harm them?

ACADEMIA, TRUTH AND GOODNESS

Christianity has benefited very greatly from the universities in various ways, apart from the work of natural and social scientists. These are critical biblical

---

33. van Asselt and Sarot, "Can Human Friendship," 190.
34. van Asselt and Sarot, "Can Human Friendship," 184-86.
35. van Asselt and Sarot, "Can Human Friendship," 186.

studies, powerful doctrinal theologies, philosophy, comparative religion, and ethics. For the wider goodness project the benefits are even greater, potentially covering every aspect of our existence. The first part of this book told about the important move I made as an academic from religious studies to comparative and applied ethics and to the founding directorship of my university's new ethics center. Among the benefits of the move was having to grapple with ethical challenges in academic life itself. Initially this took place just at my own university but soon I received invitations to work on academic ethics for two other South African universities, which later led to an invitation from one of them to contribute to a book about this subject. Here is an edited extract from my chapter showing something of the importance of academia contributing to the goodness project and also, from academic centers of Christian studies, to the renewal of the Jesus movement for greater goodness:

"Universities, cultural diversity, and inclusivity

"The contention of this part of the chapter is that the multicultural university of the twenty-first century, as a center of thought leadership that creates and imparts conceptual and practical knowledge, is by its very nature ethical. There are three reasons for this contention. The first one asserts that the business of creating and sharing knowledge is itself a core form of ethical practice (as distinct from teaching about ethics, which may have no real impact on actual practice). Knowledge must be true to count as knowledge, and in every value-system in the study of global ethics, truth is judged to be a central moral value. So to be in the knowledge business is to be in the ethics business, whether our universities acknowledge this explicitly or not. Thought that is characterized by factual error, mere opinion, illogicality and partisanship, and that is untested by the critical assessment of qualified peers, is not thought leadership but an unpardonable waste of resources.

"The second reason derives its moral status from both beneficence and integrity. It is that academics are key ethics players in their roles as researchers, as teachers and in their community service. The examples they set both personally and in how they do their work are noted by their students, their colleagues and the public, and send out clear ethical (and sometimes unethical) messages. So we can ask how well our academics and administrators are equipped for their role in providing moral influence in the academy and beyond.

"Like everybody else, university staff members all have the right to be religious or not, but the notion that they have the right to be professionally amoral if they choose, or that the right to freedom means that what they do off campus, like cheating on their income tax or on their partners, is nobody's business but their own, must be firmly rejected as a violation of the ethical principles of integrity and responsibility. How can it make sense to claim the right to be wrong?

"The third reason for asserting that universities worthy of the name are by their nature ethical relates to beneficence. Universities are inherently social. They are places which cannot function without cooperation and inter-personal reliability. Staff members who prefer to let their self-interest outweigh their duty to act supportively towards their students and colleagues when that is needed harm this essential requirement. Universities are not places for the selfish any more than for the dishonest. The duty to increase knowledge is of course non-negotiable, but nobody ever does this entirely alone, without recourse to laboratories, libraries, learned journals, administrative departments and those who run them. It will be clear that in drawing on these resources and those who work there, academics who do so respectfully and considerately will help maintain the spirit of helpfulness that is essential for success, just as rude or inconsiderate behavior damages that spirit.

"Having set out these three reasons for defining the university as by its nature ethical, it is now possible to identify the most important opportunities facing universities in connection with the further development of a global ethic. They are the inter-disciplinary and multi-cultural development of a maximally inclusive, multicultural value system; the development of a values-driven pedagogy that will incorporate the values of the developing global ethic; and thirdly to develop leaders in any field imbued with those values, so fitting them for a moral impact in a globalizing, richly multi-cultural world.

"The operations and structures of an ethically excellent, multi-cultural university will embody and practice agreed, basic ethical values and avoid the opposites of those ethical qualities, above all dishonesty, injustice, mediocrity, selfishness, disrespect and laziness."[36]

Partly as a result of the work of our universities, we now know that the most serious threat to the planet at this time is grave damage to the natural

---

36. Prozesky, "Universities," 84–85.

environment through our contribution to climate change and the way we are polluting our fresh waters, skies, soils, and the oceans. The threat to life is serious enough to give rise to warnings by scientists that we may already be in the process of triggering an eighth mass extinction of life. We therefore now have a global situation that offers both the ethical academy and the faith communities, and all others, an unprecedented opportunity for co-operative ethical action, which brings me to the final words of this chapter.

TOGETHER SAVING THE EARTH

Saving the environment is the most urgent challenge now facing the world and it needs all the support the churches, other faith communities and all other agencies can give it. The Christianity envisaged in this book can offer a spiritual invitation here to those who remain part of the old mental world of Conservative Christianity, more concerned with saving souls than saving the soil, to be part of this unprecedented and urgent mission of world salvation. They too can adopt and promote as Scripture an eleventh commandment, additional to the original ten, which goes as follows:

> "Thou shalt inherit the Holy Earth as a faithful steward, conserving its resources and productivity from generation to generation. Thou shalt safeguard thy fields from soil erosion, thy living waters from drying up, thy forests from desolation, and protect thy hills from overgrazing by thy herds, that thy descendants may have abundance forever. If any shall fail in this stewardship of the land, thy fruitful fields shall become sterile stony ground and wasting gullies, and thy descendants shall decrease and live in poverty or perish from off the face of the earth."[37]

Could there be a more important way for people of faith to serve both the supreme goodness at the heart of religion, and the goodness project, and the beloved earth itself than this?

---

37. Freudenberger, *Gift of Land*, 23, quoting W.C. Loudermilk.

Epilogue

THE DEAD SING NO praises, write no Creeds and produce no theologies. The living experience sunshine, storm and snow; they find new life and new loves; endure heat and cold, and find food; they survive injury and illness, and have many other blessings. These reveal the reality of an often precarious but always real goodness. For survivors there is always an excess of benefit over harm, a relieved, grateful sense of dependence on a mysterious power that is able to give or withhold the blessings we by nature desire. What is truly wonderful is that the goodness so experienced is inexhaustible, for we never reach a point when there is no possibility whatsoever of discerning its presence, sometimes in the most unexpected ways. Jesus showed this in the Gospel narrative of his noble spirit of forgiveness even in the agonies of an impending and truly terrible death.

Trusting the strengths of tradition, the good ship *Ecclesia* ploughs on through the night across the waters of a challenging new world until, in the small hours, she hits the massive iceberg called critical, modern knowledge, coupled with the finest global values. Unlike the *Titanic*, she does not sink, kept afloat even as she ships water by the buoyancy of the goodness that is her deep structure. She can get to harbor if helped by other vessels, but needs extensive repairs if she is to sail on, there to prepare herself for future service to the world.

No cumulative tradition of scriptures, creeds, theologies and patterns of worship can exhaust the great goodness underlying the concept of Godhead, nor close the books on its inexhaustible value and meaning. The conservative church can either continue gazing heavenward in a world crying out for all the ethical help it can get, or it can embrace its neglected core mission, founded by Christ, of inclusive, this-worldly salvation. To this end

I myself can only offer such resources of experience and study as I have been given, and caring encouragement.

Somebody has to ask the unwelcome questions. Somebody has to think the unthinkable. Progressive Christians are doing that. I have tried to do so too, in order to give the best I can to the Christianity that gave me so much, in the mode of what Don Cupitt has called the artist and not the solider,[1] seeking creativity in the power of goodness, not obedience to a beloved past. And so I find myself resonating to some words about Jesus, the rediscovered Jesus of the world's goodness project, as he resumes his mission today, words with which Albert Schweitzer ended his great work, *The Quest for the Historical Jesus*.

> "He comes to us as One unknown, without a name, as of old, by the lakeside. He came to those who knew Him not. He speaks to us the same word: "Follow thou me!" and sets to us the tasks which He has to fulfil for our time. He commands. And to those who obey Him, whether they be wise or simple, He will reveal Himself in the toils, the conflicts, the sufferings which they shall pass through in His fellowship, and, as an ineffable mystery, they shall learn in their own experience Who He is."[2]

---

1. Cupitt, Personal communication dated September 10, 2013.
2. Schweitzer, *Quest*, 401.

Bibliography

Abbot, Eric. *Flatland.* London: Seeley, 1884.
Altizer, Thomas. *The Gospel of Christian Atheism.* London: Collins, 1967.
Ariarajah, S. Wesley. "Jesus the Christ—the *Only* Way to God and Human Flourishing." *Journal of Ecumenical Studies* (2017) 57-59.
Armstrong, Karen. *The Case for God: What Religion Really Means.* London: Bodley Head, 2009.
———. *A History of God.* London: Mandarin, 1993.
———. *The Spiral Staircase: A Memoir.* London: Harper Perennial, 2005.
———. *St Paul: The Misunderstood Apostle.* London: Atlantic Books, 2015.
Ashbrook, J., and C.R. Albright. *The Humanizing Brain: Where Religion and Neuroscience Meet.* Cleveland: The Pilgrim Press, 1997.
Aslan, Reza. *God: A Human History.* London: Bantam Press, 2017.
Baker, John. *The Foolishness of God.* London: Darton, Longman and Todd, 1970.
Balcomb, Anthony O. "Of Iron Cages, Double Binds, Epistemological Crises, and Environmental Destruction: The Fragmentation of the Western Worldview and Gestures Towards Another Way of Being in the World." *Religion and Theology* 21 (2014) 358-79.
Banton, Michael. *Anthropological Approaches to the Study of Religion.* London: Tavistock, 1966.
Barnhouse, Ruth. *Identity.* Philadelphia: Fortress, 1984.
Barrett, Peter. "The Emergence of Imagination and Altruism in Human Evolution: Key Elements in a New-Style Natural Theology." *Journal of Theology for Southern Africa* 153 (November 2013) 29-45.
Barton, John, ed. *The Cambridge Companion to Biblical Interpretation.* Cambridge: Cambridge University Press, 1998.
Battson, C.D., and Ventiss, W. Larry. *The Religious Experience.* New York: Oxford University Press, 1982.
Bauckham, Richard. *The Bible in the Contemporary World: Exploring Texts and Contexts—Then and Now.* London: SPCK, 2016.
Bebbington, David, and Jones, David. *Evangelicalism and Fundamentalists in the United Kingdom during the Twentieth Century.* Oxford: Oxford University Press, 2013.
———. *Evangelicalism in Modern Britain: A History from the 1730s to the 1980s.* London: Taylor and Francis, 1988.
Bellah, Robert N, and Joas, Hans, eds. *The Axial Age and its Consequences.* Cambridge, Massachusetts: Belknap, 2012.

———. *Religion in Human Evolution: From the Paleolithic to the Axial Age.* Cambridge, Massachusetts: Bellknap Press, 2011.
Biggar, Nigel. *In Defence of War.* Oxford: Oxford University Press, 2013.
Blaisdell, Chuck. "I'm Not so Sure about a God whose Book Seems so Contradictory." *Encounter* 76 (2016) 3–7.
Bockmuehl, Markus, ed. *The Cambridge Companion to Jesus.* Cambridge: Cambridge University Press, 2001.
———. "Resurrection." In *The Cambridge Companion to Jesus,* edited by Markus Bockmuehl, 102–18, Cambridge: Cambridge University Press, 2001.
Bonhoeffer, Dietrich. *Ethics.* Minneapolis: Fortress, 2005.
Book of Common Prayer According to the use of The Episcopal Church. New York: The Church Hymnal Corporation, 1979.
Boon, Mike. *The African Way: The Power of Interactive Leadership.* Sandton: Zebra, 1996.
Borg, Marcus. *Jesus, A New Vision: Spirit, Culture and the Life of Scholarship.* San Francisco: Harper, 1991.
———. *Jesus in Contemporary Scholarship.* Valley Forge: Trinity, 1994.
———. *Jesus: Uncovering the Life, Teachings and Relevance of a Religious Revolutionary.* London: SPCK, 2011.
——— and N.T. Wright. *The Meaning of Jesus: Two Visions.* San Francisco: Harper, 1998.
———. *Meeting Jesus for the First Time.* San Francisco: Harper, 1994.
———. *Putting away Childish Things: A Novel of Modern Faith.* San Francisco: HarperOne, 2010.
Bowden, John. *Voices in the Wilderness.* London: SCM, 1977.
Bredenkamp, Vic. *What and Why? Answers to 101 Questions on the Bible and Religions.* Cape Town: Methodist Publishing House, 2011.
Brown, Judith M. "Gandhi: A Man for our Times?" *Journal for the Study of Religion* 31 (2018) 96–111.
———, and Martin Prozesky, eds. *Gandhi and South Africa: Principles and Politics.* Pietermaritzburg: University of Natal Press, 1996.
———. *Gandhi: Prisoner of Hope.* New Haven: Yale University Press, 1989.
Brown, Peter. *Authority and the Sacred: Aspects of the Christianization of the Roman World.* Cambridge: Cambridge University Press, 1995.
———. *The Rise of Western Christendom: Triumph and Diversity AD 200–1000.* Malden, Massachusetts: Blackwell, 1997.
Brown, Raymond E. *The Church the Apostles Left Behind.* New York: Paulist Press, 1984.
Bruggemann, Walter. *The Excess of Divine Fidelity and the Command of the Common Good.* London: SCM, 2017.
Burkill, T.A. *The Evolution of Christian Thought.* Ithaca: Cornell University Press, 1971.
———. *Faith, Knowledge and Cosmopolitanism. An Inaugural Lecture at the University of Rhodesia.* Salisbury: University of Rhodesia, 1971.
Calder, Todd. "Evil." In *Stanford Encyclopedia of Philosophy,* 2013: https://plato.standford.edu accessed on 13 February 2018.
Carpenter, Humphrey. *Jesus.* Oxford: Oxford University Press, 1980.
Cassidy, Michael. *Chasing the Wind.* London: Hodder and Stoughton, 1985.
———. *Witness Forever: The Dawn of Democracy in South Africa. Stories Behind the Story.* London: Hodder and Stoughton, 1995.

Charton, Nancy. *The Calling: The Story of a Pioneering Woman Priest*. Pietermaritzburg: Cluster Publications, 2009.
Cheetham, David. *Ways of Meeting and the Theology of Religions*. Farnham, Surrey: Ashgate, 2013.
Chilton, Bruce. "Friends and Enemies." In *The Cambridge Companion to Jesus*, edited by Markus Bockmuehl, 72–76. Cambridge: Cambridge University Press, 2001.
Chomsky, Noam. *Cartesian Linguistics: A Chapter in the History of Rationalist Thought*. New York: Harper and Row, 1966.
———. *Language and Mind*. New York: Harcourt, Brace and World, 1968.
Cobb, John B. Jr. *Beyond Dialogue: Towards a Mutual Transformation of Christianity and Buddhism*. Philadelphia: Fortress, 1982.
———. *A Christian Natural Theology: Based on the Thought of Alfred North Whitehead*. London: Lutterworth, 1966.
———, and David Ray Griffin. *Process Theology: An Introductory Exposition*. Belfast: Christian Journals, 1977.
———. *Sustaining the Common Good: A Christian Perspective on the Global Economy*. Cleveland, Ohio: Pilgrim, 1994.
Coplestone, Frederick. *A History of Philosophy: Volume I, Part I, Greece & Rome*. New York: Image Books, 1962.
———. *A History of Philosophy. Volume VII, Part II. Schopenhauer to Nietzsche*. New York: Image Books, 1965.
Cox, Harvey. *The Secular City: Secularization and Urbanization in Theological Perspective*. London: SCM, 1965.
Craig, Robert. *Social Concern in the Thought of William Temple*. London: Gollancz, 1963.
Crook, John H. *The Evolution of Human Consciousness*. Oxford: Clarendon, 1980.
Crossan, John, and Marcus Borg. *First Light: Jesus and the Kingdom of Heaven*. Phoenix, Arizona: Living the Questions, 2009 (DVD series).
———. *How to Read the Bible and Still be a Christian: Struggling with Divine Violence from Genesis through Revelation*. San Francisco: HarperOne, 2015.
Cupitt, Don. *After God: The Future of Religion*. London: Weidenfeld and Nicolson, 1997.
———. *The Nature of Man*. London: Sheldon, 1979.
———. *Radicals and the Future of the Church*. London: SCM, 1989.
———. *Solar Ethics*. London: SCM Press, 1995.
———. *Taking Leave of God*. London: SCM, 1980.
Daly, Herman E., and John B. Cobb Jr. *For the Common God: Redirecting the Economy towards Community, the Environment, and a Sustainable Future*. Second edition. Boston: Beacon, 1994.
Daly, Mary. *Gyn/ecology: The Metaethics of Radical Feminism*. London: Women's Press, 1979.
Davidson, James, and William Rees-Mogg. *The Sovereign Individual: The Coming Economic Revolution: How to Survive and Prosper in it*. London: Macmillan, 1997.
Dawkins, Richard. *The God Delusion*. London: Bantam, 2006.
———. *The Selfish Gene*. Second edition. Oxford: Oxford University Press, 1989.
D'Costa, Gavin. *Christian Uniqueness Reconsidered: The Myth of a Pluralistic Theology of Religions*. Maryknoll, NY: Orbis, 1990.
De Beer, Wynand. "Being Human, Becoming Like God: Patristic Perspectives on Humankind." *Journal of Theology for Southern Africa* 148 (March 2014) 65–82.

de Gruchy, John W. *Being Human: Confessions of a Christian Humanist*. London: SCM, 2006.

———. *John Calvin: Christian Humanist & Evangelical Reformer*. Wellington, South Africa: Lux Verbi BM, 2009.

Denis, Philippe. "Thirty Years Later: Albert Nolan on the *Kairos Document* and its Relevance Today." *Journal of Theology for Southern Africa* 151 (March 2015) 6–23.

———. "Timeboundness and Prophetism in the Theology of Albert Nolan." *Journal of Theology for Southern Africa* 156 (November 2016) 5–19.

Dewey, Art. "No more Potemkin Theology," editorial in *The Fourth R*, 30 (September-October 2017). www.westar@weststarinstitute.org, accessed on 26 October 2017.

Donovan, Vincent J. *Christianity Rediscovered: An Epistle from the Masai*. London: SCM, 1982.

Earl, Douglas S. *The Joshua Delusion? Rethinking Genocide in the Bible*. Cambridge: James Clarke, 2010.

Elton, G.R. *England under the Tudors*. Third edition, London: Routledge, 1991.

Esler, Philip E. "Patterns of Political Rule and Influence." In Houlden, J.L., ed. *Jesus in History, Thought and Culture: An Encyclopedia*. 2 vols. Santa Barbara: ABC Clio, 2003, 467–470.

Fernandez-Armesto, Felipe. *So You Think You're Human? A Brief History of Humankind*. Oxford: Oxford University Press, 2004.

Feuerbach, Ludwig. *The Essence of Christianity*. Translated by George Elliot. New York: Harper Torchbooks, 1957.

FitzGerald, Frances. *The Evangelicals: The Struggle to Shape America*. New York: Simon and Shuster, 2017.

Flew, Antony. *God and Philosophy*. London: Hutchinson, 1966.

Fowler, James. *Stages of Faith: The Psychology of Human Development and the Quest for Meaning*. San Francisco: Harper and Row, 1981

Frankfort, Henri, et al. *Before Philosophy: The Intellectual Adventure of Ancient Man*. Baltimore: Penguin, 1971.

Freeman, Charles. *A New History of Early Christianity*. New Haven, Yale University Press, 2009.

Frege, Gottlob. *Collected Papers on Mathematics, Logic and Philosophy*. Oxford: Blackwell, 1984.

Freudenberger, C. Dean. *The Gift of Land: A Judeo-Christian Perspective on Lifestyle Change in a Threatened World*. Los Angeles: Franciscan Communications, 1981.

Freyne, Sean. "Galilee and Judaea in the First Century." In *The Cambridge History of Christianity. Volume 1. Origins to Constantine*, edited by Margaret M. Mitchell and Frances M. Young, 37–51.Cambridge: Cambridge University Press, 2006.

Funk, Robert W., et al. *The Gospel of Jesus: According to the Jesus Seminar*. Salem, Oregon: Polebridge, 1999.

Galbraith, John. *The Anatomy of Power*. Boston: Houghton Mifflin, 1983.

Gandhi, M.K. *An Autobiography: The Story of my Experiments with Truth*. Ahmedabad: Navajivan, 1948.

Geering, Lloyd. *Christian Faith at the Crossroads*. Salem, Oregon: Polebridge, 2001.

———. *Coming Back to Earth: From Gods, to God, to Gaia*. Salem, Oregon: Polebridge, 2009.

———. *Creating the New Ethic*. Wellington: St Andrew's Trust for the Study of Religion and Society, 1991.

———. *Faith's New Age*. London: Collins, 1980, revised as *Christian Faith at the Crossroads*. Salem, Oregon: Polebridge, 2001.
———. *Reimagining God: The Faith Journey of a Modern Heretic*. Salem, Oregon: Polebridge, 2014.
———. *Resurrection: A Symbol of Hope*. London: Hodder and Stoughton, 1971.
———. *Wrestling with God: The Story of My Life*. Wellington: Bridget Williams Books, 2006.
Geras, Norman. *Marx and Human Nature: Refutation of a Legend*. London: Verso, 1983.
Gilligan, Carol. *In a Different Voice: Psychological Development and Women's Development*. Cambridge, Massachusetts: Harvard University Press, 1993.
Gould, Graham. Review of Bebbington, David, and David Jones. *Evangelicalism and Fundamentalists in the United Kingdom during the Twentieth Century*. *Journal of Theological Studies* 65 (April 2014) 361–63.
Grayling, A.C. *The God Argument: The Case against Religion and for Humanism*. New York: Bloomsbury, 2013.
Green, Joel B. "Crucifixion." In *The Cambridge Companion to Jesus*, edited by Markus Bockmuehl, Cambridge: Cambridge University Press, 2001.
Green, Michael. *The Meaning of Salvation*. London: Hodder, 1965.
Grillmeier, Alois. *Christ in Christian Tradition: From the Apostolic Age to Chalcedon*. London: Mowbrays, 1975.
Grudem, Wayne A. *Christian Beliefs: Twenty Basics Every Christian Should Know*. Grand Rapids: Zondervan, 2005.
Guy, Jeff. *The Heretic: A Study of the Life of John William Colenso 1814–1883*. Pietermaritzburg: University of Natal Press, 1983.
Hamer, Dean. *The God Gene: How Faith is Hardwired into our Genes*. New York: Doubleday, 2004.
Hamilton, William, and Thomas J. Altizer. *Radical Theology and the Death of God*. Harmondsworth: Penguin, 1968.
Hardy, Alister. *The Divine Flame: An Essay towards a Natural History of Religion*. London: Collins, 1966.
———. *The Spiritual Nature of Man: A Study of Contemporary Religious Experience*. Oxford: Clarendon Press, 1979.
Harris, Harriet. *Fundamentalism and Evangelicalism*. Oxford: Oxford University Press, 2008.
———. ed. *God, Goodness and Philosophy*. Aldershot: Ashgate, 2011.
Harris, Sam. *Letter to a Christian Nation*. New York: Knopf, 2006.
Hartshorne, Charles. *Omnipotence and other Mistakes*. Albany: State University of New York Press, 1983.
Harvey, A.E. "Jesus as a Historical Figure." In Houlden, J.L., ed. *Jesus in History, Thought and Culture: An Encyclopedia*. 2 vols. Santa Barbara: ABC Clio, 2003, 446–454.
Harvey, Susan, and David G. Hunter. *The Oxford Handbook of Early Christian Studies*. Oxford: Oxford University Press, 2010.
Heim. S. Mark. *Salvations*. New York: Orbis, 1995.
Hendel, Charles W., ed. *Hume: Selections*. New York: Scribners, 1927.
Hick, John. *Evil and the God of Love*. London: Macmillan, 1977.
———. *Faith and Knowledge*. Second edition. London: Macmillan, 1974.
———. *God Has Many Names: Britain's New Religious Pluralism*. London: Macmillan, 1980.

---. *The Interpretation of Religion: Human Responses to the Transcendent.* London: Macmillan, 1989.

--- and Paul M. Knitter, eds. *The Myth of Christian Uniqueness: Towards a Pluralistic Theology of Religions.* Maryknoll, New York: Orbis, 1987.

---. ed. *The Myth of God Incarnate.* London: SCM, 1977.

---. *The New Frontier of Religion and Science: Religious Experience, Neuro-science and the Transcendent.* Basingstoke: Palgrave Macmillan, 2006.

---. *Philosophy of Religion.* 3rd edition. Englewood Cliffs: Prentice Hall, 1973.

---. *Problems of Religious Pluralism.* London: Macmillan, 1985.

---. *The Rainbow of Faiths: Critical Dialogues on Religious Pluralism.* London: SCM, 1995.

Hind, Robert A. *Why Good is Good: The Sources of Morality.* London: Routledge, 2002.

Holder, Rodney. Review of *Faithful to Science: The Role of Science in Religion*, by Andrew Steane. *Journal of Theological Studies*, New Series 6 (October 2015) 897–900.

Hood, Adam. "John Oman on Feeling and Theology." *Religious Studies* 49, March 2013, 5–17.

Horsley, Richard A. *Jesus and the Powers; Conflict, Covenant, and the Hope of the Poor.* Minneapolis: Fortress, 2011.

---. *Jesus in Context: Power, People and Performances.* Minneapolis: Fortress, 2008.

Houlden, J.L., ed. *Jesus in History, Thought and Culture: An Encyclopedia.* Santa Barbara: ABC Clio, 2003.

Huddleston, Trevor. *Naught for Your Comfort.* London: Fontana, 1960.

Hutchinson, John A. *Paths of Faith.* Third edition. New York: McGraw-Hill, 1981.

James, William. *The Varieties of Religious Experience: A Study in Human Nature.* London: Longmans, 1902.

Jaspers, Karl. *The Origin and Goal of History.* Greenwood: Westport, Connecticut, 1976.

Jenkins, David E. *The Calling of a Cuckoo.* London: Continuum, 2003.

---. *Living with Questions: Investigations into the Theory and Practice of Belief in God.* London: SCM, 1969.

Joas, Hans. *The Genesis of Values.* Cambridge: Polity, 2000.

Jürgensmeyer, Mark. *Terror in the Mind of God: The Global Rise of Religious Violence.* Berkeley: University of California Press, 2000.

Kant, Immanuel. *Critique of Pure Reason.* Translated by Norman Kemp Smith, London: Macmillan, 1929.

Kaufmann, W., ed. *The Portable Nietzsche.* New York: Penguin, 1982.

Kee, Alistair. *The Way of Transcendence: Christian Faith without Belief in God.* Harmondsworth: Penguin, 1971.

Keller, Catherine. "The Love of Postcolonialism: Theology in the Interstices of Empire." In *Postcolonial Theologies: Divinity and Empire*, edited by Catherine Keller et al., 221–42. St Louis: Chalice, 2004.

Kelly, J.N.D. *Early Christian Creeds.* Harlow: Longmans, 1972.

---. *Early Christian Doctrine.* San Francisco: Harper, 1978.

Kershaw, Ian. *Hitler: 1889–1936: Hubris.* London: Penguin, 1999.

Kidder, Rushworth M. *How Good People Make Tough Choices: Resolving the Dilemmas of Ethical Living.* New York: Simon and Schuster, 1986.

---. *Moral Courage.* New York: William Morrow, 2005.

---. *Shared Values for a Troubled World: Conversations with Men and Women of Conscience.* San Francisco: Jossey-Bass, 1994.

King, Ursula, ed. *Faith and Praxis in a Postmodern Age*. London: Cassell, 1998.
———. *Spirit of Fire: The Life and Vision of Pierre Teilhard de Chardin*. Maryknoll, New York: Orbis, 2015.
———, ed. *Spirituality and Society in the New Millennium*. Brighton: Sussex University Press, 2001.
———. "Teilhard de Chardin's Vision of Science, Religion and Planetary Humanity: A Challenge to the Contemporary World." *Journal for the Study of Religion* 31 (2018) 135–58.
Kirchschlaeger, Peter G. "The Moral-Theological Dimension of Jesus' Way of Life. In *Making Sense of Jesus: Experiences, Interpretations and Identities*, edited by D.F. Tolmie and R. Venter, 196–216. Bloemfontein: SUN Press, 2017,
Klauck, Hans-Josef. "The Roman Empire." In *The Cambridge History of Christianity. Volume 1. Origins to Constantine*, edited by Margaret M. Mitchell and Frances M. Young, 69–83. Cambridge: Cambridge University Press, 2006.
Klemm, David E. and William Schweiker. *Religion and the Human Future: An Essay on Theological Humanism*. Chichester: Wiley-Blackwell, 2008.
Knight, John. *Liberalism versus Postliberalism: The Great Divide in Twentieth Century Theology*. Oxford: Oxford University Press, 2013.
Kohlberg, Lawrence. *The Psychology of Moral Development: The Nature and Validity of Moral Stages*. San Francisco: Harper, 1984.
Küng, Hans and Karl Josef Kuschel, eds. *A Global Ethic: The Declaration of the Parliament of the World's Religions*. London: SCM, 1993.
———. *A Global Ethic for a Global Politics and Economics*. London: SCM, 1997.
———. *Infallible? An Inquiry*. Garden City NY: Doubleday, 1971.
Laszlow, Erwin. *The Systems View of the World*. New York: George Braziller, 1972.
Levy, Neil. *What Makes us Moral? Crossing the Boundaries of Biology*. Oxford: Oneworld, 2004.
Lewis, C.S. *Mere Christianity*. London: Collins, 2016.
Lewis Williams, David. *Conceiving God: The Cognitive Origin and Evolution of Religion*: London: Thames and Hudson, 2010.
Lilley, Christopher, and Daniel J. Pedersen, eds. *Human Origins and the Image of God: Essays in Honor of J. Wentzel van Huysteen*. Grand Rapids: Eerdmans, 2017.
Lovin, Robin W. *An Introduction to Christian Ethics: Goals, Duties, and Virtues*. Nashville: Abingdon, 2011.
Lucas, F.L. *Style*. London: Cassell, 1964.
Luther, Martin. *Luther's Works. Volume 30*. Jaroslav Pelikan, ed., Walter A. Hansen, Associate editor. St Louis: Concordia, 1967.
———. *Luther's Works. Volume 36*. Abdel Ross Wentz, ed., Philadelphia: Fortress, 1959.
Luthuli, Albert. *Let my People Go*. New York: McGraw, 1962.
MacCulloch, Dairmaid. *Reformation: Europe's House Divided 1490–1700*. London: Allen Lane, 2003.
Macquarrie, John. *Principles of Christian Theology*. London: SCM, 1977.
Macqueen, Ian M. *Black Consciousness and Progressive Movements under Apartheid*. Pietermaritzburg: University of KwaZulu-Natal Press, 2018.
Marcus, John. "Jewish Christianity." In *The Cambridge History of Christianity. Volume 1. Origins to Constantine*, edited by Margaret M. Mitchell and Frances M. Young, 87–102. Cambridge: Cambridge University Press, 2006.

Marean, Curtis W. "The Most Invasive Species of all." *Scientific American* (August 2015) 33-39.
———. "When the Sea Saved Humanity." *Scientific American* 165 (August 2011) 55-61.
Marx, Karl. *On Religion*. Saul K. Padover, ed. New York: McGraw-Hill, 1974.
———. "Theses on Feuerbach" In Karl Marx. *On Religion*. Saul K. Padover, ed. New York: McGraw-Hill, 1974.
Matolino, Bernard. *Personhood in African Philosophy*. Pietermaritzburg: Cluster Publications, 2014.
McCarthy, Terence, and Bruce Rubidge. *The Story of Earth and Life: A Southern African Perspective on a 4.6 Billion-year Journey*. Cape Town: Struik, 2005.
McDonough, Richard. "Religious Fundamentalism: A Conceptual Critique." *Religious Studies* 49 (December 2013) 561-79.
McGrath, Alister E. *Christian Theology: An Introduction*. Fourth edition. Oxford: Blackwell, 2007.
———. *Evangelicalism and the Future of Christianity*. London: Hodder, 1994.
———. *The Great Mystery: Science, God and Human Quest for Meaning*. London: Hodder, 2017.
McKim, Donald K., ed. *The Cambridge Companion to John Calvin*. London: Cambridge University Press, 2004.
Meeks, Wayne A. *The Moral World of the First Christians*. London: SPCK, 1987.
———. "Social and Ecclesial Life of the Earliest Christians." In *The Cambridge History of Christianity. Volume 1. Origins to Constantine*, edited by Margaret M. Mitchell and Frances M. Young, 145-73. Cambridge: Cambridge University Press, 2006.
Micklethwaite, John, and Adrian Wooldridge. *God is Back: How the Global Rise of Faiths is Changing the World*. London: Allen Lane, 2009.
Miller, Donald. *The Case for Liberal Christianity*. London: SCM, 1981.
———. "Liberalism." In Richardson, Alan and John Bowden, eds. *A New Dictionary of Christian Theology*. London: SCM, 1983, 324-25.
Miller, Ken. *Finding Darwin's God: A Scientist's Search for Common Ground between God and Evolution*. New York: Harper, 2002.
Mitchell, Margaret M. and Frances M. Young, eds. *The Cambridge History of Christianity. Volume 1. Origins to Constantine*. Cambridge: Cambridge University Press, 2006.
———. "The Emergence of the Written Record." In *The Cambridge History of Christianity. Volume 1. Origins to Constantine*, edited by Margaret M. Mitchell and Frances M. Young, 177-94. Cambridge: Cambridge University Press.
Moral Regeneration Movement *Charter of Positive Values*. Website: https://mrm.org.za with link to the *Charter of Positive Values*.
Murove, Munyaradzi, ed. *African Ethics: An Anthology of Comparative and Applied Ethics*. Pietermaritzburg: University of KwaZulu-Natal Press, 2009.
———. *African Moral Consciousness. An Inquiry into the Evolution of Perspectives and Prospects*. London: Austin Macauley, 2016.
Murphy, Nancy, and George Ellis. *On the Moral Nature of the Universe*. Minneapolis: Fortress, 1996.
Nicolson, Ronald. *The Church and Same-Sex Marriage*. Pietermaritzburg: Cluster Publications, 2008.
———. "O worship the Lord in the Beauty of Holiness: Let the Whole Earth Tremble Before Him (Psalm 96:9)." *Journal for the Study of Religion* 31 (2018) 237-49.

Nietzsche, Friedrich. *Thus Spoke Zarathustra*. Cambridge: Cambridge University Press, 2006.
Nineham, Dennis. *New Testament Interpretation in an Historical Age*. London: Athlone Press, 1976.
———. *The Use and Abuse of the Bible: A Study of the Bible in an Age of Rapid Cultural Change*. London: Macmillan, 1976
Nolan, Albert. *Jesus before Christianity: The Gospel of Liberation*. Cape Town: David Philip, 1976.
———. *Jesus Today: A Spirituality of Radical Freedom*. Cape Town: Double Storey, 2006.
Nürnberger, Klaus. *Martin Luther's Message for us Today*. Pietermarizburg: Cluster Publications, 2011.
———. *Richard Dawkins' God Delusion: A Repentant Refutation*. (No place) Ex Libris, 2010.
Nuttall, Michael. *Number Two to Tutu: A Memoir*. Pietermaritzburg: Cluster Publications, 2003.
Opincar, John T. *Ethical Intelligence: The Foundation of Leadership*. Houston, Texas: Cultural Fire, 2016.
Otto, Rudolph. *The Idea of the Holy*. Oxford: Oxford University Press, 1936.
Oxtoby, Richard. *The Two Faces of Christianity: A Psychological Analysis*. Winchester, UK: Christian Alternative Books, 2014.
Palmer, Richard. *Hermeneutics: Interpretation Theory in Schleiermacher, Dilthey, Heidegger and Gadamer*. Evanston, Illinois: Northwestern University Press, 1969.
Pappe, Ilan. *The Ethnic Cleansing of Palestine*. London: Oneworld, 2006.
Penelhum, Terence. Review of Schellenberg's work. *Religious Studies*, Volume 49, June 2013, 249–55.
Percy, Martyn. *The Future Shapes of Anglicanism: Currents, Contours, Charts*. London: Routledge, 2017.
———. *Why Liberal Churches are Growing*. London: Clark, 2006.
Piaget, Jean. *The Origin of Intelligence in Children*. New York: International Universities Press, 1956.
Pityana, B., M., et al. *The Bounds of Possibility: The Legacy of Steve Biko and Black Consciousness*. Cape Town: David Philip, 1991.
Plantinga, Theodore. *Learning to Live with Evil*. Grand Rapids: Eerdmans, 1982.
Potgieter, Cheryl. Opening address at an international conference on corruption, School of Social Sciences, University of KwaZulu-Natal, Pietermaritzburg, 14 January 2013.
Potgieter, P.C. "Ander Weë tot God? Calvyn oor nie-Christelike Godsdienste." *Acta Theologia Supplementum* 10 (2008) 108–19.
Powell, Mark. *Jesus as a Figure in History: How Modern Historians View the Man from Galilee*. Louisville, Kentucky: John Knox Westminster, 1998.
Prozesky, Martin. "After the Hegemony of White Calvinists on the State, What Will Follow?" *Sunday Tribune* (May 20, 1990).
———, ed. *Christianity Amidst Apartheid: Selected Perspectives on the Church in South Africa*. London: Macmillan, 1990. Published in South Africa as *Christianity in South Africa*. Bergvlei: Southern Book Publishers, 1990.
———. "Christology and Cultural Relativity." *Journal of Theology for Southern Africa* 35 (June 1981) 44–67.

———. *Conscience: Ethical Intelligence for Global Well-Being.* Pietermaritzburg: University of KwaZulu-Natal Press, 2007.

———. "Context and Variety in Religious Language." *Scottish Journal of Theology* 29 (1976) 201–13.

———. "A Critique of Traditional Theistic Religion." *South African Journal of Philosophy* 4 (1985) 55–61.

———. "The Divine Absentee: Karl Barth and the 'Death of God' Theologians." *Theoria* 57 (October 1981) 39–50.

———. "The Emergence of Dutch Pietism." *Journal of Ecclesiastical History* 28 (January 1977) 29–37.

———. *Frontiers of Conscience: Exploring Ethics in a New Millennium.* Pietermaritzburg: Equinym, 2003.

———. "A Holistic Model of Human Existence as Governed by a Drive to Conceptualize, Symbolize and Realize Maximum Well-Being." Pretoria: Unpublished HSRC Research Report, 1989.

———. "Homo Ethicus: Understanding the Human Nature that Underlies Human Rights and Human Rights Education." *Journal for the Study of Religion. Special Edition in Honour of Cornelia D. Roux* 27 (2014) 283–301.

———. "Is the Secular State the Root of our Moral Problems in South Africa?" *Alternation, Special Edition* 3 (2009) 237–53.

———. *A New Guide to the Debate about God.* London: SCM, 1992.

———. "A New Home for Questioning Christians." *The Witness* (September 9, 2010).

———. "Reading and Misreading the Bible." *The Witness* (May 15, 2014).

———. *Religion and Ultimate Well-Being: An Explanatory Theory.* London: Macmillan, 1984.

———. "The Return of the Comet." *The Witness* (October 18, 2017).

——— and Felicity Edwards. Review of *Beyond Dialogue: Towards a Mutual Transformation of Christianity and Buddhism*, by John B. Cobb Jr. *Journal of Theology for Southern Africa* 56 (September 1986) 67–73.

———. *Soulscapes: A Book of Spiritual Explorations.* Pietermaritzburg: Tamarisk, 1997.

———. "Universities, Cultural Diversity and Global Ethics: Opportunities for Moral Leadership" In *Ethics in Higher Education: Values-driven Leaders for the Future*, edited by Divya Singh and Christoph Stückelberger, 79–90. Geneva: Globethics. net, 2017.

———. *Warring Souls: When Religious Faith is Governed by Ethical Passion—and When it Isn't.* Johannesburg: Porcupine, 2017.

———. "When Great Rivers Converge." *The Natal Witness* (April 25, 1992).

———. "The Young Schleiermacher: Advocating Religion to an Age of Critical Reason." *Journal of Theology for Southern Africa* 37 (December 1981) 50–75.

Pünjer, B. *Über die Religion: Reden an die Gebildeten unter Ihren Verächtern*, by Friedrich Schleiermacher. Critical edition. Braunschweig, 1879.

Ramsey, Ian T. *Religious Language: An Empirical Placing of Theological Phrases.* London: SCM, 1973.

Richardson, Alan, and John Bowden, eds. *A New Dictionary of Christian Theology.* London: SCM, 1983.

Richmond, James. "Liberal Protestantism," In *A New Dictionary of Christian Theology*, edited by Alan Richardson, and John Bowden, 325–28. London: SCM, 1983.

Robinson, John A.T. *But That I Can't Believe!* London: Collins Fontana, 1967.

———. *Can we Trust the New Testament?* London: Mowbrays, 1977.
———. *Christian Morals Today*. Philadelphia: Westminster, 1966.
———. *Honest to God*. London: SCM, 1963.
———. *The New Reformation*. London: SCM, 1965.
Robinson, Richard. *An Atheist's Values*. Oxford: Blackwell, 1964.
Rolston, Holmes. *Genes, Genesis and God: Values and their Origins in Human and Natural History*. Cambridge: Cambridge University Press, 1999.
Rossouw, Deon, with van Vuuren, Leon. *Business Ethics*. Cape Town: Oxford University Press, 2004.
Rubenstein, Richard. *After Auschwitz: Radical Theology and Contemporary Judaism*. New York: Bobbs-Merrill, 1966.
Ruether, Rosemary. *Sexism and God-Talk. Towards a Feminist Theology*. Boston: Beacon, SCM, 1983.
———. *Women Healing Earth: Third World Women on Ecology, Feminism and Religion*. London: SCM, 1996.
Russell, Bertrand. *Power: A New Social Analysis*. London: Routledge, 2004.
———. *Why I Am Not a Christian, and Other Essays on Religion and Related Subjects*. London: Unwin, 1975.
Sacks, Jonathan. *Not in God's Name: Confronting Religious Violence*. London: Hodder, 2016.
Sagan, Carl, and Ann Druyan. *Shadows of Forgotten Ancestors: A Search for Who We Are*. London: Century, 1992.
Sanders, E.P. *The Historical Figure of Jesus*. London: Penguin, 1995.
Schellenberg, J.L. *Divine Hiddenness and Human Reason*. Ithaca: Cornell University Press, 1993.
———. *Evolutionary Religion*. Oxford: Oxford University Press, 2013.
———. "My stance in philosophy of religion." *Religious Studies* 49 (June 2013) 144-50.
Schleiermacher, Friedrich. *The Christian Faith*. Edinburgh: Clark, 1928.
———. *Christmas Eve: Dialogue on the Incarnation*. English translation by T.N. Tice. Richmond: Fortress, 1967.
———. *On The Highest Good*. Translated by H. Victor Froese. Lewiston: Edwin Mellen, 1992.
———. *On Religion: Addresses in Response to its Cultured Despisers*. Translated by Terrence N. Tice. Richmond: John Knox, 1969.
———. *On Religion: Speeches to its Cultured Despisers*. Translated by John Oman. New York: Harper, 1958.
Schlesinger, Eugene R. "Schleiermacher on the Necessity of the Church." *Journal of Theological Studies* New Series 66 (April 2015) 235-44.
Schopenhauer, Arthur. *The Essential Schopenhauer*. London: Unwin, 1962.
Schweitzer, Albert. *The Quest for the Historical Jesus: A Critical Study of its Progress from Reimarus to Wrede*. London: Adam and Charles Black, 1948.
Scott, Ted. "Being Homo Spiritus," Blog dated July 8, 2017. www.http:/tedscott.ampersand.com/ accessed July 9, 2017.
———. *Ethics*. Unpublished paper, 1999.
———, and Phil Harker. *Humanity at Work*. Luscombe, Queensland: Phil Harker, 1998. Reprinted as *The Myth of Nine to Five: Work, Workplaces and Workplace Relationships*. North Sydney: Richmond, 2002.
Seliger, W. "Frontier Theology." *The Episcopalian* (March 1971) 10–12.

Sereny, Gitta. *Into that Darkness: From Mercy Killing to Mass Murder.* London: Pimlico, 1995.
Service, Robert. *Stalin: A Biography.* Cambridge, Massachusetts: Bellknap, 2004.
Sharpe, R.A. *The Moral Case against Religious Belief.* London: SCM, 1997.
Shutte, Augustine. *Ubuntu: An Ethic for a New South Africa.* Pietermaritzburg: Cluster Publications, 2001.
Singer, Peter. *The Expanding Circle: Ethics and Sociobiology.* Oxford: Clarendon Press, 1981.
———. *Practical Ethics.* Third edition. Cambridge: Cambridge University Press, 1993.
Singh, Divya, and Christoph Stückelberger, eds. *Ethics in Higher Education: Values-driven Leaders for the Future.* Geneva: Globethics.net, 2017.
Skinner, B.F. *Beyond Freedom and Dignity.* New York: Knopf, 1971.
Smart, Ninian. *Beyond Ideology: Religion and the Future of Western Civilization.* London: Collins, 1981.
———. *The Religious Experience of Mankind.* London: Collins, 1971.
———, and Richard D. Hecht, eds. *Sacred Texts of the World: A Universal Anthology.* London: Macmillan, 1982.
Smit, Dirk J. "On Constructing Ethical Discourses." In *Human Origins and the Image of God: Essays in Honor of J. Wentzel van Huyssteen,* edited by Christopher Lilley and Daniel J. Pedersen, 273–313. Grand Rapids: Eerdmans, 2017.
Smit, Johannes A., and Denzil Chetty, eds. "Festschrift for Martin Prozesky." *Journal for the Study of Religion,* 31, 2018.
Smith, Wilfred. *Faith and Belief.* Princeton: Princeton University Press, 1979.
Smuts, Jan. *Holism and Evolution.* London: Macmillan, 1926.
Spong, John. *The Sins of Scripture: Exposing the Bible's Texts of Hate to Reveal the God of Love.* New York: Harper Collins, 2005.
Stacey, David. *Interpreting the Bible.* London: Sheldon, 1976.
Starbuck, Edwin D. *The Psychology of Religion: an Empirical Study of the Growth of Religious Consciousness.* 4th ed. London: Walter Scott, 1914.
Steane, Andrew. *Faithful to Science: The Role of Science in Religion.* Oxford: Oxford University Press, 2014.
Stegmann, Robert N. and Marilyn Faure. "Reading Scripture in a Post-Apartheid South Africa." *Religion and Theology* 22 (2015) 219-49.
Stenmark, Mikael. "Religious Naturalism and its Rivals." *Religious Studies* 49 (December 2013) 529–50.
Studebaker, Steven M. "Review of Thiselton, Anthony C. *The Holy Spirit: In Biblical Teaching, Through the Centuries, and Today.* London: SPCK, 2013." *Journal of Theological Studies New Series* 65 (October 2014) 814–17.
Thakur, Shivesh. *Religion and Rational Choice.* London: Macmillan, 1981.
Thangaraj, M. Thomas. "Jesus the Christ—the *Only* Way to God and to Human Flourishing." *Journal of Ecumenical Studies* 52 (Winter 2017) 44–49.
Theissen, Gerd, and Annette Merz, *The Historical Jesus: A Comprehensive Guide.* London: SCM, 1998.
Thiselton, Anthony C. *The Holy Spirit: In Biblical Teaching, Through the Centuries, and Today.* London: SPCK, 2013.
Thomasson-Rosingh, Anna-Claara, et al. *Re-imagining the Bible for Today.* London: SCM, 2017.
Tillich, Paul. *Dynamics of Faith.* New York: Harper, 1957.

———. *Morality and Beyond*. London: Collins, 1969.
Tolmie, D.F., and R. Venter, eds. *Making Sense of Jesus: Experiences, Interpretations and Identities*. Bloemfontein: SUN Press, 2017.
Torrey, E. Fuller. *Evolving Brains, Emerging Gods: Early Humans and the Origins of Religion*. New York: Columbia University Press, 2017.
Tutu, Desmond. *God is Not a Christian: Speaking Truth in Times of Crisis*. London: Rider, 2013.
van Asselt, Willem, and Marcel Sarot. "Can Human Friendship Yield Knowledge of God?" *Religion and Theology* 24 (2017) 180–203.
van Biema, David. "Blunt Bishop: How Peter Akinola's Rejection of Liberal 'Sins' Could Push the Anglican Church to Split." *Time* (February 19, 2007) 48–50.
Van Buren, Paul M. *The Secular Meaning of the Gospel*. London: SCM, 1963.
van der Walt, Etienne. "The Limbic System and the 'Religious Brain.'" In *Homo Transcendentalis? Transcendence in Science and Religion: Interdisciplinary Perspectives*, edited by Cornel du Toit, 23–39. Pretoria: Research Institute for Theology and Religion, University of South Africa, 2010.
van Huysteen, J. Wentzel, and Erik P. Wiebe, eds. *In Search of Self: Perspectives on Personhood*. Grand Rapids: Eerdmans, 2011.
Vawter, Bruce. "Original sin." In *A New Dictionary of Christian Theology*, edited by Alan Richardson, and John Bowden, 429. London: SCM, 1983.
Vermes, Geza. *The Changing Faces of Jesus*. London: Penguin, 2000.
———. *Jesus: Nativity, Passion, Resurrection*. London: Penguin, 2010.
Vorster, Nico. "John Calvin on the Status of Women in Church and Society." *Journal of Theological Studies New Series* 68 (April 2017) 178–211.
Ward, Graham. *How the Light Gets In: Ethical Life I*. Oxford: Oxford University Press, 2016.
———. *Unbelievable: Why we Believe and Why we Don't*. London: Tauris, 2014.
Ward, Keith. *Christ and the Cosmos: A Reformulation of Trinitarian Doctrine*. New York: Cambridge University Press, 2015.
———. "The Dignity and Distinctiveness of the Human Person." In *Human Origins and the Image of God: Essays in Honor of J. Wentzel van Huysteen*, edited by Christopher Lilley and Daniel J. Pedersen, 113–30. Grand Rapids: Eerdmans, 2017.
———. *Is Religion Dangerous?* Oxford: Lion Books, 2006.
———. *A Vision to Pursue: Beyond the Crisis in Christianity*. London: SCM, 1991.
———. *What the Bible Really Teaches: A Challenge to Fundamentalists*. London: SPCK, 2004.
Welby, Justin. *Dethroning Mammon: Making Money Serve Grace*. London: Bloomsbury, 2016.
West, Gerald O. "The Co-optation of the Bible by 'Church Theology' in Post-Liberation South Africa: Returning to the Bible as a Site of Struggle." *Journal of Theology for Southern Africa* 157 (March 2017) 185-98.
Whitehead, Alfred. *Dialogues of Alfred North Whitehead*. Recorded by Lucien Price. New York: Mentor, 1954.
———. *Modes of Thought*. New York: Free Press, 1968.
———. *Process and Reality*. Edited by David Ray Griffin and Donald W. Sherburne. New York: Free Press, 1978.
———. *Science and the Modern World: Lowell Lectures, 1925*. London: Collins, 1975.

Wilde, Simon. *Caught: The Full Story of Cricket's Match-Fixing Scandal.* London: Aurum, 2001.
Williams, Rowan. *God With Us: The Meaning of the Cross and Resurrection, Then and Now.* London: SPCK, 2017.
———. *Meeting God in Paul.* London: SPCK, 2015.
Williams, Trevor. "Schleiermacher, F.D.E. (1768–1834)." In *Jesus in History, Thought and Culture: An Encyclopedia*: 757–64.
———. "What makes you think Theology is a Subject?" In *Journal for the Study of Religion* 31 (2018) 250–59.
Wittgenstein, Ludwig. *Culture and Value.* Oxford: Blackwell, 1980.
Wright, N.T. *Jesus and the Victory of God.* Minneapolis: Fortress, 1996.
———. *Simply Christian.* London: SPCK, 2006.
———. *Who was Jesus?* London: SPCK, 1992, 1993.
Yogananda, Paramahansa. *Autobiography of a Yogi.* London: Rider, 1950.
Young, Frances M. "Monotheism and Christology." In *The Cambridge History of Christianity. Volume 1. Origins to Constantine*, edited by Margaret M. Mitchell and Frances M. Young, 452–69. Cambridge: Cambridge University Press, 2006,
———. "Prelude." In *The Cambridge History of Christianity. Volume 1. Origins to Constantine*, edited by Margaret M. Mitchell and Frances M. Young, 1–34. Cambridge: Cambridge University Press, 2006.
Young, J.Z. *Introduction to the Study of Man.* Oxford: Clarendon Press, 1971.

Index

Abbot, Eric, 124
Abelard, Peter, 16, 234, 243
Abrahamic faiths, 108, 129, 147
Acts of the Apostles, 147, 153, 227, 240, 256
Allah, 6, 99, 195, 214, 221, 250, 259
America, xvi, xxi, 27-31, 48, 133, 139, 149, 157, 171, 180, 190, 267, 271
Anglican, Anglicans, xvii, 12, 14, 15, 21, 23, 30, 50, 58, 59, 67, 68, 71, 72, 137, 157, 191, 226, 246, 267
Anselm of Canterbury, 208, 210, 220
Anti-Semitism, xxiv, 174, 233
apartheid, xx, 23, 25, 34, 38, 41, 42, 43, 52, 55, 56, 61, 65, 79, 110, 169, 193, 270
  as un-Christian, 12-15, 18, 23, 26, 33, 38, 47, 55, 189
  Christian support for, 18, 47, 55, 128, 169, 192, 257
Apostles Creed, xxiii
Aquinas, Thomas. *See* Thomas Aquinas
astronomy, love of, xiii, 9-11, 204
atheism, atheists, xxi, xxv, 20, 35, 39, 47, 54, 67, 122, 130, 135, 137, 195, 196, 214, 221
atonement, theories of, 244, 243
authoritarianism, 164, 175, 179, 191
Axial Age, 104-106, 108, 163

Baker, John Austin, 3-5, 21, 91, 92, 167
Barth, Karl, 53, 68

Battson, C.D., and Ventiss, F. Larry, 124-25, 183, 196
Bayle, Pierre, 87, 99
beauty, xvi, 3-4, 5, 6, 7, 22, 29, 63, 70, 98, 110, 146, 161, 195, 204, 215
belief. *See especially* xxi, xxiii, xxv, 12, 13, 20, 24, 27, 44, 46, 70, 73, 84, 104, 122, 126, 131, 132, 140, 162, 205, 206, 201, 213, 215, 225, 228, 235, 243, 244, 256, 259, 262, 269, 271-72
  defined, 89
  formation and nature, 89-95, 116-19, 126-40
  in Conservative Christianity, xxxiii-xxiv, 11, 145-59, 162-85, 224, 261
  in Liberal Christianity, 185-86, 188-92, 193-97
Bellah, Robert, 104
Bible, xix, 5, 10, 28, 22
  authority, 60, 147, 149, 254, 261
  canon, xxiii, 17, 147, 155, 184, 226
  critical approach, 16, 254
  development, 147, 155, 259
  holy, 129, 157, 176, 244, 259, 261
  human creation, 183, 188
  in Conservative Christianity, xxiv, 11, 12, 68, 146, 150, 155-57, 166, 168, 183, 255, 269
  in Liberal Christianity, 188, 192
  in Progressive Christianity, xxiv, 6, 10, 18, 206, 216, 239, 253-64
  inspiration, xxxiii, 10, 17, 156, 171, 174, 260

Bible *(continued)*
  mistaken views, 55, 171–77, 261
  patriarchy, 172–73
  sacramental view, 259–60
  sexual orientation, 173–74
  violence, 129, 171–74, 254
  Word of God, 157, 259

Biko, Steve, 238
Bonhoeffer, Dietrich, 26, 186, 188, 275
Borg, Marcus, xvi, 68, 224, 232, 236–37, 240–42, 251
brain science, 100–101, 108, 111, 119, 132, 243
Bredenkamp, Vic, xi, 40–43, 155–56, 225
Buddha, 6, 19, 69, 104, 219, 250
Buddhism, 43, 49, 50–51, 105, 109, 117, 120, 129, 147, 181, 226

Caesar
  in history, xi, 2, 164, 247, 252
  today's equivalent, xi, 247, 252
Calvin, John, Calvinism, xvi, 58–59, 61, 127, 131, 148, 153–54
Cassidy, Michael, 50, 146, 258
Chalcedon, Council of, 148
Chomsky, Noam, 115, 119–120, 133, 145, 183
Christian atheism, 39–40
Christianity, xv, xix, xx, xxi, xxv, 5, 16, 23, 46, 75, 89, 127, 133, 259, 278
  as a belief-system, 134, 145, 150–51
  Christians against apartheid, 12–15, 18, 23, 26, 33, 38, 47, 55, 189
  Christians supporting apartheid, 18, 47, 55, 128, 169, 192, 257
  Conservative Christianity described, xxiii, 50, 127, 146–49, 151–57, 237, 243
  Conservative Christianity evaluated, xxiii, xxiv, 38, 52, 86, 90, 128, 129, 132, 134, 158–84, 205, 206, 210, 213, 222, 227, 251, 259
  ethical character, 205, 251–52
  ethical evaluation, 158–84, 201

  evangelical, xx, xxii, xxiii, xxiv, 122, 127, 146, 149–50, 157, 166, 179, 182, 189, 192, 255, 268–70
  fundamentalist, xxi, xxiii, xxiv, xxv, 149–50, 157, 166, 179, 182, 268–70
  Liberal Christianity described, 67–69, 185–90
  Liberal Christianity evaluated, 191–97
  patriarchy, 57–60
  Progressive Christianity, xvi, 96, 137–41, 199–207, 213, 220, 239, 242, 244, 245, 252–53, 260–75
Christology, 45–46, 152, 192
Cobb, John B. Jr., 48–50, 186
Communism, 23, 24, 34, 56
conscience, xxvi, 5, 7, 10–11, 34, 38, 40. 43, 54, 89, 97, 109, 121, 172, 247, 249
conscientious objection, 24
Conservative Christianity. *See* Christianity
cosmos, 5, 9, 11, 85–89, 98, 99, 100, 106, 117, 136, 203, 204, 211–15, 219, 220, 231, 261
Cox, Harvey, 39
Creeds. *See* Apostles and Nicene
Crossan, John Dominic, xvi, 6, 68, 216, 224, 239, 241, 242, 251, 267
Crucifixion of Jesus. *See* Jesus
culture. *See especially* 17, 25, 27, 39, 49, 60, 69–70, 78, 82–83, 84, 91, 96, 97, 101, 104, 105, 118, 127, 160, 167 177, 181, 189, 214, 220, 223, 225, 228, 231, 245, 258, 262, 274
Cupitt, Don, 39, 43, 44, 49, 50, 186, 215, 217, 280

Dalai Lama, 7, 43, 132
Daly, Mary, 57
Daniel, Book of, 10, 72, 75
Dawkins, Richard, xxi, 47, 103, 132
deep and surface structures, xxvi, 115, 119, 137, 183
de Gruchy, John, 131, 150, 186
Descartes, René, 14, 67

Deuteronomy, 171–72, 256
domination, 57, 58, 61, 62, 112, 113, 162, 163, 167, 173, 189, 227, 230, 232, 275

Ellwood, Robert, 127
Ellis, George. *See* Murphy, Nancey
Enlightenment period, xxiii, 6, 81, 105, 184, 185
environment, xi, 47, 48, 49, 95, 130, 171, 182, 218, 233, 246, 253, 278
Episcopal, Episcopalian, xvii, 22, 27, 139, 157, 171, 246, 267–68, 271
Episcopal Theological School, 22, 27
ethics, xvii, xxv, 10, 38, 49, 51, 56, 57, 65, 66–67, 74, 95, 220, 247, 248
and brain science, 100-101, 111–112
and Progressive Christianity, 209, 213, 252
core values, xxiv, 61, 96, 97, 98, 151
definition, 10, 73, 95, 97–98, 100–102, 106, 112–13, 161
environmental ethics, 48, 87, 95, 130, 171, 182, 233, 246, 278
global, 97, 160–61, 249
historical stages, 103–106
in Christianity, xxiv, 151, 158–64, 251, 255, 265–66, 275
macro-, meso- and micro-ethics, 106, 182, 251
of Conservative Christianity, 158, 165–84, 213
of Liberal Christianity, 185–207, 210
older than religion, 99–100
personal stages, 107–108
practical ethics, 74–75, 81, 102–103, 276–78
Evangelical. *See* Christianity
Evil. *See especially* xx, 10–11, 34, 35, 38, 43, 53, 55, 57, 62, 95, 100, 108–12, 126, 130, 152–53, 168, 173, 175, 182, 188, 213, 221, 222, 224, 227, 233, 234. 242, 243, 247, 253, 269, 272

faith. *See especially* xx, xxi, xxii, xxiv, 11,17, 45, 54, 92, 95, 115, 118–20, 121, 122, 126, 187, 192, 201, 202, 206, 208, 218, 252, 256, 268, 278
according to John Hick, 118, 191
according to W.C. Smith, 119, 221
and belief, 119–20
and cumulative traditions, 119, 183, 259
as orientation to transcendence, 119, 205, 259
defined, 118–20, 126, 192, 201, 203
Feuerbach, Ludwig, 93
First Corinthians, 58, 173, 235, 259
First Thessalonians, 235
First Timothy, 173
forgiveness, xxiv, 231, 253, 266, 267, 279
Fowler, James, 104, 121, 182
Francis of Assisi, xviii, 19, 23, 275
Frankfort, Henri, 92
freedom, 4, 81, 83–84, 87, 92, 93, 98, 125, 159, 160, 185, 187, 211, 233, 277
Frege, Gottlob, 93, 94, 133, 183, 208
Freudenberger, C. Dean, 96
friendship, 11, 21, 22, 23, 26–27, 43, 46, 57, 78, 122, 138, 146, 203, 228, 229, 250, 273, 274–75
fundamentalism. *See* Christianity

Galatians, 58, 105
Galbraith, John Kenneth, 112, 247
Gandhi, Mahatma, ix, xviii, 6, 25, 108, 122–23
Gautama Siddhartha. *See* Buddha
Geering, Lloyd, ix, xvi, 39, 46 48, 93, 103–106, 138, 180, 191, 215, 216, 236, 240, 241, 264
gender justice, 16, 57–59, 138, 160, 173
genocide in Scripture, 171–74, 23, 244, 25
Gilligan, Carol, 107
global ethics. *See* ethics
global goodness project, 246–61

God. *See especially* xiii, xv, xxiii, xxiv,
    11, 21, 27, 64, 84, 91, 94, 120,
    133, 145, 156, 176, 208, 210–13,
    215, 230
  as Godhead, xii, 218–79
  as perfect goodness and love, xv,
    18, 52, 74, 93, 117, 145, 162, 167,
    168, 170, 172, 173, 193, 204, 209,
    216
  as personal, 147, 209, 210, 214
  as Trinity, xxiii, 68, 151, 168, 209
  as ultimacy, 208–17
  concepts of, xxvii, xxiii, 47, 48, 53,
    70, 116, 132, 134, 163, 189, 192,
    208
  Conservative Christian views, xix,
    112, 150, 164, 166–67, 169, 206,
    210–13
  Islamic, 221
  Liberal Christian views, 186, 188,
    189, 192, 194
  Progressive Christian views, xiii,
    113, 201, 206, 216–18, 218–79
  traditional attributes, 151, 178,
    210–213
Golden Rule, 160
Good, Goodness. *See especially* xv, xvi,
    xix, xxvi, 13, 19, 20, 22, 28, 38,
    49, 54, 55, 60, 63, 72, 84, 97, 99,
    108, 127, 136, 158, 161, 173, 192,
    201, 202, 209, 213, 221, 223, 232,
    234, 238, 242, 253, 257, 259, 261,
    264, 273, 274, 275–78
  and God, Godhead, 218–220, 233
  defined, xix, 4–8, 87, 100, 109, 197,
    203–207, 229, 264–66
  global goodness project, 246–52,
    270, 280
  J.A. Baker's account, 3–4
Gospels, xxiii, 147, 154, 225, 226, 227,
    231, 235, 240, 242, 255, 259
Grayling, A.C., 47, 133
Green, Michael, 50, 146
Grudem, Wayne, 154, 156, 261

Hardy, Alister, 44, 84, 213, 216
Hebrew Scriptures, 6, 16, 35, 155, 166,
    168, 171, 213, 214, 228

hell, xxiii, 138, 153, 154, 166, 167.
    170, 179, 188, 219, 244, 271, 272
Hick, John, ix, xx, 43, 44, 45, 46, 47,
    50, 87, 92, 93, 109, 111, 118, 151,
    188, 190, 191, 193, 215, 242
Hinduism, 117, 120, 122, 129, 147,
    169, 209, 214
holism, holistic, 85, 85, 98, 203, 219,
    245, 258
homo ethicus, 76, 97, 99, 100, 117
Honest to God, 21, 53, 188
Horsley, Richard, 224, 241
Huddlestone, Trevor, 12, 13
human nature, 76–86, 97, 117, 223,
    225
  and brain science, 100–101, 108,
    111, 119
  and well-being, 4, 11, 77, 78–79
  creativity, 77, 80, 203
  relatedness, 80–82
  sentience, 77, 84
  spiritual nature, 84–85, 117
  valorizing ability, 77
Hutchinson, John A., 126

imperialism, 227, 228
Incarnation, 122, 126, 209, 216, 245,
    253
infanticide in Scripture, 259
Islam, 22, 54, 104, 105, 116, 128, 147,
    148, 151, 169, 177, 214, 221, 259

James, William, 44, 84, 85, 116, 125,
    136, 187, 213
Jaspers, Karl, 104
Jenkins, David E., 21, 64, 186, 210
Jesus. *See especially* xv, xvi, xix, xxii, 6,
    45, 121, 128, 139, 148, 181, 205,
    206, 240, 251, 259, 266, 273
  as ethical revolutionary, 223-45
  as Godhead incarnate, 45, 130
  as goodness incarnate, 223, 230,
    234
  as historical figure, 68, 69, 228, 239,
    262, 266, 280
  Conservative Christian beliefs
    about, 90, 145, 152–56, 167,
    169–71, 182, 205, 211, 237

Crucifixion, 25, 188, 228, 235, 238
first followers, xxiv, 6, 147, 226,
  229, 231, 236, 237, 238, 263, 274
historical context, 227–28
Jesus and global goodness, 246–52
leadership, 229, 238, 239, 245, 274
Liberal Christians beliefs about,
  188, 189
Lord, 232
Messiah and Christ, 232
opposition, 228, 229, 232, 233
Progressive Christian views of, 139,
  188, 219, 223–45
Resurrection, 234–38
Son of God, 45, 90, 138, 177, 232
Jesus Movement, xi, xvi, 146, 178,
  201, 227, 228, 229, 235, 237, 245,
  246, 247, 249, 251–54, 262, 263,
  268, 269, 270, 273, 274
Jesus Seminar, 239
Joas, Hans, 96
John's Gospel, 5, 74, 154, 165, 170,
  223, 226, 240, 255, 259, 263, 274
John the Baptist, 238
Judaism, 6, 16, 19, 35, 116, 127, 130,
  134, 147, 151, 152, 211
Justice. *See especially* xi, xx, xxiv, 4, 6,
  12, 16, 24, 35, 57, 59, 60, 62, 67,
  98, 132, 138, 140, 151, 157, 159,
  160, 161, 165, 166, 167, 170, 173,
  177, 178, 184, 189, 206, 209, 257,
  272, 273

Kant, Immanuel, 14, 26, 60, 90, 102,
  158, 186, 187
Kee, Alistair, 93
Kidder, Rushworth M., 97, 102, 160
King, Martin Luther, 7, 140
King, Ursula, 57, 186
Kohlberg, Lawrence, 95, 107
Küng, Hans, 97, 102, 160, 186, 192

Laszlow, Erwin, 81, 86, 87
Leviticus, 174
Lewis, C.S., xv, xx, 146, 231
Lewis-Williams, David, 84, 86, 129,
  132, 133
Liberal Christianity. *See* Christianity

Lord's Prayer, 241
Love. *See especially* xx, xxiv, xxv, 4, 5,
  18, 31, 52, 68, 70, 73, 74, 83, 91,
  109, 115, 116, 121, 123, 125, 140,
  145, 146, 151, 157, 159, 161, 162,
  165, 167, 169, 170, 171, 176, 178,
  184, 186, 202, 209, 201–13, 215,
  218, 219, 233, 229, 231, 243, 246,
  253, 256, 257, 266, 267, 269, 272,
  273, 279
Luke's Gospel, 172, 244, 255
Luther, Martin, xxiv, 7, 17, 57–58,
  114, 131, 148, 177

Macquarrie, John, xxv
Mandela, Nelson, 7, 13, 95
Mark's Gospel, 121, 172, 244, 255, 262
Marx, Karl, 6, 34, 47, 66, 102
Marxism, Marxists, 23, 34, 35, 39, 60,
  81, 99, 131, 150
Matthew's Gospel, 57, 154, 157, 170,
  255
McGrath, Alister, xx, 50, 146, 148,
  149, 153, 243
Meeks, Wayne, 228
methods of this book, 90, 224–27,
  229, 236
Moltmann, Jürgen, 83, 84, 275
Moore, Basil, 18, 30, 33, 56
moral courage, 20, 22, 26, 68, 158,
  186, 191, 229, 243
Moral Regeneration Movement
  (MRM), 67
Moses, 6, 13, 35, 60, 211, 214, 233,
  236, 256
Muhammad, Prophet, 6, 22, 123, 181,
  219, 227, 259
Murphy, Nancey, 98, 106
mystical experience, 13, 52, 72, 204

Nazism, 24, 26, 68, 128
Nicene Creed, xxiii, xxiv, 45, 148, 151,
  152, 154, 163, 166, 187, 239, 271
Nietzsche, Friedrich, 39, 47, 109
Nineham, Dennis, 16, 17
Nolan, Albert, 45, 223, 224, 239, 241

Old Testament, 16, 21, 34, 156, 172, 173, 184
Oosthuizen, Daantjie, 18, 26, 30, 74
other religions, xviii, xxv, 116, 122, 130, 147, 149, 150, 166, 191, 195, 216, 220, 253
Otto, Rudolf, 38
Oudtshoorn, South Africa, 9, 13, 18, 19
Oxford University, ix, xvii, 19, 21–27, 44, 49, 64, 84, 91, 123, 217, 224, 256

Paul the Apostle, 12, 58, 60, 105, 147, 157, 163, 173, 174, 181, 225, 227, 232, 236, 240, 255, 256, 259, 263
phenomenological method, 40, 146, 225, 228
philosophy, xviii, xix, xxv, xxvi, 13, 18, 20, 26, 37, 48, 50, 66, 68, 70, 77, 80, 89, 101, 112, 163
Piaget, Jean, 94, 95, 107, 120, 121
power, ethics of, 112–12, 248
practical ethics. *See* ethics
Price, Lucien, 87
process philosophy, 50, 77
process theology, 48, 68, 112, 113, 116, 167, 186, 216
Progressive Christianity. *See* Christianity

Qur'an, 6, 22, 132, 221, 250, 258, 259, 275

Reformation, 17, 57, 59, 60, 185, 253
Religion. *See especially* xix, xxiv, 20, 27, 34–35, 38, 43, 46, 70, 76, 79, 84, 88, 96, 115–16, 120, 147, 218, 222, 242
 defined, 44, 99, 114, 135–36, 216, 217
 dimensions, 127, 249
 explanations, 50, 68, 100, 126, 135–36, 258
 historical stages, 44, 103–105, 180
 orientations within, 124–26
 personal stages, 120–22

religion and ultimate well-being, 85, 100, 117, 118, 135
 unethical aspects, 34–35, 52, 57, 66, 128–31, 133, 134, 164–65
religious experience, 44, 84, 108, 114, 115, 116, 125, 126, 127, 131, 136, 187, 196, 203, 213
religious pluralism, 43, 117, 188, 190, 193, 196, 220–22, 271
revelation, doctrine of, 68, 90, 116, 151, 168, 169, 170, 175, 179, 188, 209, 214, 258
Resurrection of Jesus. *See* Jesus
Rhodesia, 19, 33, 34, 35, 37, 38, 39, 40, 41, 43, 47, 56
Robinson, John A.T., 21, 39, 40, 53, 186, 188, 247, 263, 268, 273
Robinson, Richard, 4, 5, 35, 134, 135
Rolston, Holmes, 103
Roman Catholic, xvii, 25, 45, 59, 127, 128, 148, 150, 154, 166, 173, 184, 186, 192, 223, 239, 246, 275
Romans, Epistle, 12, 174
Rossouw, Deon, 106, 110, 182
Rubenstein, Richard, 128, 134, 135
Ruether, Rosemary Radford, 57, 186
Russell, Bertrand, 47, 112

Sacks, Jonathan, 7, 132
salvation, 52, 147, 183
 Conservative Christian beliefs, xxiii, xxiv, 122, 130, 152, 153–54, 167–70, 179, 242, 243, 244, 272
 Liberal Christian beliefs, 67, 115, 188, 189, 193
 Progressive Christian perspectives, 213, 242–53, 278, 279
Samuel, First Book of, 16, 213
Sanders, E. P. 224
Satan, Satanism, 18, 108, 109, 111, 243
Schellenberg, J.E., 47, 84, 88, 202, 217, 218
Schleiermacher, Friedrich, xvi, xxii, 27, 36, 37, 114, 115, 126, 127, 148, 186, 188, 191, 195, 205, 262–63
 on religion, 27, 44, 114–17, 205

on Scripture, 262–63
theology, 44, 46
Schweitzer, Albert, 186, 224, 241, 280
Scott, Ted, 83, 98, 107, 108, 164, 182
secular humanism, 54, 131
secular state in South Africa, 60–63
secularism, 50, 131, 148, 193, 194, 195, 197, 221
sexism, 55, 57, 100, 174, 189
sexual orientation, 102, 109, 140, 156, 173, 174, 189, 264
sin, sinful, sinners, xix, xxiii, 12, 20, 152–53, 154, 166, 171–73, 188, 211, 229, 243, 253, 255
Singer, Peter, 81, 102–103, 105
Skinner, B.F., 81
slavery, 6, 16, 38, 109, 110, 128, 162, 163, 255
Smith, Wilfred Cantwell, 115, 117, 118–19, 120, 133, 183, 221, 259
soul, concept of, 7, 35, 68, 84, 89, 121, 122, 128, 131, 189, 205, 234, 244, 268, 269, 275, 278
Spinoza, Baruch, 91
spiritual development, 120–122, 181, 182
Spong, John Shelby, xvi, 171, 173, 261
Stacey, David, 17, 260
Stalin, Joseph, 24, 63, 109, 110
Starbuck, Edwin, 44
symbols in religion, 120, 209, 271

Teilhard de Chardin, Pierre, 202, 217
Ten Commandments, 6, 165, 175, 182, 262
Thomas Aquinas, 93, 118
Tillich, Paul, 53, 99, 120, 186, 188, 192, 252
transcendence, 93, 104, 107, 126–27, 217
Trinity College, Oxford, ix, 19, 21, 23
Trinity, the Holy, xxiii, 94, 148, 151, 152, 155, 156, 168, 169

Tutu, Desmond, xiii, xxi, 7, 37, 71, 132, 148, 229, 251, 273

Ubuntu, 80, 292
ultimacy, 208–22
Unilever Ethics Centre, 65, 74
universal salvation, 195
University of KwaZulu-Natal, ix, 33, 75, 112
University of Natal, xviii, 33, 40, 41–50, 127, 192, 225, 272
University of Rhodesia, 33, 34–40, 50
University of the Free State, ix, 75, 274
USA. *See* America

van Buren, Paul, 18, 39
Ventiss, W. Larry. *See* Battson
Vermes, Geza, 240, 241
violence in Scripture. *See* Bible
von Moltke, Count Helmuth James, 25, 26

Ward, Graham, xvi, 150
Ward, Keith, xviii, 186, 215, 250, 256, 261, 264, 268, 271
ways of being religious, 124–26
Welby, Justin, 130
West, Gerald, 254
Westar Institute, 239
Whitehead, Alfred North, xix, 14, 48, 70, 80, 81, 86–87, 112, 164, 186, 245
women's liberation, 60
worship, xxiii, 63, 67, 68, 69, 120, 121, 129, 145, 146, 162, 163, 176, 177, 178, 180, 189, 195, 217, 251, 252, 263, 267, 271, 273 279
Wright, N.T., 50, 146, 224, 230, 232, 233, 236, 241

Young, J.Z. 91

Zimbabwe, 19, 36, 90, 209, 248

www.ingramcontent.com/pod-product-compliance
Lightning Source LLC
Chambersburg PA
CBHW061428300426
44114CB00014B/1583